THE NATIONAL TRUST
HANDBOOK
A GUIDE FOR
MEMBERS AND VISITORS
MARCH 1991 to MARCH 1992

STANDEN

THE NATIONAL TRUST
36 Queen Anne's Gate, London SW1H 9AS

Registered Charity No. 205846

STOWE LANDSCAPE GARDENS *Lake Pavilions*

Editor: Alison Honey
Illustrations by: Norman Charlton, F. N. Colwell, Brian Delf, John Dyke, Brin Edwards, Sue Grimshaw, Peter Morter, Claude Page, David Peacock, Neil Rutherford, Eric Thomas, Soun Vannithone, Margaret Wetherbee

Front cover: Anglesey Abbey, Cambridgeshire (see p. 42). 1991 marks the 25th anniversary of the Trust's acquisition of this garden. Photo: National Trust Photographic Library/Nick Meers

Back cover: Ightham Mote, Kent (see p. 136). Photo: National Trust Photographic Library/Ian Shaw. This property is undergoing a major restoration programme. The Ightham Mote Appeal aims to raise £500,000 to help finance this work. Further information from the Special Appeals Manager, the National Trust, 36 Queen Anne's Gate, London SW1H 9AS

Designed by Pardoe Blacker Ltd, Lingfield, Surrey
Phototypeset in Monotype Lasercomp Photina Series 747
by Southern Positives and Negatives (SPAN), Lingfield, Surrey
Printed by Richard Clay (The Chaucer Press) Ltd, Bungay, Suffolk

Contents

KEDLESTON HALL *Wall-sconce*

From the Director-General

I am pleased to introduce the Handbook for the new season. 1991 has been chosen as National Trust Gardens Year and it is therefore particularly appropriate that from May, Biddulph Grange Garden in Staffordshire will be opening to members and the public for the first time on a regular basis. This remarkable Victorian garden was acquired by the Trust in 1988 in a state of advanced dilapidation. Its opening marks the culmination of three years of restoration work. If you are able to visit Biddulph Grange you will discover it ranks among the most spectacular and imaginatively planned gardens of its time.

With the help of this Handbook I hope you will be able to plan visits to many other National Trust properties. The following pages should give some idea of the variety which the Trust has to offer you.

Thank you for your support of the National Trust. It is much appreciated.

Angus Stirling

BIDDULPH GRANGE GARDEN *Cheshire Cottage*

The National Trust

Since 1895 the National Trust has worked for the preservation of places of historic interest or natural beauty in England, Wales and Northern Ireland. Under the National Trust Act of 1907 it is empowered to declare its land and buildings inalienable, and subsequent legislation gave it the right to appeal to Parliament against a compulsory purchase order on its inalienable land. Nearly all its properties are inalienable which means that they cannot be sold or mortgaged. If the Trust so wishes, and subject to the approval of the Charity Commission, inalienable land may be leased.

Today the Trust – which is not a government department but a charity depending on the voluntary support of the public and its members – is the largest private landowner and conservation society in Britain. Wherever you go, you are close to land that is protected and maintained by the National Trust. 140,000 acres of fell, dale, lake and forest belong to the Trust in the Lake District alone; its care extends to prehistoric and Roman antiquities; downs and moorlands, fens, farmland, woods and islands; nature reserves; lengths of inland waterways – even all or a significant part of 51 villages. NT coast and countryside properties are open to the public at all times subject only to the needs of farming, forestry and the protection of wildlife.

How to use this Handbook

Please read the following sections before visiting any of the properties in this book.

The National Trust Handbook gives you details on how to visit National Trust properties open to the public. These include stately homes, gardens, castles, barns, dovecotes and even two lighthouses. There is also a section at the beginning of most county entries giving a selection of the Trust's coast and countryside properties. The county maps show the location of buildings and gardens and, as far as possible, the coastal and countryside properties mentioned in the text.

There are two editions of the Handbook. The members' edition is on lightweight paper to reduce the cost of postage to members. The trade edition is sold through retail outlets in this country and distributed overseas by the British Tourist Authority and is printed on a heavier weight paper. The Trust is grateful to Ford Motor Co. for helping to defray some of the costs of producing this Handbook.

Under each main entry you will find a brief description of the property, with its postal address, a telephone number (wherever possible) and details of the facilities available on site. A key to the symbols used in the entries is on page 24. Please be sure to read the opening arrangements carefully as these vary from property to property and take into account the careful balancing of public access and conservation. Last admissions are usually half an hour before the stated closing time. Properties which are open during the winter months are usually closed on Christmas Day, Boxing Day and New Year's Day. If you have any doubts or queries about your visit please phone the property direct.

Information in this Handbook is valid until the end of March 1992. Although details are correct at the time of going to press, they are subject to revision.

Important Notes for National Trust Members

Membership of the National Trust allows you free entry to most properties open to the public, during normal opening times and under normal opening arrangements *on presentation of a valid membership card.* Please check that you have your card with you before you set out on your journey as you can not be admitted free of charge without it, and the Trust cannot normally refund members' entrance charges subsequently. If your card is lost or stolen, please write to or telephone the Membership Department, Bromley (address on page 22) which will send a replacement either to your home address or to a temporary address if this is more convenient. Membership cards are not transferable.

Exceptions to free entry

If members visit a property when a special event is in progress they may be required to pay an additional charge. Likewise when a property is opened especially for a National Gardens Scheme open day members are liable to pay the admission fee. There is also a small number of properties where members are asked to pay because the management is not under the Trust's direct control. Some properties in this guide are owned by the National Trust but maintained and administered by English Heritage or Cadw (Welsh Historic Monuments). In these cases members of the National Trust and English Heritage or Cadw members are admitted free of charge.

Other benefits

Members are also admitted free to properties of the National Trust for Scotland. Details of these are found in *The National Trust for Scotland's Guide to Over 100 Properties* which can be obtained by sending £1 and a self-addressed adhesive label to the National Trust for Scotland, 5 Charlotte Square, Edinburgh EH2 4DU.

Reciprocal arrangements exist with overseas National Trusts including Australia, New Zealand, Barbados, Bermuda, Canada, Jersey and Guernsey. For a full list of participating organisations please send a s.a.e. to the London office (see page 22).

Admission fees

Unless otherwise stated the normal adult admission fee is given. Prices quoted are inclusive of VAT and are liable to change if the VAT rate is altered.

Reduced admission charges apply as follows
Children: under 5 free. Under 17 (accompanied by an adult, if not, at the Trust's discretion) half price, unless otherwise stated.
Pensioners: As a charity, the National Trust is unable to offer reductions for pensioners. Some properties not directly managed by the NT and those under the

guardianship of English Heritage or Cadw (Welsh Historic Monuments) admit pensioners at a reduced rate.

Disabled visitors: These visitors are charged the usual rate but the necessary companion of a disabled or visually handicapped visitor is admitted free.

Parties: Reductions are usually available for pre-booked groups of 15 or over. Please contact the relevant property for details.

School parties: Reductions are available at most properties for groups of school children aged under 19. School Corporate members are admitted free (see page 11 for details). Teachers are invited to make a free preliminary visit by prior arrangement with the property.

Free Entry Day

Each year the National Trust and the National Trust for Scotland organise a day when all visitors are admitted free to many of their properties. This year's free entry day is set for Wednesday 15 May.

How to get there

At the end of each main entry is a brief description of location together with a grid reference. Car parking is usually available within 100 yards of the property.

The majority of National Trust properties are in rural surroundings which are not always well serviced by public transport. However, where possible we give details of how to reach them by train or bus. Please note that no indication of frequency of transport services is given, so please check the times of services before setting out. 'Passing BR' (NIR in Northern Ireland) indicates the bus service passes the station entrance or approach road and 'passing close BR' indicates that a walk is necessary. Unless otherwise stated bus services pass the property, and the railway station name is followed by the distance from the property. Information on the existence of taxi ranks is regrettably not available.

Wheelchair visitors travelling by train should note that some stations are unstaffed. These are followed by a (U).

The Trust is grateful to Barry Doe, a life member, for this travel information. If you experience difficulties following this information or have suggestions to make, he will be glad to reply to your comments. Please contact him at: Travadvice, 25 Newmorton Road, Moordown, Bournemouth, Dorset BH9 3NU. Tel. Bournemouth (0202) 528707.

Conservation and security measures at National Trust properties

Please read these notes before visiting any National Trust property.

Owing to the fragile and valuable nature of the contents of many of the Trust's properties we must ask visitors to observe certain restrictions for reasons of conservation and security. These measures, which have been introduced after a great deal of research and thought, are essential to the safekeeping of properties under the Trust's care. By respecting these few regulations you will be helping the Trust to ensure that its houses and contents are preserved for future generations. Symbols indicating restrictions are positioned to the right-hand side on the line following the property name.

HOW TO USE THIS HANDBOOK

Shoes ⌧
Sharp-heeled shoes are not permitted. Any heel which covers an area smaller than a postage stamp causes irreparable damage to all floors, carpets and rush matting. When necessary plastic slippers are provided for visitors with unsuitable or muddy footwear.

Large bags 🎒
At some properties visitors will be asked to leave large items of hand luggage behind while they make their visit. This is to protect furniture and contents from accidental damage as well as for reasons of security. This restriction includes rucksacks, large handbags, carrier bags and bulky shoulder bags. These can usually be left at the entrance desk during your visit.

Prams, pushchairs and baby back carriers
Prams, pushchairs and back carriers for babies are not usually allowed inside properties for the same reason as the note above. At some properties front slings are available on loan.

Photography 📷
Flash photography, the use of tripods and video cameras are not permitted inside properties. At certain properties no form of photography is allowed and this is indicated by the 📷 symbol. Commercial photographers should always contact the relevant regional office for prior permission.

Environmental control
Blinds are wholly or partly drawn in most rooms to protect contents from fading and decay caused by daylight. Light levels are carefully monitored to ensure reasonable viewing conditions and good preventive conservation.

Smoking
Smoking is not permitted inside NT properties.

Heavily visited properties
Some properties are extremely popular on Bank Holidays and at weekends during the summer. These are shown by the ▦ sign. In some cases timed tickets may be issued and all visitors (including NT members) are required to use this system. This practice is in the interests of conservation and for the visitor's better enjoyment of the property. In extreme cases entry to the property may not be possible.

Dogs
Dogs (except guide dogs) are not allowed inside National Trust houses and restaurants and seldom in gardens. Some properties have no suitable areas for dogs and these are indicated by the symbol 🐕. The symbol 🐕 indicates properties which welcome dogs on leads in their grounds (not gardens). In these cases it is essential that dogs are kept on the lead at all times to protect deer and grazing livestock.

Dogs are welcome at most countryside properties providing they are kept under control. However, in a few cases the Trust has introduced a restriction on dogs at family beaches during the busy summer months. A list of these sites can be obtained from the London office (address page 22).

Health and safety

The National Trust endeavours to provide a healthy and safe environment for visitors at its properties as far as is reasonably practicable. You can help the Trust by observing all notices and signs relating to this subject during your visit and by wearing appropriate clothing and footwear at outdoor properties.

Visitors with special needs

Disabled and visually handicapped visitors.

The Trust warmly welcomes these visitors to its properties and wherever possible will give advice and assistance. Although it is rare for a building or garden to be wholly accessible to visitors using wheelchairs most Trust properties are accessible to some degree. A brief note on the extent of access is given in relevant property entries following the ⓑ symbol. Some properties have one or more wheelchairs for visitors' use ⓑ. Adapted lavatories are shown by ⓑ WC.

⬥ indicates special attractions or facilities for visually handicapped visitors. Braille and tape guides are available at some properties. Guide dogs and trainee guide dogs are welcomed inside properties unless otherwise stated. The same applies to hearing dogs for deaf visitors.

For general information and a free booklet about access and facilities, please write (enclosing a stamped addressed adhesive label) to Mrs Valerie Wenham, Adviser, Facilities for Disabled Visitors at the London Office (address page 22).

Visitors with babies and toddlers

The symbol 🜂 shows where there are facilities for visitors with babies and toddlers. Details of these, such as baby feeding areas, nappy changing facilities and high chairs, are given in the appropriate entries. At some properties where there are restrictions on pushchairs and carriers (please read the section on page 8) front sling baby carriers are available for loan.

SMALL COPPER

9

Volunteers

There are over sixty different volunteer opportunities within the National Trust to suit practically all ages and interests. Volunteers help the Trust as chaplains, pilots, accountants, surveyors, gamekeepers and calligraphers besides the better known occupations of room stewarding and lecturing. If you are interested in helping the Trust locally or wish to join a National Trust Volunteer Group or a property support group please contact the Regional Volunteer Co-ordinator at your nearest National Trust Regional Office (addresses on page 22).

The Trust also organises residential working holidays for people aged 16 and over. Full details of these are given in a brochure *National Trust Acorn Projects and other Working Holidays 1991*. For your free copy please send a stamped (41p) addressed envelope 12 × 9 inches to the National Trust Volunteer Unit, PO Box 12, Westbury, Wiltshire BA13 4NA (tel. Westbury (0373) 826826).

COMMON GREY SEAL

Join the Trust and help its work

Membership subscriptions are an increasingly vital source of the Trust's income. If you join the Trust you will contribute to its conservation work and the protection of important historic buildings and outstanding countryside. You will also gain free entry to most properties in the care of the Trust and each year will receive the Handbook, three colour magazines, a mail order catalogue, the annual report and two regional newsletters. If you are a member already why not give membership to a friend as a novel present?

Please remember, the Trust is a charity independent of government and depends on your help and support.

The different categories of membership are listed below. If you decide to join please return the form overleaf to: The National Trust Membership Department, PO Box 39, Bromley, Kent BR1 1NH. Alternatively you may join and pay by credit card by telephoning 081-464 1111.

Annual categories

Individual: £21. *Additional:* £12 (for each person living at the same address as a member). Each receives an individual membership card.

Family Group: £38 – one card gives free admission to both parents (or partners) and their children aged under eighteen living at the same address.

Under 23: £8. Independent membership for under-23 year olds.

School Corporate: £40. For schools and youth organisations. A single card gives free entry to up to 60 admissions to no more than one property on the same day. Please write for details to the Membership Department in Bromley.

Life categories

Individual: £500 (£325 for those retired and aged 60 or over). Lifetime privileges and one card admitting a guest free.

Joint: £575 for lifetime partners. (£400 if either partner is retired and aged 60 or over). Each receives one card for personal admission.

Benefactors: £2,000 or more entitles a member to be known as a benefactor of the Trust. Card also admits one guest.

NOTE: Life members who took out their membership before 1968 have cards which admit one person only, whereas life members who joined after 1968 have cards which admit the member and a guest.

Pre-1968 life members wishing to exchange 'admit one' for 'admit two' cards, or who wish to transfer from individual to joint life membership should contact the Membership Department for the scale of charges.

FORM A

Application for membership

TO: THE NATIONAL TRUST, PO BOX 39, BROMLEY, KENT BR1 1NH

Twelve-month memberships

☐ **Individual:** £21. For each additional member of the household at the same address: £12. One card for each member
☐ **Family Group:** £38 for both parents and all their children under 18. One card covers the family
☐ **Under 23:** £8. Please give date of birth..............................

Life memberships

☐ **Individual:** £500 (£325 for those retired and aged 60 or more). The card admits the member and a guest
☐ **Joint:** £575 for lifetime partners (£400 if either partner is retired and aged 60 or more).
Separate card each, admitting one person

	INITIALS	SURNAME (BLOCK CAPITALS)
MR/MRS/MS/MISS	★	
FULL ADDRESS (BLOCK CAPITALS)		
		∨
POSTCODE		

ADDITIONAL MEMBERS	MR/MRS/MS/MISS	MR/MRS/MS/MISS
	MR/MRS/MS/MISS	MR/MRS/MS/MISS

12

National Trust Associations and Centres

The Associations and Centres listed below are formed and run by National Trust members enabling people to meet and share common interests. A small subscription is usually charged to cover costs. Activities include lectures and visits to properties as well as fundraising for Trust projects. There are also many opportunities for members to become involved in volunteer activities at Trust properties.

If you are a member and would like to join one of these groups please contact the Honorary Secretary of the Association nearest you (please enclose s.a.e. when writing). If you can see no convenient Association please write to the Deputy Secretary at the London address on page 22 to find out whether there is any likelihood of one being formed in your vicinity.

Honorary Secretaries, October 1990

SOUTH-WEST ENGLAND

Axe Valley L. E. H. Lovejoy, Charlecote, 27 Lydgates Rd, Seaton, Devon EX12 2BX (Seaton 21997)

Bath Mrs F. M. Poole, 24 Audley Park Rd, Bath BA1 2XL (Bath 426275)

Blackmore Vale & Yeovil Mrs E. D. Wells, 7 Acreman Ct, Sherborne, Dorset DT9 3PW (Sherborne 812563)

Bournemouth Mrs W. Gasson, 2 Barrington Ct, 5 Cavendish Pl, Bournemouth BH1 1RQ (Bournemouth 556720)

Bristol Mrs R. Booker, 4 Hurle Rd, Clifton, Bristol BS8 2SY (Bristol 733453)

Christchurch & New Forest N. G. Lake, Holmhurst, Brighton Rd, Sway, Lymington, Hants SO41 6EB (Lymington 683058)

Cornwall Mrs M. Burford, Chyvandowr, St Martin, Helston, Cornwall TR12 6DF (Mawgan 632)

Culm & Exe Valleys Mrs N. Clemerson, 17 The Fairway, Post Hill, Tiverton, Devon EX16 4NF (Tiverton 254765)

Dorset Miss Edwina Hart, 13A Dunbar Rd, Bournemouth BH3 7AZ (Bournemouth 290154)

East Dorset Miss M. B. Goodman, 50 Ryan Cl, Ferndown, Wimborne, Dorset BH22 9TP (Ferndown 896028)

Exeter & District Mrs Pauline Feneck, 11 Denmark Rd, Exeter EX1 1SL (Exeter 59632)

Golden Cap/West Dorset G. J. Whitehouse, 5 Culverhayes, Beaminster, Dorset DT8 3DG (Beaminster 862508)

Haldon Mrs A. E. Archer, 5 Brimley Ct, Lower Brimley, Teignmouth, Devon TQ14 8LW (Teignmouth 775232)

Hembury J. Popkess, Lower Wick Fm, Wick, Luppitt, Honiton, Devon EX14 0TY (Luppitt 891208)

Mid-Devon H. J. A. Fernbank, 2 Elder Grove, Crediton, Devon EX17 1DE (Crediton 2765)

Minehead & West Somerset Miss M. Girling, Millhaven, Mill Gdns, Dunster, Somerset TA24 6SP (Dunster 821251)

Newton Abbot Mrs D. Priestley, 65 Church Rd, Newton Abbot, Devon TQ12 1AN (Newton Abbot 53061)

North Cornwall C. Matthews, 36 Trelyn, Rock, Cornwall PL27 6LZ (Trebetherick 863606)

North Devon Mrs E. M. Cooke, Astral House, Instow, Bideford EX39 4LZ (Instow 861188)

North Wiltshire Miss F. E. Bull, 5 Wharfside, Couch Lane, Devizes, Wilts SN10 1EB (Devizes 752200)

Penwith Miss E. M. Floyd, 2 Cornwall Tce, Penzance, Cornwall TR18 4HN (Penzance 50245)

Plymouth Miss B. Eccles, 8 Green Close, Kingsbridge, Devon TQ7 1NH (Kingsbridge 852107)

Purbeck J. Morgan, Satara, Swanage Rd, Studland, Swanage, Dorset BH19 3AE (Swanage 44207)

Quantock D. J. Bastable, 54 Manor Rd, Taunton, Somerset TA1 5BQ (Taunton 284545)

Raleigh W. E. Swann, West Gleams, 151 Parkside Dr, Exmouth EX8 4LZ (Exmouth 274734)

NATIONAL TRUST ASSOCIATIONS AND CENTRES

Salisbury & South Wiltshire Mrs W. J. E. Sandford, Beechwood, Salisbury Rd, Coombe Bissett, Salisbury, Wilts SP5 4JT (Coombe Bissett 397)

Sidmouth J. Mitchell, 'Briarleigh', Yardlands Cl, Sidmouth, Devon EX10 9LL (Sidmouth 515409)

South Hams R. Kessel, Limecroft, Shute Hill, Malborough, Kingsbridge, Devon TQ7 3SF (Kingsbridge 560089)

Torbay L. Womersley, Kohinur, Old Mill Rd, Chelston, Torquay, Devon TQ2 6HW (Torquay 605508)

Upper Thames & Ridgeway G. Haines, 23 Farleigh Crescent, Swindon, Wilts SN3 1JY (Swindon 538964)

Wells & District D. Nicholson, The Garden House, New St, Wells, Somerset BA5 2LQ (Wells 73710)

West Devon Mrs E. Morris, 6 Willow Tree Close, Okehampton EX20 1NL (Okehampton 52549)

Weston-super-Mare and District Mrs P. Curtis, 7 St Jude's Tce, Weston-super-Mare, Avon BS22 8HB (Weston-super-Mare 622112)

SOUTH & EAST ENGLAND

Adur Arun (Worthing) P. Patten, 32 Brook Barn Way, Goring-by-Sea, Worthing, W. Sussex BN12 4DW (Worthing 44121)

Arun Valley Mrs B. Willcocks, 19 Beech View, Dapper's Lane, Angmering, W. Sussex BN16 4DE (Rustington 786749)

Brighton & South Downs Mrs E. Churchill, 1 The Paddock, The Droveway, Hove, East Sussex BN3 6LT (Brighton 551923)

Cambridge Mrs T. Capes, 30 Queensway, Sawston, Cambridge CB2 4DJ (Cambridge 833417)

Chelmsford & District Miss E. Ward, 5 Crossways, Chelmsford, Essex CM2 9EP (Chelmsford 265636)

Chichester A. W. R. Ambrose, 64 Kelsey Av, Southbourne, Emsworth, Hants PO10 8NG (Emsworth 371561)

Colchester & Essex S. Sheppard, Silverlea, Scotland St, Stoke-by-Nayland, Colchester, Essex CO6 4QF (Colchester 262765)

Darent Cray Miss Audrey Miller, 78 Moultain Hill, Swanley, Kent BR8 8BU

East Kent Mrs E. Stoydin, 23 Ersham Rd, Canterbury, Kent CT1 3AR (Canterbury 463661)

East Suffolk W. R. Wright, 18a Fonnereau Rd, Ipswich, Suffolk IP1 3JP (Ipswich 218058)

Hastings & St Leonards Miss B. Dickinson, 41 Collinswood Dr, St Leonards on Sea, E. Sussex TN38 0NU

Herts & Essex Border E. Allen, 25 Gilby Cres, Stansted, Essex CM24 8DS (Stanstead 816729)

Isle of Wight Miss S. Higgins, 116 Great Preston Rd, Ryde, IoW PO33 1BA (IoW 65277)

Lewes Mrs E. Eley, 26 Sadlers Way, Ringmer, Lewes, East Sussex BN8 5HG

Mid-Kent Mrs G. Golborn, 45 Littlebourne Rd, Maidstone, Kent ME14 5QP (Maidstone 673604)

Mid-Sussex Miss J. H. Ashworth, 10 Grey Alders, Lindfield, Haywards Heath, W. Sussex RH16 2AF (Lindfield 74261)

Norfolk Miss D. K. Powlett, 24 Bracondale, Norwich NR1 2AF (Norwich 627917)

North Hampshire D. Colclough, 18 Oaklea Gdns, Bramley, Basingstoke, Hants RG26 5QY (Basingstoke 880029)

North Sussex Miss W. S. Learoyd, 29 Chesworth Cres, Horsham, W. Sussex RH13 5AN (Horsham 64303)

Portsmouth & District Mrs M. E. Rosier, 71 Greenfield Cres, Cowplain, Portsmouth PO8 9EL (Horndean 595367)

Royston & Saffron Walden W. Hitchcock, 12 Echo Hill, Royston, Herts (Royston 247651)

Rye & Winchelsea P. G. Armitage, 39 Fair Meadow, Rye Hill, Rye, E. Sussex TN31 7NL (Rye 223488)

Seaford J. S. Greenwood *(Membership Secretary)* 6 Ladycross Cl, Seaford, E. Sussex BN25 4DD (Seaford 891808)

Sevenoaks Area Mrs M. Morley, 43 Bradbourne Park Rd, Sevenoaks, Kent TN13 3LJ (Sevenoaks 460308)

Seven Sisters, Eastbourne & District Miss J. W. Peskett, Ambleside, 131 Hollingdean Tce, Brighton BN1 7HF (Brighton 550784)

Southampton & District Mrs J. Ballard, 3 Pentire Way, Shirley, Southampton SO1 2RW (Southampton 785202)

South-East Surrey Mrs D. Knapp, 48 Oakwood Cl, Redhill, Surrey RH1 4BD (Redhill 763421)

South-East Sussex Mrs M. Hooper, Firlend, 11 Firle Rd, Bexhill-on-Sea, E. Sussex TN39 3TJ (Cooden 2637)

Southend-on-Sea & District *(Membership Secretary)* Miss M. Whittaker, 40 Vardon Dr, Leigh-on-Sea, Essex SS9 3SR (Leigh-on-Sea 557707)

Weald of Kent R. J. Knapp, 38 Heskett Park, Pembury, Tunbridge Wells TN2 4JG

West Norfolk Miss M. Hodgkinson, 31 Ashwicken Rd, Pott Row, King's Lynn PE32 1BZ (King's Lynn 630387)

West Suffolk F. Lloyd, 19 Holly Cl, Horringer, Bury St Edmunds IP29 5SZ (Horringer 634)
West Surrey W. N. Coates, Woodborough, Grosvenor Rd, Godalming GU7 1NZ (Godalming 7071)
Winchester Miss E. M. Wicks, Sundial, 1 Fairdown Cl, Winchester, Hants SO23 8JU (Winchester 62510)

LONDON & HOME COUNTIES

Abingdon & District Mrs D. Murphy, 3 Park Cr, Abingdon, Oxon OX14 1DF (Abingdon 20073)
Amersham Mrs R. Cree, 10 Whielden Green, Whielden St, Amersham, Bucks HP7 0JE (Amersham ,726240)
Aylesbury Mrs C. Egan, Southways, 17 Station Rd, Tring, Herts HP23 5NG (Tring 3136)
Barnet D. C. B. Wright, 10 Cadogan Gdns, Finchley, London N3 2HN (081-346 3254)
Beaconsfield Mrs E. Y. Ashford, Chatterings, Christmas Lane, Farnham Common, Bucks SL2 3JF (Farnham Common 4992)
Beckenham & Bromley R. F. McNab Jones, 52 Oakwood Av, Beckenham, Kent BR3 2RT (081-650 0217)
Bedford R. Newbery, 23 Hartshill, Bedford MK41 9AL (Bedford 62264)
Croydon & District L. P. Hawkes, 15 Yew Tree Rd, Dorking, Surrey RH4 1ND (Dorking 883699)
Dacorum H. Checkley, 37 Hill View, Berkhamsted, Herts HP4 1SA (Berkhamsted 874095)
Ealing K. Goff, 41 Gloucester Rd, Ealing, London W13 4JA
Edgware & District Miss R. Joseph, 4 Hill Cl, Stanmore, Middx HA7 3BS (081-954 3902)
Enfield Miss M. Larrett, 20 The Grove, Enfield, Middlesex EN2 7PY (081-366 0394)
Epsom, Ewell & District Miss L. J. Maxey, 24 Briavels Ct, Downs Hill Rd, Epsom, Surrey KT18 5HP (Epsom 725992)
Gerrards Cross & Chalfonts Miss G. M. Hollier, 2 Long Grove, Seer Green, Beaconsfield, Bucks HP9 2YL (Beaconsfield 676413)
Hampstead Miss S. A. Wilson, Flat 39, 5 & 7 Belsize Grove, London NW3 4UT (071-586 9821)
Harrow Mrs M. Williams, 15 Compton Rise, Pinner, Middx HA5 5HS (081-866 9272)
Havering & District Miss E. Thompson, 4 Ferguson Ct, Ferguson Av, Gidea Park, Romford, Essex RM2 6RJ (Romford 20564)
Hertford Mrs M. Halfhide, 61 Roselands Ave, Hoddesdon, Herts EN11 9BA (Hoddesdon 466125)
Ilford Miss P. Jolley, 109A Woodbridge Rd, Barking, Essex IG11 9EU (081-594 8531)
Kensington & Chelsea *(Membership Secretary)* 4 Knightsbridge Chambers, 5 Brompton Rd, London SW3 1ED (071-373 2536)
London Miss P. Farries, 49 Lebanon Rd, Croydon CRO 6UT (081-656 2337)
Maidenhead Mrs B. A. Smith, 8 Birdwood Rd, Maidenhead SL6 5AP (Maidenhead 24337)
Marlow Mrs K. Arch, 20 Primrose Lea, Marlow, Bucks SL7 2QL (Marlow 74573)
Milton Keynes Mrs S. Coombes, Emperor Cottage, Weston Underwood, Olney, Bucks MK46 5JS
Newbury Mrs J. Turner, Hopwood, Peasmore, Newbury, Berks RG16 0JF (Newbury 248490)
North Hertfordshire Miss J. Carey, 81 Westwood Avenue, Hitchin, Hertfordshire SG4 9LL (Hitchin 52507)
Orpington & Chislehurst P. J. Reader, 75 Kingsway, Petts Wood, Kent BR5 1PN (Orpington 32911)
Oxford Mrs E. M. Crampton, 48 Mill St, Eynsham, Oxford OX8 1JU (Oxford 880309)
Reading *(Membership Secretary)* H. Boddington, Flat 6, The Firs, 11 Bath Rd, Reading, Berks RG1 6HN (Reading 586945)
Richmond Miss J. Houghton, 21 Ashley Rd, Richmond, Surrey TW9 2TG (081-940 4615)
St Albans & District A. C. Longstaff, 7 Augustus Close, St Albans, Herts AL3 4JH (St Albans 66044)
South Bedfordshire Dr H. E. Davies, 8 Church Ave, Leighton Buzzard LU7 7AD (Leighton Buzzard 383566)
South East Berkshire D. Hunt, 3 Moore's Green, Wokingham, Berks RG11 1QC (Wokingham 786642)
Watford & District *(Membership Secretary)* Miss R. Russell, 37 Bushey Mill Cres, Watford, Herts WD2 4RA (Watford 31204)
Welwyn Hatfield District Mrs M. Hodson, 38 Fordwich Rd, Welwyn Garden City, Herts AL8 6EY (Welwyn Garden 323561)
Wembley & District Mrs M. Sinclair, 140 Chalkhill Rd, Wembley Park, Middx HA9 9AJ (081-904 8381)
West Middlesex *(Membership Secretary)* Mrs B. Jeffery, 55 Chamberlain Way, Pinner, Middx HA5 2AU (081-866 0337)
Wimbledon Mrs E. Brockbank, 2A Rougemont Ave, Morden, Surrey SM4 5PZ (081-640 4855)
Windsor & District M. J. Gorton, 11 Duncannon Cres, Windsor, Berks SL4 4YN (Windsor 869173)
Woodford Green D. S. Zoers, 41 Wordsworth Av, S. Woodford, London E18 2HD (081-989 2590)
Wycombe Mrs C. Vaizey, 44 Walton Dr, High Wycombe, Bucks HP13 6TT (High Wycombe 440752)

NATIONAL TRUST ASSOCIATIONS AND CENTRES

MIDLANDS

Banbury & District R. Everitt, 101 Courtington Lane, Bloxham, Banbury, Oxfordshire (Banbury 720472)

Cheltenham & Gloucestershire A. Bruce, Cleadon House, Cleeve Hill, Cheltenham, Glos GL52 3QG (Cheltenham 529433)

Coventry Miss M. B. Smith, 7 Lamerton Cl, Wyken, Coventry CV2 3AL (Coventry 455579)

Herefordshire & Marches Miss P. M. Allen, 8 Orchard Cl, Moreton-on-Lugg, Hereford HR4 8DG (Hereford 760587)

Leicester Miss B. A. Hewitt, 7 Westleigh Avenue, Fosse Rd South, Leicester LE3 0HG (Leicester 546280)

Lincolnshire Miss J. K. Jefferson, 2 Wiseholme Rd, Skellingthorpe, Lincoln LN6 5TF (Lincoln 687837)

Mansfield Mrs A. Gibson, 40 Highfield Rd, Clipstone, Nottinghamshire NG21 9ER

Midland (Birmingham) Mrs M. E. Stoddart, 78 Prince of Wales Lane, Warstock, Birmingham BI4 4JY (021-474 3631)

Mid-Warwickshire Miss J. Johnstone, Rocklands, Stoneleigh Rd, Blackdown, Leamington Spa, Warwickshire CV32 6QR (Leamington Spa 24841)

Northamptonshire Mrs D. Campbell, 5 Courteenhall Village, Roade, Northampton NN7 2QE (Northampton 863741)

North Cotswolds V. Aylott, Rosebank, Old Rectory Gdns, Longborough, Moreton-in-Marsh, Glos GL56 0QF (Bourton-in-the-Water 30317)

North Staffordshire Mrs M. Richards, 6 Geneva Dr, Westlands, Newcastle-under-Lyme ST5 2QG

Nottingham C. B. Huthwaite, 11 Grange Rd, Woodthorpe, Nottingham NG5 4FU (Nottingham 609565)

Peterborough & Stamford Miss S. A. Green, 3 Beaufort Ave, Market Deeping, Peterborough PE6 3JD (Market Deeping 347489)

Rugby D. C. Eastwood, 1 Grays Orchard, Thurlaston, Rugby, Warwicks CV23 9LB (Rugby 810481)

Shropshire E. Stephenson, 'Paroma', Batch Lane, All Stretton, Church Stretton, Shropshire SY6 6JR (Church Stretton 722401)

Solihull H. D. Kettle, Broadmead, 7 Cawdon Gr, Dorridge, Solihull B93 8EA (Knowle 772901)

South Derbyshire Mrs J. Harris, 50 Spring Terrace Rd, Stapenhill, Burton-on-Trent, Staffs DE15 9DU (Burton-on-Trent 66888)

Staffordshire L. Ashton, 20 Fallowfield, Wildwood, Stafford ST17 4QU

Stratford-upon-Avon *(Chairman)* K. Allen, 6 Bishopton Lane, Stratford-upon-Avon, Warwickshire (Stratford-upon-Avon 204105)

Sutton Coldfield Mrs G. Hutchinson, 22 Roberts Ct, Chester Rd, Erdington, Birmingham B24 0BX (021-373 3187)

Walsall H. R. Taylor, 17 Squirrel Wk, Little Aston, Sutton Coldfield B74 3PX (021-353 8845)

Wolverhampton Mrs S. Allsop, 34 Willow Rd, Finchfield, Wolverhampton WV13 3ST

Worcester/Malvern Mrs D. Hopkin-Morgan, 58 Wedderburn Road, Malvern WR14 2DQ (Malvern 62764)

Wyre Forest & District P. D. Dingley, 16 Cheviot Cl, Astley Cross, Stourport on Severn DY13 0NX (Stourport 4746)

NORTHERN ENGLAND

Bolton Mrs K. Gorse, 15 Kinloch Dr, Heaton, Bolton BL1 4LZ (Bolton 47849)

Chester C. D. Rodway, 12 Kipling Way, Crewe, Cheshire CW1 1JQ (Crewe 582803)

Cleveland S. Morgan, 29 Matfen Ave, Nunthorpe, Middlesbrough TS7 0EQ (Middlesbrough 319431)

County Durham Miss J. D. Yates, 40 Whaggs Lane, Whickham, Newcastle-upon-Tyne NE16 4SE

Crosby Mrs I. Horsfall, 118 Moor Dr, Crosby, Liverpool L23 2UT (051-924 2626)

Dales Mrs N. Purvis, The Shoulder of Mutton, Kirkby Malzeard, Ripon, N. Yorks HG4 3RT (Kirkby Malzeard 619)

Doncaster Miss A. Walton, 39 Old Hexthorpe, Doncaster, S. Yorks DN4 0JD (Doncaster 854307)

East Cheshire (Stockport area) Mrs W. Luxon, 73 Dairyground Rd, Bramhall, Stockport SK7 2QW

East Yorkshire Mrs G. M. Brooke, 82 Westbourne Ave, Hull HU5 3HS (Hull 493146)

Frodsham Mrs M. Dodd, 48 SBJ Park, Chester Rd, Helsby WA6 0EZ

Greater Manchester Miss Joan K. Bateson, 96 Kingsway, Alkrington, Middleton, Manchester M24 1HN (061-643 2505)

Heswall Mrs J. Cussons, 6 Lester Dr, Irby, Wirral L61 4XS (051-648 1814)

Holme & Calder Mrs B. Kennedy-Skipton, 9 Marling Rd, Fixby, Huddersfield, W. Yorks (Elland 74237)

16

Lake District Members' Club Mrs H. Edwards, Barbary Hill, Spooner Vale, Windermere, Cumbria (Windermere 5075)
Liverpool Miss M. J. Moulson, 44 Venables Dr, Poulton, Bebington, Merseyside L63 9LT (051-334 4801)
Lunesdale & Kent Estuary Mrs E. M. C. Dean, 83 Greenwood Ave, Bolton le Sands, Lancs LA5 8AW (0524 824085)
Maghull Mrs L. Wheeler, 12 Kendal Dr, Maghull, Merseyside L31 9AZ (051-526 2567)
Mid-Yorkshire Miss D. Chant, 11 Mount Pisgah, Burras Lane, Otley LS21 3DX (Otley 463273)
North Cheshire Mrs M. Birchall, 1 Tolland Lane, Altrincham, Cheshire WA15 0LD (061-980 7351)
North Cumbrian Club Mrs S. Cumming, Midtown House, Greysouthen, Cockermouth CA13 0UL (Cockermouth 825438)
North Northumberland G. Harris, Greystones, Stable Green, Mitford, Morpeth NE61 3QA (Morpeth 513150)
Ormskirk & District J. Watson, 'San Remo', 38 Ruff Lane, Ormskirk, L39 4QZ (Ormskirk 572656)
Peak District Mrs J. M. Griffiths, 3A Red Lane, Disley, Stockport SK12 2NP (Disley 65240)
Pendle Forest C. Parkinson, 2 Lawrence Av, Simonstone, nr Burnley, Lancs BB12 7HX
Ribble T. Heathman, 7 Fulwood Heights, Preston, Lancashire PR2 4AW (Preston 701499)
Ryedale A. H. Ansell, 5 Millfield Rise, Easingwold, York YO6 3NE (Easingwold 22555)
St Helens Miss E. Thomas, 11 Springfield Lane, Eccleston, St Helens, Merseyside WA10 5EL (St Helens 34524)
Sheffield G. Hampton, 23 Top Rd, Worrall, Sheffield, S. Yorks S30 3AQ (Oughtibridge 3441)
Tyneside Miss R. Parkinson, 6 Howick Av, Gosforth, Newcastle upon Tyne NE3 2NA (091-285 6418)
West Lancashire R. Hipkins, 54 Hampton Rd, Southport PR8 6QA (Southport 538692)
West Yorkshire P. Askwith, 316 Bradford Rd, Otley, W. Yorks LS21 3LT (Otley 463436)
York W. B. Taylor, 4 The Courtyard, Bishopthorpe, York YO2 1RD (York 707063)

WALES

Abertawe Mrs B. A. Garnham, 57 Caemawr Rd, Morriston, Swansea SA6 7EA (Swansea 773072)
Cardiff J. Long, Greenacre, Llantwit Rd, Cowbridge, S. Glam CF7 7AU (Cowbridge 772320)
Chirkland R. Harrison, 54 Llanforda Rise, High Lea, Oswestry (Oswestry 666216)
Dyffryn Clwyd Mrs F. Sasse, Hendy, Afonwen, Mold, Clwyd CH7 5UP (Mold 720220)
Eryri M. Hickman, Douglas House, Mynydd, Llandegai, Bangor Gwynedd
Gwent Mrs B. Moon, 11 Barton Bridge Cl, Raglan NP5 2JN (Raglan 690317)
Menai Mrs K. Thorpe, c/o Plas Newydd, Llanfairpwll, Anglesey, Gwynedd LL61 6EQ
Merioneth W. R. Holton, Ty'r Gof, Heol y Bryn, Lon Uchaf, Harlech, Gwynedd (Harlech 780161)
North Wales E. W. Stanley, Evergreens, 15 Bryn-y-Mor Rd, Rhos on Sea, Colwyn Bay, Clwyd LL28 4EF (Colwyn Bay 46569)
Powis J. Gleave, Abernant, Fron, Powys SY15 6RZ (0686 640494)
Wrexham D. R. Dutton, Inglenook, 3 Camberley Dr, Wrexham, Clwyd LL12 7LN (Wrexham 263831)

NORTHERN IRELAND

Belfast David Smith, Knockleigh, Shaw's Bridge, Belfast 9.
North Coast D. G. Hanns, Brookville, 15 Main St, Castlerock, Coleraine, Co. Londonderry BT51 4RA (Coleraine 848294)

SLOES

National Trust Enterprises

The National Trust's shops, restaurants, tea-rooms and holiday cottages are all managed by National Trust Enterprises Ltd and are an important source of income for the Trust contributing £4 million to National Trust funds in 1989.

Shopping with the National Trust

Most National Trust properties have shops offering a wide range of merchandise – much of which is exclusive to the National Trust. These shops and their opening times are indicated in relevant property entries by the ⬜ symbol. Many of these shops are also open for Christmas shopping and dates are given in the appropriate entries. In addition the Trust now operates a number of shops in towns (listed below) which are usually open during normal trading hours.

Town shops

AVON
Bath: Marshall Wade's House, Abbey Churchyard, Bath BA1 1LY (0225 460249)
Bristol: 77 Queen's Road, Clifton, Bristol BS8 1QP (0272 264798)

BERKSHIRE
Windsor: 14 High St, Windsor SL4 1LD (0753 850433)

CAMBRIDGESHIRE
Cambridge: 9 King's Parade, Cambridge CB2 1SJ (0223 311894)

CHESHIRE
Chester: 5 Northgate St, Chester CH1 2HA (0244 313465)

CORNWALL
Penzance: The Egyptian House, 6 Chapel St, Penzance TR18 4AJ (0736 64378)
Truro: 9 River St, Truro TR1 2SQ (0872 41464)

CUMBRIA
Hawkshead: The Square, Hawkshead, Ambleside LA22 0NZ (09666 471)

DEVON
Dartmouth: 8 The Quay, Dartmouth TQ6 9PS (0803 833694)
Exeter: 18 Cathedral Yard, Exeter EX1 1HB (0392 74102)
Sidmouth: Old Fore St, Sidmouth EX10 8LS (03955 78107)
Totnes: The Plains, Totnes TQ9 5DW (0803 863475)

DORSET
Dorchester: Williams House, 65 High West St, Dorchester, Dorset DT1 1XA (0305 267535)

DURHAM
Durham: Durham Information Centre & Shop, 61 Saddler St, Durham City DH1 3NU (091-384 5285)

GLOUCESTERSHIRE
Tewkesbury: 39 Church St, Tewkesbury GL20 5SN (0684 292919) (closed end Jan to end March)

ISLE OF WIGHT
Newport: 35a St James's St, Newport PO30 1LB (0983 526445)

KENT
Canterbury: 24 Burgate, Canterbury CT1 2HA (0227 457120)

LONDON
Westminster: The Blewcoat School, 23 Caxton St, London SW1H 9AH (071-222 2877)

NORFOLK
Norwich: (shop & tea-room) 3–5 Dove St, Norwich NR1 1DE (0603 610206)

NORTHUMBERLAND
Hexham: 25/26 Market Pl, Hexham, Northumberland NE46 3PB (0434 607654)
Seahouses: 16 Main St, Seahouses, Northumberland NE68 7RQ (0665 721099)

SHROPSHIRE
Shrewsbury: 42 High St, Shrewsbury SY1 1ST (0743 50354)

SOMERSET
Wells: 16 Market Place, Wells, Somerset BA5 2RB (0749 77735)

SUSSEX, EAST
Brighton: The Vokins Store, 43 Ship St, Brighton, E. Sussex BN1 1FD (0273 23211)
Rye: 87 High St, Rye, E. Sussex TN31 7JN (0797 224295)

WILTSHIRE
Melksham: 5 Church St, Melksham, Wiltshire SN12 6LS (0225 706454)
Salisbury: House of Steps, 41 High St, Salisbury, Wiltshire SP1 2PB (0722 331884)

YORKSHIRE
York: 32 Goodramgate, York YO1 2LG (0904 659050)

SOUTH WALES
Monmouth: 5 Church St, Monmouth, Gwent NP5 3BX (0600 3270)
Pembroke: Westgate House, 3 Main St, Pembroke, Dyfed SA71 4JS (0646 684197)
St David's: Captain's House, High St, St David's, Haverfordwest, Dyfed SP62 65D (0437 720385)
Solva: Main Street, Solva, Dyfed SA62 6UU (0437 720661)

NORTHERN IRELAND
Belfast: 86 Botanic Ave, Belfast BT7 1JR (0232 230018)

National Trust Enterprises produce an annual catalogue for mail-order shopping which is sent to all members in the autumn. If you are not a member and would like to receive a catalogue please write to the Mail Order Customer Services Manager, PO Box 101, Melksham, Wiltshire SN12 8EA (tel. Melksham (0225) 705676).

National Trust restaurants and tea-rooms

The National Trust runs over 100 restaurants and tea-rooms at its properties. Many specialise in serving local specialities, some are licensed and all concentrate on home cooking. The ▣ indicates where refreshments are available and lists opening times.

Holidays with the National Trust

The National Trust has over 200 holiday cottages in some of the most beautiful parts of England, Wales and Northern Ireland. These range form a converted water tower to a Cornish mansion with 11 acres of gardens. Some have been specially adapted for disabled visitors.

These cottages are especially popular during the main holiday period and it is wise to book as far in advance as possible. Out of the main season short weekend breaks are available. Full details of properties with prices and booking contracts are given in a colour 72-page brochure *National Trust Holiday Cottages 1991.* This is available from National Trust (Enterprises) Ltd, PO Box 101, Western Way, Melksham, Wiltshire SN12 8EA (tel. Melksham (0225) 705676). Please include a

19

cheque/postal order for 50p made payable to National Trust (Enterprises) Ltd to cover the cost of post and packing.

If you would like details of the many National Trust tenants who offer Bed and Breakfast accommodation please write to the London address on page 22 (enclosing s.a.e.) for a leaflet.

If you are interested in self-catering holidays in Scotland please contact the National Trust for Scotland, 5 Charlotte Square, Edinburgh, EH2 4DU (enclosing s.a.e.).

The Landmark Trust also offers self-catering holiday accommodation in unusual historic buildings. The Landmark Trust is based at Shottesbrooke, Maidenhead, Berkshire SL6 3SW (tel. Maidenhead (0628) 825925).

Publications

The Trust produces an increasingly wide range of books, guidebooks and children's literature. Most of these are available in National Trust shops and good book shops but you can also order them from the mail order address above (see Shopping with the National Trust). If you would like a full list of National Trust publications please write to the Trust's London address (enclosing s.a.e.)

Listed below are National Trust books you may find particularly useful when planning a visit.

The National Trust Atlas with colour photographs and gazetteer entries is invaluable (£9.95).

The National Trust Guide (fourth edition) is illustrated throughout with colour photographs and is a fascinating guide to properties and countryside in the Trust's care (£18.95).

Properties of the National Trust gives a comprehensive list of all Trust properties and is revised every 5 years. Copies are available on application to the Membership Department, Bromley (see page 22).

The National Trust Family Handbook lists a selection of Trust properties best suited for family visiting and is illustrated with lively cartoons (£3.50).

The National Trust Gardens Handbook is published in May 1991 and concentrates on the great variety of gardens in the Trust's care with practical details for getting the most out of your visit (£3.95).

MONTACUTE *Skimmington Ride*

Legacies

Please consider mentioning the Trust in your Will. When you make a legacy – no matter how modest – you can be certain that your gift will provide a lasting safeguard for the countryside and buildings in the Trust's care. If you would like to consider leaving a legacy to the Trust the following are two acceptable wordings for use in a new Will or a Codicil to your existing Will.

I bequeath to The National Trust (HB) for Places of Historic Interest or Natural Beauty of 36, Queen Anne's Gate in the City of Westminster a (state the fraction chosen) of the residue of my estate.

or

I bequeath to The National Trust (HB) for Places of Historic Interest or Natural Beauty of 36, Queen Anne's Gate in the City of Westminster the sum of £XXX (inflation linked to the Retail Price Index from the date of this Will).

If you would like to be sent a leaflet with other suggestions for wording to pass on to your professional adviser or if you have any queries about leaving a legacy to the National Trust please write to the Head of the Legacies Unit at the London address (page 22) or telephone 071-222 9251.

The Royal Oak Foundation

More than 15,000 Americans are involved with the work of the National Trust through membership of the Royal Oak Foundation. Royal Oak is a tax-exempt US organisation providing strong support for the Trust's work and has contributed more than US $1m to the restoration of National Trust properties.

In addition to helping the Trust, ROF members receive many benefits: a quarterly newsletter; the National Trust magazine, catalogue and Handbook; invitations to lectures, parties, exhibitions and special events in the United States; free admission to all National Trust properties and to those belonging to the National Trust for Scotland.

For information on how to join please write to The Royal Oak Foundation, 285 West Broadway, New York, NY 10013, USA or tel. 010 1 212 966 6565.

MONTACUTE *Parlour Plasterwork*

Useful Addresses

London Office: 36 Queen Anne's Gate, London SW1H 9AS (071-222 9251)

London Information Centre: Blewcoat School, 23 Caxton Street, London SW1

Membership: PO Box 39, Bromley, Kent BR1 1NH (081-464 1111)

Finance; Internal Audit; Enterprises; Volunteer Unit: Heywood House, Westbury, Wiltshire BA13 4NA (Westbury, Wilts (0373) 826826)

1 **Cornwall:** Lanhydrock, Bodmin PL30 4DE (Bodmin (0208) 74281)

2 **Devon:** Killerton House, Broadclyst, Exeter EX5 3LE (Exeter (0392) 881691)

3 **Wessex** *(Avon, Dorset, Somerset, Wiltshire)* Stourton, Warminster, Wiltshire BA12 6QD (Bourton, Dorset (0747) 840224)

4 **Southern** *(Hampshire, Isle of Wight, South-Western Greater London, Surrey and West Sussex)* Polesden Lacey, Dorking, Surrey RH5 6BD (Bookham (0372) 453401)

5 **Kent & East Sussex** *(includes South-Eastern Greater London)*, The Estate Office, Scotney Castle, Lamberhurst, Tunbridge Wells, Kent TN3 8JN (Lamberhurst (0892) 890651)

6 **East Anglia** *(Cambridgeshire, Essex, Norfolk, Suffolk)* Blickling, Norwich NR11 6NF (Aylsham (0263) 733471)

7 **Thames & Chilterns** *(Buckinghamshire, Bedfordshire, Berkshire, Hertfordshire, London north of the Thames, and Oxfordshire)* Hughenden Manor, High Wycombe, Bucks HP14 4LA (High Wycombe (0494) 528051)

8 **Severn** *(Gloucestershire, Hereford & Worcester, Warwickshire, part of West Midlands)* Mythe End House, Tewkesbury, Glos GL20 6EB (Tewkesbury (0684) 850051)

9 **South Wales:** *(Dyfed, Gwent, West Glamorgan, southern part of Powys)* The King's Head, Bridge Street, Llandeilo, Dyfed SA19 6BB (Llandeilo (0558) 822800)

10 **North Wales:** *(Clwyd, Gwynedd, northern part of Powys)* Trinity Square, Llandudno, Gwynedd LL30 2DE (Llandudno (0492) 860123)

11 **Mercia** *(Cheshire, Merseyside, Shropshire, Greater Manchester, most of Staffordshire part of West Midlands)* Attingham Park Shrewsbury, Shropshire SY4 4TP (Upton Magna (074 377) 343)

12 **East Midlands** *(Derbyshire, Leicestershire, Lincolnshire, Northamptonshire, Nottinghamshire, South Humberside and those parts of Cheshire, Greater Manchester, Staffordshire, South Yorkshire and West Yorkshire within the Peak National Park)* Clumber Park Stableyard, Worksop, Notts S80 3BE (Worksop (0909) 486411)

13 **Yorkshire** *(includes North, South and West Yorkshire, Cleveland and North Humberside)* Goddards, 27 Tadcaster Road, Dringhouses, York YO2 2QG (York (0904) 702021)

14 **North-West** *(Cumbria and Lancashire)* Rothay Holme, Rothay Road, Ambleside, Cumbria LA22 0EJ (Ambleside (05394) 33883)

15 **Northumbria** *(Durham, Northumberland, and Tyne & Wear)* Scots' Gap, Morpeth, Northumberland NE61 4EG (Scots' Gap (067 074) 691)

16 **Northern Ireland:** Rowallane House, Saintfield, Ballynahinch, Co. Down BT24 7LH (Saintfield (0238) 510721)

Regional Offices

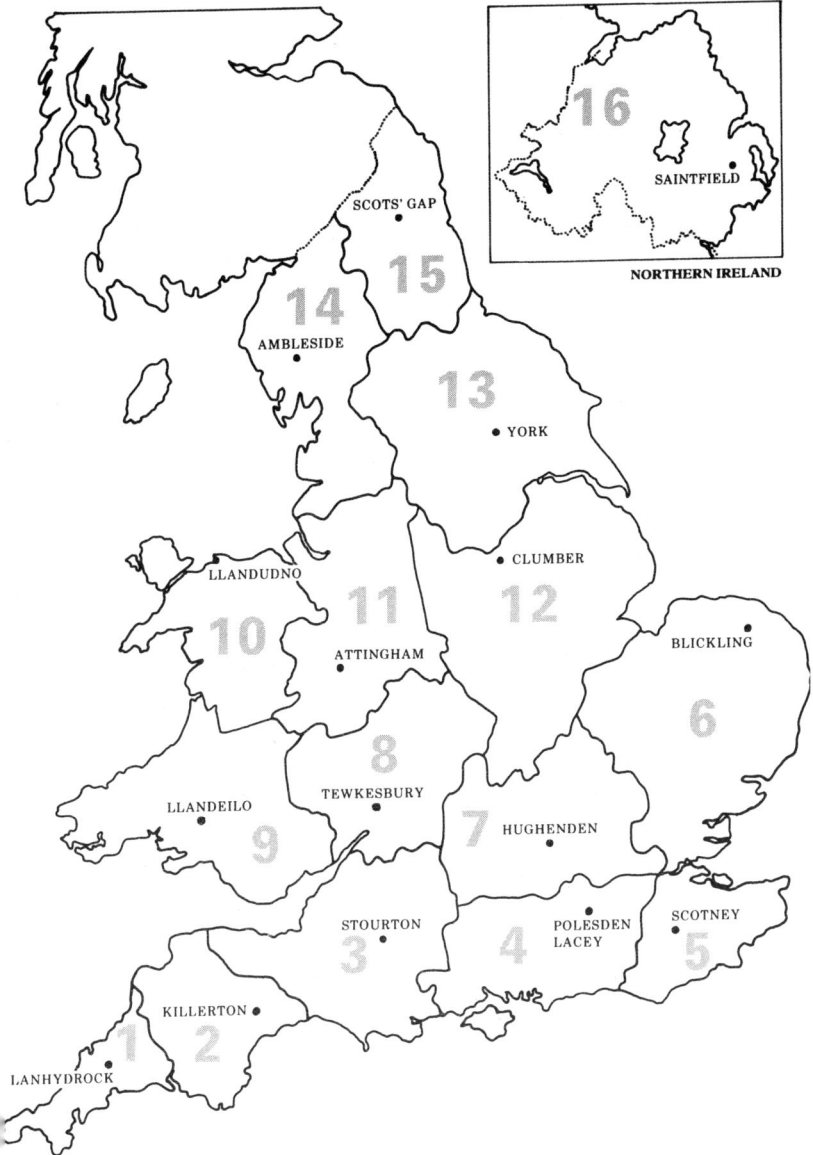

SCOTS' GAP

16

SAINTFIELD

NORTHERN IRELAND

15

14

AMBLESIDE

13

YORK

LLANDUDNO

11

12

CLUMBER

10

ATTINGHAM

BLICKLING

6

8

TEWKESBURY

LLANDEILO

9

7

HUGHENDEN

STOURTON

3

4

POLESDEN
LACEY

SCOTNEY

5

KILLERTON

1

2

LANHYDROCK

Key to symbols

Castle

Historic house

Other buildings

Mill

Church, chapel etc

Garden

Park

Countryside

Coast

Prehistoric/Roman site

Industrial archaeology

Farm/farm animals

Nature reserve

Country walk*

Open

Guided tours**

Winter opening
(varying dates from
Dec 1991 to March 1992)

Heavily-visited property

No sharp heels in building

No interior photography

No bulky bags

Admission details

Wheelchair access

Wheelchair available

For visually
handicapped visitors

Mother & baby facilities

For children

Dogs admitted on leads

No dogs please

Refreshments

How to find the property

Shop

Map symbols:
▲ Buildings & gardens
■ Coast & country

*The Trust's countryside is freely open to walkers, subject to farming or forestry restrictions;
the walks indicated by ⓘ in the entries are those which are waymarked or specially
recommended.
**The symbol ⓘ on the top line of an entry indicates that guided tours only are the rule; in
the left hand margin it indicates that guided tours are available at certain times or by
arrangement.

Avon

COUNTRYSIDE

At **Rainbow Wood** [172: ST777630] on Claverton Down, and **Smallcombe Wood** and fields [172: ST764640], at Bathwick, 524 acres of wood and farmland are part of the **Bath Skyline Walk**. A leaflet describes an 8-mile (or shorter) walk, past Iron Age field enclosures, ancient woodland and remains of the 18th-century expansion of Bath under Ralph Allen with breathtaking views across the city. Leaflet from NT Shop, Abbey Churchyard, Bath.

The Avon Gorge Nature Reserve on the west bank of the River Avon is approached from Bristol across the Clifton Suspension Bridge [172: ST560734]. This large area of woodland has flowers and fungi peculiar to the gorge, and an Iron Age hill-fort.

Blaise Hamlet, 4m N of central Bristol, W of Henbury village, just N of B4057 [172: ST559789], is a hamlet of ten different cottages designed in 1809 for John Harford by John Nash for Blaise Estate pensioners. Free access to the Green, cottages not open.

COAST

A coastal path traverses the Trust properties of **Sand Point** at Kewstoke, north of Weston-super-Mare [182: ST325660] and the adjoining two miles of coastline at **Middle Hope**. The limestone headland of **Sand Point** includes 'Castle Batch', thought to be a Norman motte. The **Monk's Steps** at Kewstoke give views over the Severn estuary [182: ST336632]. Views from Middle Hope over the Bristol Channel to the Welsh mountains and to the Mendip Hills.

BATH ASSEMBLY ROOMS

Alfred Street, Bath BA1 2QH (tel. Bath (0225) 461111)

Designed by John Wood the Younger in 1769; bombed in 1942 and re-opened 1963; restored and redecorated in 1979 and 1990; Museum of Costume (not NT) housed in basement

March to end Oct: Mon to Sat 9.30–6, Sun 10–6. Nov to end Feb 1992: Mon to Sat 10–5, Sun 11–5. Closed 25 & 26 Dec

Please contact property for details of admission charges

N of Milsom Street, E of the Circus [156: ST749653] *Bus:* frequent from BR Bath Spa and surrounding areas (tel. Bath (0225) 464446)
Station: Bath Spa ¼m

CLEVEDON COURT

Clevedon BS21 6QU (tel. Clevedon (0272) 872257)

Home of the Elton family; 14th-century manor house, once partly fortified; with 12th-century tower and 13th-century hall; collection of Nailsea glass and Eltonware; beautiful terraced garden

31 March to end Sept: Wed, Thur, Sun & BH Mon 2.30–5.30. Last admissions 5

£2.50, children £1.30. Children under 17 must be accompanied by an adult. Parties of 20 or more and guided evening tours by prior arrangement; no reduction. Coaches by appointment. Unsuitable for trailer caravans

Tea-room in Old Kitchen 2.30–5 (not NT)

1½m E of Clevedon, on Bristol road (B3130), signposted from exit 20 M5 [172: ST423716] *Bus:* Badgerline X7, 360–3, 661–3 Bristol–Clevedon; X23/4, 823 from Weston-super-Mare, alight Triangle, ¼m (tel. Bristol (0272) 297979) *Station:* Yatton 3m

DYRHAM PARK

Dyrham, nr Chippenham SN14 8ER (tel. Abson (027582) 2501)

Mansion built for William Blathwayt, Secretary at War and Secretary of State to William III, between 1691 and 1710; the rooms have been little changed since they were furnished by Blathwayt and their contents recorded in his housekeeper's inventory; 263 acres of ancient parkland with herd of fallow deer

Park: all year: daily 12–5.30 or dusk if earlier. **House & garden:** 30 March to 3 Nov: daily except Thur & Fri 12–5.30. Last admissions ½hr before closing

£ House, garden & park £4. Park only £1.20. Coaches by appointment only

Ground floor and terrace only; parking by house. Taped guide to house

Dog walking area provided. No dogs in deer park

Light lunches & afternoon teas in Orangery. 25 March to 3 Nov: daily except Thur & Fri 12–5.30; last orders 5; (tel. Abson (027582) 4293). Picnics welcome in park

→ 8m N of Bath, 12m E of Bristol; approached from Bath-Stroud road (A46), 2m S of Tormarton interchange with M4, exit 18 [172: ST743757]
Station: Bath Spa 8m

HORTON COURT

Horton, nr Chipping Sodbury, Bristol BS17 6QR

A Cotswold manor house with 12th-century Norman hall and early Renaissance features; Late Perpendicular ambulatory detached from house. Norman hall and ambulatory only shown

O 30 March to 2 Nov: Wed & Sat 2–6 or dusk if earlier. Other times by written appointment with tenant

£ £1.20. No reduction for children or parties. Unsuitable for coaches. No WCs

Ambulatory only accessible; special parking facilities on application to tenant

→ 3m NE of Chipping Sodbury, ¼m N of Horton, 1m W of the Bath-Stroud road (A46) [172: ST766851] *Station:* Yate 5m

Bedfordshire

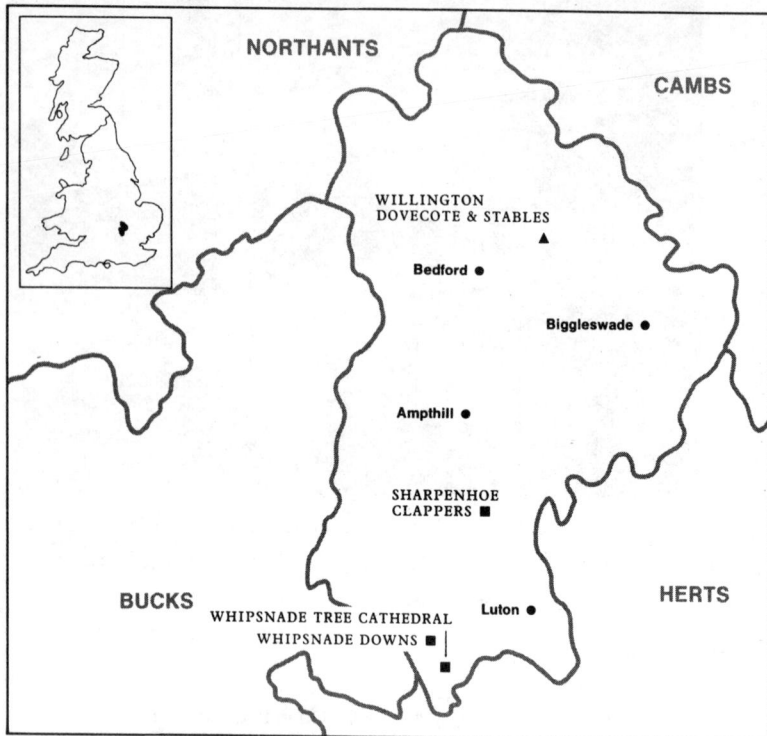

COUNTRYSIDE

At **Whipsnade Downs**, near Dunstable [166 & 165: TL000190], the Trust owns a 250-acre farm on the plateau and 50 acres of the chalk grassland on the scarp slope. There are views north towards Dunstable and west towards Ivinghoe Beacon (see Pitstone Windmill, p. 38). On this stretch of unimproved downland, the Trust has re-introduced sheep grazing, the traditional form of management of these slopes. The effect has been to conserve the open grassland habitat which supports a rich variety of plants and insects. There is unrestricted access to the chalk downland; but only by footpaths across farmland. A car park is signposted off the B4540.

Whipsnade Tree Cathedral [166: TL008182] is one of the Trust's most unusual countryside properties. Many species of trees have been planted out in the traditional pattern of a cathedral, with grassy avenues for nave and transepts. This quiet, peaceful area may be reached from Whipsnade village green, beside which there is a car park.

At the eastern end of the Chilterns, south-west of Barton-le-Clay are the steep slopes of **Sharpenhoe Clappers** [166: TL067300]. The hill top was the site of an Iron Age hill-fort.

This stretch of the Chiltern scarp contains a wide variety of habitats, ranging from unimproved chalk grassland with its richly varied flora and fauna, through incipient and mature hawthorn scrub, to beech and ash woodland. Access to the viewpoint is from the car park beside the Streatley road, half a mile to the south.

WILLINGTON DOVECOTE & STABLES 🏠

Willington, nr Bedford

16th-century stables and stone dovecote lined internally with nesting boxes for 1,500 pigeons

Note: The dovecote may be closed during the nesting season

[O] 30 March to end Sept: by appointment with Mrs J. Endersby, 21 Chapel Lane, Willington MK44 3QG (tel. Bedford (0234) 838278)

[£] [🐴] £1. No reduction for parties. Car park 30yds. No WCs

[♿] Accessible but floors uneven [◄] Guide dogs admitted by arrangement

[→] 4m E of Bedford, just N of the Sandy road (A603) [153: TL107499]
Bus: United Counties 176–8 Bedford–Biggleswade (passing BR Bedford St John's & Biggleswade and close BR Sandy), alight Willington crossroads, ½m (tel: Bedford (0234) 262151) *Station:* Bedford St John's (U), not Sun, 4m; Sandy 4½m; Bedford 5m

COMMON BLUE

Berkshire

OXON   BUCKS

■ COCK MARSH

■ LOUGH DOWN   Maidenhead
LARDON CHASE ■   PINKNEY'S GREEN ■ ●
AND THE HOLIES

BASILDON PARK ▲   MAIDENHEAD   Windsor ●
PANGBOURNE MEADOW   THICKET
Reading ●

● Newbury

FINCHAMPSTEAD RIDGES,   ● Bracknell
HEATH POOL & SIMONS WOOD

■ ■ WELLINGTONIA
AVENUE

SURREY

HANTS

COUNTRYSIDE

Glimpses of Berkshire, Hampshire and Surrey may be seen from the steep, heather-clad ridge of **Finchampstead Ridges** [175: SU808634], 4 miles south of Wokingham, south of the B3348. The ridge overlooks the valley of the River Blackwater. North of the Ridges is **Simons Wood** [175: SU814637], a heathland and woodland area with a rich variety of tree species, including clumps of Scots pine over a century old. A popular walk is to **Heath Pool**, not far from a Roman ride known as 'The Devil's Highway'. The course of the London to Silchester Roman road also crosses the wood. The area has many attractions for naturalists and bird watchers, with siskins and spotted fly catchers among the species which may be sighted. You may park beside the B3348 at the Ridges, and further east along the same road there is a signposted car park in Simons Wood. Nearby is the impressive **Wellingtonia Avenue**, which forms part of the B3348. As its name suggests, it is lined by mature species of what is one of the world's tallest trees.

Common land on the south bank of the Thames at Maidenhead and Cookham provides a range of pleasant country walks. One of the features of **Maidenhead Thicket** [175: SU855810] is a prehistoric Belgic farm enclosure known for some reason as 'Robin Hood's Arbour'. The Thicket is perhaps at its most attractive in springtime, when a mass of primroses bloom here. Visitors may be fortunate enough to hear a nightingale.

Parts of **Cock Marsh** [175: SU890869], on the south bank of the Thames facing Bourne End, provide a fine example of a lowland marsh, a habitat which is increasingly at risk in Britain today. A group of burial barrows remains as evidence of Cock Marsh's ancient history. Adjoining Maidenhead Thicket to the north is **Pinkney's Green**, and in the same area the Trust also owns **Cookham Dean** village green, **Cookham Moor**, **Widbrook (or Whitebrook) Common**, **Bigfrith** and **Tugwood Commons**, and **North Town Moor**, half a mile north of Maidenhead and Winter Hill. Residents of the area bought and gave all these pleasant open spaces to the Trust in 1934. Today they continue to be enjoyed by local people and visitors alike. There are several small car parks in the area, some of which are signposted.

The Holies [174: SU594797], **Lardon Chase** [174: SU588809] and **Lough Down** [174: SU588813] all lie on the west side of the Goring Gap where the Thames divides the Chilterns from the North Wessex Downs. The car park at the top of Streatley Hill [174: SU583806] gives access to all these properties, from which there are magnificent views. The chalk grassland is managed for its nature conservation interest. The Holies comprises grassland, heathland and woodland. A short distance away, just below Pangbourne Bridge, east of the B471 is **Pangbourne Meadow** [175: SU640768], a seven-acre area with some interesting flora, on the south bank of the Thames.

BASILDON PARK 🏠 ❀ ♠   ✄ ▨ ▨

Lower Basildon, Reading RG8 9NR (tel. Reading (0734) 843040)

Classical 18th-century house by John Carr of York, in beautiful setting overlooking the Thames Valley; the focal point of the interior is an unusual Octagon room; fine plasterwork; important pictures and furniture; decorative Shell room; garden and woodland walks

○   30 March to end Oct: Wed to Sat 2–6; Sun & BH Mon 12–6. Closed Wed following Bank Holiday. Last admissions 5.30

▣ ❀   Shop open 30 March to end Oct: Wed to Sat 2–5.30; Sun & BH Mon 1.30–5.30; 1 Nov to 15 Dec: Fri 12–4; Sat & Sun 11–5 (tel. Upper Basildon (0491) 671738)

£   House and grounds £2.80. Grounds only £1.80. Party rates on application to Administrator; parties must book (no parties on Sun or BH Mon). Parking in grounds, 400yds downhill from house

♦   High chair available in tea-room

♿   Garden via gravel paths; tea-room accessible via 2 low steps. Shop in stable yard; level access. House largely unsuitable. Special parking facilities; please collect pass at ticket office; ♿ WC in car park

🐕   In grounds only, on leads

◗♿   Tea-room same months as house: teas Wed to Sun, also light lunches Sat, Sun & BH Mon; Wed to Fri 2–5.30; Sat, Sun & BH Mon 12–5.30. Also 1 Nov to
❀   15 Dec: Sat & Sun 12–4. Tel. Reading (0734) 844080. Picnic area by car park

→   Between Pangbourne and Streatley, 7m NW of Reading, on W side of A329; leave M4 at Jn 12 [175: SU611782] *Bus:* Oxford/Bee Line 5 Reading–Oxford (passing BR Pangbourne) (tel. Reading (0734) 581358 or Oxford (0865) 711312) *Station:* Pangbourne 2½m; Goring & Streatley 3m

PLEASE REFER TO PAGES 5–9

STONECHAT

31

Buckinghamshire

NORTHANTS

BEDS

● Milton Keynes

▲ BUCKINGHAM CHANTRY CHAPEL

● Buckingham

STOWE LANDSCAPE GARDENS

▲ CLAYDON HOUSE

OXON

ASCOT T ▲

PITSTONE
WINDMILL

WADDESDON MANOR
▲

BOARSTALL DUCK DECOY ▲
BOARSTALL TOWER ▲

Aylesbury ● ▲
KING'S HEAD

LONG CRENDON COURTHOUSE ▲

HERTS

■ COOMBE HILL AND LOW SCRUBS

■ PULPIT WOOD

PRINCES RISBOROUGH ▲
MANOR HOUSE

■ BRADENHAM

WEST WYCOMBE HILL ▲ HUGHENDEN MANOR
& VILLAGE
WEST WYCOMBE ▲ ■ ● High Wycombe
PARK

CLIVEDEN ▲

● Beaconsfield
▲ DORNEYWOOD
GARDEN

Marlow ●

GREATER LONDON

BERKS

COUNTRYSIDE

The charming village of **Bradenham** [165: SU823970] to the north-west of High
Wycombe belongs almost entirely to the Trust. There are over 1,000 acres of Chiltern
beech woodland, hills and farmland to be explored. A network of paths provides easy
access for the rambler. The church and 17th-century manor house provide an impressive
backdrop to the sloping village green. The manor house, which is let and not open to the
public, was once the home of Isaac Disraeli, whose Prime Minister son Benjamin lived at
Hughenden Manor nearby (see p. 37). Car parking is available at the village green.

🚶 **Coombe Hill** [165: SP849066], $3\frac{1}{2}$ miles north-east of Princes Risborough, is the
highest viewpoint in the Chilterns, rising to 852 feet. There are extensive views over the
Vale of Aylesbury, towards the Berkshire Downs, to the Cotswolds north of Oxford and

the woodland in which is set Chequers, the official country house of the Prime Minister. (The monument on Coombe Hill is not NT property.) During winter, sheep graze the chalk downland turf. In 1906, the then owner of Coombe Hill put fences on his property to keep the public out. However, the outraged people of nearby Wendover tore down the barriers and eventually public rights of way were legally established.

Adjoining Coombe Hill is **Low Scrubs**, bought by the National Trust in 1985. It includes an area of ancient beech coppice which was used for centuries by local poor people to provide fuel. There is a car park for both properties off the Dunsmore road [165: SP852063].

Pulpit Wood [165: SP832048], south of Coombe Hill, is a typical Chiltern beechwood, on which a hill-fort may be seen. This recent acquisition gives fine views over the Vale of Aylesbury. There is a small car park by the roadside [165: SP834045].

West Wycombe Hill and Village (see p. 41) [175: SU829947] is situated 2 miles west of High Wycombe with fine views over West Wycombe Park (see p. 41) and the surrounding countryside. The hill, on which is an Iron Age defended settlement, was given to the National Trust in 1935 just after the acquisition of most of the village a year earlier.

ASCOTT 🏠🍀 ⊠⬚⬚⬚

Wing, nr Leighton Buzzard LU7 0PS (tel. Aylesbury (0296) 688242)

Anthony de Rothschild collection of fine pictures, French and Chippendale furniture, exceptional Oriental porcelain; garden contains unusual trees, flower borders, topiary sundial, naturalised bulbs and water-lilies

⭘ **House & garden:** April to 9 May & 1–29 Sept: Tues to Sun 2–6; also BH Mon 1 April & 6 May 2–6 (but closed Tues 2 April & 7 May)
Garden only: 15 May to 28 Aug: every Wed & last Sun in each month & BH Mon, 27 May & 26 Aug 2–6. Last admissions 5.30

£ House & garden £3.80; children £2. Grounds only £2.20. No reduction for parties which must book. Parking 220yds

♿ Ground floor only; limited access to garden; special parking by prior arrangement

🐕 In car park only

➡ ½m E of Wing, 2m SW of Leighton Buzzard, on S side of A418 [165: SP891230] *Bus:* Aylesbury Bus/Bee Line 65, X14/15, Routemaster 5 Aylesbury–Leighton Buzzard (passing close BR Aylesbury & Leighton Buzzard) (tel. Aylesbury (0296) 84919 or 382000) *Station:* Leighton Buzzard 2m

BOARSTALL DUCK DECOY 🦆🚶

Boarstall, nr Aylesbury (tel. Brill (0844) 237488)

An 18th-century duck decoy in working order; in 13 acres of natural woodland; nature trail

⭘ Good Fri 29 March to 26 Aug: Wed 2–5; Sat, Sun & BH Mon 10–5. School parties by arrangement Wed am. Talk/demonstration when Warden is available, Sat, Sun & BH Mon at 11 & 3. Exhibition Hall *continued*

£	£1.50. Parties of six or more, which must book in advance, £1
♿	Nature trail, bird hide and decoy accessible in dry weather; ramps
🐕	In car park only
→	Midway between Bicester and Thame, 2m W of Brill [164 or 165: SP624151] *Station:* Bicester Town, (U), not Sun, 6½m; Bicester North, 7½m

BOARSTALL TOWER 🏠

Boarstall, nr Aylesbury HP18 9OX

The stone gatehouse of a fortified house long since demolished; it dates from the 14th century and retains its crossloops for bows; almost surrounded by a moat

◯	By written appointment with tenant. May to end Sept: Wed 2–6
£	£1. No reduction for parties. No WCs
♿	Access to garden and ground floor of house (1 step); car park near house
🐕	In car park only
→	Midway between Bicester and Thame, 2m W of Brill [164 or 165: SP624141] *Station:* as for Boarstall Duck Decoy above

BUCKINGHAM CHANTRY CHAPEL 🏠 ✈ ⌧

Market Hill, Buckingham

Rebuilt in 1475 and retaining a fine Norman doorway; restored by Gilbert Scott in 1875, at which time it was used as a Latin or Grammar School

◯	30 March to end Oct: by written appointment with the Buckingham Heritage Trust Ltd, The Old Gaol, Market Hill, Buckingham MK18 1EW
£	Free. No WC. ♿
→	On Market Hill [152 or 165: SP693340] *Bus:* Aylesbury Bus 2, 66 from Aylesbury (passing close BR Aylesbury) (tel. Aylesbury (0296) 84919); Paynes 32, 51 from Milton Keynes (passing close BR Milton Keynes Central) (tel. Buckingham (0280) 817761) *Station:* Wolverton 10m

CLAYDON HOUSE 🏠✠ ⌧ 📷

Middle Claydon, nr Buckingham MK18 2EY
(tel. Steeple Claydon (0296) 730349/730693)

18th-century house, containing a series of magnificent and unique rococo staterooms with important carving; museum with mementoes of Florence Nightingale and the Verney family

Notes: Certain rooms have no electric light. Visitors wishing to make a close study of the interior should avoid dull days early and late in the season. All Saints Church, in the grounds, is open to the public, not NT

☉ 30 March to end Oct: Sat to Wed & BH Mon 1–5. Last admissions 4.30

£ £2.80. Parties must book; rates on application to Custodian

✚ Nappy-changing facilities

♿ Car park close to front door. 3 steps to front door; ramps; then all ground floor
rooms accessible. Access to garden via 2 steps; ramps. Half-price admission to
ground floor only; ♿ WC. Guided tours for groups of visually handicapped
people by arrangement: Braille guide

🐕 In park on leads only

♿ Teas open as house

Events: Claydon concert series: tel. Steeple Claydon (0296) 730252. ♿

➡ In Middle Claydon 13m NW of Aylesbury, 3½m SW of Winslow; signposted
from A413, A421 & A41; entrance by N drive only [165: SP720253]
Bus: Aylesbury Bus 15 from Aylesbury (passing close BR Aylesbury)
(tel. Aylesbury (0296) 84919)

CLIVEDEN (Bucks & Berks) ✿♠🏛 ⊠

Taplow, Maidenhead, Berkshire SL6 0JA (tel. Burnham (0628) 605069)

*Set on cliffs 200 feet above the Thames; the present house built in 1851, and once the home
of Nancy, Lady Astor, is now let as an hotel to Blakeney Hotels Ltd; the 375 acres of garden
and woodland include a magnificent parterre a water garden and miles of woodland walks
with spectacular views of the Thames*

☉✿ **Grounds:** March to end Oct: daily 11–6; Nov & Dec: daily 11–4. **House (three
rooms open):** April to Oct: Thur & Sun 3–6. Last admissions 5.30. Entry by
timed ticket from information kiosk   *continued*

⬜ ❄ Shop in Old Grape House adjacent to main car park. Open Good Fri 29 March to end Oct: Wed to Sun & BH Mon 1–5.30; 1 Nov to 15 Dec: Wed to Sun 12–4. Tel. Burnham (0628) 665946

£ Grounds £2.80. House £1 extra. Party rates on application to Administrator; parties must book (no parties on Sun or BH Mon). Car parking 400yds from house

Note: Mooring charge on Cliveden Reach £5 per 24hrs (up to 4hrs £2) (incl. NT members) but excl. admission fee to Cliveden. Tickets available from River Warden. Mooring at suitable locations for more than $\frac{1}{2}$m downstream from Cliveden boathouse

♿ Grounds largely accessible; maps with suggested routes available. Access to house by special arrangement. Shop in Old Grape House accessible. ♿ WC. Car park 200yds from house but special arrangements available, please enquire

🐕 Dogs in specified woodlands only; not in garden (except guide dogs)

🍴 ♿ Morning coffee, light lunches, teas and vegetarian dishes 29 March to end Oct:
❄ Wed to Sun & BH Mon (incl. Good Fri) 11–5 in Orangery restaurant. Also 9 Nov to 15 Dec: Sat & Sun 12–2. 🪑 High chairs available. Parties of more than 20 must book. Tel. Burnham (0628) 661406

Events: 26 June to 7 July, Open Air Theatre Festival; s.a.e., please, for details. ♿

➡ 3m upstream from Maidenhead, 2m N of Taplow; leave M4 at Jn 7 onto A4 or M40 at Jn 4 onto A404 to Marlow and follow signs. Entrance by main gates opposite Feathers Inn [175: SU915851] *Bus:* Bee Line 68 Slough–Maidenhead (passing close BR Taplow & Slough) (tel. Maidenhead (0628) 21344) *Station:* Taplow, not Sun, 2$\frac{1}{2}$m; Burnham 3m

DORNEYWOOD GARDEN ❄ 🪑

Dorneywood, Burnham SL1 8PY

The house was given to the Trust as an official residence for either a Secretary of State or Minister of the Crown; only the garden is open

🅾 Wed 10 & 17 July, Sat 3 & 17 Aug: 2–6 by appointment in writing to the Secretary, Dorneywood Trust, at the above address. Also open Whit Sun 26 May as part of National Gardens Scheme when no appointment necessary

£ £1.80. No reduction for parties. ♿ Part of garden only

➡ SW of Burnham Beeches, 1$\frac{1}{2}$m N of Burnham village, 2m E of Cliveden. On Dorneywood road from Burnham village, take Beaconsfield road, 1st rt outside village; or from M40, Jn 2, take A355 to Slough, 1st rt to Burnham, 2m, then 2nd left after Jolly Woodman PH [175: SU938848] *Bus:* London Country NW 704 High Wycombe–Heathrow Airport (passing close BR Slough & Beaconsfield), alight Farnham Common, 1$\frac{1}{2}$m walk through Burnham Beeches (tel. High Wycombe (0494) 464647) *Station:* Burnham 2$\frac{1}{2}$m

PLEASE REFER TO PAGES 5–9

HUGHENDEN MANOR 🏛️ ❄️ ♠️   ✉️ 📷

High Wycombe HP14 4LA (tel. High Wycombe (0494) 532580)

Bought in 1847 by Disraeli, who refashioned the house and grounds and lived here until his death in 1881; contains many Disraeli relics, including much furniture, pictures and books. Access to woodland on Hughenden Manor Estate; Hanging and Flagmore Woods contain remnants of Disraeli's tree planting schemes; Great and Little Tinkers Woods form a backdrop to Disraeli's monument

O March: Sat & Sun only 2–6. April to end Oct: Wed to Sat 2–6; Sun & BH Mon 12–6. Closed Good Fri. Last admissions 5.30

🛍️ ❄️ Shop open as house. Also Nov to 15 Dec: Wed to Sun 12–4. Tel. High Wycombe (0494) 440718

£ £2.80. Parties must book; rates on application to Custodian; no parties Sat, Sun or BH Mon. Coach parking: space for only one coach at a time; car park 200yds from house

♿ Ground floor and grounds only; special car parking arrangements; ♿ WC. Braille leaflet and taped guide

🐕 In Park and car park only

➡️ 1½m N of High Wycombe; on W side of the Great Missenden road (A4128) [165: SU866955] *Bus:* Bee Line 323/4 High Wycombe–Aylesbury, (passing close BR High Wycombe) (tel. High Wycombe (0494) 520941) *Station:* High Wycombe 2m

KING'S HEAD 🏠

The Market Square, Aylesbury HP20 1TA (tel. Aylesbury (0296) 415158)

An hotel, partly mid-15th-century; the large contemporary window in the parlour contains fragments of figures of angels holding shields – some of which bear the arms of Henry VI and his wife, Margaret of Anjou

O ✻ During licensing hours

🍵 Bar food daily; à la carte restaurant Mon to Fri & Sat evening, (advanced booking recommended)

➔ At NW corner of Market Square. *Bus:* from surrounding areas (tel. Aylesbury (0296) 84919) *Station:* Aylesbury; few min. walk

LONG CRENDON COURTHOUSE 🏠   ⊠ ⊠

Long Crendon, nr Thame HP18 9AN

A 14th-century building of two storeys, partly half-timbered, probably first used as a wool store; the manorial courts were held here from the reign of Henry V until recent times; the ground floor, re-arranged as a flat, is let

O Upper floor only 30 March to end Sept: Wed 2–6; Sat, Sun & BH Mon 11–6

£ £1. No reduction for parties. No WCs

🍵 Teas in Church House nearby every Sun and most Sat (not NT)

➔ 2m N of Thame, via B4011, close to the church [165: SP698091] *Bus:* Aylesbury Bus/Oxford 260/1, Aylesbury – Thame (passing BR Haddenham & Thame Parkway) (tel: Aylesbury (0296) 84919) *Station:* Haddenham & Thame Parkway 2m by footpath, 4m by road

PITSTONE WINDMILL ⊠   ⊠

Ivinghoe

One of the oldest post mills in Britain; in view from Ivinghoe Beacon

O May to end Sept: Sun & BH Mon 2.30–6. Last admissions 5.30

£ 60p. No reduction for parties; for details of arrangements for parties, contact I. A. Horn, 1 Wellcroft, Ivinghoe, Leighton Buzzard, Beds (tel. Cheddington (0296) 668227). Parking 200yds (by B488). Not suitable for disabled or visually handicapped visitors. No WCs

➔ $\frac{1}{2}$m S of Ivinghoe, 3m NE of Tring, just W of B488 [165: SP946158] *Bus:* Luton & District 61 Aylesbury–Luton (passing close BR Aylesbury & Luton) (tel. Aylesbury (0296) 84919). *Station:* Tring 2$\frac{1}{2}$m; Cheddington 2$\frac{1}{2}$m

PLEASE REFER TO PAGES 5–9

PRINCES RISBOROUGH MANOR HOUSE 🏠 ☒

Princes Risborough HP17 9AW

17th-century red brick house with Jacobean oak staircase

O **✱** House & garden by written appointment only with tenant, Wed 2.30–4.30. Last admissions 4. Principal rooms and staircase shown

£ **&** £1. No reduction for parties. Public car park 50yds

♞ Admitted by arrangement with tenant

➔ Opposite church, off market square in town centre [165: SP806035]
Bus: Bee Line 323/4 High Wycombe–Aylesbury (passing close BR Aylesbury) (tel. High Wycombe (0494) 20941) *Station:* Princes Risborough 1m

STOWE LANDSCAPE GARDENS ✚ 🏠 ♣

Buckingham MK18 5EH (tel. Buckingham (0280) 822850)

One of the supreme creations of the Georgian era; the first, formal layout was adorned with many buildings by Vanbrugh, Kent and Gibbs; in the 1730s Kent designed the Elysian Fields in a more naturalistic style, one of the earliest examples of the reaction against formality leading to the evolution of the landscape garden; miraculously, this beautiful garden survives; its sheer scale must make it Britain's largest work of art continued

◯ ✳ 23 March to 14 April, 29 June to 1 Sept, 18–27 Oct, 14–24 & 27–31 Dec, 1–5 Jan 1992: daily 10–6 or dusk if earlier. Last admissions 1hr before closing. During summer & autumn terms telephone above no. for details of additional openings on answering machine. Closed Good Fri (29 March), 25 & 26 Dec

Notes: Visitors are advised to allow plenty of time, as complete route takes 2hrs to walk. The main house belongs to Stowe School, and the building may be open during Stowe school holidays at an additional charge of £2 (including NT members)

£ £2.80. Pre-booked party visits available all year: please contact Administrator: no reduction

♿ Limited access; some paths suitable for wheelchairs; self-drive Batricars available (advance booking recommended); details from Administrator

🐕 Dogs on leads only

🍴♿ Light refreshments and teas. Same days as gardens 12–5 (Dec & Jan 12–4)

➔ 3 miles NW of Buckingham via Stowe Avenue, off A422 Buckingham/Banbury road [152: SP665366] *Bus:* Paynes 32 Milton Keynes–Buckingham (passing BR Milton Keynes Central & Bletchley) (tel. Buckingham (0280) 817761); Aylesbury Bus 2, 66 Aylesbury–Buckingham (tel. Aylesbury (0296) 84919). On all, alight Buckingham, thence 3m

---

WADDESDON MANOR ⬤ ✳ 🏠   ✈

Waddesdon, nr Aylesbury HP18 0JH (tel. Aylesbury (0296) 651211)

In 1874 Baron Ferdinand de Rothschild acquired the Buckinghamshire hilltop which became the site for the Destailleur-designed château, around which is set one of the finest of late Victorian formal gardens and parks designed by Lainé. Restoration plans for the gardens include shrubberies and additional bedding to the fountain terrace. The elegant cast iron rococo-style aviary, built in 1889, contains mainly softbill birds and some parrots

House closed for refurbishment during 1991 and 1992. Re-opening in 1993. Grounds, aviary, gift shop and tea-room will remain open during 1991 and 1992

◯ ✳ **Grounds and aviary only:** 20 March to 21 Dec: Wed to Sun & BH Mon 12–5

🗖 ✳ Gift shop, which includes Christmas shopping, open as grounds

🚶 Hourly free guided tours of the grounds and aviary (to include information about refurbishment) will be available to visitors, weather permitting

£ Grounds and aviary only: £2.50. Free entry to stables for gift shop and tea-room. Free parking near stables

🛝 Play area for young children

♿ Gift shop and tea-room easily accessible. Most of garden and grounds easy; some gravel. ♿ WC

🍴♿ Light lunches and teas in tea-room, open as grounds. Enquiries to Aylesbury (0296) 651211. Picnics welcome except on lawns in front of house

➡️ 6m NW of Aylesbury, on A41, 11m SE of Bicester, entrance in Waddesdon village [165: SP740169] *Bus:* Aylesbury Bus 1, 15–17 from Aylesbury (passing close BR Aylesbury) (tel. Aylesbury (0296) 84919) *Station:* Aylesbury 6m

WEST WYCOMBE PARK 🏛️ ✳️ ♠️   ✉️

West Wycombe HP14 3AJ (tel. High Wycombe (0494) 524411)

Palladian house with frescoes and painted ceilings, fashioned for Sir Francis Dashwood in the mid 18th century; landscape garden and lake laid out at the same time with various classical temples, including the recently reconstructed Temple of Venus

Note: The West Wycombe Caves and adjacent café are privately owned, and National Trust membership cards are therefore not accepted for entry to these

🅾️ **Grounds only:** April & May: Sun & Wed 2–6; Easter, May & Spring BH Sun & Mon 2–6. **House and grounds:** June, July & Aug: Sun to Thur 2–6. Weekday
🎟️ entry by timed ticket. Last admissions 5.15. Guided tours, depending on visitor numbers

💷 House & grounds £3.80. Grounds only £2.20. No reduction for parties, which must book. Parking 250yds. Pushchairs and wheelchairs not admitted to house

♿ Grounds only; special parking; 🦮 guide dogs in car park only

🐕 In car park only

➡️ At W end of West Wycombe, S of the Oxford road (A40) [175: SU828947] *Bus:* From surrounding areas (passing close BR High Wycombe) (tel. High Wycombe (0494) 20941). Also Green Line 290 London–Oxford (tel. High Wycombe (0494) 464647) *Station:* High Wycombe 2½m

WEST WYCOMBE VILLAGE AND HILL 🏠 ✝️

Chilterns village with buildings representing six centuries, including fine examples from 16th–18th centuries. The hill is part of the 18th-century landscape of West Wycombe Park; it is surmounted by an Iron Age hill-fort, in which stands the church, and commands fine views

Note: The church, mausoleum and caves do not belong to the National Trust

🅾️ ✳️ All year. Parking available at top of hill and in village. Village architectural trail leaflet available in village store

🍽️ George and Dragon, Plough, and Swan public houses

➡️ 2m W of High Wycombe, on both sides of A40 *Public transport:* as for West Wycombe Park above

Cambridgeshire

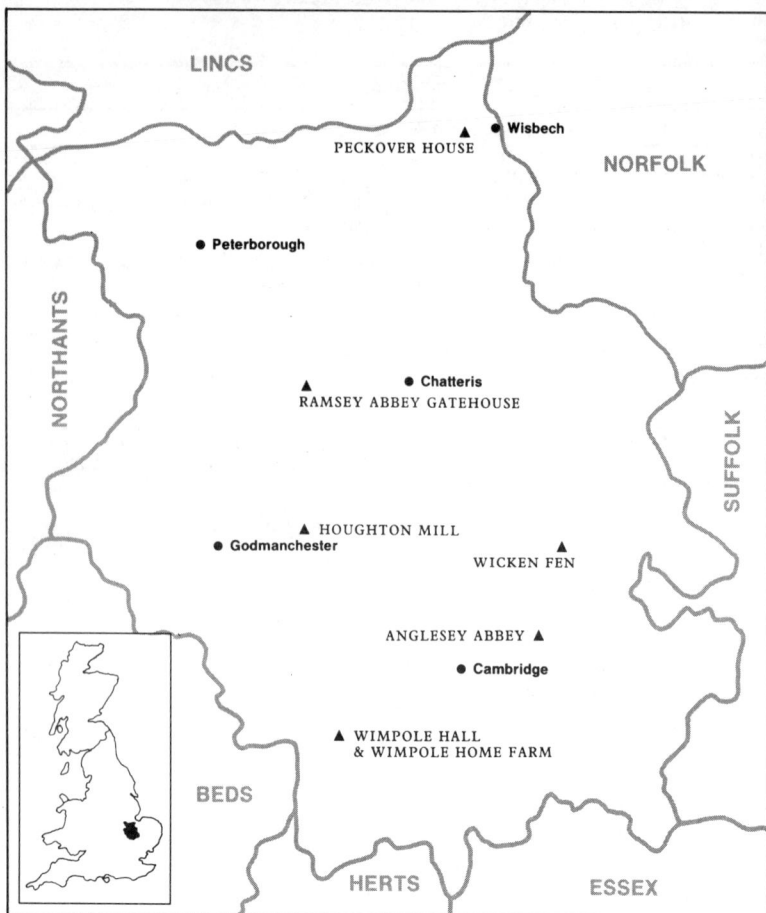

LINCS

PECKOVER HOUSE ▲ ● Wisbech

NORFOLK

● Peterborough

NORTHANTS

▲   ● Chatteris
RAMSEY ABBEY GATEHOUSE

SUFFOLK

▲ HOUGHTON MILL
● Godmanchester

▲
WICKEN FEN

ANGLESEY ABBEY ▲

● Cambridge

▲ WIMPOLE HALL
& WIMPOLE HOME FARM

BEDS

HERTS   ESSEX

ANGLESEY ABBEY 🏛 ✚ ✠ ✿   ✖ ✕ ⊘

Lode, Cambridge CB5 9EJ (tel. Cambridge (0223) 811200)

Outstanding 100-acre garden laid out this century; house built about 1600, with associations with the Augustinian order; Fairhaven collection of paintings and furniture; the machinery in Lode Mill is demonstrated first Sunday in each month; Visitors' Centre includes restaurant, shop, plant centre and display showing how this unique garden was developed

O — **House:** 30 March to 13 Oct: Wed to Sun & BH Mon 1.30–5.30. **Garden:** 30 March to 14 July: Wed to Sun & BH Mon 11–5.30; 15 July to 10 Sept: daily 11–5.30; 11 Sept to 13 Oct: Wed to Sun 11–5.30. **Lode Mill:** 30 March to 13 Oct: Sat, Sun & BH Mon 1.30–5.30

⬛ ✳ — Shop & Plant Centre open 30 March to 13 Oct: Wed to Sun & BH Mon (daily 15 July to 10 Sept) 11–5.30. Also open 17 Oct to 22 Dec: Thur to Sun 11–4; 4 Jan to end March 1992: Sat & Sun only 11–4. Tel. Cambridge (0223) 811175

£ — House & garden £4.50. Parties £3.50. Garden only £2. Lode Mill free. Parties please book with s.a.e. to Administrator

✚ ▲ — Children's guide to house. Baby slings available

♿ ◉ — Special entrance arrangements: please contact Administrator at least 24hrs in advance. Garden level; (house difficult; only 3 rooms accessible via 3 stone steps). ♿ WC. Hyacinth garden in spring. Braille guide to house only

▦ ♿ ✳ — Lunches and teas (table licence) in restaurant by car park, 30 March to 13 Oct: Wed to Sun & BH Mon 11–5; 17 Oct to end March 1992: same days as shop 11–3.30. Kiosk open on Mon & Tues from 15 July to 10 Sept. Picnic area

➔ — In village of Lode, 6m NE of Cambridge on B1102 [154: TL533622] *Bus:* Cambus 111/122 from Cambridge (frequent services link BR Cambridge and bus station) (tel. Cambridge (0223) 423554) *Station:* Cambridge 6m

LODE MILL

HOUGHTON MILL ☒ ⬚   ⬚

Houghton, nr Huntingdon (tel. St Ives (0480) 301494)

A large timber-built watermill on an island on the River Great Ouse, two miles downstream from Huntingdon; much of the 19th-century machinery is intact and is demonstrated on open days; corn is ground on 1st & 3rd Sun in each month throughout season, and the flour sold; art gallery

○   **Mill:** 30 March to 27 May & 9 Sept to 13 Oct: Sat, Sun & BH Mon 2–5.30. 28 May to 8 Sept: Sat to Wed 2–5.30. Last admissions 5.15. Parties at other times by arrangement with Custodian. **Art Gallery:** June to end Sept: Sat & Sun 2.30–5.30

⬚ ✿   Small shop open 30 March to 13 Oct: Sat & Sun 2–5, BH Mon 11–5. Also open for Christmas shopping. Contact property for details

£   £1.60. No reduction for parties. Car park on adjacent private land (no street parking); charge £1 (NT members 25p). Coaches must park 300yds away in village

⬚   Ground floor only; steep wooden stairs

⬚   Children's discovery trail in mill

➔   In village of Houghton, signposted off A1123 to St Ives [153: TL282720] *Bus:* United Counties 73/4, Whippet 1A, 4 from Huntingdon (passing close BR Huntingdon) (tel. Huntingdon (0480) 453159 or 63792) *Station:* Huntingdon 3½m

PECKOVER HOUSE ⬚ ✿ ⬚   ⬚ ⬚

North Brink, Wisbech PE13 1JR (tel. Wisbech (0945) 583463)

Town house, c.1722; fine plaster and wood rococo decoration; collection of Cornwallis family portraits; notable 2-acre Victorian garden with unusual trees; 18th-century stables

○   **House & garden:** 30 March to 27 Oct: Sat, Sun & BH Mon 2–5.30. **Garden only:** 1 April to 23 Oct: Mon to Wed 2–5.30

£   £2 (£1 on garden only days). Parties £1.50. For special party bookings (min. 20) please contact Custodian. *Note:* Members may, by written appointment with the tenants, view Nos. 14 and 19 North Brink

⬚ ✿   Garden only, on prior application to Custodian. Scented flowers and plants

⬚   Teas in Old Kitchen when house is open

➔   On N bank of River Nene, in Wisbech (B1441) [143: TF458097] *Bus:* BR Rail Link coach Peterborough–King's Lynn. (See BR timetable, table 26A); Eastern Counties 46, 794 from King's Lynn (passing close BR King's Lynn) (tel. King's Lynn (0553) 772343) *Station:* March 9½m

PLEASE REFER TO PAGES 5–9

RAMSEY ABBEY GATEHOUSE 🐘 ❌

Abbey School, Ramsey, Huntingdon

Remains of 15th-century gatehouse of the Benedictine Abbey

⭕ 30 March to end Oct: daily 10–5. Other times by written application to Curator

💷 Free (but collection box for contributions). No WCs

➡️ At SE edge of Ramsey, at point where Chatteris road leaves B1096, 10m SE of Peterborough [142: TL291851] *Bus:* Enterprise 330/1 Peterborough–Huntingdon (passing close BR Peterborough & Huntingdon) (tel. Chatteris (03543) 2504) *Station:* Huntingdon 10m

WICKEN FEN 🐦❌🚶 ❌

Lode Lane, Wicken, Ely CB7 5XP (tel. Ely (0353) 720274)

600 acres of wetland reserve, undrained remnant of East Anglia's Great Fens; particularly rich in plant and insect life; wide variety of habitats for birds of scrub, marsh, reeds and water; display in William Thorpe Building of history of Fen's evolution; stout footwear essential in winter and spring but $\frac{3}{4}$m board walk gives easy access; traditional cottage built using natural materials from the fen, furnished as it might have been in 1930s

⭕✴️ **Fen:** all year: daily except Christmas Day. The nature of the property means that parts of the Fen can be waterlogged and to minimise damage visitors are advised that some areas may be temporarily closed. However, the $\frac{3}{4}$ mile boardwalk trail together with access to the Tower Hide will be open at all times.
Fen Cottage: April to Oct: Sun 2–5. Other times by appointment

💷 Fen & Cottage: £2. Cottage only: 50p. Pre-booked parties £1.50, School/educational groups 75p by arrangement with the Education Officer (tel. Ely (0353 723095 or write enclosing s.a.e.). Special facilities available. Simple self-catering accommodation available for parties of up to 30

♿ Raised $\frac{3}{4}$m boardwalk for disabled visitors; special parking by previous arrangement. Ramp into William Thorpe building. Limited access to Fen Cottage. ♿ WC (closed Dec to end March, but alternative unadapted WCs available)

🐕 Admitted only if kept under very strict control. Not allowed in Fen Cottage *continued*

YELLOW FLAG

45

➡️ S of A1123, 3m W of Soham (A142), 9m S of Ely, 17m NE of Cambridge via A10 [154: TL563705] *Bus:* Cambus 116/122 from Cambridge, Ely & Newmarket, alight Soham Downfields, 3m; 109 Cambridge–Ely, alight Stretham 3½m. All pass BR Ely. (tel. Cambridge (0223) 423554)
Station: Ely 9m

WIMPOLE HALL 🏠🌳👤🏠❋✝

Arrington, Royston, Hertfordshire SG8 0BW (tel. Cambridge (0223) 207257)

The most spectacular mansion in Cambridgeshire in a restrained 18th-century style; rooms intimate and formal with work by Gibbs, Flitcroft and Soane; servants' quarters including housekeeper's room, butler's pantry and basement corridor; 350-acre park landscaped by Bridgeman, Brown and Repton; includes a grand folly and Chinese bridge; walks through park (leaflet); restored Victorian stableblock with heavy horses

🅾️ 30 March to 3 Nov: Tues, Wed, Thur, Sat & Sun 1–5 (BH Sun & Mon 11–5)

🛍️❋ Shop open same days as house 10.30–5. Also 4 Nov to 22 Dec & 4 Jan to end March 1992: Tues, Wed, Thur, Sat & Sun 11–4

💷 Hall & Garden £4. Parties £3, Tues to Thur only, please send s.a.e. to Administrator. Joint ticket with Home Farm £5. Car park 200yds

🔺👶 Children's guide. Mothers' room in stable block; baby slings available

♿🦽 Apply to Reception for special access. Staff may be available to lift wheelchairs up steps to ground floor of house, which is then level and fully accessible. ♿ WC open 10.30–5.30 at the stable block; 12–5.30 at the Hall. Braille guide

🐕 In park only, on leads

🍴♿ Light lunches and teas in Great Dining Room same days as house (and Fri in July & Aug) 12–5. Also 4 Nov to 22 Dec and 4 Jan to end March 1992: Tues to Thur, Sat & Sun 11–3.30. Table licence for wines. Light refreshments in stables same days as house & Fri in July & Aug 10.30–5. ♿ access by arrangement. Picnic area

Events: For details of musical and other events send s.a.e. to Administrator

→ 8m SW of Cambridge (A603), 6m N of Royston (A1198) [154: TL336510]
Bus: Whippet 175 Cambridge–Biggleswade (passing close BR Biggleswade &
Cambridge) (tel. St Ives (0480) 63792) *Station:* Shepreth 5m

WIMPOLE HOME FARM 🔊 ✝ ♣ ✈

As Wimpole Hall, above

*Wimpole Home Farm was built in 1794 as a model farm; the Great Barn, designed by Sir
John Soane, houses a collection of farm machinery of the kind used here over 200 years; 350
acres of parkland are grazed by rare breeds of animals also to be viewed in paddocks and the
thatched buildings; video film in loft*

🔘 30 March to 3 Nov: Tues, Wed, Thur, Sat & Sun (but open BH Mon) 10.30–5

💷 NT members £1.50. Non-members £3. Children over 3 half-price. Parties £2,
Tues to Thur only, please book with s.a.e. to Administrator, Wimpole Hall.
Joint ticket for Hall & Farm £5. School parties especially welcome (£1) and part
of a building is reserved for their use. Parking 400yds, at Hall

📷 Shop for sweets, gifts etc; also leaflets about the Farm

🅰 A special area is set aside as a children's corner; woodland adventure
playground; children's publications

♿ 🔘 Level access throughout Farm and ramps to some animal sheds; klaxon at
Farm gate to summon assistance. ♿ WC at stable block. Braille guide

☕ Simple refreshments only; or see Hall entry, above

→ As Wimpole Hall, above

PORTLAND SHEEP

Cheshire

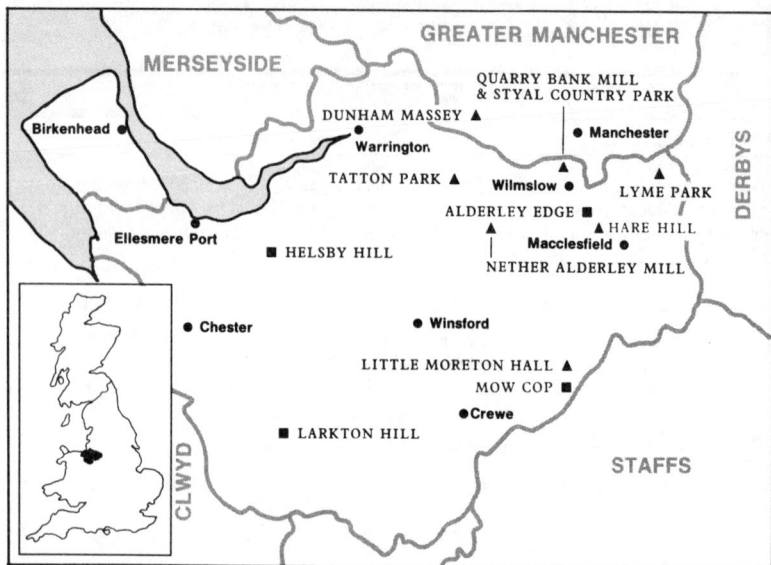

COUNTRYSIDE

Several of the Trust's beauty spots in this county are very near the great industrial conurbations that fringe its northern and eastern boundaries. **Alderley Edge** [118: SS860775] is within easy reach of Manchester and Macclesfield and gives splendid views of the Cheshire Plain. It is 600ft high and its wooded sandstone escarpment once harboured a large Neolithic settlement. Bronze Age pottery and tools have been found here. A footpath has been created which is linked to the Trust's nearby Hare Hill Estate. There is a signed path from the car park suitable for wheelchairs (but a strong pusher is needed) along the Edge, giving fine views. WC. A mile away is **Nether Alderley Mill** (see p. 52).

About 20 miles due west of Alderley Edge is **Helsby Hill** [117: SJ491752], a sandstone outcrop overlooking the Mersey, and giving views of the mountains of North Wales. The climb to the summit takes about five minutes and you will pass an Iron Age hill-fort near the top.

On the Staffordshire border, a hill rises to nearly 1100ft above sea level. It is topped by a Gothic folly in the shape of a castle, now ruined. **Mow Cop** [118: SJ857573] marks the beginning of the Staffordshire Way footpath and gives views towards Alderley Edge and beyond to Manchester to the north, north-east to the Peak District, south to Cannock Chase and Shropshire and west to Wales and the Berwyn Mountains. From Mow Cop you can walk 3 miles to the timber-framed **Little Moreton Hall**, Congleton (see p. 50).

In the centre of the county lies **Larkton Hill** [117: SJ497526] at the southern tip of the Peckforton Hills – over 160 acres of mixed woodland, heathland and fields accessible by public footpath. The Peckforton Hills are a wooded red sandstone ridge running from Maiden Castle, an Iron Age fort in the south, to the 13th-century Beeston Castle in the north. The Sandstone Trail, a 30-mile long-distance footpath, traverses the length of the hills from Grindley Brook to Frodsham, passing a variety of dwellings from black and white cottages to prehistoric hill-forts.

DUNHAM MASSEY 🏠🌸🍀🏠❎🚶 ✉️🖼️

Altrincham WA14 4SJ (tel. 061–941 1025)

18th-century mansion in 250-acre wooded deer park; until 1976 home of the 10th and last Earl of Stamford; over 30 rooms open; collections of furniture, paintings and silver; library, kitchen, laundry and stables; on site of a Tudor building whose moat provides power for a working Elizabethan mill; large garden extensively replanted with shade-loving and waterside plants, attractive woodland; park with formal avenues; fallow deer

🅾️🌸 30 March to 3 Nov: **House:** Sat to Thur 1–5 (Sun & BH Mon 12–5). Last admissions 4.30. **Garden:** daily 12–5.30 (Sun & BH Mon 11–5.30). The mill machinery will normally operate on Wed & Sun. Park always open

📷🌸 Shop open as house 12–5.30 (Sun & BH Mon 11–5.30). Also open 7 Nov to 15 Dec: Thur to Sun 12–4; 4 Jan to 22 March 1992: Sat & Sun 12–4

💷 House & garden £3.50. Family ticket £8.75. Garden only £1.50. Reduced rate for booked parties. Evening opening for pre-booked parties £4.50 per person incl. guided tour (min. charge £200). Park only, £1 per car (NT members free). Car park 250yds; coaches free; bicycles in car park only

♿ Some steps to ground floor of house; garden, park, outbuildings and shop, via cobbled area; special car parking by prior arrangement; wheelchair path from car park to canal; ♿ WC

🐕 In park only, on leads

continued

⬛ ✳ Licensed self-service restaurant on first floor of stable block, for lunches & teas; open as shop (30 March to 3 Nov from 10.30); also open for booked parties, functions, etc. by arrangement (tel. Catering Manager 061-941 2815)

Events: Programme available from Administrator; please send s.a.e.

➡ 3m SW of Altrincham off A56; junction 19 off M6; junction 7 off M56 [109: SJ735874] *Bus:* North Western/GM Buses 38 BR Altrincham Interchange–Warrington (tel. Chester (0244) 602666) *Station:* Altrincham 3m; Hale 3m

HARE HILL ✳ ♠   ✖

nr Macclesfield SK10 4QB

Walled garden with pergola, rhododendrons and azaleas; parkland; link path to Alderley Edge

🅾 ✳ 30 March to 27 Oct: Wed, Thur, Sat, Sun & BH Mon 10–5.30. Special opening to see rhododendrons and azaleas: 20 May to 7 June: daily 10–5.30. 2 Nov to end March 1992: Sat & Sun 10–5.30

£ £1. Entrance per car £1 refundable on entry to garden. Parties by appointment in writing with Head Gardener, Garden Lodge; not suitable for school parties

♿ Gravel paths, some help needed

➡ Between Alderley Edge and Prestbury, turn off north at B5087 at Greyhound Road [118: SJ875765] *Bus:* Cheshire Bus E17 Macclesfield–Wilmslow (passing BR Wilmslow & Prestbury), to within ¼m (tel. Chester (0244) 602666) *Station:* Alderley Edge 2½m; Prestbury 2½m. Link path 2m in each direction from Alderley Edge. Free car parking at Alderley Edge

LITTLE MORETON HALL 🏠 ✳ ✝   ✖ 🏛

Congleton CW12 4SD (tel. Congleton (0260) 272018)

Begun in the 15th century; one of the most perfect examples of a timber-framed moated manor house in the country; long wainscoted gallery, chapel, great hall and knot garden

🅾 🗝 March & Oct: Sat & Sun 1.30–5.30. April to end Sept: daily except Tues 1.30– 5.30; BH Mon 11.30–5.30 Last admissions 5. School parties April to end Sept: mornings only, not Tues, by prior arrangement with Administrator. Optional guided tours most afternoons

🗂 Shop as house, but closes 5.15

£ Weekends & Bank Holidays £2.90; other days £2.30. Family ticket £7. Pre-booked parties by arrangement. Parking 150yds, £2, refundable on entry to Hall (NT members free); car park open from 11 weekends; 12 weekdays

♿ Ground floor; includes Great Hall, Parlour, Chapel, tea-room, shop, exhibition room. Cars may be driven to entrance, but then must park in car park. Garden accessible. Electric mobility vehicle and wheelchair available

🐕 In car park and on grass area in front of Hall only

▣⬛ Refreshments and home-made teas (waitress service); licensed; limited seating – no reservations. Closes 5. Picnic area adjacent to car park

Events: Details from Administrator, s.a.e. please; **⬛**

➜ 4m SW of Congleton, on E side of A34 [118: SJ832589] *Bus:* Cheshire Bus 312 Congleton–Hanley (passing close BR Kidsgrove & Congleton), alight Brownlow Heath 1½m (tel. Chester (0244) 602666) *Station:* Kidsgrove 3m; Congleton 4¼m

---

LYME PARK ⬛⬛⬛⬛ ◻◻◻◻   ✉

Disley, Stockport SK12 2NX (tel. Disley (0663) 762023)

Home of the Legh family for 600 years; part of the Elizabethan house survives, but altered in the 18th century by Giacomo Leoni and later by Lewis Wyatt. 18th- and 19th-century interiors; visitors are welcomed by staff who reconstruct the life of Edwardian servants at Lyme; English clock collection; Dutch garden; red deer in 1,300-acre park on the edge of the Peak District

NT members please note: Lyme Park is financed and managed by Stockport MBC. All NT members are subject to park admission charges, and are also charged for entrance to special events

◯ **Hall:** Good Fri, 29 March to 1 Oct. *Free flow:* 25 May to 9 June and 16 July to 1 Sept: daily except Mon & Fri (but open BH Mon) 2–5. Also open Sun throughout season 2–5. Last admissions 4.15. *Guided tours only:* 29 March to 23 May, 11 June to 14 July & 3 Sept: Tues to Thur 2–4 (hourly); Sat 2–4 (every ½hr). Evening openings on Thur in May (except 16 May). Guided tours at 7, 7.30 & 8. Also special Christmas openings, please telephone for details.

✹ **Garden:** all year daily except 25 & 26 Dec. Summer (29 March to 1 Oct) 11–5; winter (Oct to end March) 11–4

◻ Shop in Hall open same times as Hall

£ Hall £1.50, children and OAPs £1. Park & Garden: pedestrians free, car/minibus (up to 12 seats) £3 (NT members incl.), motorcycle (incl. occupants) £2. Coach passengers (NT members incl.): Hall, Park & Garden £1.50. Season ticket available

⬛⬛ High chairs available in Servants Hall tea-room. Backpacks allowed in Park only; may be left under staff supervision. Adventure playground. Education services; school visits with special concessionary rates. Children's tours available during school holidays. Contact Education Officer for details

⬛ Some parts of Hall, garden & park. Special arrangements, please telephone in advance; **⬛** WC by lakeside; parking at Hall on request

⬛ In park under control, and on leads in garden

▣⬛ Light lunches & teas in Servants Hall tea-room from 12.30 when Hall is open. Kiosk in car park: weekends, school holidays, June to Aug daily 11–5

Events: For details of concerts, Hall tours, park events, guided walks etc, please contact the Manager; special charges may apply   *continued*

Notes: Visitor Centre; Countryside Centre; pitch and putt course; fishing and horse riding permits; details from Manager. Orienteering course (open all year)

→ On S side of A6; 6½m SE of Stockport, entrance on W outskirts of Disley [109: SJ965825] *Bus:* From surrounding areas (tel. 061-228 7811) *Station:* Disley ½m from Park entrance

NETHER ALDERLEY MILL ⊠ ⊠

Congleton Road, Nether Alderley, Macclesfield

A fascinating overshot tandem wheel watermill, originally 15th-century, with a stone-tiled low pitched roof; the machinery was derelict for 30 years, but has now been restored to full working order; grinds flour occasionally for demonstrations

◯ 31 March to end June & Oct: Wed, Sun & BH Mon 2–5.30. July to end Sept: daily except Mon, but open BH Mon 2–5.30

£ £1.40. Parties (max. 20) by prior arrangement with Mrs Pamela Ferguson, 7 Oak Cottages, Styal, Wilmslow SK9 4JQ (tel. Wilmslow (0625) 523012). Ladder stairs. Unsuitable for disabled visitors. Parking space for one coach at a time; must book. No WCs

→ 1½m S of Alderley Edge, on E side of A34 [118: SJ844763] *Bus:* C-Line 129/ 130, 150 Manchester–Macclesfield (passing BR Alderley Edge) (tel. Chester (0244) 602666) *Station:* Alderley Edge 2m

QUARRY BANK MILL & STYAL COUNTRY PARK

QUARRY BANK MILL ⊠ ⊠ ⊠ ⊠ ⊠

Wilmslow SK9 4LA (tel. Wilmslow (0625) 527468)

Major Georgian cotton mill restored as working museum of the cotton industry now running under waterpower; demonstrations of weaving and spinning; galleries illustrate the millworkers' world, textile finishing processes, and the Gregs as pioneers of the factory system; Apprentice House (recently restored) shown as lived in by mill apprentices in 1830

The Mill is managed for the National Trust by the tenant, Quarry Bank Mill Trust Ltd

◯ ✳ Mill: March & Oct to end March 1992: Tues to Sun 11–4. April to end Sept: daily 11–5. Pre-booked parties from 9.30 throughout the year (except Sun or BH Mon) and also specified evenings from May to end Sept 6.30–10. Visitors wishing to avoid crowds are advised not to visit on BH and Sun afternoons in spring and summer
Mill Kitchen: March & Oct to end March 1992: Tues to Sun 10.30–4.30. April to end Sept: daily 10.30–5.30
Apprentice House and Garden: 23 March to 7 April, July, Aug, and 26 Dec to 5 Jan 1992 as Mill. Rest of year as Mill but closed Mon (open BH Mon) and open from 2 on Tues to Fri. *Note:* Due to fire and safety regulations a maximum of 30 people can be admitted to the Apprentice House at any one time. Admission by timed ticket only (NT members incl.) available from Mill Reception. School groups should telephone for separate information leaflet Mill, Mill Kitchen, Apprentice House and Garden all open on BH but closed 24 & 25 Dec

▢ ✳ Mill shop open as Mill Kitchen. Selling goods made from cloth woven in mill

£ Mill and Apprentice House £4, students/children £3, family £10. Mill only £3, students/children £2, family £8. Apprentice House & garden only £2, students/children £1.50, family £6. NB: NT members will be expected to pay the special charges which will apply to certain events during the year. Advance booking essential for all parties of 10 or more (please apply for booking form at least 3 weeks in advance; guides may be booked at same time). Reduction: one visitor in every 20 free (not Jun & July)   *continued*

♿ Exterior and special route through part of interior, using step lift. Please telephone for special access details and leaflet; cars may set down passengers at mill. Sympathetic Hearing Scheme operates in Reception. 🔊 WC by Styal Workshop. Mill unsuitable for guide dogs

🍴 ❀ Available at all times when Mill is open; licensed tea-room/restaurant for morning coffee, home-made soup, hot meals, regional dishes and vegetarian food; tea; may be booked for dinners & evening functions; also Pie Shop for hot & cold snacks, beverages and ice cream; parties should book at least 3 weeks in advance

Note: Conservation and display developments are often under way and may cause some slight disruption for visitors

➡ 1½m N of Wilmslow off B5166, 1m from M56, exit 5, 10m S of Manchester [109: SJ835835] *Station:* Styal, ½m

---

STYAL COUNTRY PARK 🏛🛏✝✖🏠

Wilmslow SK9 4JQ (tel. Wilmslow (0625) 523012)

Part of the valley of the river Bollin combining natural beauty with historic interest; pleasant riverside walks in fine woodlands; the Country Park includes Quarry Bank Cotton Mill (see entry on p. 52), the factory colony village of Styal and associated farmland

🔘 ❀ All year during daylight hours

£ 🐕 Admission to country park £1 per car refundable on entry to Mill

♿ A circular woodland route is available from the Twinnies Bridge end of the country park. (Not from the main car park)

🚶 Guided tours of woodlands and village from main car park on 2nd Sun in each month at 2.30

🍴 ❀ Available from Mill whenever open

➡ As for Quarry Bank Mill p. 52

TATTON PARK 🏛❀🌳🏠👟🚶   ✖

Knutsford WA16 6QN (tel. Knutsford (0565) 654822)

Over 1,000 acres of deer park; 19th-century Wyatt house containing collections of pictures, furniture, china, glass and silver; cellars; 60-acre garden with authentic Japanese garden, orangery, fernery, rose garden and arboretum; rhododendrons and azaleas; restored Italian garden; medieval old hall; 1930s' farm; many varieties of wildfowl

Members please note: Tatton Park is financed, administered and maintained by Cheshire County Council. All NT members are subject to car park charges and are also charged for entrance to events (listed below) where it is impossible to separate access arrangements. Annual members also charged for Old Hall and Farm

🔘 29 March to 30 Sept: Mansion, Garden, Old Hall, Farm: daily except Mon (but open BH Mon) 12–4. Park: daily except Mon (but open BH Mon) 11–6.

❄ Oct to end March 1992: Garden: daily except Mon 12–3. Farm: Sun only 12–3. Park: daily except Mon 11–4. Mansion and Old Hall: open for 'Tatton at Christmas' (see Events)

Note: Certain rooms in the Mansion are occasionally closed during events

Parties: All attractions may be visited outside normal opening times by prior arrangement and on payment of an additional charge

🏠❄ Shop open 29 March to end Sept same days as Mansion 11.30–5.30; Oct to end March 1992 Sun only 11.30–4.30

£ All-in ticket £5 (incl. admission to Park). Mansion £2, Garden £2. NT Annual Members included for following charges: Old Hall £1.50, Farm £1.50. Admission to Park £1.70 per car (incl. all NT members), coaches, bicycles and pedestrians free

🧒🏚 Adventure playground. Nursing mothers invited to use emergency rest room

♿ Parking in stableyard and at Home Farm. Easy access to Mansion ground floor, garden & shop. ♿ WC

🐕 In garden on leads and in park under close control

☕❄ All meals catered for in Stableblock; bookings Knutsford (0565) 632914. Open as shop

Events: All NT members will be expected to pay the special charges which apply to the following events: 23 Feb: Point to Point (Park); 31 March, 1 April: Oriental Gardens weekend; 8, 9 June: Italian weekend and Orchid Show (Garden); 15, 16 June: Carriage Driving Trials (Park). Special Christmas opening days (telephone for details). Please send s.a.e. for calendar of events

→ 3½m N of Knutsford, 4m S of Altrincham, 3½m from M6 at Manchester interchange No. 19, or leave M56 at jn. 7, travel S on A556 and look for signposts to Tatton Park; entrance on Ashley Road, 1½m NE of jn. A5034 with A50 [109 & 118: SJ745815] *Bus:* Cheshire Bus X2 BR Altrincham Interchange–Chester, Sun only otherwise from surrounding areas to Knutsford, thence 2m (tel. Chester (0244) 602666) *Station:* Knutsford 2m

Cleveland

COUNTRYSIDE

The bent pinnacle of Roseberry Topping [93: NZ575126) has been described as a miniature Matterhorn. The summit rises to 1,057 feet and provides panoramic views over the Cleveland Hills and across Teesside to the North Sea.

Roseberry Topping has a long and romantic history. Prehistoric herdsmen and hunters occupied the site and to the Vikings it was a sacred hill. The Topping was used as a beacon station at the time of the Spanish Armada and during the Napoleonic Wars. Captain James Cook, one of the world's great navigators, worked with his father at Aireyholme Farm on the Topping's southern slopes. The Topping lies on the northern edge of the North York Moors National Park, south-west of Guisborough, and about 8 miles south-east of Middlesbrough. Access is from the car park on the A173, 1 mile north-east of Great Ayton [93: NZ571128]. The Trust's purchase of **Roseberry Common** and part of Roseberry Topping in 1985 included the northern and eastern slopes of the hill, as well as a stretch of heather moorland and an oak wood on its western flank; a total of 267 acres.

Some 5 miles to the north-west is **Ormesby Hall** (see entry below).

ORMESBY HALL 🏠✻🏠♠   ✖🗹

Ormesby, Middlesbrough TS7 9AS (tel. Middlesbrough (0642) 324188)

*Mid 18th-century house; opulent decoration inside includes fine plasterwork by
contemporary craftsmen; a Jacobean doorway with a carved family crest survives from the
earlier house on the site; the stable block, attributed to Carr of York, is a particularly fine mid
18th-century building with an attractive courtyard leased to the Mounted Police; garden*

O 30 March to 2 April: daily 2–5.30. April to Oct: Wed, Sat, Sun & BH Mon
⫪ 2–5.30. Also open Thur in July, Aug & Sept. Last admissions 5. Guided tours
most days. School groups and special parties on weekdays by arrangement
with Administrator

⌂✻ Shop as house. Also Nov to 15 Dec: Sat & Sun 2–5

£ £1.60. Parties £1.30; children 70p. Parking 100yds

⫪ Baby-changing facilities. Pushchairs may be left at entrance

♿ Ground floor of house, shop, tea-room & garden; cars may bring disabled
visitors to front door; please notify Administrator in advance of visit; ♿ WC
opposite car park

☕ Tea-room open as house

Events: For a detailed programme and inclusion on the mailing list, send s.a.e.
to the Administrator

➔ 3m SE of Middlesbrough, W of A171 [93: NZ530167] *Bus:* From
Middlesbrough (passing close BR Middlesbrough) (tel. Middlesbrough (0642)
210131) *Station:* Marton (U), not Sun, except May to Sept, 1½m;
Middlesbrough 3m

PLEASE REFER TO PAGES 5–9

Cornwall

COAST

The Trust's countryside holdings in Cornwall are mainly of truly spectacular coastline – more than 110 miles, including some of the most famous and beautiful holiday stretches.

On the north coast between the Devon border and Bude the Trust owns three blocks of coastline. The most northerly, centred on **Morwenstow** [190: SS2015] has associations with the celebrated 19th-century cleric and poet, Hawker of Morwenstow. The Trust property from north of **Duckpool** to south of **Sandy Mouth** [190: SS2011] extends inland up the **Coombe Valley**. ⓘ There is a café, WCs and a car park at **Sandy Mouth** where, at low tide, the beach lives up to its name. A narrow strip at **Maer Cliff** [190: SS2008] runs between Northcott Mouth and Crooklets Beach.

Crackington Haven [190: SX1497] is flanked by **Dizzard Point** where there is a stunted oak wood; **Penkenna Point**; and **High Cliff**, the loftiest height on the Cornish coast at 731ft. **Trevigue Farm** has a shop, café and information point.

At **Boscastle** [190: SK1091] the Trust owns both sides of the picturesque harbour, a

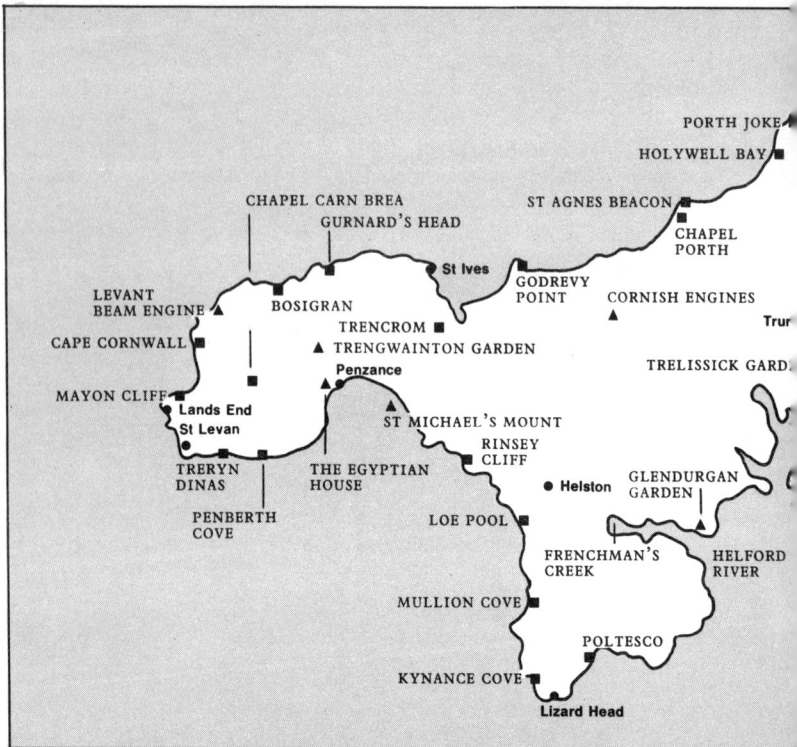

PORTH JOKE

HOLYWELL BAY

CHAPEL CARN BREA

GURNARD'S HEAD

ST AGNES BEACON

CHAPEL PORTH

St Ives

LEVANT BEAM ENGINE

BOSIGRAN

GODREVY POINT

CORNISH ENGINES

Trur

CAPE CORNWALL

TRENCROM

TRENGWAINTON GARDEN

Penzance

TRELISSICK GARD

MAYON CLIFF

Lands End

St Levan

ST MICHAEL'S MOUNT

RINSEY CLIFF

TRERYN DINAS

THE EGYPTIAN HOUSE

Helston

GLENDURGAN GARDEN

PENBERTH COVE

LOE POOL

FRENCHMAN'S CREEK

HELFORD RIVER

MULLION COVE

POLTESCO

KYNANCE COVE

Lizard Head

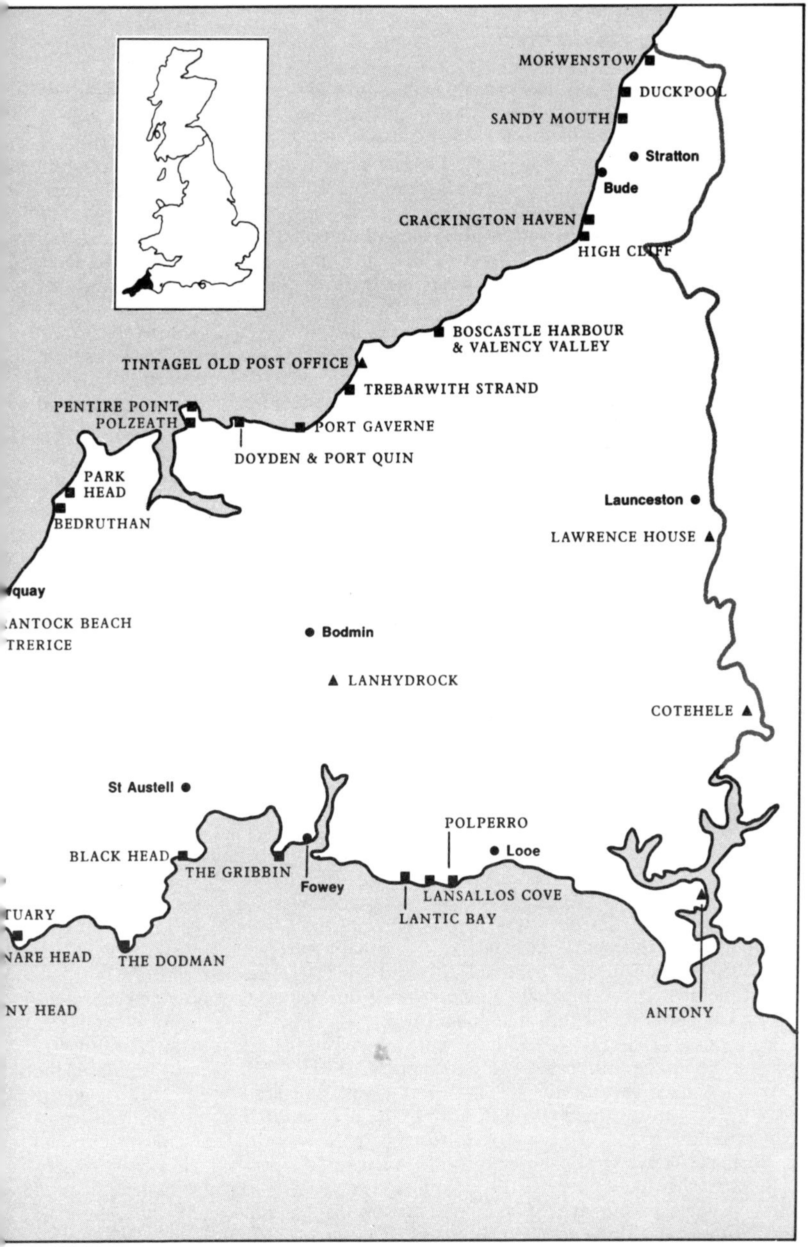

MORWENSTOW

DUCKPOOL

SANDY MOUTH

● Stratton

Bude

CRACKINGTON HAVEN

HIGH CLIFF

BOSCASTLE HARBOUR
& VALENCY VALLEY

TINTAGEL OLD POST OFFICE

TREBARWITH STRAND

PENTIRE POINT
POLZEATH

PORT GAVERNE

DOYDEN & PORT QUIN

PARK
HEAD

Launceston ●

LAWRENCE HOUSE ▲

BEDRUTHAN

quay

ANTOCK BEACH
TRERICE

● Bodmin

▲ LANHYDROCK

COTEHELE ▲

St Austell ●

POLPERRO

BLACK HEAD

THE GRIBBIN

● Looe

Fowey

LANSALLOS COVE

TUARY

LANTIC BAY

NARE HEAD

THE DODMAN

NY HEAD

ANTONY

natural haven still used by fishermen. [&] The NT shop and information centre is open in summer in the Old Smithy. [i] The Trust owns land up the wooded **Valency Valley** towards St Juliot, rich with Thomas Hardy connections.

Visitors to **Tintagel Old Post Office** (see page 69) can walk out to the cliffs to see **Willapark** [200: SX0689], where there is a cliff castle; **Barras Nose**, the Trust's earliest coastal acquisition in England; or the lengthy stretch of coast extending from Tintagel south to **Trebarwith Strand**. The old cliffside slate quarries are worth seeing, and at **Glebe Cliff** a viewpoint has wheelchair access [&]. The Trust owns a cluster of old fish 'cellars' and the foreshore at **Port Gaverne**.

The next highlight is the wonderful 6-mile stretch from **Port Quin** to **Polzeath** [200: SW9380]. The main features are **Pentire Point; the Rumps** with its cliff castle – probably the finest on the Cornish coast; **Lundy Bay; Doyden Castle**, a 19th-century folly; and **Port Quin** itself where there is a car park and a clutch of NT holiday cottages.

The remote, convoluted coastline at **Park Head** [200: SW8471], with its seabird breeding colonies, is the perfect foil for the more gregarious pleasures to be found at **Bedruthan** [200: SW8569]. The justly famous beauty spot of Bedruthan Steps (not NT) can be viewed from the Trust's clifftop land. NT shop and information centre, café and WCs in the car park.

Immediately west of Newquay the trio of sandy beaches, **Crantock Beach, Porth Joke** and **Holywell Bay** are backed and separated by an extensive Trust hinterland [200: SW7760]. This is wonderful walking country.

The high ground of **St Agnes Beacon** (629ft) is Trust owned, and the whole area is rich in industrial relics from mining days. **Chapel Porth** [203: SW7050] is another fine beach, at low tide; the ruin of **Towanroath engine house** stands prominently above it.

Between **Gwithian** and **Portreath** the Trust owns over 6 miles of almost continuous coastline [203: SW6545 to 5842]. The awesome drop at **Hell's Mouth** and the headlands of **Godrevy** and **Navax Points** are the most dramatic features.

Not on the coast, but only 2 miles inland from Carbis Bay, is **Trencrom Hill** [203: SW5236], a 64-acre granite eminence rather like a Dartmoor tor. Two main rock piles are surrounded by lesser outcrops which are linked by an Iron Age wall, and the remains of stone dwellings can be seen.

Once west of St Ives the character of the landscape changes. This is West Penwith, a coastline of rocky headlands and coves backed by a flattish plateau of small fields where traditionally managed farms are overlooked by a serrated ridge of granite outcrops called carns. The Trust owns a number of the headlands, as well as larger areas at **Treveal, Rosemergy** and **Bosigran** [203: SW4237]. A walk out to **Zennor** and **Gurnard's Head** will give the visitor a flavour of this very Celtic, unspoilt coast.

Cape Cornwall [203: SW3532], England's only cape, was acquired in 1987.

The three properties nearest to Land's End are the ½ mile of **Polpry Cove** [203: SW3630], to the north of Whitesand Bay; the ¾ mile of **Mayon** and **Trevescan Cliffs** [203: SW3526] between Sennen Cove and Land's End; and **Chapel Carn Brea** [203: SW3828], a 53-acre hilltop reaching 657ft, 2 miles inland from Whitesand Bay, which claims the widest sea view from the British mainland.

Once round Land's End the south coast of Cornwall begins, and the first Trust property encountered is the point called **Pedn-men-an-mere** [203: SW3821] which protects the open-air Minack Theatre (not NT) from south-westerly gales. Beyond **Porthcurno** the Trust owns 2 miles, passing the little fishing cove of **Penberth**, perhaps Cornwall's most perfect fishing cove [203: SW4023]. Between the two is the thrusting cock's comb peninsula of **Treryn Dinas**; the famous 66-ton Logan Rock perched on its rocky crest.

St Michael's Mount (see page 68) is the first Trust property east of Penzance, followed by three detached sites at **Cudden Point, Lesceave Cliff** and **Rinsey Cliff**, the last-named having a restored 19th-century mine engine house on the cliff slope.

Once east of Porthleven the extensive **Penrose Estate** [203: SW6425] spreads inland to the outskirts of Helston and south to **Gunwalloe Church Cove**. ⓘ It contains the remarkable and beautiful **Loe Pool**, Cornwall's largest natural freshwater lake, separated from the sea by the shingle barrier of Loe Bar. A 5-mile footpath follows the edge of the lake, and a bird hide looks out onto the reed bed. **Gunwalloe Towans** is a fine sweep of sand dunes now used by Mullion Golf Club.

Trust ownership along the west-facing Lizard coast is fragmented into a number of properties. South of Poldhu the **Marconi Memorial** site marks Guglielmo Marconi's first trans-Atlantic wireless message. **Mullion Cove** and **Island** [203: SW6617] are owned by the Trust. About a mile to the south, at **Predannack Head**, the 674-acre Predannack holding spreads inland almost to the A3083. Biologically, this is one of the Trust's most interesting sites. **Kynance Cove** [203: SW6913] offers good bathing at low tide, and the Trust has just landscaped and improved the clifftop car park. The $\frac{1}{2}$ mile of rugged coast to the east of Lizard Point includes **Pistil Meadow** where the bodies of 200 people are buried – drowned in one of the worst wrecks off this most treacherous point.

On the east-facing Lizard coast, on either side of the stone and thatch village of **Cadgwith** [203: SW7214], where fishermen still winch their brightly-coloured craft up the beach, the Trust owns several miles of cliff land. Of particular interest are the remains of the 19th-century serpentine works – serpentine is the local stone – at **Poltesco**. Three detached properties at **Beagles Point, Black Head** and **Lowland Point** flank the next village along the coast, Coverack [204: SW7818].

The shores of the **Helford River** [204: SW7626], probably Cornwall's most beautiful estuary, together with its subsidiary **Gillan Creek**, are protected by the Trust along several miles of its length, and at the northern approach, **Rosemullion Head** [204: SW8028]. One of these safeguarded areas is the enchanting **Frenchman's Creek**, the location of Daphne du Maurier's novel. **Glendurgan Garden** (see page 66) fronts the mouth of the estuary. Between the Helford River and Falmouth is a mile of open cliff on either side of the popular beach of **Maenporth**.

Trelissick Garden (see page 69) and estate straddles the western approach to the King Harry Ferry on the B3289, and **Turnaware Point** [204: SW8338] on the east side marks the end of Carrick Roads and the beginning of the Fal Estuary. Facing Carrick Roads, the Trust owns 2 miles to the south of **St Just** [204: SW8434]. **Newton Farm** was bought after a local appeal in 1988.

TOWANROATH MINE

61

♿ **St Anthony Head** and **Zone Point** [204: SW8631] form the once-fortified eastern approach to Falmouth harbour. The old defences are largely cleared away, but some of the accommodation is available as holiday lets (see p. 19), with wheelchair access and facilities in the cottages. A viewfinder approached by a path suitable for wheelchair users on the highest point identifies the features in the wide-ranging panorama.

East of here, Trust ownership extends from the sea on both sides of **Porthmellin Head** [204: SW8732] across the waist of the St Anthony peninsula to the creek and estuary waterfronts facing St Mawes. This is largely farmland, but paths give good access to the main places of interest. Another property fronts the **Percuil River** further up.

Nare Head [204: SW9137] is the focus for a concentration of Trust properties, with a 4½ mile coastline, and extending to about 900 acres. The off-lying **Gull Rock** was presented to the Trust in 1989. A Trust car park at **Penare** was part of a major tidying-up scheme ♿. A wheelchair ramp and picnic area overlook **Kiberick Cove**.

The Dodman [204: SX0039] is the grandest headland on the south Cornish coast. The remains of an Iron Age promontory fort can be seen across its broad back and there are Bronze Age barrows. To the east and west are the detached properties of **Lambsowden Cove** and **Maenease Point**, and further on, **Turbot Point** or **Bodrugan's Leap**, where Sir Henry Trenowth of nearby Bodrugan is said to have jumped into the sea to make his escape by boat to France. Within St Austell Bay is **Black Head**, where yet another Iron Age earthwork can be seen, together with a rifle range from more recent times.

Much of the coastline to the east and west of Fowey is owned by the Trust. **Gribbin Head** [200: SX1050] with its boldly striped navigational daymark begins the sequence of properties. There is a gap at **Polridmouth Cove** (always called Pridm'th) where the Trust owns only the east side of the cove, then a wide strip of mostly Trust land to the outskirts of Fowey. Upstream, overlooking the china clay loading quays, the Trust safeguards the 31 acres of woods and meadow at **Station Wood** [200: SW1252]. Across Fowey harbour is the tree-fringed creek of **Pont Pill** [200: SX1451] where the lovely **Hall Walk** passes through the woods. Once beyond Polruan, Trust ownership follows the coast for several miles to beyond the village of **Lansallos** [201: SX1751], and extends some distance inland. There are attractive beaches at **Lantic Bay** and **Lansallos Cove**.

On each side of **Polperro** [201: SX2151] the Trust has one mile of coastline. The eastern strip was willed to the Trust by Miss Angela Brazil, the author of school stories for girls, and another mile of Trust land projects into the Channel at **Hore Point** [201: SX2451].

Trust ownership east of Looe consists of smallish properties at **Millendreath, Trethill Cliffs, Higher Tregantle Cliffs** and **Sharrow Point**, where there is a cliffside folly called Sharrow Grot [201: SX3952].

EDIBLE CRAB

A series of detailed leaflets, with maps, has been produced about the Trust's coastal properties. They are available from NT shops in Cornwall or from the Regional Trading Manager (see address on page 22; please include a donation to cover postage).

No. 1	Bude to Morwenstow	60p
No. 2	Crackington Haven	40p
No. 3	Boscastle	60p
No. 4	Tintagel	60p
No. 5	Polzeath to Port Quin	50p
No. 6	Bedruthan and Park Head	50p
No. 7	Crantock to Holywell Bay	50p
No. 8	St Agnes and Chapel Porth	40p
No. 9	Godrevy to Portreath	50p
No. 10	West Penwith: St Ives to Pendeen	80p
No. 11	West Penwith: Cape Cornwall to Logan Rock	60p
No. 12	Loe Pool and Gunwalloe	60p
No. 13	The Lizard, West Coast: Gunwalloe Church Cove to Kynance	60p
No. 14	Kynance Cove	50p
No. 15	The Lizard, East Coast: Landewednack to St Keverne	60p
No. 16	Helford River	60p
No. 17	Trelissick	60p
No. 18	The Roseland Peninsula	50p
No. 19	St Anthony Head Battery	50p
No. 20	Nare Head and the Dodman	60p
No. 21	Fowey	80p
No. 22	Lantic Bay to Sharrow Point	60p

ANTONY 🏠 🏡 ♿ 𝐈 ✈ ✗ ✉

Torpoint PL11 2QA (tel. Plymouth (0752) 812191)

One of Cornwall's finest early 18th-century houses, built of silvery-grey Pentewan stone, offset by colonnaded wings of red brick; fine garden with national collection of day lilies, magnolias and summer borders; extensive grounds; 18th-century dovecote; 1789 Bath Pond House; family history exhibition

⦿ April to end Oct: Tues, Wed, Thur & BH Mon 2–6; also Sun in June, July & Aug 2–6. Last guided tour of house 5.30. Bath Pond House can be seen on previous written application to Administrator and only when house is open

🗐 Shop open as house

£ £3. Pre-arranged parties £2.40; organisers please notify the Administrator

♿ House accessible via a flight of steps; then all on one level. Garden largely accessible

➔ 5m W of Plymouth via Torpoint car ferry, 2m NW of Torpoint, N of A374, 16m SE of Liskeard, 15m E of Looe [201: SX418564] *Bus:* Western National 81 from Plymouth (passing close BR Plymouth), alight Great Park Estate, ¼m, (tel. Plymouth (0752) 664011) *Station:* Plymouth 6m via vehicle ferry. *Ferry:* Torpoint 2m

CORNISH ENGINES 🔧🕯 ✈

Pool, nr Redruth (tel. Redruth (0209) 216657)

Impressive relics of the tin-mining industry, these great beam engines (one with a cylinder 7½ft in diameter) were used for pumping water from over 2,000ft deep, and for winding men and ore; the engines exemplify the use of high-pressure steam patented by the Cornish engineer Richard Trevithick in 1802

🅾   29 March to end Oct: daily 11–6 or sunset if earlier (closes 5 in Oct). Last admissions ½hr before closing

🛍   Shop open same times

💷   £1.40. No reduction for parties. No WCs. Unsuitable for disabled or visually handicapped visitors

         Note: A further engine is preserved at a mine which is still working and can only be seen when visits can be arranged to fit in with normal mine routine; arrangements must be sought beforehand from the Manager, South Crofty (tel. Redruth (0209) 714821)

➡   At Pool, 2m W of Redruth on either side of A3047 [203: SW672415] *Bus:* From surrounding areas (some passing BR Redruth) (tel. Truro (0872) 40404) *Station:* Redruth 2m; Camborne 2m

THE LEVANT BEAM ENGINE 🔧🕯

Trewellard, Pendeen, nr St Just
(Tourist Amenity Manageress, Geevor Mine, (0736) 788662)

The oldest engine in Cornwall (1840–1930) currently undergoing restoration

🅾   Open Easter weekend then Fri, Sun & BH Mon 24 May to 15 Sept 11–4

💷   Admission free but donations invited. Stewarded by volunteer members of the Trevithick Society

➡   1m W of Pendeen, on B3306 St Just–Zennor road [203: SW368346] *Bus:* Western National 10A from BR Penzance (tel. Penzance (0736) 69469) *Station:* Penzance 7m

COTEHELE 🏠❄✈🔧🕯   ✈✉🏛🎦

St Dominick, nr Saltash PL12 6TA (tel. Liskeard (0579) 50434; information 51222)

Built 1485–1627, home of the Edgcumbe family for centuries, it contains original furniture, armour and needlework; gardens on several levels; medieval dovecote; Cotehele Mill, restored to working condition with adjoining cider press; Cotehele Quay on the Tamar with 18th- and 19th-century buildings; outstation of National Maritime Museum; restored Tamar sailing barge Shamrock

PLEASE REFER TO PAGES 5–9

House: 29 March to end Oct: daily except Fri (open Good Fri) 11–6 (11–5 in Oct). Last admissions 5.30 or dusk if earlier. **Garden:** 29 March to end March 1992: daily 11–6 or dusk if earlier. **Mill:** 29 March to end Oct: daily 11–6 or dusk if earlier. A timed ticket system may be operated on BH weekends which may lead to delays in admission to the house

Shop open as house. Also limited daily opening Nov to Christmas. Tel. Liskeard (0579) 50072

House, garden & mill £4.40. Garden & mill only £2.20. Pre-arranged parties £3.50 by prior written arrangement only with Administrator. Coach party organisers are advised to obtain a copy of the route from Administrator. No parties Sun or BH Mon. Schools resource pack available

Parents' & babies' room

Hall and kitchen only; most of garden unsuitable as very steep; special parking and entrance arrangements; some loose gravel; ramps available at house and restaurant; WC

Coffee, lunches and teas in the Barn (closed Fri) and on Cotehele Quay (open Fri) during season, and limited opening Nov to Christmas. Please enquire for ramp. Tel. Liskeard (0579) 50652

Note: There is no electric light in the rooms; visitors wishing to make a close study of tapestries and textiles should avoid dull days early and late in the season

→ On W bank of the Tamar, 1m W of Calstock by footpath (6m by road), 8m SW of Tavistock, 14m from Plymouth via Saltash Bridge; 2m E of St Dominick, 4m from Gunnislake (turn at St Ann's Chapel); can be reached from Plymouth by water (contact Plymouth Boat Cruises Ltd – tel. Plymouth (0752) 822202) [201: SX422685]
Station: Calstock (U), not Sun (except May–Sept), 1¼m, Cotehele is signposted from station

COTEHELE KITCHEN

THE EGYPTIAN HOUSE 🏠🏠

6 Chapel Street, Penzance TR18 4AJ (tel. Penzance (0736) 64378)

A flamboyant façade well worth seeing, c.1830; owned and restored by Landmark Trust; NT shop on ground floor

O ✿ April to 24 Dec: Mon to Sat 9–5; Jan to end Mar: daily except Sun & Wed 10–4

→ *Bus:* From surrounding areas (tel. Penzance (0736) 69469) *Station:* Penzance, few minutes walk

GLENDURGAN GARDEN ✿ ✗

Helford River, Mawnan Smith, nr Falmouth TR11 5JZ
(Enquiries tel. Bodmin (0208) 74281)

Valley garden of great beauty; fine trees and shrubs, walled and water gardens; a wooded valley runs down to the tiny village of Durgan on the river; house is tenanted and not open

O March to end Oct: Tues to Sat & BH Mon (closed Good Fri) 10.30–5.30. Last admissions 4.30

£ £2. No reduction for parties

🜨 Maze and Giant's Stride (a pole with ropes to swing from)

→ 4m SW of Falmouth, ½m SW of Mawnan Smith, on road to Helford Passage [204: SW772277] *Bus:* Western National 32 from Falmouth (passing BR Penmere) (tel. Truro (0872) 40404) *Station:* Penmere (U) 4m

LANHYDROCK 🏠✿♣ 🛉 ✗

Bodmin PL30 5AD (tel. Bodmin (0208) 73320)

A 17th-century house largely rebuilt after a fire in 1881; the gatehouse (1641) and north wing, including a 116ft gallery with fine plaster ceiling, are unaltered; 36 rooms open; formal and shrub gardens of interest and beauty in all seasons; large park on River Fowey; walks

O ✿ 29 March to end Oct: **Garden** daily; **House** daily except Mon, but open BH Mon 11–6 (closes 5 in Oct). Last admissions to house, ½hr before closing. Nov to end March 1992: garden only, open daily during daylight hours

🏠✿ Shop open daily 29 March to end Oct. Also limited opening in Nov & Dec. Tel. Bodmin (0208) 74331

£ £4.20. Garden and grounds only £2.40. Pre-arranged parties £3.40; organisers please book visits and arrange meals beforehand with Administrator. Car park at end of long drive, 600yds. Schools resource pack available

🛉 Mothers' room

♿ Disabled visitors may be driven to house; special parking, for assistance please consult car park attendant; access to house via loose gravel and shallow steps then most ground floor rooms easily accessible; small lift to first floor; ramp to restaurant; ♿ WC. Shop has some steps. Garden has gravel paths, some sloping, and steps

🐕 In park only, on leads

🍴♿ Coffee, lunches and snacks. April to end Oct: daily; limited opening in Nov & ❄ Dec. Tel. Bodmin (0208) 74331. ♿ access via steps; ramp available

Events: April, Cornwall Gardens Society Spring Flower Show; open-air theatre and other events in summer; Music Festival in Nov; tel. Bodmin (0208) 73320 for details

→ 2½m SE of Bodmin, overlooking valley of River Fowey; follow signposts from either A38, Bodmin-Liskeard, or B3268, Bodmin-Lostwithiel roads [200: SX085636] *Station:* Bodmin Parkway 1¾m by original carriage-drive to house, signposted in station car park; 3m by road

---

LAWRENCE HOUSE 🏛

9 Castle Street, Launceston PL15 8BA (tel. Launceston (0566) 772640)

Local history museum; the house was given to the Trust to help preserve the character of the street and leased to the Council as a museum and civic centre

Lawrence House is leased to Launceston Town Council

🅾 April to mid Oct: Mon to Fri 10.30–4.30 (closes 12.30–2.30 in April, May, Sept & Oct). Open BH Mon. Other times by appointment

💷 Free, but visitors are invited to contribute towards museum expenses

→ [201: SX330848] *Bus:* Infrequent Western National service from Callington with connections from Plymouth (tel. Plymouth (0752) 664011)

ST MICHAEL'S MOUNT 🏰✝   ✗ ✗ ✗

Marazion, nr Penzance TR17 0HT (tel. Penzance (0736) 710507)

Originally the site of a Benedictine chapel established by Edward the Confessor; the spectacular castle on its rock dates from the 14th century; fine views towards Land's End and The Lizard

29 March to end Oct: Mon to Fri 10.30–5.45. Last admissions 4.45. Nov to end March: guided tours or free flow, as tide, weather and circumstances permit (no regular ferry service during this period; ferries may only operate in favourable boating conditions at any time of year). The Mount is open most weekends during the season; these are special charity open days, when NT members are asked to pay for admission

Special educational visits for schools and organisations on Tues from March to end May, weather permitting, by prior arrangement with Mr O. Bartle, Manor Office, Marazion. Schools resource pack available

The times stated above apply from the visitors' entrance on the island, therefore ample time should be allowed for travel to the island.

Notes: Owing to narrow passages within the castle it may be necessary to restrict numbers; visitors are warned that some delays may occur at the height of the season. On Sun from June to Sept a short non-denominational service is held in the Castle Chapel at 11; seating is limited. The causeway and paths are cobbled, and therefore unsuitable for wheelchairs, prams or pushchairs

Shop open 29 March to end Oct daily

£2.80. Family ticket £7.50

Island café, 29 March to end Sept: Mon to Fri. 'The Sail Loft' restaurant, 29 March to end Oct: daily; limited out of season service

→ ½m S of A394 at Marazion, whence there is access on foot over the causeway at low tide or, during summer months only, by ferry at high tide (return ferry tickets should not be taken) [203: SW515298] *Bus:* Western National 2, 2A Penzance–Falmouth (passing BR Penzance) (tel. Penzance (0736) 69469) *Station:* Penzance 3m

TINTAGEL OLD POST OFFICE 🏠   ✉ ⛪

Tintagel PL34 0DB

Small and fascinating 14th-century stone house built to plan of medieval manor house, with a large hall; used in the 19th century for nearly fifty years as the letter-receiving office for the district and now restored as such

Note: Visitors may find the building partly closed for repairs during 1991 season

⏺🛍 29 March to end Oct: daily 11–6 (closes 5 in Oct). Shop

£ £1.60. No reduction for parties

→ In centre of village [200: SX056884] *Bus:* Fry's service from Wadebridge (tel. Camelford (0840) 770256)

TRELISSICK GARDEN 🍀♣🔱🧍

Feock, nr Truro TR3 6QL (tel. Truro (0872) 862090; information 865808)

Large garden, lovely at all seasons; rare shrubs and plants; extensive park, woods and farmland; beautiful views over Fal Estuary and Falmouth harbour; woodland walks beside river Fal; house not open; Art and Craft Gallery by the Home Farm Courtyard

⏺🍀 March to end Oct: Mon to Sat 11–6; Sun 1–6; (closes 5 in March & Oct). Woodland walk also open Nov to end March

🛍 Shop and plant sales open as garden

£ £2.50. No reduction for parties. £1 car park fee refundable on admission

♿🔊 Upper parts of garden accessible, but loose gravel paths; special parking; ♿ WC near shop & car park. Small walled garden, specially planted with aromatic plants

🐕 In woodland walk and park only, on leads

🍴♿ Coffee, lunches and teas in Trelissick Garden Barn on garden open days, Mon 🍀 to Sat 11–6; Sun 12–6; (closes 5 in March & Oct); additional limited daily opening in Nov & Dec. Tel. Truro (0872) 863486

Events: Programme of theatrical and musical events; details from Administrator

→ 4m S of Truro, on both sides of B3289 above King Harry Ferry [204: SW837396] *Bus:* Western National 85 from Truro, (passing close BR Truro) (tel. Truro (0872) 40404) *Station:* Truro 5m; Perranwell (U), not Sun, except May to Sept, 4m

TRENGWAINTON GARDEN ✿ ✖

nr Penzance TR20 8RZ (tel. Penzance (0736) 63021)

Large shrub garden with view over Mounts Bay; particularly colourful in spring and early summer; the walled garden has many tender plants which cannot be grown in the open elsewhere in England

O March to end Oct: Wed to Sat, BH Mon & Good Fri 11–6 (closes 5 in March & Oct)

£ £1.80. No reduction for parties

♿ Special car parking on request. ♿ WC

♨♿ Teas usually available at Trengwainton Farm

→ 2m NW of Penzance, ½m W of Heamoor on Penzance-Morvah road (B3312), ½m off St Just road (A3071) [203: SW445315] *Bus:* Western National D Penzance–Madron; 10 Penzance–St Just (both passing BR Penzance), thence ¼m (tel. Penzance (0736) 69469) *Station:* Penzance 2m

TRERICE 🏠 ✿ ✖ ✖

nr Newquay TR8 4PG (tel. Newquay (0637) 875404)

A delightful small secluded Elizabethan manor house, built in 1571; containing fine fireplaces and plaster ceilings, oak and walnut furniture; tapestries; a small museum in the barn traces the development of the lawn mower. A summer garden with some unusual plants and an orchard

O 29 March to end Oct: daily except Tues 11–6 (closes 5 in Oct). Last admissions ½hr before closing

🛍 Shop open as house

£ £3.20. Pre-arranged parties £2.60

♿ Ground & upper (via grass slope) floors of house & shop accessible; some loose gravel and cobbles; garden more difficult; special parking by prior arrangement with Administrator. ♿ WC

♨♿ Coffee, lunches and teas in the Barn. Organisers of parties should arrange for meals beforehand with the Administrator

→ 3m SE of Newquay via A392 and A3058 (turn right at Kestle Mill) [200: SW841585] *Bus:* Western National 90 Newquay–Truro, alight Kestle Mill, ¾m (tel. Truro (0872) 40404) *Station:* Quintrell Downs (U), not Sun, except May to Sept, 1½m

Cumbria

SCOTLAND   NORTHUMBERLAND

NT owned land within
the National Park

SOLWAY COMMONS   ● Carlisle
■ WETHERAL
  WOODS

WORDSWORTH HOUSE

Cockermouth

DURHAM

● Workington   ▲▲   *Bassenthwaite Lake*   ● Penrith   ▲ ACORN BANK
                                                            GARDEN
CRUMMOCK WATER   ■ CASTLERIGG STONE CIRCLE
LOWESWATER●   ● Keswick
● Whitehaven   *Derwentwater*   *Ullswater*
                                            ▲ KELD CHAPEL
Ennerdale   BUTTERMERE
Water   *Haweswater*

                    HAWKSHEAD COURTHOUSE
                    STAGSHAW GARDEN
WASTWATER   ▲   ▲ TOWNEND
BEATRIX POTTER GALLERY ▲
STEAM YACHT GONDOLA ▲   HILL   *Lake Windermere*
            TOP
Coniston Water   ▲ SIZERGH CASTLE
            ■
            FELL FOOT PARK

            ▲ CARTMEL PRIORY
              GATEHOUSE
SANDSCALE   ■ ARNSIDE KNOTT
HAWS   ▲ DALTON
        CASTLE   N. YORKS
● Barrow-in-Furness
                LANCS

LAKE DISTRICT LANDSCAPE

The Trust's most important work in Cumbria is the conservation of more than one quarter of the Lake District National Park. Almost all the central fell area and the major valley heads are owned or held on lease by the Trust, and six of the main lakes and much of their shoreline are also fully protected. These 140,000 acres are about a quarter of the Trust's entire holding throughout the country and by far the largest portion of any National Park protected by the Trust.

The Trust bought its first property in the Lake District, **Brandelhow Woods** [89: NY250200], in 1902 to guarantee public access to the shore of Derwentwater. Some of the most important of the Trust's 7,000 acres of woodland in the National Park are in the Borrowdale Valley: **Great Wood** [89: NY2721], with a well-screened car park and lake access, **Manesty Wood** [89: NY251191] with its caravan site run by the Caravan Club, and **Johnny Wood** [89: NY252142] a Site of Special Scientific Interest. Ruskin called the view from **Friar's Crag** [89: NY264223], on the north shore of Derwentwater, one of the finest in Europe: his memorial stands upon the crag which itself is a memorial to Canon Hardwicke Rawnsley whose inspiration and energy began the great work of the Trust ⓘ. Nearby at the Keswick boatlandings is a National Trust information centre and shop. To the east of Keswick on a magnificent site is **Castlerigg Stone Circle** [89: NY293236], a free-standing megalithic circle of 40 stones.

Loweswater [89: NY1221], **Crummock Water** [89: NY1518] and **Buttermere** [89: NY1815] are all under Trust protection: a boat can be hired on all three lakes for fishing. Around these lakes the Trust is increasing the native hardwoods, planting predominantly oak. **Scale Force** [89: NY150171] south-west of Crummock Water, is the highest waterfall in a district renowned for its falls.

Much of the northern and all of the southern shore of **Ennerdale Water** [89: NY1015], is protected by the Trust, as are all the high fells to the west and south.

Further south still is dramatic **Wasdale**, arguably the wildest of all the valleys [89: NY1606], almost entirely protected by the Trust: from **Scafell Pike** [89: NY215071], England's highest mountain, and **Great Gable** [89: NY215106] at its head, to the awesome screes sliding down into **Wastwater**, England's deepest lake. Even the bed of the lake is in the Trust's care.

There are dramatic views of the lakeless Eskdale from the top of **Hardknott Pass** [89: NY230015]. In this valley alone the Trust protects 3,750 acres of land, including the summit of **Bowfell** [89: NY247064] and all the surrounding fells. One of the Trust's 12 isolated holiday cottages, Bird How, is situated in this quiet and beautiful valley.

Dunnerdale [96: SD2093], beloved of the poet Wordsworth (whose birthplace in Cockermouth is under Trust care and open to the public, see p. 80), with the tumbling River Duddon, scattered woods and steep side-valleys, leads up to **Wrynose Bottom** [89: NY260020], where much work has recently been done in repairing dilapidated dry stone walls.

Wrynose Pass leads down to the Langdale Valleys. **Great Langdale** [89: NY3006] is climbing country: here the Trust runs a permanent campsite. For those less hardy the Old Dungeon Ghyll Hotel [89: NY286060] provides much more comfortable accommodation. Evidence of some of the huge amount of footpath repair undertaken in recent years can be seen just a short walk up the fell from the well-screened and landscaped car park beneath **Stickle Ghyll** [89: NY295064]. 16,842 acres of land in this area are held on lease from the 7th Earl of Lonsdale until 1996 or his death, whichever is the longer. This large area includes the famous **Langdale Pikes**, together with all the highland from **Seat Sandal** on the slopes of Helvellyn to the head of Great Langdale, the bed of **Grasmere Lake**, and part of **Rydal Water**, **White Moss** and **Elterwater Commons**.

Moving to the softer hills of the south, Trust ownership around Coniston is centred on the vast Monk Coniston Estate which includes **Tarn Hows** [89: NY3300]; (car park charge for non-members). This was bought by Beatrix Potter, better known locally as Mrs William Heelis. She sold half at cost to the Trust, and then bequeathed to it the other half. Restored and relaunched by the National Trust in 1980 the Victorian steam yacht **Gondola**, first launched in 1859, gently plies the length of Coniston Water (see p. 79). In

Hawkshead village there is a National Trust shop [96: SD352982] and the **Beatrix Potter Gallery**, with a selection of her original watercolours on display (see p. 75). **Hill Top** [89: SD370956], Beatrix Potter's first acquisition in the Lake District, in Near Sawrey, is best visited at off-peak times (see p. 77).

It was through money raised by Beatrix Potter that the Trust was able to purchase **Cockshott Point** [96: SD396965] on the shore of Windermere. On this lake, the most popular of all, the Trust protects some 90% of the land from which the public has free access to the shore. On the west side is **Low Wray Campsite** [89: NY372011] and **Claife Woods**, along some 3 miles of shore stretching from near Ferry Nab to Wray Castle [96: SD3898]. At the southern tip of the lake, near Newby Bridge, is **Fell Foot Country Park** [96: SD382870], with picnic areas, boats for hire and a boathouse café (see p. 76).

Bridge House, perched over Stock Ghyll in Ambleside, once home to a family of six, is now the Trust's oldest Information Centre and smallest shop [89: NY375045]. ⓘ ♿ Between Ambleside and Grasmere lies **White Moss Common** (car park charge for non-members) [89: NY348065] where the Trust has provided a wheelchair path leading from the car park to the river. **Church Stile** houses a Trust shop and Information Centre [89: NY336074] in Grasmere village, while at the head of the valley the Trust has pitched a totally new footpath up Helm Crag to overcome the massive erosion problems and provide a more attractive route to the summit of this family favourite.

Aira Force [89: NY399205]; (car park charge for non-members); provides a glimpse of a landscaped Victorian park with dramatic waterfalls, arboretum and rock scenery. There is also a café. After a walk along this shore of Ullswater Wordsworth wrote 'I wandered lonely as a cloud'. Trust purchase in 1913 ensured that this area would not be developed into a housing estate.

In the small area of the Lake District are tranquil lakes, quiet valleys, gently rolling vales and awesome mountains, each individual and with its own special character. Today it is still a working community of farmers and sheep where the Trust's protection of so much of this glorious landscape is aimed at maintaining the delicate balance between man and nature. In the past three years the Trust has planted 135,000 trees in the Lake District, the majority native hardwoods, predominantly sessile oak. In the past ten years 23 major footpath rebuilding projects have been completed as well as many smaller projects right across the Lake District. Since 1985 major works have been completed on well over half of the Trust's 80 Lake District farms, and less extensive repairs and improvements have been carried out to nearly every farm the Trust owns. Many miles of walls have also been repaired by Trust gangs, although with an estimated 2,000 miles of wall on Trust land alone, there is still a lot to do.

YEW TREE FARM

73

THE REMAINDER OF CUMBRIA

While most of the countryside under the Trust's protection lies within the National Park, there are some outstanding areas in other parts of Cumbria. Near Carlisle **Wetheral Woods** [86: NY470533] provides riverside walks by the River Eden, while at the other end of the county the limestone escarpment of **Arnside Knott** [89: SD456774] offers wonderful views over Morecambe Bay [⚐]. Only two miles from Barrow is **Sandscale Haws** (car parking [96: SD200756] signed Roanhead off A595, just north of Dalton-in-Furness) an internationally renowned nature reserve, with beach, dunes and flora-rich marshes, the breeding site of the rare Natterjack toad and with a strong population of the Coral Root orchid. Nearby stands **Dalton Castle**, a 14th-century pele tower in the main street of Dalton-in-Furness (see p. 76). Three miles from Kendal is the **Sizergh Castle Estate** [89: SD498878] with not only the castle and its extensive garden (see p. 78), but also long walks through surrounding woods and hills. On a smaller scale is **Keld Chapel** [90: NY554145] (see p. 78), a charming pre-Reformation building near Shap. **Cartmel Priory Gatehouse** (see p. 76) also dates from before the Reformation and is the only building, other than the church, which remains of the Augustinian Priory. At the opposite end of the county is **Acorn Bank Garden** [91: NY612281] (see p. 75), a fascinating contrast of well established herb garden and newly opened-up woodland. The furthermost north-west of the Trust's properties are the **Solway Commons** [85: NY3156], 170 acres of common land and 1½ miles of coastline with a solitary beauty and magnificent views of the estuary and of the mountains of Galloway.

Holiday Cottages. The National Trust's 12 holiday cottages in the Lake District do not attempt to be anything but homely and reasonably comfortable bases from which to explore. The cottages can be conveniently categorised as either fell or waterside. The waterside cottages stand within yards of lakeshores and river banks. They tend to be of easier access and slightly more modern in their facilities than the fell cottages. As their name implies the fell cottages are at a higher level, often at the end of rough tracks; some are quite isolated and offer a rather more spartan habitation.

[♿] Restharrow Cottage, on the quiet western shore of Windermere, has been adapted for disabled visitors, who will be given booking preference. For a leaflet or bookings for all cottages, contact the Bookings Secretary, Fell Foot Park (address below).

Farm Accommodation. For self-catering or dinner, bed and breakfast accommodation at many of the Trust's 80 fell farms, please ask for a free leaflet from the Bookings Secretary, Fell Foot Park (address below).

Boating and Fishing. A leaflet detailing the boating and fishing available on National Trust waters in the Lake District is available from NT Information Centres or from the Bookings Secretary, Fell Foot Park, Newby Bridge, nr Ulverston, Cumbria LA22 8NN (please send s.a.e.). NT rowing boats are available for hire on Buttermere, Crummock Water, Loweswater and Windermere.

[♿] Tarn Hows, White Moss Common, Fell Foot Park, Castlerigg Stone Circle and Friar's Crag have special provision for disabled visitors: details are given in a special leaflet.

PLEASE REFER TO PAGES 5–9

ACORN BANK GARDEN ✿

Temple Sowerby, nr Penrith CA10 1SP (tel. Kirkby Thore (07683) 61893)

2½-acre garden protected by fine oaks under which grow a vast display of daffodils; inside the walls are two orchards with fruit trees; surrounding the orchards are mixed borders with shrubs, herbaceous plants and roses. The herb garden has the largest collection of culinary and medicinal plants in the north; the red sandstone house is let to the Sue Ryder Foundation. Newly opened woodland walk beside the Crowdundle Beck. Mill under restoration but not yet open to visitors

🅾	29 March to 3 Nov: daily 10–6. Last admissions 5.30. Admission to the house by written application to the Sue Ryder Foundation
🗂	Small shop and plants for sale, open same times as garden
£	£1.20. Pre-arranged parties 80p. Car parking within grounds
🧍	Baby-changing facilities
♿	Newly restored greenhouse, herb garden and herbaceous borders. ♿ WC
🐕	Dogs admitted, but not to walled garden
➡	Just N of Temple Sowerby, 6m E of Penrith on A66 [91: NY612281] *Station:* Langwathby (U) 5m; Penrith 6m

BEATRIX POTTER GALLERY 🏠   ✖ ✖ ✖ ✖

Main Street, Hawkshead LA22 0NS (tel. Hawkshead (09666) 355)

An award winning exhibition of a selection of Beatrix Potter's original drawings and illustrations of her children's story books (to be changed annually), together with a display telling the story of her life as an author, artist, farmer and determined preserver of her beloved Lake District; the building was once the office of her husband, the solicitor William Heelis; the interior remains largely unaltered since his day

🅾	29 March to 1 Nov: Mon to Fri & BH Sun 10.30–4.30. Last admissions 4
🗂 ✿	Shop 30yds open daily 9–5.30, except Tues out of season; Feb & March: weekends only
£	£2. No reduction for parties. Car and coach parking in town car park 200yds. We regret the Gallery is not suitable for baby backpacks, pushchairs or wheelchairs
🍴	Available in Hawkshead
➡	In The Square [96: SD352982]. *Bus & Station:* As Hawkshead Courthouse p. 77

CARTMEL PRIORY GATEHOUSE 🏠✝ 🏛

Cavendish Street, Cartmel, Grange-over-Sands (tel. Cartmel (05395) 36602)

All that is left, apart from the church, of the Augustinian priory, dating from about 1330; a picturesque building which served as a grammar school from 1624–1790

🅾 29 March to 3 Nov: Tues to Sun 11–5. If closed on stated opening days tel. Cartmel (05395) 36691 for accompanied visit

£ Parking in the village

➔ [96: SD378788] *Bus:* CMS 530–3, G1–3, Kendal–Grange-over-Sands (passing BR Grange-over-Sands) (tel: Kendal (0539) 733221) *Station:* Cark (U) 2m

DALTON CASTLE 🏠

(Tel. Ambleside (05394) 33883)

A 14th-century tower in the main street of Dalton

🅾 30 March to end Sept: Sat 2–5. Key also available daily June to Sept: 10–4 from Mr I. Whitehead, 18 Market Place, Dalton (tel. Barrow-in-Furness (0229) 66271)

➔ In main street of Dalton [96: SD226739] *Bus:* From surrounding areas (tel. Barrow-in-Furness (0229) 821325) *Station:* Dalton ¼m

FELL FOOT PARK 🌳🚣

Newby Bridge, Ulverston LA12 8NN (tel. Newby Bridge (05395) 31273)

An 18-acre country park with lakeshore access and magnificent views; ideal for a day's outing; car parking, touring caravans, fishing, boat launching (no power boats), picnics, also furnished self-catering chalets, café, information centre and shop, rowing boats for hire; booking for holiday cottages in the Lake District

🅾🌼🏕 **Park:** all year: 10 to dusk. **Caravan site:** March to end Oct. **Chalets:** weekend before Easter to end Oct. **Café, Information Centre, shop and boat hire:** Easter to end Oct; daily incl. Good Fri (shop and café 10.30–5)

£ No admission fee. Car park £2 (NT members free). Coaches £8

♿🐕 Accessible but please be careful; slopes and unfenced water; guide dogs admitted but not to chalets overnight. ♿ WC beside café; special parking for 3 cars

🐕 Dogs admitted, but not to chalets

🍽♿ Coffee, light lunches and teas in boathouse café, Easter to end Oct. Picnic sites in park

➔ At the extreme S end of Lake Windermere on E shore, entrance from A592 [96/97: SD381869] *Bus:* CMS 518 Ulverston–Grasmere (passing BR Windermere) (tel. Kendal (0539) 733221) *Station:* Grange-over-Sands 6m

HAWKSHEAD COURTHOUSE 🏠 ✈️ ✂️

Hawkshead, nr Ambleside, Cumbria
(tel. Regional Office, Ambleside (053 94) 33883)

Dating from the 15th century, the Courthouse is all that is left of the manorial buildings of Hawkshead once held by Furness Abbey

O 29 March to 3 Nov: daily 10–5, by key from NT shop, The Square, Hawkshead. May occasionally be in use by the local community

£ Free. No WCs. No parking facilities

→ At junction of Ambleside and Coniston roads, ½m N of Hawkshead on B5286 [96/97: SD349987] *Bus:* CMS 505, 516 from Ambleside (connections from BR Windermere) (tel. Kendal (0539) 733221) *Station:* Windermere 6½m via vehicle ferry

HILL TOP 🏠 ❋ ✈️ ✂️ 🚭 👜

At Near Sawrey, Ambleside LA22 0LF (tel. Hawkshead (09666) 269)

Beatrix Potter wrote many Peter Rabbit books in this little 17th-century house, which contains her furniture and china

Notes: The cottage is so small that numbers of visitors may have to be limited at peak times. We regret the cottage is not suitable for baby backpacks, pushchairs or wheelchairs. A selection of Beatrix Potter's original drawings on display in Beatrix Potter Gallery, Main Street, Hawkshead (see p. 75)

O Good Fri 29 March to 3 Nov: Mon to Wed, Sat & Sun 11–5 (closed Thur & Fri except Good Fri). Last admissions 4.30

🏠 Shop daily 10–5 during season

£ £2.90; children £1.50. No reduction for parties. Parking 100yds; no parking for coaches

♿ Unsuitable for disabled visitors; visually handicapped people with escorts are welcome, but are advised to visit outside peak times (weekends and BH) as house is so small and approach paths are narrow. Guide dogs admitted

🍽 Bar lunches and evening bar meals at the Tower Bank Arms (NT owned, and let to tenant) next door, during licensing hours (tel. Hawkshead (09666) 334)

→ 2m S of Hawkshead, in hamlet of Near Sawrey, behind the Tower Bank Arms [96/97: SD370955] *Bus:* Frequent from BR Windermere to Bowness Pier, thence ferry & 2m walk (tel. Kendal (0539) 733221) *Station:* Windermere 4½m via vehicle ferry

PLEASE REFER TO PAGES 5–9

KELD CHAPEL ✚

Shap, nr Kendal

Small pre-Reformation building, still used for occasional services

🅾️ ❄️ At all reasonable hours; key available in village; notice on chapel door

💷 Free. Unsuitable for coaches. No WCs

➡️ 1m SW of Shap village, close to River Lowther [90: NY554145]
Station: Penrith 10m

SIZERGH CASTLE 🏰 ❀   ✈️ ✖️ 🎣

nr Kendal LA8 8AE (tel. Sedgwick (053 95) 60070)

The Strickland family home for more than 700 years; impressive 14th-century pele tower; extended in Tudor times, with some of the finest Elizabethan carved overmantels in the country; good English and French furniture and family portraits; surrounded by gardens (including the Trust's largest limestone rock garden) of beauty and interest; good autumn colour

🅾️ **Castle:** 31 March to end Oct: Sun to Thur 1.30–5.30. **Garden:** as Castle from 12.30. Last admissions 5

🏪 Shop open as garden

💷 £2.80. Garden only £1.40. Parties of 15 or more £2 by arrangement with Administrator (not BH). Car park 100yds. We regret the Castle is not suitable for baby backpacks or pushchairs

♿ 👁️ Most of garden mainly via gravel paths. Lower Hall & tea-room accessible. Adapted WC at Peppercorn Lane car park, near Abbot Hall, Kendal, 3m. Garden & first floor suitable for accompanied visually handicapped visitors

📁🔥 Tea-room in basement of pele tower open 1.30. Picnic tables in car park

➡️ 3½m S of Kendal NW of interchange A590/A591 [97: SD498878] *Bus:* CMS
555 Keswick–Lancaster (passing close BR Kendal) (tel. Kendal (0539)
733221) *Station:* Oxenholme 3m; Kendal (U) 3½m

STAGSHAW GARDEN ✵   ✖

Ambleside LA22 0HE (tel. Ambleside (053 94) 33883)

*This woodland garden was created by the late C.H.D. Acland, Regional Agent for the Trust;
fine collection of azaleas and rhododendrons, planted to give good blends of colour under the
thinned oaks on the hillside; many trees and shrubs, including magnolias, camellias and
embothriums*

🅾️ 29 March to end June: daily 10–6.30. July to end Oct: by appointment with
NT North West Regional Office (see p. 22). Please send s.a.e.

💷 £1. No reduction for parties. Parking very limited; access dangerous; visitors
may park at Waterhead car park and walk to Stagshaw. No access for coaches
which may drop visitors at end of drive, and park in Waterhead car park,
Ambleside. No WCs

➡️ ½m S of Ambleside on A591 [90: NY380030] *Bus:* CMS 518, 555–7, W1/2
from BR Windermere (tel. Kendal (0539) 733221) *Station:* Windermere, 4m

STEAM YACHT GONDOLA   ✖

Coniston Water (tel. Coniston (053 94) 41288)

*The steam yacht Gondola, first launched in 1859, and now completely renovated by the
Trust, provides a steam-powered passenger service, carrying 86 passengers in opulently
upholstered and heated saloons; travel aboard Gondola is an experience in its own right, and
a superb way to see Coniston's scenery*

🅾️ **Sailings:** Steam Yacht *Gondola* sails to a scheduled daily timetable during the
season, weather permitting, starting at 11, except Sat, when sailings start at
12.05. 1991 sailings begin on 27 March and continue to 3 Nov. The Trust
reserves the right to cancel sailings in the event of high winds or lack of
demand. Piers at Coniston, Park-a-Moor at SE end of the lake and Brantwood
(not NT). Parties from Coniston Pier only

💷 Ticket prices on application and published locally. No reduction for NT
members as *Gondola* is an enterprise and not held solely for preservation.
Parties & private charters: *Gondola* Bookings, Pier Cottage, Coniston, Cumbria
LA21 8AJ (tel. Coniston (053 94) 41288). Contact may be made direct
between 8.30am & 10.30am; answerphone in operation at other times

&♿ Disabled and visually handicapped people may travel on *Gondola* at own risk;
access not easy, but help available from crew; guide dogs admitted

➡️ Coniston (¾m to Coniston Pier). *Bus:* CMS 505 from Ambleside, (connections
from BR Windermere); (tel. Kendal (0539) 733221) *Station:* Foxfield (U), not
Sun, 10m; Windermere 10m via vehicle ferry

TOWNEND 🏠   ✗ ✗ ✗

Troutbeck, Windermere LA23 1LB (tel. Ambleside (053 94) 32628)

An exceptional relic of Lake District life of past centuries; a 'statesman' (wealthy yeoman) farmer's house, built about 1626, containing carved woodwork, books, papers, furniture and fascinating domestic implements of the past, collected by the Browne family who lived here from that date until 1944

🔘   29 March to 3 Nov: Tues to Fri, Sun & BH Mon, 1–5 or dusk if earlier. Last admissions 4.30

£   £2. No reduction for parties which must be pre-booked. Townend and the village are unsuitable for coaches; 12 & 15 seater minibuses are acceptable; permission to take coaches to Townend must be obtained from the Highways Dept, Cumbria CC, Carlisle, Cumbria. Car park (no coaches)

     Note: We regret that Townend is not suitable for baby backpacks, pushchairs or wheelchairs

➡   3m SE of Ambleside at S end of village [90: NY407020] *Bus:* From surrounding areas (many passing BR Windermere) to within 1m (tel. Kendal (0539) 733221) *Station:* Windermere 3m

WORDSWORTH HOUSE 🏠 ❀   ✗ ✗ ✗

Main Street, Cockermouth CA13 9RX (tel. Cockermouth (0900) 824805)

North-country Georgian town house, built in 1745, birthplace of William Wordsworth (1770); seven rooms furnished in 18th-century style, with some personal effects of the poet; also his childhood garden with terraced walk; video display in old stables

🔘   29 March to 3 Nov: daily except Thur 11–5 (Sun 2–5). Last admissions 4.30

🛍 ❀   Shop same days as house 10–5 (Sun 2–5). Also 4 Nov to end March 1992 10–5 (closed Thur, Sun & week after Christmas)

£   £2. Parties £1.40 by arrangement, not Sun. Parking in the town. We regret the house is not suitable for baby backpacks, pushchairs or wheelchairs

👁   Unsuitable for disabled people, but suitable for escorted visually handicapped visitors

☕   Light lunches (licensed); teas in the old kitchen

➡   [89: NY118307] *Bus:* CMS 34–6 Keswick–Workington (passing close BR Workington); 58 from Maryport (passing close BR Maryport) (tel. Workington (0900) 603080) *Station:* Maryport 6½m

Derbyshire & Peak District

GTR MANCHESTER
● Glossop
DERWENT MOORS
■ KINDER SCOUT
S. YORKS
■ HIGH PEAK ESTATE
■ MAM TOR
LONGSHAW ESTATE ▲ ■
■ RILEY GRAVES
CHESHIRE
● Buxton
● Chesterfield
HARDWICK HALL ▲
▲ ● Winster
WINSTER MARKET HOUSE
SOUTH PEAK ESTATE ■
Alfreton ●
NOTTS
MANIFOLD VALLEY ▲
ILAM PARK ▲■
■ DOVEDALE
● Ashbourne
▲ THE OLD MANOR
● Ilkeston
▲ KEDLESTON HALL
Derby ●
▲ SUDBURY HALL
STAFFS
▲ CALKE ABBEY
LEICS

NT owned land within the National Park

COUNTRYSIDE

Derbyshire is a county of contrasts – gentle river valleys, pastures, woodland and the high peat moorlands and towering limestone crags of the Peaks.

The Trust's holdings here, primarily in Derbyshire, Staffordshire and South Yorkshire, amount to some 12 per cent of the Peak District National Park, the first of ten to be designated in England and Wales by Government in the 1950s and '60s. While the Trust and the National Park Authorities work closely together they are entirely separate bodies; the National Parks are statutory authorities, and the Trust is an independent charity. The Trust's extensive ownership in the Peak District is managed in three estates.

High Peak Estate (tel. Estate Office: Hope Valley (0433) 70368).
An important part of the Trust's High Peak Estate is in South Yorkshire; the Derwent Moors extend to some 5,000 acres, with an extra 1,400 acres which spill over into

81

Derbyshire (110: SK1944]. This vast stretch of moorland on the east bank of the River Derwent, rises to 1,775ft and overlooks the three main reservoirs in the Peak District, created at the turn of the century by flooding the dales – the Ladybower, the Derwent and the Howden.

By far the largest single holding of the Trust's 36,500 acres in Derbyshire is the **Hope Woodlands**, 16,500 acres, 12 miles west of Sheffield [110: SK135935]. This has less woodland than its name suggests; it is largely lonely and dramatic Pennine moorland adjoining Kinder Scout and giving superb views over the Peak District. The moors are open except on published grouse-shooting days. The property is crossed by the Pennine Way.

Kinder Scout [110: SK0888] came to the Trust in 1982. Probably the most famous landmark in the Peak District at 2,000ft high, known not only for its magnificence, but because of the mass trespass here in 1932 when ramblers campaigned, eventually with some success, for the right of access to uplands in England.

[⚡] The Kinder estate marches with the Trust's holdings in Edale, where several hill farms are owned with viewpoints such as **Lord's Seat** and **Lose Hill Pike** [110: SK153853]. But perhaps the most fascinating landmark here is **Mam Tor** – the 'shivering mountain' of which Celia Fiennes said in 1697 '... a high hill that looks exactly round but on the side next Castleton ... it's all broken that it looks just in resemblance as a great Hayricke thats cut down one halfe ... and on that broken side the sand keeps trickling down all wayes ...' This description fits today, and there are views from its 1,700-ft summit towards Kinder and the High Peak [110: SK1383].

Next to Mam Tor is the spectacular limestone gorge of **Winnats Pass** close to the Blue John mines of Treak Cliff (not NT) which yield an amethyst-coloured stone from which ornaments have been made since the 18th century.

Longshaw Estate (tel. Hope Valley (0433) 31708 Visitor Centre/31757 Estate Office). (See also entry on p. 85).
At **Longshaw** near Hathersage the Trust owns nearly 1,600 acres of moor, pasture and woodland on the Burbage Brook which varies from a raging torrent in wet weather to a babbling brook in summer. In a disused quarry are half-finished millstones – a reminder of the end of the millstone-making industry centred here about a hundred years ago.

In 1665 the Plague came to Eyam near Tideswell, carried there from London in some clothing. When it was discovered, the villagers – led by their rector – took a terrible decision: they isolated the village and no-one was allowed in or out until the infection had burnt itself out. Three-quarters of the inhabitants died and seven members of one family, the Hancocks, are buried in the **Riley Graves** in a meadow called the Righ Lea. The Trust owns the graves and protects the meadow [110: SK229766].

South Peak Estate (tel. Estate Office: Thorpe Cloud (033 529) 503).
This area of outstanding natural beauty in the southern limestone region of the Peak District extends to 3,200 acres and consists of **Ilam Hall** (now a Youth Hostel) its grounds and parkland (see p. 198); **Dovedale**, internationally famous for its ashwoods and geological features [♿]; parts of **Wolfscote** and **Biggin Dales**, and some areas of the **Manifold and Hamps Valleys**. There is an Information Shelter at Milldale.

Ilam Hall is at the centre of **Ilam Country Park**, where there are very pleasant walks (leaflet available; address on p. 198), also an Information Centre/Shop and the Manifold Restaurant, (tel. Thorpe Cloud (033 529) 245); also a Day Visit Room, bookable for use by visiting groups; book in advance via the National Park Study Centre, Losehill Hall, Castleton, Derbyshire (tel. Hope Valley (0433) 20373).

PLEASE REFER TO PAGES 5–9

CALKE ABBEY 🏚 ❄ 🏠 ♣ ✚ 🅿 👤   ✉ 🏛

Ticknall DE7 1LE (tel. Melbourne (0332) 863822 – general enquiries;
864444 – 24hr recorded information service)

*'The house that time forgot'; Baroque mansion, built 1701–3 for Sir John Harpur; virtually
unaltered since the death of the last baronet in 1924; natural history collections; unique
Caricature Room; gold and white drawing room; early 18th-century state bed unpacked and
displayed in house for first time; extended visitor route in house for 1991; carriage display in
stable block; walled gardens and pleasure grounds; early 19th-century church; Portland sheep
in park*

Notes: One-way system operates in the Park; access only via Ticknall entrance. Due to
large numbers visiting Calke, entry to the house is by timed ticket (incl. NT members).
Waiting time may be spent in the park, garden, church, stables, restaurant or shop;
visitors are advised that on busy days the delay in gaining admission to the house may
be considerable, and very occasionally admission may not be possible

[O] **House, garden and church:** 30 March to end Oct: Sat to Wed incl. BH Mon.
House 12.30–5. Church and garden open from 11. Last admissions 4.30.
Ticket office open same days as house 11–5. Admission to house for all visitors
(incl. NT members) is by timed ticket (obtain on arrival). This gives the time of
entry to the house, but does not restrict the time visitors may spend on their
tour

[❄] **Park:** open during daylight hours all year. Vehicle charge, £1 (refundable on
purchase of house ticket); NT members free

[🏠][❄] Shop and Information Room open same days as house 11–5. Also Nov to
22 Dec: Sat & Sun 12–4

[👤] Guided tours for parties may be arranged outside normal open hours, Sat, Mon,
Tues, Wed mornings (not BH weekends). Tours last approx. 1hr 20 min; (extra
charge incl. NT members). Parties must book through Calke office (tel. 0332
863822)

[£] £3.70; children £1.80.
No discount for parties

[👶][🎠] Parent and baby facilities.
Play area near restaurant;
log cabin for younger
children
continued

DERBYSHIRE & PEAK DISTRICT

   Access above ground floor difficult. Moderate access to garden and church (some steps), good access to stables and all visitor facilities. Leaflet available detailing vehicle access for disabled visitors

   In park only, on leads (not in garden, house or church, except guide dogs)

   Licensed restaurant open as shop serving wide variety of home-cooked hot and cold lunches 12–2 and teas 2–5 (2–4 Nov & Dec)

   9m S of Derby, on A514 at Ticknall between Swadlincote and Melbourne [128: SK356239] *Bus:* Trent 68 from Derby (passing close BR Derby) (tel. Derby (0332) 292200); long walk along drive to house *Station:* Derby 8½m; Burton-on-Trent 9m

HARDWICK HALL

Doe Lea, Chesterfield S44 5QJ (tel. Chesterfield (0246) 850430)

Late 16th-century 'prodigy house' designed by Robert Smythson for Bess of Hardwick; outstanding contemporary furniture, tapestries and needlework, many pieces identified in an inventory of 1601; Needlework Exhibition (permanent); walled courtyards enclose fine gardens, orchards and herb garden; Country Park contains Whiteface Woodland sheep and Longhorn cattle; Information Point in Country Park

Note: The remains of Hardwick Old Hall in the grounds are in the guardianship of English Heritage

   Hall: 30 March to end Oct: Wed, Thur, Sat, Sun & BH Mon 12.30–5, or sunset if earlier. Last admissions 4.30.
Garden: 30 March to end Oct: daily 12–5.30. Car park gates close 6.30.
Country park open daily throughout the year, dawn to dusk
Note: To avoid congestion, access to the house may be limited at peak periods

   Shop open as Hall

   Hall & garden £4.50, children £2.20. Garden only £1.80. No reduction for parties; parties of 10 or more only by prior arrangement in writing with Administrator; school parties Wed and Thur only; please send s.a.e. To avoid congestion parties are limited to two per day. Car park charge for Country Park to non-members 20p

   Garden and some parts of park accessible; access to house limited to ground floor via several steps to main entrance. Herb and flower garden particularly recommended

   In Country Park only, on leads, not in garden

   Lunches 12–1.45 & teas 2.30–4.45 in licensed restaurant in the Great Kitchen on days Hall is open (access by several steps). Party bookings by written application only; s.a.e. please

   6½m W of Mansfield, 9½m SE of Chesterfield; approach from M1 (exit 29) via A6175 [120: SK463638] *Bus:* E Midland X2 Sheffield–Nottingham, 63 Chesterfield–Nottingham, 48 Chesterfield–Bolsover (all passing within 30-min walk of BR Chesterfield), alight Glapwell 'Young Vanish' 2m (tel. Derby (0332) 292200 *Station:* Chesterfield 9½m

ILAM HALL & COUNTRY PARK see STAFFORDSHIRE

KEDLESTON HALL 🏛️➕✳️🌳   ✉️

Derby DE6 4JN (tel. Derby (0332) 842191)

Palladian mansion set in classical park landscape; built 1759–65 for Nathaniel Curzon, 1st Baron Scarsdale, whose family has lived at Kedleston since the 12th century; the house has the most complete and least altered sequence of Robert Adam interiors in England; the rooms still contain their original great collection of family portraits and old masters, and their original furniture and other contents; Indian Museum houses objects collected by Lord Curzon when Viceroy of India (1899–1905); Adam bridge and fishing pavilion in the park; garden and pleasure grounds

⭕✳️ **House:** 30 March to end Oct: Sat to Wed 1–5.30 (last admissions to house 5). **Garden:** same days as house 11–6. **Park:** April to end Oct: daily 11–6; Nov to 22 Dec: Sat & Sun only 12–4 (vehicle entry charge £1, on Thur & Fri and during Nov & Dec)

🛍️✳️ Shop open as house. Also Nov to 22 Dec: Sat & Sun only 12–4

💷 £3.50; children £1.70. Reduced rate for booked parties on application

♿ Difficult steps for wheelchairs; please telephone Administrator in advance of a visit

🐕 In park only, on leads

🍽️♿ Licensed restaurant same days as house 12–5

➡️ 3m NW of Derby, signposted from roundabout where A38 crosses A52 close to Markeaton Park *Bus:* Trent 1/2 from Derby (passing close BR Derby), alight Allestree Lane End, 2m (tel. Derby (0332) 292200) *Station:* Duffield (U) $3\frac{1}{2}$; Derby $5\frac{1}{2}$m

LONGSHAW ESTATE 🏠🍴🚶🔭🎁

Sheffield S11 7TZ (tel. Hope Valley (0433) 31708)

1,600 acres of open moorland, woodland and farms in the Peak National Park; dramatic views and varied walking; stone for the Derwent and Howden Dams was quarried from Bolehill, and millstones may be seen in quarries on the estate; quarry winding house above Grindleford station; the Duke of Rutland's former shooting lodge is not open

Estate: open at all times. Lodge is converted into flats and is not open. **Visitor Centre (café, shop and information centre):** weekends throughout year incl. BH Mon 11–5 or sunset if earlier. Also open Wed & Thur from Easter to end Sept 11–5. Closed 23 Dec to 3 Jan 1992. Booked parties at other times by arrangement. Guided walks around the estate may be booked by groups: contact Head Warden (tel. Hope Valley (0433) 31757)

£ Car park 200yds from Visitor Centre; access difficult for coaches; no coaches at weekends or BH. Car parks for Estate at Haywood [110/119: SK256778] and Wooden Pole [110/119: SK267790]. Riding permits available. Longshaw Walks leaflet from Visitor Centre

Carriage drives only suitable; disabled visitors may be driven to Visitor Centre and 🚻 WC; drivers must, however, return and park in main car park, unless only visiting WC. No car parking at Centre or at adjacent lodge

On leads only; no dogs in Visitor Centre

Light lunches and teas at Visitor Centre

Events: 5–7 Sept, Longshaw Sheepdog Trials

→ 7½m from Sheffield, next to A625 Sheffield-Hathersage Road; Woodcroft car park is off B6055, 200yds S of junction with A625 [110/119: SK266802] *Bus:* S Yorkshire 240 Sheffield–Bakewell (passing BR Grindleford); 272 Sheffield–Castleton (passing BR Hathersage); Whites X65 Sheffield–Buxton (passing BR Grindleford & close BR Buxton). All pass close BR Sheffield (tel. Buxton (0298) 23098) *Station:* Grindleford (U) 2m

THE OLD MANOR 🏠🐴❄️✝️   ✉️

Norbury, Ashbourne DE6 2ED

Stone-built 13th- to 15th-century hall with rare king post roof, undercroft and cellars; hall of specialist architectural interest only; also late 17th-century red-brick manor house, incorporating fragments of an earlier Tudor house, tenanted (and not open); church (not NT) well worth a visit

Medieval Hall by written appointment only with the tenant Mr C. Wright. 30 March to end Sept: Tues, Wed & Sat afternoons

£ £1

→ *Bus:* Stevensons 409 Uttoxeter–Ashbourne (passing close BR Uttoxeter), alight Ellastone, ¾m (tel. Derby (0332) 292200) *Station:* Uttoxeter (U) 7½m

SUDBURY HALL 🏛️✳️🏠 ✉️

Sudbury DE6 5HT (tel. Sudbury (028 378) 305)*

One of the most individual of late 17th-century houses; begun by George Vernon c.1661; the rich decoration includes wood carvings by Gibbons and Pierce; superb plasterwork; mythological decorative paintings by Laguerre; family portraits; furniture; Museum of Childhood (see below) with Ballantyne collection of modern ceramics and study room

🅾️   30 March to end Oct: Wed to Sun & BH Mon (closed Tues following BH) 12.30–5 or sunset if earlier. Last admissions to Hall 4.30

🛍️✳️   Shop open as Hall. Also Nov to 22 Dec: Sat & Sun only 12–4. Pots study room open by arrangement with Administrator

💷   Hall £2.80. Parties £2; all parties (of 15 or over) must book; please contact Administrator. Museum of Childhood open similar to Hall (separate admission charge, incl. NT members)

🧒🖼️   Museum of Childhood (Derbyshire County Council) contains displays about children in the Victorian period and houses the Betty Cadbury collection in the Toybox Gallery. Backpack baby carriers accepted in Museum only. Chimney climbs for the adventurous youngster. Special facilities for pre-booked school parties in both Museum and Hall, by arrangement with Administrator

♿   Hall difficult, but arrangements can be made for access to the ground floor with prior notice. Museum, grounds & tea-room accessible; for special arrangements and for parties, please contact Administrator; ♿ WC in Museum

🐕   In grounds only

🍴♿   Refreshments and teas in Coach House tea-rooms (licensed) 12–5 (last orders 4.45) on open days (tel. Sudbury (028 378) 305*). Lakeside picnic area

    Events: Concerts & special events; details from Administrator; please send s.a.e.

➡️   6m E of Uttoxeter at the crossing point of A50 Derby-Stoke and A515 Lichfield-Ashbourne roads [128: SK160323] *Bus:* Stevensons 401 Burton-on-Trent–Uttoxeter (passing BR Tutbury & Hatton and close BR Burton-on-Trent (tel. Derby (0332) 292200) *Station:* Tutbury & Hatton (U) 5m

WINSTER MARKET HOUSE 🏠 ✉️

nr Matlock (tel. Thorpe Cloud (033 529) 245)

Market house of late 17th or early 18th century; ground floor of stone with original five open arches filled in; upper storey of brick with stone dressings; bought in 1906 and restored; now NT Information Room

🅾️   30 March to end Oct: Sat & Sun (daily during July & Aug) 10–6

💷   Free. No WCs

➡️   4m W of Matlock on S side of B5057 in main street of Winster [119: SK241606] *Bus:* Hulley's 170 Chesterfield–Matlock (passing close BR Chesterfield & Matlock) (tel. Buxton (0298) 23098) *Station:* Matlock (U) 4m

*Tel. no. will change during summer to Burton (0283) 585305

Devon

HIGHVEER POINT
HOLDSTONE DOWN | FORELAND POINT,
ILFRACOMBE | COUNTISBURY HILL
DAMAGE CLIFFS | & WATERSMEET
LUNDY
MORTE POINT | GREAT HANGMAN
Woolacombe | LITTLE HANGMAN
BAGGY POINT
SOMERSET

Barnstaple

THE
BROWNSHAMS
PEPPERCOMBE VALLEY
CLOVELLY

Torrington

Tiverton

Holsworthy

Okehampton

DORSET

Exeter

LYDFORD GORGE
BRANSCOMBE
PEAK HILL &
SALCOMBE HILL
Exmouth

CORNWALL

Torquay
Brixham
Kingswear
Plymouth | Dartmouth
HIGHER BROWNSTONE FARM
WEMBURY CLIFFS | Kingsbridge | LITTLE DARTMOUTH
YEALM ESTUARY
BOLT TAIL | Salcombe
PORTLEMOUTH DOWN
BOLT HEAD | PRAWLE POINT & GAMMON HEAD
& SNAPES POINT

DEVON

The Trust owns a total of 78 coastal miles in Devon.

On the south coast, near Plymouth, $5\frac{1}{2}$ miles of cliff and woodland are owned, on both sides of the **Yealm Estuary**. **Wembury Cliffs** extend for $1\frac{1}{2}$ miles from Wembury Head (see also p. 98) [201: SX530480].

From **Bolt Tail** [202: SX6639] to **Overbecks** near Salcombe (see p. 98) are 6 miles of rugged cliffland traversed by the coast path which dips to give access to safe bathing at **Soar Mill Cove**, **Starehole Bay** and at **Bolberry Down** car park a path leads to the west and is suitable for wheelchair users 🦽. **Bolt Head** and **Bolt Tail** are the best places from which to observe seabirds. The Trust's first property in the Kingsbridge Estuary, **Snapes Point** [202: SX745394] has a footpath around the unspoilt headland, and a small car park 🚶.

Another extensive holding lies between **Portlemouth Down** [202: SX740375] and

88

Prawle Point [202: SX773350]. 330 acres of low cliffs with walks, views and sandy coves. The walker can choose whether to use higher or lower paths, and the cliffs grow higher and more craggy further east towards **Gammon Head** [202: SX765355].

In the beautiful estuary of the river Dart, the Trust protects, on the Dartmouth side, woodland, hilltop and 165 acres at **Little Dartmouth** [202: SX880490] – cliff and farmland forming the western approach to Dartmouth Harbour for $1\frac{1}{2}$ miles from the Dancing Beggars rocks off Warren Point to the harbour entrance [⚡]. Across the estuary at Kingswear, 298 acres at **Higher Brownstone Farm** [202: SX901505] gives access to paths to the coast, and the recent acquisition of the **Coleton Fishacre Estate** (see p. 93) has added a further 970 acres of coastal land; the Trust has created a coastal footpath here and car parking is provided. There are two popular beaches at Man Sands and Scabbacombe along this stretch of coast between Kingswear and Brixham.

The Trust owns **Peak Hill** [192: SY109871] and **Salcombe Hill** [192: SY143882], buttresses to the town of Sidmouth. Further east, farmland, cliffs and foreshore are protected from development at **Lincombe, Weston Combe and Branscombe** [192: SY2188], including some cottages, a forge and a bakery (now a tea-room and baking museum) at Branscombe.

On the north coast the Trust's ownership begins not far from the Somerset border at Countisbury where it protects about 1,500 acres of **Foreland Point, Countisbury Hill** and the wooded valley of **Watersmeet** [180: 557449]. There is an information point at **Watersmeet House** (see p. 100) and many miles of signposted footpaths traverse the property.

The Trust has recently acquired 187 acres of spectacular coastline between Heddons Mouth and Woody Bay, including **Highveer Point** [180: SS655498] and two areas of woodland. [⚡] There is already a circular walk here, and there is access to the Roman Signal Station at Martinhoe, which is on the property. The Trust now protects over three miles of continuous coastline between Woody Bay and Trentishoe. More cliff and moorland is owned at **Holdstone Down** [180: SS620475] with car parking at Trentishoe, and the **Great Hangman** and **Little Hangman** [180: SS601480/584481].

Two hundred and sixty acres at **Ilfracombe** [180: SS5047] include most of the coastal land from the town's outskirts to the village of Lee, where the Trust owns 5 miles of fine coastline as far as **Woolacombe,** including **Morte Point** [180: SS554445] and **Damage Cliffs** [180: SS470465]. [♿] South-west to Croyde more coastal holdings include the view-point of **Baggy Point** where there is a path suitable for wheelchair users [180: SS4241].

Lundy's vessel, *Oldenburg*, sails from Bideford and Ilfracombe to the island in the Bristol Channel (see p. 97). At Bideford Bay between **Abbotsham** and **Bucks Mills** the Trust owns 5 miles of spectacular coastline, acquired in 1988, and the wooded **Peppercombe Valley** which slopes down to the sea [190: SS384238]. Footpaths are being upgraded. Further west at **Clovelly** more than 600 acres of cliff, farm and woodland – with two ancient farmhouses at **The Brownshams** [190: SS285260] – are protected by the Trust.

A series of leaflet maps has been produced, giving details of coast and countryside properties in Devon. These are on sale at National Trust shops, or from the Regional Information Office (address on p. 22).

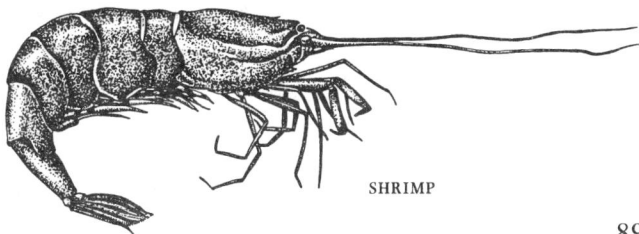

SHRIMP

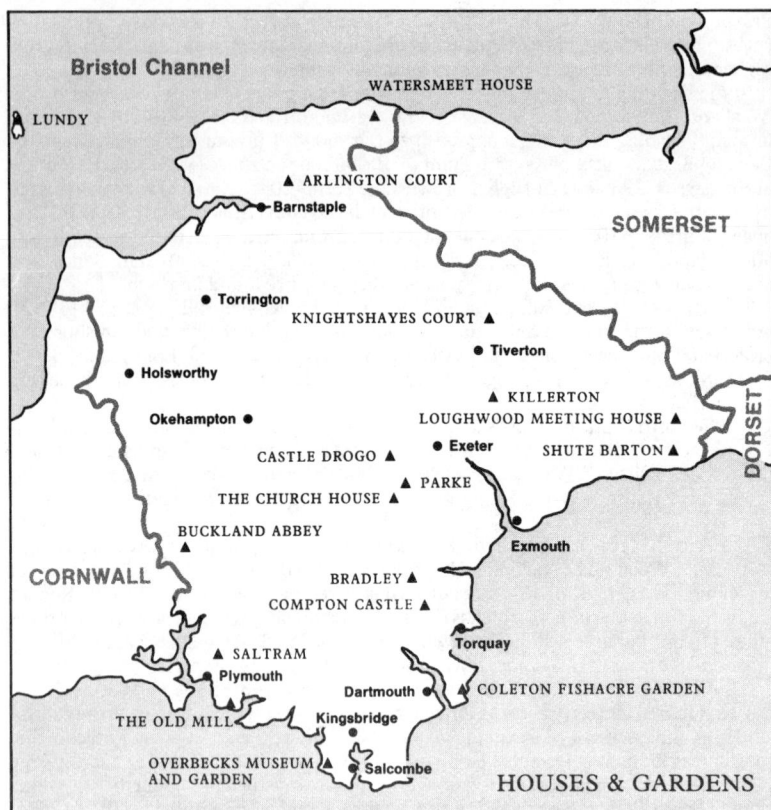

Bristol Channel

LUNDY

WATERSMEET HOUSE ▲

▲ ARLINGTON COURT

● Barnstaple

SOMERSET

● Torrington

KNIGHTSHAYES COURT ▲

● Tiverton

● Holsworthy

▲ KILLERTON

LOUGHWOOD MEETING HOUSE ▲

Okehampton ●

CASTLE DROGO ▲   ● Exeter   SHUTE BARTON ▲

DORSET

▲ PARKE

THE CHURCH HOUSE ▲

BUCKLAND ABBEY
▲

Exmouth ●

CORNWALL

BRADLEY ▲

COMPTON CASTLE ▲

▲ SALTRAM

Torquay ●

● Plymouth

Dartmouth ●   ▲ COLETON FISHACRE GARDEN

THE OLD MILL

Kingsbridge
●

OVERBECKS MUSEUM ▲
AND GARDEN   ● Salcombe

HOUSES & GARDENS

ARLINGTON COURT 🏠🦢🌳❄️📷🧍 ✉️🚫♿

Arlington, nr Barnstaple EX31 4LP (tel. Barnstaple (0271) 850296)

In beautiful steep wooded country west of Exmoor; park is grazed by Shetland ponies and Jacob sheep; the house, built in 1822, contains a fascinating medley of small objets d'art; model ships, shells, pewter and furniture and fittings of the last century; stables with large collection of horse-drawn vehicles; carriage rides from front of house

🅾️ ❄️ **House and Victorian Garden:** 29 March to end Oct: daily except Sat but open Sat of BH weekends 11–6 (Oct: 11–5). Last admissions ½hr before closing. **Park:** footpaths across parkland open all year

📷 ❄️ Same days as house 11–5. Also Nov to 22 Dec & Jan 1992: Wed to Sun 11–5; Feb & March 1992: Sat & Sun 11–5. Tel. Barnstaple (0271) 850348

£ £4. Garden only £2. Pre-arranged parties of 15 or more paying visitors £3. Organisers please book visits and arrange meals beforehand with Administrator. Parking 300yds

♿ Table in ladies' WC available for nappy-changing

♿ House, garden (gravel paths), grounds & shop accessible. Special parking arrangements; disabled visitors may be driven to house by arrangement with Administrator. ♿ WC

🐕 In grounds only, on leads

◧♿ Licensed restaurant and tea-room at house, open same days as house, 11–½hr
❄ before closing. Tea-room open Nov to end March 1992: as shop. Open for pre-booked Christmas lunches. Tel. Barnstaple (0271) 850629

➡ 7m NE of Barnstaple on A39 [180: SS611405] *Bus:* Red Bus 310 Barnstaple – Lynton (passing close BR Barnstaple), alight Blackmoor Gate, 3m (tel. Barnstaple (0271) 45444) *Station:* Barnstaple 8m

---

BRADLEY 🏠🔔 ✕✕✕

Newton Abbot TQ12 6BN

A small medieval manor house set in woodland and meadows

Bradley is occupied by Commander and Mrs A. H. Woolner

◯ April to end Sept: Wed 2–5; also Thur 4 & 11 April, 19 & 26 Sept 2–5. Last admissions 4.45

£✗ £2. No party reduction; parties over 15 by written appointment only with Secretary. Lodge gates are too narrow for coaches. No WCs. Chapel closed for restoration

➡ On outskirts of town, on Totnes road (A381), drive gate (with small lodge) is about 100yds inside 30mph limit, opposite Old Totnes Road junction [202: SX848709] *Bus:* From surrounding areas to bus station, ¾m (some pass closer) (tel. Torquay (0803) 613226) *Station:* Newton Abbot 1½m

---

BUCKLAND ABBEY 🏠✝❄🏠 ✕

Yelverton PL20 6EY (tel. Yelverton (0822) 853607)

The spirit of Sir Francis Drake is rekindled at his home with new exhibitions of his courageous adventures and achievements throughout the world; originally a 13th-century monastery, the Abbey was ingeniously transformed into a family residence by Sir Richard Grenville of Revenge fame before Drake bought it in 1581; additional monastic, farm buildings and craft workshops are now open; countryside walks

Buckland Abbey is jointly managed by the National Trust and Plymouth City Council

◯❄ 29 March to end Oct: daily except Thur 10.30–5.30 (Oct: 10.30–5). Nov to end March 1992: Sat & Sun 2–5 (also Wed for pre-arranged parties only). Closed 23 Dec to 3 Jan   *continued*

🏠 ❄️ Shop open 29 March to end Oct: as house. Nov to 22 Dec: Sat & Sun 12–5. 4 Jan to end March 1992: Sat & Sun 2–5. Craft workshops open throughout year daily except Thur: 29 March to end Sept 10.30–5.30; Oct to end March 1992 10.30–5 (please check for Christmas opening dates)

💷 £3.60. Grounds only £1.60. Pre-arranged parties £2.80; school parties £1.40. Organisers please book visits beforehand with Administrator. Workshops only free. NB: There may be an increased charge on certain days (NT members incl.) when special events are in progress. See Events below. Car park 150yds, £1 refundable on admission

♿ 👁️ Disabled visitors may be set down at the Abbey after ticket purchase at main Reception. Car park area for disabled drivers near Reception. Site steep and difficult with lower levels only accessible. Motorised buggy. Braille house guide; scented herbs and plants in garden. Advice leaflet on request

🐕 Dogs in car park only on leads

🍴 ♿ ❄️ Licensed restaurant and tea-room open as shop (but opens at 12 from Jan to March 1992). Last servings ½hr before closing. Also open for pre-booked Christmas lunches and candlelit dinners in Dec. Tel: Yelverton (0822) 855024. Picnics in car park

Events: Please contact Administrator for details. An additional entrance charge may be applied on certain days including 28 & 29 June, Summer Craft Fair and for Living History Days

➡️ 6m S of Tavistock, 11m N of Plymouth: turn off A386 ¼m S of Yelverton [201: SX487667] *Bus:* Western National 55 from Yelverton (with connections from BR Plymouth) (tel. Plymouth (0752) 664011) *Station:* Bere Alston (U) not Sun (except May to Sept), 4½m

---

CASTLE DROGO 🏰🍴🌼❄️✝️👤 ✖️ ⊠

Drewsteignton EX6 6PB (tel. Chagford (0647) 433306)

This granite castle, built between 1910 and 1930, is one of the most remarkable works of Sir Edwin Lutyens; it stands at over 900ft overlooking the wooded gorge of the River Teign with beautiful views of Dartmoor

⭕ **Castle:** Good Fri 29 March to end Oct daily except Fri (open Good Fri) 11–6 (Oct 11–5). **Garden:** daily as castle. Last admissions ½hr before closing

💷 Castle, garden & grounds £3.80. Garden & grounds only £1.60. Pre-arranged parties £3. Organisers please book visits and arrange meals beforehand with Administrator. Car park 400yds

🏠 ❄️ Shop and plant centre by car park open as garden. Also Nov to 22 Dec & Jan 1992: Wed to Sun 11–5; Feb & March 1992: Sat & Sun 11–5. Tel. Chagford (0647) 433563

♿ 👁️ Limited access to part of castle; garden accessible. Special parking and access by arrangement at shop. ♿ WC near shop. 👁️ Scented plants

🍴 ❄️ Licensed restaurant at castle. Tea-room in grounds. Restaurant open same days as castle 29 March to end Sept: 12–5.30 (Oct: 12–5). Tea-room open daily from 10.30; also open Nov to end March 1992 as shop

Note: The restored croquet lawn is open; equipment for hire from Visitor Reception

➔ 4m S of A30 Exeter–Okehampton road via Crockernwell (car access only); coaches must turn off A382 Moretonhampstead–Whiddon Down road at Sandy Park [191: SX721900] *Bus:* Devon Services 359 from Exeter (passing close BR Exeter Central) (tel. Totnes (0803) 864161) *Station:* Yeoford (U) 8m

THE CHURCH HOUSE 🏠

Widecombe-in-the-Moor, Newton Abbot TQ13 7TA (tel. Widecombe (03642) 321)

Former village school; originally a brewhouse dating back to 1537; leased as a village hall and occasionally open to the public; the Sexton's Cottage is an NT and Information Centre and shop

🅾 June to mid Sept: Tues & Thur 2–5

🏠❋ Shop in Sexton's Cottage open daily March to end Sept 10–6; Oct to 24 Dec 10–5; Feb & March 1992 10–5. Closed Jan

£ Church House free (donation box)

➔ In the centre of Dartmoor, N of Ashburton, W of Bovey Tracey [191: SX718768]

COLETON FISHACRE GARDEN ❋🏛 ⚓

Coleton, Kingswear, Dartmouth TQ6 0EQ (tel. Kingswear (080 425) 466)

An 18-acre garden in a stream-fed valley set within the spectacular scenery of this Heritage Coast; the garden was created by Lady Dorothy D'Oyly Carte between 1925 and 1940, and is planted with a wide variety of uncommon trees and rare and exotic shrubs

🅾 3, 10, 17 & 24 March: 2–5. 29 March to end Oct: Wed, Thur, Fri & Sun 11–6 or dusk if earlier

£ £2. Parties £1.50 *continued*

93

⬧ ⬧ Limited access, steep slopes. Scented herbs and plants

➡ 2m from Kingswear; take Lower Ferry road, turn off at toll house
[202: SX910508] *Bus:* Devon General 22 Brixham–Kingswear (with
connections from BR Paignton), alight ¾m SW of Hillhead, 1½m (tel. Torquay
(0803) 613226) *Station:* Paignton 8m; Kingswear (Dart Valley Rly) 2¼m by
footpath, 2¾m by road

COMPTON CASTLE 🏰✝   ✉✉

Marldon, Paignton TQ3 1TA (tel. Paignton (0803) 872112)

*A fortified manor house with curtain wall; built at three periods: 1340, 1450 and 1520, by
the Gilbert family; home of Sir Humphrey Gilbert (1539–1583), coloniser of Newfoundland
and half-brother to Sir Walter Raleigh; the family still lives here*

Compton Castle is occupied and administered by Mr & Mrs G. E. Gilbert

🅾 April to end Oct: Mon, Wed and Thur 10–12.15 and 2–5, when the courtyard,
restored great hall, solar, chapel, rose garden and old kitchen are shown. Last
admissions ½hr before closing

💷 £2. Parties £1.60; organisers should please notify Secretary. Additional
parking and refreshments at Castle Barton opposite entrance

⬧ Limited access for wheelchair users

➡ At Compton, 4m W of Torquay, 1m N of Marldon; from the Newton Abbot–
Totnes road (A381) turn left at Ipplepen crossroads and W off Torbay ring road
via Marldon [202: SX865648] *Bus:* Devon General 7 BR Paignton–Marldon,
thence 1½m (tel. Torquay (0803) 613226) *Station:* Torquay 3m

KILLERTON 🏠✳🏠🌳🚶🏛✝   ✉

Broadclyst, Exeter EX5 3LE (tel. Exeter (0392) 881345)

*The house, home of the Aclands, was rebuilt in 1778 to the design of John Johnson; it houses
the Paulise de Bush collection of costumes shown in a series of room tableaux of different
periods; the tableaux are changed each year, and range from the 18th century to the present
day; 15 acres of hillside garden containing rare trees and shrubs; walks in Ashclyst Forest;
19th-century chapel; estate exhibition*

🅾✳ **House:** 29 March to end Oct: daily except Tues 11–6 (Oct: 11–5). Last
admissions ½hr before closing. **Park & garden:** open all year during daylight
hours

🛍✳ Shop and plant centre in Stable Courtyard. Open daily 29 March to end Sept
11–6; Oct to 22 Dec 11–5; Jan to end March 1992 11–4. Tel. Exeter (0392)
881912

💷 £3.60; garden only £2.20; Garden & park winter rate £1. Pre-booked parties
£2.80; organisers please book visits and arrange meals beforehand with
Administrator

🚼 Table & chair in ladies' WCs near Stable Courtyard, and at house

⚿ 3 steps to house, accessible ground floor. Lower levels of garden accessible, but gravel paths and grass. Motorised buggies with drivers available for tour of higher levels. ⚿ WCs. Apply at ticket office for special parking and access arrangements; special parking for disabled drivers; passengers may be set down at house; ⚿ wheelchair lift to upper level of shop

🐕 In park only

💷⚿ Licensed restaurant open same days as house 12–5.30 (Oct: 12–5) and for pre-booked Christmas lunches. Tel. Exeter (0392) 881345. Tea-room in Stable Courtyard open 29 March to 22 Dec: daily 10.30–5.30; Jan to end March 1992: Sat & Sun only 11–4

➡ On W side of Exeter-Cullompton road (B3181 – formerly A38) entrance off B3185; from M5 northbound, exit 28 via Broadclyst and B3181 [192: SX9700] *Bus:* Devon General 54/A from Exeter (passing close Exeter Central), alight Killerton Turn ¾m; 55/A/B, Exeter–Tiverton (passing close BR Exeter Central), alight Silverton 2½m (tel. Exeter (0392) 56231) *Station:* Pinhoe (U), not Sun, 4½m; Whimple (U), not Sun, 6m; Exeter Central & St David's, both 7m

KNIGHTSHAYES COURT 🏠 ❄ ♠   ✉

Bolham, Tiverton EX16 7RQ (tel. Tiverton (0884) 254665)

Begun in 1869, a rare survival of the work of William Burges; the house with its richly decorated Victorian interior stands on the east side of the Exe valley; one of the finest gardens in Devon with specimen trees, rare shrubs, spring bulbs, summer flowering borders

🅾 29 March to end Oct: **Garden:** daily 11–6 (Oct: 11–5); **House:** daily, except Fri (but open Good Fri) 1.30–6 (Oct: 1.30–5). Last admissions ½hr before closing.
❄ Nov & Dec: Sun 2–4 for pre-booked parties only; please note that some items normally on view may not be displayed due to conservation work

📋❄ Shop and plant centre open 29 March to end Oct: daily 11–6; Nov to 22 Dec: daily 11–5; Jan to end March 1992: Wed to Sun 11–4. Tel. Tiverton (0884) 259010
continued

£ £4; garden & grounds only £2.20. Pre-booked parties £3. Organisers please book visits and arrange for meals beforehand with Administrator. Parking 450yds. Visitor Reception and information: tel. Tiverton (0884) 257381

Changing facilities in ladies' WC

House and garden accessible. Small lift to first floor suitable for ambulant disabled people only. Disabled drivers may park near house; or disabled passengers may be set down by house entrance. NB All tickets must please be purchased initially at the Visitor Reception point in the Stables. ● Scented plants. ● WC

In park only, on leads

Licensed restaurant for coffee, lunches and teas daily 29 March to end Sept: daily 10.30–5.30; Oct daily: 11–5; Nov & Dec: Wed to Sun 11–5; Jan to end March 1992: Wed to Sun 11–4. Also open for pre-booked Christmas lunches. Restaurant bookings: tel. Tiverton (0884) 259416. ● Picnic area in car park. ● High chair available

→ 2m N of Tiverton; turn right off Tiverton-Bampton road (A396) at Bolham [181: SS960151] *Bus:* Tiverton & District 373/4 from BR Tiverton Parkway (tel. Barnstaple (0271) 45444; Devon General 55/A/B Exeter–Tiverton (passing close BR Exeter Central) (tel. Exeter (0392) 56231). On all alight Tiverton 1¼m. *Station:* Tiverton Parkway 8m

LOUGHWOOD MEETING HOUSE ✠

Dalwood, Axminster EX13 7DU

Built c.1653 by Baptist congregation of Kilmington; interior fitted in early 18th century

○ ❄ All year

£ Free (donation box provided)

→ 4m W of Axminster; turn right on Axminster/Honiton road (A35), 1m S of Dalwood, 1m NW of Kilmington [192 & 193: SY253993] *Station:* Axminster 2¼m

LUNDY 🏰🧺🐦✝🎮🏛 ✈

Bristol Channel EX39 2LY (tel. Ilfracombe (0271) 870870

Leased to the Landmark Trust; unspoilt island; rocky headlands; interesting animal and bird life; no cars; a place to explore for a day trip; small island community with church, tavern and castle. There is a steep climb to the village from the landing stage

Lundy is financed, administered and maintained by the Landmark Trust

🅾️ ❄️ Always

💷 £2.50 (waived for passengers on MS *Oldenburg*)

♿ Disabled visitors are very welcome but should telephone in advance so that disembarkment arrangements may be made

🍴 Food and drink at The Marisco Tavern
Accommodation: 23 holiday cottages; camping site for up to 30 people. For bookings, apply to The Landmark Trust, Shottesbrooke, Maidenhead, Berkshire SL6 3SW (tel. Maidenhead (0628) 825925)

➡️ 11m N of Hartland Point, 25m from Ilfracombe, 30m S of Tenby [180: SS1345] *Bus:* Frequent Red Bus services (from BR Barnstaple to Bideford or Ilfracombe (tel. Barnstaple (0271) 45444) *Station:* Barnstaple, 8½m to Bideford, 12m to Ilfracombe. *Sea Passages:* From Bideford, all year round, also from Ilfracombe in the summer season by the island vessel, MS *Oldenburg*, 300 tons, 267 passengers, refreshments and shop on board. For sailing details, contact Bideford (0237) 470422/477676, or Ilfracombe (0271) 63001

LYDFORD GORGE 🧺🚶

The Stables, Lydford Gorge, Lydford, nr Okehampton EX20 4BH (tel. Lydford (082 282) 441/320)

This famous gorge is 1½ miles long; the deep ravine scooped by the River Lyd into a succession of potholes, including the exciting Devil's Cauldron, emerges into a steep-sided oak-wooded valley providing an enchanting riverside walk to the 90ft high White Lady waterfall

🅾️ ❄️ 29 March to end Oct: daily 10.30–6. Nov to March 1992: daily 10.30–4, but from waterfall entrance as far as waterfall only

Note: There are delays at the Devil's Cauldron during busy periods

🏬 ❄️ Shop at main entrance open as gorge March to end Oct. Nov to 22 Dec: Sat & Sun 11–5. Small shop at far end of gorge 29 March to end Oct only

💷 £2.20. Pre-arranged parties, £1.60; organisers please notify Administrator

👶 Facilities for nappy-changing in ladies' WC

♿ Gorge unsuitable for disabled visitors; accessible picnic area; ♿ WC

🐕 Must be on leads

🍴 Main entrance; light refreshments 29 March to end Sept: daily 12–5. Oct: Sat & Sun 12–4   *continued*

97

DEVON

→ At W end of Lydford village; halfway between Okehampton and Tavistock, 1m W off A386 opposite Dartmoor Inn; main entrance at W end of Lydford; second entrance near Manor Hotel [191 & 201: SX509846] *Bus:* Down's 118 from Tavistock – with connections from Plymouth (tel. Mary Tavy (082 281) 242)

THE OLD MILL 🏠🖼️📷

Wembury Beach, Wembury PL9 0HP (tel. Plymouth (0752) 862314)

Café and shop housed in former mill house standing on a small beach near the Yealm estuary

🅾️❄️ **Shop** 29 March to end Oct: daily 10.30–5.30. Tel. Plymouth (0752) 863164.
📷 Limited opening Nov & Dec. Parking charge to non-members
🐕 Admitted, except to café

💭 Drinks, refreshments, ice cream, etc; take-away service; open as shop

→ At Wembury, nr Plymouth [201: SX517484] *Bus:* Western National 48 from Plymouth, thence ½m (tel. Plymouth (0752) 664011) *Station:* Plymouth 10m

OVERBECKS MUSEUM AND GARDEN 🌸🏠🖼️ ✖️✖️

Sharpitor, Salcombe TQ8 8LW (tel. Salcombe (054 884) 2893)

Beautiful 6-acre garden; many rare plants, shrubs and trees; spectacular views over Salcombe estuary; elegant Edwardian house contains collections of local photographs taken at the end of the last century; local ship-building tools; model boats, shells, birds and eggs, animals and other collections; 100-year-old polyphon; exhibition showing natural history of Sharpitor

🅾️❄️ **Museum:** 29 March to end Oct daily 12–5. Last admissions 4.30. **Garden:** daily throughout year 10–8 or sunset if earlier

📷 Shop same days as museum 10–5

💷 Museum & garden £2.60; garden only £1.80. No party reduction. Small car park; charge refundable on admission. Roads leading to Overbecks are narrow and therefore unsuitable for coaches

🅰️ Secret room; dolls, toys and other collections, quiz guide

♿ The garden is largely accessible with a strong pusher; details of parking available from Administrator. Ground floor of museum, shop and tea-room accessible via steps

💭 Tea-room for snacks and light refreshments 2–4.30. Picnicking allowed in garden

→ 1½m SW of Salcombe, signposted from Malborough and Salcombe [202: SX728374] *Bus:* Tally Ho! 606 from Kingsbridge (with connections from Plymouth & Dartmouth), alight Salcombe, 1½m (tel. Kingsbridge (0548) 3081)

PLEASE REFER TO PAGES 5–9

98

PARKE 🌳🔭👤

Haytor Road, Bovey Tracey TQ13 9JQ (tel. Bovey Tracey (0626) 833909)

Over 200 acres of parkland in the wooded valley of the River Bovey, forming a beautiful approach to Dartmoor; there is a series of lovely walks through woodlands, beside the river and along the route of the old railway track; National Trust and Dartmoor Park Interpretation Centre (tel. Bovey Tracey (0626) 832093)

Rare Breeds Farm: Owned and administered by Mr T. Ash. A private collection of animals, including horses, cattle, pigs, sheep and poultry, many of which have been used to provide our food for thousands of years. New interpretation centre and farm trails help people to discover yesterday's farm and bring it to life. 🅰 With baby animals and a special Pets Corner, children will have a visit they will remember. Collection of model pigs. Covered all-weather farmyard

🅾 ✳ April to end Oct: **Rare Breeds Farm** daily 10–6. Last admissions 5. **Parkland** open all year. **Shop** 10–5

💷 Parkland free. Rare Breeds Farm prices on application (NT members included)

🐾 In parkland only

🍴 In farm buildings (coffee, light lunches and cream teas). Picnic site

➡ Just W of Bovey Tracey on N side of B3344 to Manaton [191: SX805785] *Bus:* Devon General 72 from Newton Abbot (passing close BR Newton Abbot) (tel. Torquay (0803) 613226) *Station:* Newton Abbot 6m, follow brown signs from A38 Drumbridges roundabout

SALTRAM 🏠🏠🌳✳✝👤 ✉

Plympton, Plymouth PL7 3UH (tel. Plymouth (0752) 336546)

A remarkable survival of a George II mansion and its original contents, in a landscaped park; magnificent interior plasterwork and decoration; two important rooms designed by Robert Adam, fine period furniture, china and pictures, including many portraits by Reynolds; Great Kitchen; stables; gallery of West Country art in chapel; interesting garden with orangery; landscaped park

🅾 **House:** Good Fri 29 March to end Oct: daily except Fri & Sat but open Good Fri and Sat of BH weekends 12.30–6 (Oct: 12.30–5. **Art gallery, garden & Great Kitchen:** open as house but from 11. Last admissions ½hr before closing

🏠✳ Shop in stable block. 29 March to end Oct: Sun to Thur 11–6; Nov to 23 Dec: daily 11–5; Jan 1992: daily 11–5; Feb & March 1992: Sat & Sun 11–4. Tel. Plymouth (0752) 330034

💷 £4.40; garden only £1.60. Pre-arranged parties £3.40; organisers please book visits and meals with the Administrator. Parking 500yds (50p Sun only)

👤 Please ask Administrator for facilities

♿ House and garden accessible but house not suitable for powered chairs; disabled visitors may be set down at front door by prior arrangement; lift (2′2″ wide × 2′10″ deep) to first floor. 🌸 Scented plants   *continued*

⊞ Designated areas only

⊡ ⊡ Licensed restaurant in house (entrance from garden) open as garden; also open
⊞ for pre-booked Christmas lunches (tel. Plymouth (0752) 340635). ⊞ High
chair available. Drinks, light refreshments and ice cream at Coach House near
car park at peak times. Tea-room open as shop Nov to end March 1992

→ 2m W of Plympton, 3½m E of Plymouth city centre, between Plymouth/Exeter
road (A38) and Plymouth/Kingsbridge road (A379); take Plympton turn at
Marsh Mills roundabout [201: SX520557] *Bus:* Plymouth Citybus 20/A,
21, 22/A, 51 from Plymouth, alight Plymouth Road/Plympton Bypass Jn,
¼m footpath (tel. Plymouth (0752) 222221) *Station:* Plymouth 3½m

SHUTE BARTON ⊞ ⊞   ⊠

Shute, nr Axminster EX13 7PT (tel. Axminster (0297) 34692)

*Remains of a manor house, built over three centuries and completed in late 16th century;
grey stone with battlemented tower and late Gothic windows; gatehouse*

⊡ Exterior may be viewed during daylight hours. The house is tenanted; there is
access to parts of interior: April to end Oct: Wed & Sat 2–6 (Oct 2–5)

£ £1.20 Pre-arranged parties £1

→ 3m SW of Axminster, 2m N of Colyton on Honiton–Colyton road (B3161)
[177(193): SY253974] *Station:* Axminster, 3m

WATERSMEET HOUSE ⊞ ⊞ ⊞

Watersmeet Road, Lynmouth EX35 6NT (tel. Lynton (0598) 53348)

*A fishing lodge c.1832 in a picturesque valley at the confluence of the East Lyn and Hoar Oak
Water, used for information, recruiting, refreshments and NT shop; has been a tea-garden
since 1901; focal point for several beautiful walks*

⊡ ⊡ 29 March to end Oct: daily 11–6 (Oct: 11–5)

£ Free

⊞ Changing facilities in both men's and ladies' WCs

⊞ Access arrangements for disabled visitors strictly by appointment

⊞ Admitted, but not to restaurant or shop

⊡ Coffee, light lunches and teas in tea-room and garden beside the river:
10.30–5.30; (Oct: 10.30–4.30). Party catering by arrangement

→ 1½m E of Lynmouth, in valley on E side of Lynmouth/Barnstaple road (A39)
[180: SS744487] *Bus:* Red Bus 310 Barnstaple–Lynton (passing close BR
Barnstaple), alight Lynton, thence cliff lift to Lynmouth and walk through NT
Gorge (tel. Barnstaple (0271) 45444) May to Sept, Lyn Valley Community
Transport (tel. Lynton (0598) 52470/53202)

Dorset

COUNTRYSIDE

The Trust's estate at **Fontmell Down**, between Shaftesbury and Blandford [183: ST884184] includes **Melbury Beacon** and **Melbury Down** [184: ST900193], a total of 730 acres; with magnificent walks across chalk downland overlooking, to the west, the Blackmore Vale. Fontmell Down was bought by public appeal to commemorate the Dorset of Thomas Hardy. Car park at the top of Spread Eagle Hill and at Compton Abbas airfield. Refreshments available (not NT). 🚻 Limited access for disabled visitors.

🚻 Magnificent views from **Creech Grange Arch**, a folly near Corfe Castle (see p. 103) [195: SY212818] may be enjoyed by wheelchair users.

Dorset is dominated by Iron Age forts and many of these are now in the permanent care of the National Trust, including **Pilsdon Pen**, at 909ft the highest hill in Dorset, near Broadwinsor [193: ST414012], **Lambert's Castle**, north of Lyme Regis [193: SY370986] and the adjacent **Coney's Castle. Eggardon Hill, Hod Hill** and **Turnworth Down**, north-west of Blandford, are equally rewarding as archaeological sites and for superlative views.

🚻 On the **Kingston Lacy Estate** (see p. 104) the Trust has opened a number of walks (some of which are accessible to wheelchair users). The 7,000-acre agricultural estate is crossed by public footpaths, many still following Roman and Saxon tracks past medieval cottages. The estate is dominated by the Iron Age hillfort of **Badbury Rings**. Leaflets on the Kingston Lacy Estate walks and on Badbury Rings are available from the shop at Kingston Lacy and from the information caravan on Badbury Rings at weekends. Audio guide to Badbury available for hire. Point to point races are held at Badbury on four Saturdays early in the year. On these days the car park is closed to vehicles.

COAST

The Dorset coast is rich in variety; hills, coombes, cliffs, bays and islands. One such island in Poole Harbour, is **Brownsea** (see below), and immediately south is the Trust's **Studland** peninsula, part of the 7,000-acre **Corfe Castle** estate (see p. 103). This includes the whole of Studland Bay with Old Harry Rocks and Shell Bay (see p. 105). The heathland behind Studland beach is recommended to naturalists in winter because of its variety of overwintering birds. There are several public paths and two nature trails here.

[🚹] At **Golden Cap** [193: SY4092] the Trust owns more than 2,000 acres of hill, farmland, cliff, undercliff and beach (5 miles of coast) between Lyme Regis and Eypemouth. Here is the highest cliff in southern England – so named because of the yellow limestone and clumps of golden gorse near its summit. This splendid viewpoint and the remainder of the estate have 20 miles of paths for walkers including a 6-mile coastal footpath. There is a campsite at St. Gabriel's on the estate; booking through the Warden (0297) 89628. [♿] **Stonebarrow Hill** has an adapted WC for wheelchair users and paths here are accessible. Seasonal shop and information centre.

[♿] The shingle beach at **Burton Bradstock** is accessible to wheelchair users, from its grassy car park. There are riverside and cliff walks through this 83-acre Trust property which includes a stretch of the South-West Coastal Footpath [193/194: SY483893].

The Hardy Monument which overlooks the Dorset coast 6 miles south-west of Dorchester was erected in 1844 in memory of Vice-Admiral Sir Thomas Masterman Hardy, flag-captain of the *Victory* at the Battle of Trafalgar. [♿] This viewpoint is suitable for visitors in wheelchairs [194: SY613876].

BROWNSEA ISLAND 🏛🛏🐑🚹   ✈

Poole Harbour BH15 1EE (tel. Canford Cliffs (0202) 707744)

A 500-acre island of heath and woodland; nature reserve run by the Dorset Trust for Nature Conservation; wide views of Dorset coast

Access: Boats run from Poole Quay and Sandbanks. Visitors may land from their own boats at the Pottery Pier at W end of Island, accessible at all stages of the tide

[◉] 25 March to 30 Sept: daily 10–8 or dusk if earlier; check time of last boat. Oct: limited opening; ring to check

[🏠] Shop open daily 25 March to 29 Sept 10–6 (tel. Canford Cliffs (0202) 700852)

[£] [🚹] Landing fee: £1.70, children 90p. Family ticket £4.50 (2 adults & 2 children) available April, May, June & Sept. Parties £1.50, children 70p, by written arrangement with Warden. Parties wishing for guided tours please contact Dorset Trust for Nature Conservation Warden. Brownsea Island (tel. Canford Cliffs (0202) 709445)

[♿] Island paths hilly and rough, but area around Quay accessible; mainland car parking near Poole Quay; all boats will accept and help wheelchairs; [♿] WC near Island Quay

[🍽][♿] Coffee, lunches and teas in the Café Villano near landing quay (tel. Canford Cliffs (0202) 700244). Open daily 25 March to 24 May 10–5; 25 May to 8 Sept 10–5.30; 9–29 Sept 10–5. Tuck shop daily 10–6

Events: Open-air theatre, and other events in summer; check with Warden on 0207 707744

→ [195: SZ032878] *Bus:* From surrounding areas to Poole Quay. To Sandbanks: Wilts & Dorset 150 Bournemouth–Swanage (passing BR Branksome); 152 from Poole (passing close BR Parkstone) (tel. Poole (0202) 673555); Yellow Buses 12 from Christchurch, summer only (tel. Bournemouth (0202) 27272) *Station:* Poole ½m to Quay; Branksome or Parkstone 3½m to Sandbanks

CLOUDS HILL 🏠 ✖

Wareham BH20 7NQ

T. E. Lawrence (Lawrence of Arabia) bought this cottage when he rejoined the RAF in 1925; it contains his furniture and other relics

○✱ 27 March to 31 Oct: Wed, Thur, Fri, Sun & BH Mon 2–5; 10 Nov to end March 1992: Sun only 1–4 or dusk if earlier; no electric light

£ £2. No reduction for parties or children. Unsuitable for coaches or trailer caravans. No WCs

→ 9m E of Dorchester, ½m E of Waddock crossroads (B3390), 1m N of Bovington Camp [194: SY824909] *Bus:* Southern National/Bere Regis & District from BR Wool, alight Bovington, 1m (tel. Weymouth (0305) 783645) *Station:* Wool 3½m; Moreton (U) 3½m

CORFE CASTLE 🏰

Corfe Castle, Wareham BH20 5EZ (tel. Corfe Castle (0929) 480921)

One of the most impressive ruins in England; former royal castle, besieged and slighted by Parliamentary forces in 1646

○✱ March to end Oct: daily 10–5.30 or dusk if earlier. Open Good Fri and BH Mon. Nov to Feb 1992: Sat & Sun only 12–3.30

🛍✱ Shop daily 1–30 March 10–4; 31 March to 26 Oct 10–6; 27 Oct to 24 Dec 10–4; 1 Jan to end March 1992 10–4. Tel. Corfe Castle (0929) 480921

continued

DORSET

£	£2. Parties £1.70. Car & coach park (not NT) in West St, subject to a charge
🐕	On leads only
🍽	Licensed restaurant; coffee, lunch and cream teas at castle entrance open daily 2–30 March 10.30–4; 31 March to 26 Oct 10.30–5.30; 27 Oct to 23 Dec 10.30–4; 2 Jan to end March 1992 10.30–4
➔	On A351 Wareham-Swanage road [195: SY959824] *Bus:* Wilts & Dorset 142–4 Poole–Swanage (passing BR Wareham) (tel. Poole (0202) 673555) *Station:* Wareham 4½m

HARDY'S COTTAGE 🏠❀ ❌❌

Higher Bockhampton, nr Dorchester DT2 8QJ (tel. Dorchester (0305) 262366)

A small thatched cottage where the novelist and poet Thomas Hardy was born in 1840; built by his great-grandfather and little altered; furnished by the Trust

⭕🏠	25 March to end Oct: daily (except Thur) 11–6 or dusk if earlier. Approach by 10 min. walk from car park through woods. Interior by appointment with Custodian. Exterior from end of garden. Shop in Dorchester (see p. 18)
£	Interior £2. No reduction for children or parties. Schools: 6th forms only. Coaches by prior arrangement only. No WCs. Hardy's works on sale
♿	Garden only; special car parking arrangement with Custodian
➔	3m NE of Dorchester, ½m S of A35 [194: SY728925] *Bus:* Wilts & Dorset 184/6 Weymouth–Salisbury, 187/9 Bournemouth–Weymouth (All pass BR Dorchester South & close Dorchester West), alight Bockhampton Lane, ½m (tel. Poole (0202) 673555) *Station:* Dorchester South 4m; Dorchester West (U) 4m

KINGSTON LACY 🏠❀♣ 🦡

Wimborne Minster BH21 4EA (tel. Wimborne (0202) 883402)

Seventeenth-century house designed for Sir Ralph Bankes by Sir Roger Pratt; altered by Sir Charles Barry in the 19th century; outstanding collection of paintings; set in 250 acres of wooded park with a fine herd of Red Devon cattle

⭕	25 March to 3 Nov: daily except Thur & Fri. **House & Garden** 12–5.30; last admissions 4.30. **Park** 11.30–6
🏠❄	Same days as house 11.30–5.30. Also open 9 Nov to 22 Dec: Sat & Sun 12–4. Tel. Wimborne (0202) 841424
£	£4.50, children £2.20; parties (20 or more) £4. Park & garden £1.40. Parking 100yds. Parties by prior arrangement with Administrator
♿	Garden only; some thick gravel. ♿ WC; special parking by arrangement with Administrator. 🦮 Guide dogs in grounds and gardens only
🐕	Dogs in north park only, on leads

104

📧 ♿ Lunches & teas in licensed stable restaurant open same days and times as shop. Tel. Wimborne (0202) 889242. Picnics in north park only

❄️
➡️ *Bus:* Wilts & Dorset X13, 132/3/9 from Bournemouth, Poole, Shaftesbury (passing close BR Bournemouth & Poole). On all alight Wimborne Square 2½m, but occasional service to house in peak summer period (tel. Poole (0202) 673555) *Station:* Poole 8½m

STUDLAND BEACH & NATURE RESERVE 🏛️ 🚶

Studland Bay, Swanage BH19 3AX (tel. Studland (092 944) 259)

Three miles of fine sandy beaches backed by the Studland Nature Reserve, extending from the Sandbanks Ferry to the chalk cliffs of Handfast Point and Old Harry Rocks; awarded title of 'Cleanest Beach in England' in 1988

🅾️ ❄️ All year. Car parks 9–8

🛍️ Shop open 29 March to 29 Sept daily. Tel. Studland (092944) 259

£ Car parks: April, Sept & Oct £1; May & June £1.50; July & Aug £2; rest of year 50p. NT members free. Coaches £10. WCs

♿ Knoll Car Park has good access. In summer boardwalk for wheelchairs along part of Knoll beach. ♿ WCs

🐕 Must be kept on leads May to end Sept, and not allowed to foul the beach

📧 Refreshments (not all NT)

Boat Launching: Powered craft £10 per day. Others, incl. sail boards £3 per day. (NT members included)

➡️ [195: SZ036835] *Bus:* Wilts & Dorset 150 Bournemouth–Swanage (passing BR Branksome) to Shell Bay and Studland; 152 Poole–Sandbanks (passing close BR Parkstone) (tel. Poole (0202) 673555) & Yellow Buses 12 Christchurch–Sandbanks, summer only (tel. Bournemouth (0202) 27272) (Vehicle ferry from Sandbanks to Shell Bay) *Station:* Branksome or Parkstone, both 3½m to Shell Bay or 6m to Studland via vehicle ferry

County Durham

COAST AND COUNTRYSIDE

Just north of Easington, the Trust owns **Beacon Hill**, the highest point on the Durham Coast. It provides spectacular views to the North and South; access on foot through Hawthcrne Dene [88: NZ454442].

Further south, near Horden, are two denes, **Warren House Gill** and **Foxholes Dene** (the Trust owns only the southern half of this dene), connected by a narrow coastal strip; access from B1283 via footpaths [88: NZ444427]. This piece of coast marks the 500th mile acquired through the Trust's coastal appeal, Enterprise Neptune.

Inland, the Trust-owned **Moorhouse Woods** [88: NZ305460], are just to the north of Durham City; peaceful woodland walks are available on the banks of the River Wear. Access to Moorhouse Woods can be gained from Leamside across a footbridge over the A1(M). At the village of **Ebchester** [88: NZ100551] in north-west County Durham is a short woodland walk along the banks of the River Derwent.

🏠 While in County Durham, why not visit the Trust's Information Centre and Shop at 61 Saddler Street, Durham City (tel. 091-384 5285).

Essex

CAMBS

SUFFOLK

● Saffron Walden

HERTS

■ HATFIELD FOREST

PAYCOCKE'S ▲

COGGESHALL GRANGE ▲
BARN

Colchester ●

▲ BOURNE MILL

COPT HALL ■

Clacton-on-Sea

BLAKE'S WOOD ■
Chelmsford ●

LINGWOOD COMMON ■

DANBURY ■
COMMON

Blackwater Estuary

NORTHEY
ISLAND

Epping ●

GTR
LONDON

● Basildon

RAYLEIGH CASTLE
▲
●
Southend-on-Sea

COUNTRYSIDE

Five miles east of Chelmsford, **Danbury & Lingwood Commons** [167: TL7805] are a
survival of the medieval manors of St Clere and Herons, where commoners from the
settlements roundabout grazed their animals on these heath and woodland areas.
Danbury is more open with heather, bracken, broom and brambles, some oak and silver
birch, and areas of hornbeam coppice and standard trees. One clearing on this common is
one of the few known breeding grounds in this country for the Rosy Marbled moth.
Lingwood Common has more woodland, with open glades and a fine viewpoint. Near
Little Baddow, 2 miles to the north-west, the Trust owns **Blake's Wood** – more than 100
acres of hornbeam and chestnut coppice and renowned for bluebells [167: TL773067].
All these areas are Sites of Special Scientific Interest. ♿ **Hatfield Forest**, near Bishop's
Stortford, on the Herts/Essex border offers well over 1,000 acres of undulating wooded
country and open grassland for walkers and riders to explore (see p. 109). **Rayleigh Castle**
is a Domesday site in the centre of Rayleigh (see p. 110).

PLEASE REFER TO PAGES 5–9

COAST

The Trust owns the bird reserve of **Northey Island** in the Blackwater estuary. Permits to visit must be sought from the Warden, Northey Cottage, Northey Island, Maldon, Essex at least 24 hours in advance of a visit). It is a Grade 1 site for overwintering birds, and for saltmarsh plants. The island is cut off at high tide so access is limited [168: TL872058]. Eight miles south of Colchester is the **Copt Hall** estate, near Little Wigborough on the Blackwater estuary [168: TL981146]. The saltmarsh is extremely important for over-wintering birds. 1½ mile waymarked circular route. Small car park.

BOURNE MILL 🗵   🗵

Bourne Road, Colchester (tel. Colchester (0206) 572422)

Fishing lodge built in 1591, later converted into a mill; much of the machinery, including the waterwheel, is intact; 4-acre mill pond

🔘 31 March & 1 April, 5 & 6 May, 26 & 27 May 2–5.30. Also Sun & Tues in July & Aug (open BH Mon) 2–5.30

💷 £1.20. Children must be accompanied by an adult. No reduction for parties. No WCs

➡ 1m S of centre of Colchester, in Bourne Road, off the Mersea Road (B1025) [168: TM006238] *Bus:* Colchester Transport/Eastern National 7/A, 8 from Colchester (passing BR Colchester) (tel. Colchester (0206) 44449) *Station:* St Botolph's, not Sun, except May–Sept, ¼m; Colchester 2m

COGGESHALL GRANGE BARN 🏠 ❌

Grange Hill, Coggeshall, Colchester CO6 1RE (tel. Coggeshall (0376) 562226)

Oldest surviving timber-framed barn in Europe, dates from around 1140, originally part of the Cistercian Monastery of Coggeshall; restored in the 1980s by the Coggeshall Grange Barn Trust, Braintree District Council and Essex County Council

🅾️ 30 March to 27 Oct: Tues, Thur, Sun and BH Mon 1–5

💷 £1.20. Parties 80p

♿ Barn accessible

➡️ Signposted off A120 Coggeshall bypass. ¼m from centre of Coggeshall, on Grange Hill (signposted) [168: TQ850231] *Bus:* Eastern National 70, X70 Braintree–Colchester (passing close BR Marks Tey) (tel. Colchester (0206) 571451) *Station:* Kelvedon 2½m

HATFIELD FOREST 🅿️ 🐕 🚶

**Takeley, nr Bishop's Stortford, Hertfordshire
(Head Warden: tel. Bishop's Stortford (0279) 870678)**

Over 1,000 acres of ancient woodland, once part of the royal forests of Essex; the chases and rides afford excellent walks; there is good coarse fishing on the two lakes; observation hide for bird-watching; nature walk; Site of Special Scientific Interest

🅾️ ❄️ All year. Vehicle access restricted Nov to Easter and Thur throughout year

💷 Car park £2. Coaches £20; school coaches £10. Parties must book in advance with Head Warden. Special literature for teachers and school children. Dogs on leads where cattle are grazing and around lake. Riding by permit only; contact Head Warden

♿ Adapted WC and reserved car parking; accessible paths and grassland

🍴 Refreshments are available near the lake

➡️ [167: TL547208/546199] *Bus:* Eastern National 33, 133, 370 Bishop's Stortford–Braintree or BR Chelmsford, alight Takeley, 1m (tel. Bishop's Stortford (0279) 652476) *Station:* Bishop's Stortford 4m

PAYCOCKE'S 🏠 ❄️ ❌ 📷

West Street, Coggeshall, Colchester CO6 1NS (tel. Coggeshall (0376) 561305)

A merchant's house, dating from about 1500; unusually rich panelling and wood carving; display of lace for which Coggeshall was famous; pleasant garden

🅾️ 31 March to 6 Oct: Tues, Thur, Sun & BH Mon 2–5.30

💷 £1.30. Parties of 6 or more should make arrangements beforehand with the tenant. No reduction for parties. Children must be accompanied by an adult

continued

109

[access] Access to garden and ground floor; but one awkward step at front door. The house is small; please contact the tenant before a visit

[directions] Signposted off A120, on S side of West Street, about 300yds from centre of Coggeshall, on road to Braintree next to the Fleece Inn, 5½ E of Braintree [168: TL848225] *Bus:* Eastern National 133 Braintree–Colchester, (passing close BR Marks Tey) (tel. Colchester (0206) 571451 *Station:* Kelvedon 2½m

RAINHAM HALL see London, p. 151

RAYLEIGH CASTLE

Rayleigh

A four-acre site in the middle of Rayleigh Town; on this mound once stood the Domesday castle erected by Sweyn of Essex

[O] [*] All year during daylight hours

[£] Free

[directions] 6m NW of Southend, path from Rayleigh station (A129) [178: TQ805909] *Bus:* From surrounding areas (tel. Southend-on-Sea (0702) 558421] *Station:* Rayleigh 200yds

Gloucestershire

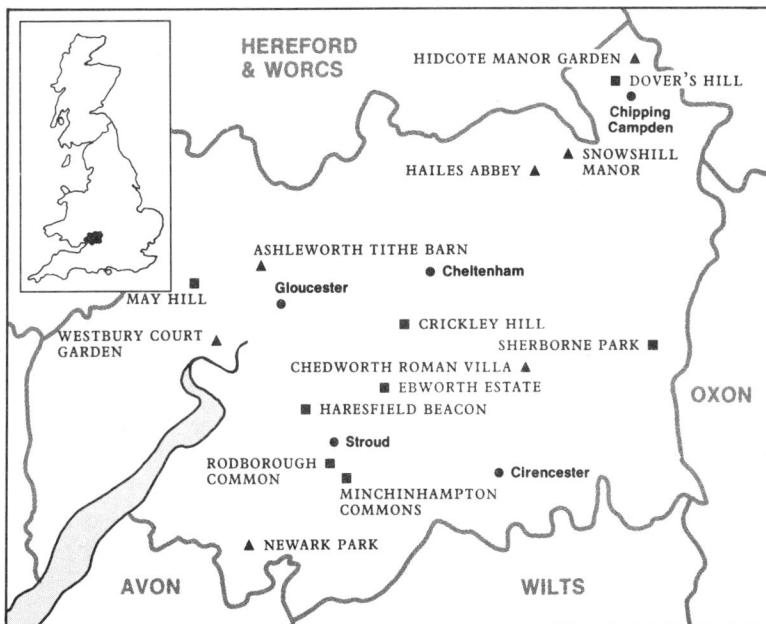

HEREFORD & WORCS

HIDCOTE MANOR GARDEN ▲

■ DOVER'S HILL

● Chipping Campden

▲ SNOWSHILL MANOR

HAILES ABBEY ▲

ASHLEWORTH TITHE BARN ▲

● Cheltenham

Gloucester ●

■ MAY HILL

WESTBURY COURT GARDEN ▲

■ CRICKLEY HILL

SHERBORNE PARK ■

CHEDWORTH ROMAN VILLA ▲

■ EBWORTH ESTATE

■ HARESFIELD BEACON

OXON

● Stroud

RODBOROUGH COMMON ■

■ MINCHINHAMPTON COMMONS

● Cirencester

▲ NEWARK PARK

AVON

WILTS

COUNTRYSIDE

Dover's Hill, 1 mile north of Chipping Campden, [151: SP137937] forms a natural amphitheatre on a spur of the Cotswolds, giving glorious views over the Vale of Evesham. The Cotswold 'Olympick Games' have been held here since 1612, and are re-enacted every year on the evening of the first Friday following Spring Bank Holiday. There is a way-marked woodland walk. Wheelchair access to viewpoint and topograph. Leaflet available on site.

Six miles to the east of Gloucester is **Crickley Hill** [163: SO930163], on the Cotswold escarpment, commanding magnificent views over the Severn Vale to the Forest of Dean and Welsh hills beyond. It is run as a country park in conjunction with adjoining land owned by the County Council; leaflets of various guided walks are available at the information point. The promontory is the site of an Iron Age and Neolithic hill-fort.

Three miles north-west of Stroud is **Haresfield Beacon** [162: SO820089]. The site of a hill-fort, and several hundred acres of nearby woodland, provide spectacular views towards the Severn estuary and across to the Forest of Dean. A topograph (signposted from a small car park) is sited on the adjoining spur known as Shortwood; it displays the area in relief and indicates the views. There are many footpaths through the woodland and the Cotswold Way long distance footpath traverses the property.

The Ebworth Estate close to Sheepscombe, 2 miles north-east of Painswick, provides

111

excellent woodland walking through magnificent beechwoods rich in wildlife. Access to Workmans Wood [163: SO897107] and Lord's and Lady's Woods [163: SO888110] is by public rights of way only and there are no parking facilities. Blackstable Wood [163: SO894097] is also accessible by public rights of way with car parking available nearby.

Two miles south of Stroud, **Minchinhampton** and **Rodborough Commons** [162: SO850010/850038] together amount to nearly 1,000 acres of high open grassland and woods for walking and other quiet recreation. The commons form a steep-sided plateau, rich in wild flowers and other wildlife, with views across the Stroud valleys which contain former wool and cloth mills, to distant hills beyond. There are a number of interesting archaeological sites including the impressive Minchinhampton Bulwarks.

Three miles south-west of Newent and 9 miles west of Gloucester are **May Hill** and **May Hill Common** [162: SO694218]. Walks to the pine trees on the 969ft summit (not NT) are signposted from the minor road below the hill. This is a wild and romantic area of heath and grassland, from which there are spectacular views in every direction.

Sherborne Park [163: SO157144] is off the A40, 3 miles east of Northleach. There are attractive waymarked walks through woods and parkland, with fine views across the valley of the river Windrush.

ASHLEWORTH TITHE BARN 🐘

15th-century tithe barn with two projecting porch bays and fine roof timbers with queenposts

⭕	30 March to end Oct: daily 9–6 or sunset if earlier. Other times by prior appointment only with Severn Regional Office, address on p. 22
💷	50p
➜	6m N of Gloucester, 1¼ E of Hartpury (A417), on W bank of Severn, SE of Ashleworth [162: SO818252] *Bus:* Swanbrook Transport Gloucester–Tewkesbury (passing close BR Gloucester), alight Ashleworth ¼m (tel. Cheltenham (0242) 574444) *Station:* Gloucester 7m

CHEDWORTH ROMAN VILLA 🏛 ✖

Yanworth, nr Cheltenham GL54 3LJ (tel. Withington (024 289) 256)

The remains of a Romano-British villa, excavated 1864–66; mosaics and two bath houses are well preserved; museum houses the smaller finds; 10-min. video programme

[O] [✷] March to end Oct: Tues to Sun & BH Mon 10–5.30. Last admissions 5. Closed Good Fri. Nov to 8 Dec: Wed to Sun 11–4

[⌂] [✷] Shop open as villa. Also 14 & 15 Dec 11–4

[£] £2.20. Family ticket £6. School and other parties are given an introduction to the site, but must be booked in advance. No reduction for parties, which must be limited to one coach at a time. Free coach and car park. Picnic area in nearby woodland, open April to end Sept

[♿] All parts accessible but some with difficulty. [♿] WC in visitors' building

[→] 3m NW of Fossebridge on Cirencester-Northleach road (A429), approached by Fossebridge-Yanworth-Withington road (coaches must avoid Withington) [163: SP053135] *Station:* Cheltenham Spa 9m

HAILES ABBEY [✝]

nr Winchcombe, Cheltenham GL54 5PB (tel. Cheltenham (0242) 602398)

Seventeen cloister arches and extensive excavated remains in lovely surroundings of an abbey founded by Richard, Earl of Cornwall, in 1246; small museum and covered display area

Hailes Abbey is in the guardianship of English Heritage

[O] [✷] Site & Museum Good Fri 29 March to end Sept: daily 10–6. Oct to end March 1992: Tues to Sun 10–4 (closed 24–26 Dec & New Year BH)

Note: Access to site daily, but museum is closed on certain days from Oct to end March for staffing reasons. To avoid disappointment please telephone the property direct or English Heritage Area Office, Bridge House, Sion Place, Clifton, Bristol BS8 4XA (tel. Bristol (0272) 734472)

[£] £1.30, children 65p (OAPs, students & UB40 holders 95p)

[♿] Access to most of site and museum. [♿] WC

[🐕] Dogs, on leads only, in Abbey grounds, but not in Museum

[→] 2m NE of Winchcombe, 1m E of Broadway road (B4632) [150: SP050300] *Bus:* Castleways from Cheltenham (passing close BR Cheltenham) alight Didbrook, 1½m, or more frequent to Greet, 1¼m by footpath (tel. Winchcombe (0242) 602949) *Station:* Cheltenham 10m

HIDCOTE MANOR GARDEN [✿]   [✖] [⎕]

Hidcote Bartrim, nr Chipping Campden GL55 6LR (tel. Mickleton (0386) 438333)

One of the most delightful gardens in England, created this century by the great horticulturist Major Lawrence Johnston; a series of small gardens within the whole, separated by walls and hedges of different species; famous for rare shrubs, trees, herbaceous borders, 'old' roses and interesting plant species

[O] 30 March to end Oct: daily except Tues & Fri 11–8 (no entry after 7pm or 1hr before sunset if earlier)   *continued*

113

⬚ ❀   Shop and plant sales centre open as garden 11–6. Shop also open 2 Nov to 15 Dec: Sat & Sun 12–4

£   £3.80. Family ticket £10.40. Parties of 15 or more by written appointment only; no reduction. No picnicking in garden. Large free coach and car park 100yds. Liable to serious overcrowding on BH Mon and fine Sun

♿   Wheelchair access to part of garden only. ♿ WC in forecourt

☕♿ ❀   Coffee, licensed lunches, cream teas in tea-room 11–5. Also open as shop in Nov & Dec. Parties to book in advance with the Catering Manageress (tel. Mickleton (0386) 438703)

➜   4m NE of Chipping Campden, 1m E of B4632 (originally A46), off B4081 [151: SP176429] *Station:* Honeybourne (U) 4½m

---

NEWARK PARK ☗ ⚔   ✈ ✉

Ozleworth, Wotton-under-Edge GL12 7PZ (tel. Dursley (0453) 842644)

Elizabethan 'standing' or hunting lodge built on the edge of a cliff by the Poyntz family, made into a four-square castellated country house by James Wyatt, 1790; house of specialist architectural interest in the course of rehabilitation by present tenant, Mr R. L. Parsons, who is responsible for the showing arrangements

◉   April, May, Aug & Sept: Wed & Thur 2–5; guided tours every half hour, last admissions 4.30

£ £1.10. No reduction for parties. Car park. Not suitable for coaches. No WCs

→ 1½m E of Wotton-under-Edge, 1½m S of junction of A4135 & B4058
[172: ST786934] *Bus:* Badgerline 309 Bristol–Dursley, alight Wotton-under-Edge, 1¼m. Frequent services link BR Bristol Temple Meads with the bus station (tel. Bristol (0272) 297979) *Station:* Stroud 10m

SNOWSHILL MANOR 🏠❀   ✈ ✖ ✉ ⊞

nr Broadway WR12 7JU (tel. Broadway (0386) 852410)

A Tudor house with a c.1700 façade; 21 rooms containing Charles Paget Wade's collection of craftsmanship, including musical instruments, clocks, toys, bicycles, weavers' and spinners' tools, Japanese armour; small formal garden and Charles Wade's cottage

Note: There is no access to the Costume Collection at present

O Easter Sat, Sun & Mon (30 March to 1 April) 11–1 & 2–6. April & Oct: Sat & Sun 11–1 & 2–5. May to end Sept: Wed to Sun & BH Mon 11–1 & 2–6. Last admissions ½hr before closing

🛍 Shop open as house

£ £3.50. Family ticket £9.60. Parties by written appointment Wed to Fri only; no party concession. School parties by previous appointment Wed to Fri mornings only. Free car park on N side of village. No coaches. No picnicking. Student and specialist photography only by prior arrangement with Administrator. Liable to serious overcrowding on Sun & BH Mon

♿ Limited access (with assistance) to house (ground floor) and part of garden

→ 3m SW of Broadway, 4m W of junction of A44 & A424 [150: SP096339]
Bus: Castleways BR Evesham–Broadway, thence 3m (tel. Winchcombe (0242) 603715) *Station:* Moreton-in-Marsh 7m

WESTBURY COURT GARDEN ❀   ✈

Westbury-on-Severn GL14 1PD (tel. Westbury-on-Severn (045 276) 461)

A formal water garden with canals and yew hedges, laid out between 1696 and 1705; the earliest of its kind remaining in England; restored in 1971 and planted with species dating from pre 1700, including apple, pear and plum trees

O ❀ 30 March to end Oct: Wed to Sun & BH Mon 11–6. Other months by appointment only

£ £1.60. Parties of 15 or more by written arrangement. Free car park. Picnic area

♿ ◈ All parts of garden accessible. ♿ WC

→ 9m SW of Gloucester on A48 [162: SO718138] *Bus:* Red & White X73 Gloucester–Cardiff (passing close BR Gloucester & Newport) (tel. Newport (0623) 265100) *Station:* Gloucester 9m

Hampshire

BERKS

SANDHAM MEMORIAL CHAPEL   THE VYNE ▲

▲ WEST GREEN HOUSE

Basingstoke ●   Aldershot ●

● Andover

WILTS   SURREY

Stockbridge ● ■ STOCKBRIDGE DOWN

LUDSHOTT COMMON & WAGGONERS' WELLS
■

Winchester ● ▲   ▲ HINTON AMPNER
WINCHESTER
CITY MILL

MOTTISFONT ▲
ABBEY GARDEN

BRAMSHAW COMMONS
■ & MANORIAL WASTES

Southampton

Fareham   Havant

Portsmouth

Hayling Island

COUNTRYSIDE

On the northern edge of the New Forest between Bramshaw, Cadnam and Plaitford, the Trust owns 1,400 acres of **Bramshaw Commons and Manorial Wastes**, [184/185: SU2717]. They consist of Cadnam and Stocks Cross Greens; Cadnam, Furzley, Half Moon, Penn and Plaitford Commons; Hale Purlieu and Millersford Plantation; and Hightown Common. They abut onto the New Forest and local grazing animals may safely stray from one area to another.

[🚶] At **Ludshott Common and Waggoners' Wells** on the Hampshire/Surrey border [186: SU855350], there is a string of man-made ponds which are a source of the River Wey (see p. 212). There are many footpaths and rides and a number of nature walks. [♿] Wheelchair access.

Some 10 miles due north of **Mottisfont Abbey Garden** (see p. 117) is **Stockbridge Down**, 1 mile east of Stockbridge [185: SU379349]. The chalk downland is rich in plant and insect life. Pleasant walks here are accessible from two car parks on the A272. [♿] Limited access.

HINTON AMPNER 🏠 ❀ ✖ ✖

Bramdean, nr Alresford SO24 0LA (tel. Winchester (0962) 771305/771023)

Remodelled by the late Ralph Dutton in 1936; a fire in 1960 gutted the house and destroyed much of his collection; he re-built and re-furnished with fine Regency furniture, 17th-century Italian pictures and porcelain; set in superb countryside, the garden combines formal design and informal planting, producing delightful walks with many unexpected vistas

Note: Visitors are asked to note that parts of the garden are currently being restored

O   Good Fri 29 March to end Sept: **garden:** Sat, Sun, Tues, Wed, Good Fri & BH Mon 1.30–5.30; **house:** Tues & Wed only also Sat & Sun in Aug 1.30–5.30. Last admissions 5

£   Garden £1.70; house £1.20 extra. Parties to house & garden £2.50 (please pre-book). Parking 200yds. Special entrance for coaches; please book in advance

♿   Most of garden accessible. Special parking in front of house. ♿ WC by house

♨ ♿   Tea-room same days as garden 2–5. Picnics in car park only

→   On A272, 1m W of Bramdean village, 8m E of Winchester [185: SU597275] *Bus:* Hampshire Bus 67 Winchester–Petersfield (passing close BR Winchester and passing BR Petersfield) (tel. Winchester (0962) 52352) *Station:* Alresford (Mid-Hants Rly) 4m: Winchester 9m

MOTTISFONT ABBEY GARDEN ❀

Mottisfont, nr Romsey; bookings and enquiries to the Head Gardener, The White House, Hatt Lane, Mottisfont, nr Romsey SO51 0LJ (tel. Lockerley (0794) 41220 during opening hours, otherwise 40757)

A tributary of the River Test flows through the garden forming a superb and tranquil setting for a 12th-century Augustinian priory, which, after the Dissolution, became a house; it contains the spring or 'font' from which the place-name is derived; the magnificent trees, walled gardens and the national collection of old-fashioned roses combine to provide interest throughout the seasons   *continued*

117

▦ **Ⓚ** *Notes on the house:* The Abbey (tenanted) contains a drawing room decorated by Rex Whistler, and the cellarium of the old priory. There are guided tours of these two rooms on Wednesday afternoons only; timed tickets should be obtained from the kiosk on arrival (NT members included). Numbers are restricted and access is not possible for all at peak times; it is best to come on Wed in April, May or September but please check with the property beforehand if planning to visit the house. Parties will find it difficult gaining admission to house in the peak season

◯ April to end Sept: Garden daily except Fri & Sat: 2–6. Last admissions 5. House (Whistler room and cellarium only) Wed afternoons only (See *Notes on the house,* above). Additional opening of Rose Garden in the evenings during rose season (usually June or early July, but please check with property first) Tues, Wed, Thur & Sun 7pm–9pm; last admissions 8.30pm

🛍 Shop open at peak times

£ Garden £2; house 50p extra. No reduction for parties; coaches please book in advance

♿ ◉ Cellarium & garden only; **♿** WCs. Special parking area available; please ask at Rose kiosk on arrival. Rose garden particularly recommended to visually handicapped visitors

🐕 In car park only

🍴 ♿ Light lunches and home-made teas at local Post Office nearby (separate car park), not NT (tel. Lockerley (0794) 40243)

Events: Open-air events in summer; for details telephone the Booking Office (Lockerley (0794) 40846)

➜ 4½m NW of Romsey, ¾m W of A3057 [185: SU327270] *Station:* Mottisfont Dunbridge (U) ¼m

SANDHAM MEMORIAL CHAPEL ✚   ✈ ⊠

Burghclere, nr Newbury, Berkshire (tel. Burghclere (063 527) 292)

A First World War memorial built in the 1920s; notable for the paintings by Stanley Spencer of war scenes in Salonica, which cover the chapel walls, 'The outstanding English monument to painting of the pioneering years of the 20th century' (Pevsner)

◯ ❄ Good Fri 29 March to end Oct: Wed to Sun & BH Mon, 11.30–6. Nov to end March 1992: Sat & Sun only, 11.30–4. Closed Christmas Day & 1 Jan. *Note:* As there is no lighting in the chapel, it is best to view the paintings on a bright day

£ £1. No reduction for parties which must book. No WCs. Road verge parking

♿ Accessible via two small sets of steps

➜ 4m S of Newbury, ½m E of A34 [174: SU463608] *Bus:* Bee Line 123/4 from Newbury (passing close BR Newbury) (tel. Newbury (0635) 40743) *Station:* Newbury 4m

PLEASE REFER TO PAGES 5–9

THE VYNE 🏠 ❀

Sherborne St John, Basingstoke RG26 5DX (tel. Basingstoke (0256) 881337)

House of diaper brickwork built by William, 1st Lord Sandys in early 16th century;
extensively altered in mid 17th century, when John Webb added the earliest Classical portico
to a country house in England; Tudor chapel with Renaissance glass; Palladian staircase;
garden with herbaceous border, lawns and lake; woodland walks

Good Fri 29 March to end Oct: daily, except Mon & Fri (open Good Fri & BH Mon but closed Tues following). **Garden:** 12.30–5.30; **house:** 1.30–5.30, BH Mon 11–5.30. Last admissions 5

Shop as garden. Also open for Christmas shopping (tel. for dates). ♿ one step into shop

House & garden £3.40; garden only £1.70. Parties £2.20, Tues, Wed & Thur only. Parking 100yds

Garden & ground floor only (2 steps to Stone Gallery); disabled visitors may be driven to door by prior arrangement *continued*

In car park only

Light refreshments and home-made teas in the Old Brew House (licensed) 12.30–2 & 3–5.30. Also open as shop pre-Christmas. Coach parties by prior arrangement with Administrator. Picnics not allowed in grounds

Events: please send s.a.e. for information

4m N of Basingstoke between Bramley and Sherborne St John [175 & 186: SU637566] *Bus:* Hampshire Bus 45A, 50/1, 150 from Basingstoke (passing BR Basingstoke), alight Sherborne St John, 1¼m on 45A & 51, Sherborne West, 1½m on 50 & 150 (tel. Basingstoke (0256) 464501) *Station:* Bramley 2½m

WEST GREEN HOUSE

Hartley Wintney, Basingstoke RG27 8JB

Small early 18th-century house of great charm in a delightful garden at its best before July

West Green House and garden will be closed for restoration work during 1991

WINCHESTER CITY MILL

1 Water Lane, Winchester. Bookings and enquiries to the Custodian, 4 Rockbourne Rd, Winchester SO22 6JS (tel. Winchester (0962) 880644)

Built over the river in 1744, the mill has a delightful small island garden and an impressive millrace; part of the property is used by the Youth Hostels Association

Good Fri 29 March to end Sept: daily except Mon & Fri, but open Good Fri & BH Mon (closed Tues following) 1.45–4.45. Last admissions 4.30. Oct to end March: by prior arrangement with the YHA Warden (tel. Winchester (0962) 53723).

Christmas shop

50p. No reduction for parties. Parking in public car park, 500yds. No WCs

Not suitable for wheelchair users; many steps; but visually handicapped visitors may enjoy the sound of rushing water

At foot of High Street, beside City Bridge [185: SU487294] *Bus:* From surrounding areas (tel. Winchester (0962) 52352) *Station:* Winchester 1m

Hereford & Worcester

A map of Hereford & Worcester showing surrounding areas SHROPSHIRE, POWYS, WARWICKS, GLOUCESTERSHIRE, GWENT, and locations including CLENT HILLS, Kidderminster, Bromsgrove, CROFT CASTLE & BIRCHER COMMON, HANBURY HALL, BERRINGTON HALL, BRADNOR HILL, Leominster, Kington, LOWER BROCKHAMPTON, HAWFORD DOVECOTE, Bromyard, THE GREYFRIARS, Worcester, WICHENFORD DOVECOTE, CWMMAU FARMHOUSE, Great Malvern, THE WEIR, MIDDLE LITTLETON TITHE BARN, Hereford, Evesham, THE FLEECE INN, BREDON BARN.

COUNTRYSIDE

Just south of Stourbridge at the south-western edge of Birmingham are the **Clent Hills**, now a Country Park and managed by the Hereford and Worcester County Council. The Trust owns over 400 acres of these hills which are covered with heathy grassland. This is ideal country for walkers and riders with superb views in every direction to the Wrekin in the north-west, the Welsh hills to the west and the Malvern and Cotswold ranges to the south. There is an excellent wheelchair path to a toposcope which explains all the views, with perching points and seats for less able people to regain their breath and enjoy the surrounding countryside [139: SO9379].

At **Croft Castle** (see p. 123), the Trust owns nearly 1,400 acres, including the high open grassland of **Bircher Common**, where local people still graze their animals. The Iron Age hill-fort of **Croft Ambrey** on a 1,000ft limestone ridge can give views over as many as 14 counties. The estate is home to hares, squirrels, fallow deer, stoats, weasels and even polecats which have ventured here from across the Welsh border. Britain's largest finch, the hawfinch, is sometimes seen feeding on hornbeam seeds on Croft Ambrey. There are walks through the park to the hill-fort; butterflies and wild flowers abound on the estate.

At **Bradnor Hill** near Kington [148: SO282584] is 340 acres of common land rising to 1,284ft with the highest golf course in Europe on the summit.

At Brockhampton near Bromyard, visitors to **Lower Brockhampton** (see p. 125) may also like to explore the woods and take in the nearby woodland nature walk at Bringsty Common which is also open to the public.

121

BERRINGTON HALL 🏠🏵 ✈ ✉ 📷 🎒

nr Leominster HR6 0DW (tel. Leominster (0568) 615721)

An elegant neo-Classical house of the late 18th century, designed by Henry Holland and set in a park landscape by 'Capability' Brown; the formal exterior belies the delicate interior with beautifully decorated ceilings and fine furniture, including the Digby collection, a recently restored bedroom suite; nursery, Victorian laundry and pretty tiled Georgian dairy; attractive garden with interesting plants and recently planted historic apple orchard in walled garden

🅾	30 March to end April: Sat, Sun & BH Mon 1.30–5.30. May to end Sept: daily except Mon & Tues (open BH Mon) 1.30–5.30. Oct: Sat & Sun 1.30–4.30. Last admissions ½hr before closing. Grounds open from 12.30
🛍 🏵	Shop open same days as house 1–5.30. Also 2 Nov to 15 Dec: Sat & Sun 1–4.30
£	£2.70. Family ticket £7.40. Grounds only £1. Parties of 15 or more by prior written arrangement only. No access to park. Free car and coach park
♿	Grounds only. ♿ WC. Disabled people may park in courtyard; please enquire at ticket office
☕	Lunches & teas in the Servants' Hall open same days as house from 12.30. No wheelchair access but special arrangements can be made if requested. Picnic tables in car park
➜	3m N of Leominster, 7m S of Ludlow on W side of A49 [137: SO510637] *Bus:* Midland Red West X92, 292 Birmingham–Hereford (passing close BR Ludlow & Leominster), alight Luston 2m (tel. 0345 212 555) *Station:* Leominster (U) 4m

BREDON BARN 🏠

14th-century barn, 132ft long with fine porches, one of which has unusual stone chimney cowling; the barn was restored with traditional materials after a fire in 1980

🅾️ 30 March to end Nov: Wed, Thur, Sat & Sun 10–6 or sunset if earlier. Dec to
Feb: by prior appointment only, with Severn Regional Office (address on p. 22)

💷 50p

➡️ 3m NE of Tewkesbury, just N of B4080 [150: SO919369] *Bus:* Spring & Son
Evesham–Cheltenham (passing close BR Evesham) (tel. Evesham (0386)
442290); Midland Red West 540 Evesham–Tewkesbury (passing close BR
Evesham) (tel. 0345 212 555) *Station:* Pershore (U) 8½m

CROFT CASTLE 🎖️🎤🎇🚹🏛️   ⊠

nr Leominster HR6 9PW (tel. Yarpole (056 885) 246)

---

*Home of the Croft family since Domesday (with a break of 170 years from 1750); walls and
corner towers date from 14th and 15th centuries; interior mainly 18th-century, when the
fine Georgian-Gothic staircase and plasterwork ceilings were added; splendid avenue of
350-year old Spanish chestnuts; Iron Age fort (Croft Ambrey) may be reached by footpath*

🅾️🎇 Easter Sat, Sun & Mon (30 March to 1 April) 2–6. April & Oct: Sat & Sun 2–5.
May to end Sept: Wed to Sun & BH Mon 2–6. Last admissions to house ½hr
before closing. Car park, picnic area, parkland and Croft Ambrey open all year

💷♿ £2.40. Family ticket £6.60. Parties of 15 or more by prior written
arrangement. Free car parking. Picnics in parkland only. Dogs in parkland
only, on leads

♿ Access to ground floor and part of grounds; special parking by castle

🍴 Lunches and teas available in restaurant at Berrington Hall, 5½m (tel.
Leominster (0568) 615721) see p. 122

➡️ 5m NW of Leominster, 9m SW of Ludlow; approach from B4362, turning N at
Cock Gate between Bircher and Mortimer's Cross; signposted from Ludlow–
Leominster road (A49) and from A4110 at Mortimer's Cross [137: SO455655]
Bus: Midland Red West X92, 292 Birmingham–Hereford (passing close BR
Ludlow & Leominster), alight Gorbett Bank, 2¼m (tel. 0345 212 555)
Station: Leominster (U) 7m

CWMMAU FARMHOUSE 🏛️   ⊠⊠

Brilley, Whitney on Wye HR3 6JP (tel. Clifford (04973) 251)

Early 17th-century timber-framed and stone-tiled farmhouse

🅾️ Easter, May, Spring & Summer Bank Holiday weekends only, (Sat, Sun & Mon
2–6). Other times by previous appointment only with tenant, Mr D. Joyce

💷 £1.60. Not suitable for coaches

➡️ 4m SW of Kington between A4111 & A438; approach by long narrow lane
leading S from Kington–Brilley road at Brilley Mountain [148: SO267514]

PLEASE REFER TO PAGES 5–9

THE FLEECE INN 🏠 ✖

Bretforton, nr Evesham (tel. Evesham (0386) 831173)

Medieval farmhouse in the centre of the village; became a licensed house in 1848, and remains largely unaltered; family collection of furniture

O ❋ Only during normal public house licensing hours

£ Car parking in village square. Coaches by written appointment only

● Lunchtime snacks

→ 4m E of Evesham, on B4035 [150: SP093437] *Bus:* Midland Red West/Spring & Son 554 from Evesham (tel. 0345 212 555) *Station:* Evesham 3m

THE GREYFRIARS 🏠 ❋ ✖

Friar Street, Worcester WR1 2LZ (tel. Worcester (0905) 23571)

Built in 1480, with early 17th- and late 18th-century additions, this timber-framed house was rescued from demolition at the time of the Second World War and has been carefully restored and refurbished; interesting textiles and furnishings add character to the panelled rooms; an archway leads through to a delightful garden – a haven of peace in the centre of a busy city

O April to end Oct: Wed, Thur & BH Mon 2–5.30. Other times by written appointment only

£ £1.30. Family ticket £3.50. Parties of 15 or more by written appointment. Public car park in Friar Street. No WCs

→ [150: SO852546] *Bus:* From surrounding areas (tel. 0345 212 555) *Station:* Worcester Foregate Street ½m

HANBURY HALL 🏠 🏠 ❋ ♠ ✖

Droitwich WR9 7EA (tel. Hanbury (0527 84) 214)

Wren-style red brick house, completed in 1701 and little altered since; a typical example of an English country house built by a prosperous local family; outstanding painted ceilings and staircase by Thornhill; the Watney Collection of porcelain; contemporary orangery; ice house

O During much of 1991 the house and grounds will be closed for major restoration and repairs. It is planned to open the house and grounds from Sat 29 June to end Oct: Sat, Sun & Mon 2–6

🗂 Shop open as house

£ 🐕 £2.40. Family ticket £6.60. Parties of 15 or more and evening visits by prior written arrangement. Free car and coach parking. Picnic area in car park. No dogs in garden and in park on footpaths only, on leads

♿ Wheelchair access to ground floor and garden; disabled visitors may be driven to front door; parking available near house. ⧉ Braille guide. ♿ WC in house

▣♿ Cream teas in tea-room in the house, open as shop, above

➔ 4½m E of Droitwich, 1m N of B4090, 6m S of Bromsgrove, 1½m W of B4091 [150: SO943637] *Bus:* Midland Red West 142/4 Worcester–Birmingham (passing close BR Droitwich Spa), alight Wychbold, 2½m (tel. 0345 212 555) *Station:* Droitwich Spa 4m

HAWFORD DOVECOTE ▣

16th-century half-timbered dovecote; access (on foot only) via the entrance drive to adjoining house

⊙ 30 March to end Oct: daily 9–6 or sunset if earlier. Other times by prior appointment only with Severn Regional Office, address on p. 22

£ 50p

➔ 3m N of Worcester, ½m E or A449 [150: SO846607] *Bus:* Midland Red West 303 Worcester–Kidderminster (passing BR Worcester Foregate Street & Kidderminster), alight Hawford Lodge, ¼m (tel. 0345 212 555) *Station:* Worcester Foregate Street 3m; Worcester Shrub Hill 3½m

LOWER BROCKHAMPTON ▣▣   ✖✖

Bringsty WR6 5UH

A late 14th-century moated manor house, with an attractive detached half-timbered 15th-century gatehouse, a rare example of this type of structure; and ruins of a 12th-century chapel

⊙ Medieval Hall & Parlour only 30 March to end Sept: Wed to Sun & BH Mon 10–1 & 2–6. Oct: Wed to Sun 10–1 & 2–4
continued

£ £1.20. Family ticket £3.30. Parties of 15 or more by prior written arrangement

& Access to all parts

→ 2m E of Bromyard on Worcester road (A44); reached by a narrow road through 1½m of woods and farmland [149: SO682546]
Bus: Midland Red West 419/20 Worcester–Hereford (passing BR Worcester Foregate Street & close BR Hereford) (tel. 0345 212 555)

MIDDLE LITTLETON TITHE BARN 🐘

Magnificent 13th-century tithe barn, built of blue lias stone, still in use as farm building

O 30 March to end Oct: daily 9–6 or sunset if earlier. Other times by prior appointment only with Severn Regional Office, address on p. 22

£ 50p

→ 3m NE of Evesham, E of B4085 [150: SP080471] *Bus:* Midland Red West X6, 146 Evesham–Birmingham (passing close BR Evesham), alight Middle Littleton School Lane, ½m (tel. 0345 212 555) *Station:* Honeybourne (U) 3½m; Evesham 4¼m

THE WEIR ✪   🗡

Swainshill, nr Hereford

Delightful riverside garden particularly spectacular in early spring; fine views over River Wye and Black Mountains

O ✪ 14 Feb to end Oct: Wed to Sun (incl. Good Fri) & BH Mon 11–6

£ £1.10; Free car park (unsuitable for coaches). No WCs

→ 5m W of Hereford on A438 [149: SO435419] *Bus:* Midland Red West 101 Hereford–Credenhill (passing close BR Hereford), thence 1½m (tel. 0345 212 555) *Station:* Hereford 5m

WICHENFORD DOVECOTE 🐘

17th-century half-timbered dovecote

O 30 March to end Oct: daily 9–6 or sunset if earlier. Other times by prior appointment only with Severn Regional Office, address on p. 22

£ 50p

→ 5½m NW of Worcester, N of B4204 [150: SO788597] *Bus:* Midland Red West 310–3 from Worcester (passing close BR Worcester Foregate Street), alight Wichenford, ½m (tel. 0345 212 555) *Station:* Worcester Foregate Street 7m; Worcester Shrub Hill 7½m

Hertfordshire

ASHRIDGE ESTATE ⬛🏠🚶

Ringshall, Berkhamsted

---

*The **Ashridge Estate** covers some 6 square miles in Hertfordshire and Buckinghamshire, running along the main ridge of the Chiltern Hills from Ivinghoe Beacon to Berkhamsted. It comprises 4,000 unspoilt acres of open spaces, commons and woodlands.*

*At the northerly end, the **Ivinghoe Hills** offer splendid views from some 700ft above sea level. This area may be reached from a car park at Steps Hill. The rest of Ashridge is an almost level area, with many fine walks through woods and open commons. The main focal point is the granite monument erected 150 years ago to the 3rd Duke of Bridgewater. Wildlife is well represented; a wide variety of birds is always in evidence; some 300 fallow and muntjac deer roam freely; badgers, foxes and the grey squirrel also abound; and almost unique to the area is the glis glis, or edible dormouse. An interesting illustrated booklet about the Ashridge Estate is available at the Information Centre near the Monument*

🅾️❄️ Estate: open all year. **Monument, Shop & Information Centre:** Good Fri 29 March to end Oct: Mon to Thur & Good Fri 2–5, Sat, Sun & BH Mon 2–5.30

Note: The Monument may be closed for essential maintenance work during the 1991 season   *continued*

127

£   Monument 50p. Parking facilities
£1 on summer weekends.
Note: for further information and
party bookings tel. Aldbury
Common (044 285) 227

♿   In monument area, on monument
drive and to Information Centre.
♿ WC. Special parking near
Information Centre. Self-drive
battery-powered vehicles available
free of charge from Information
Centre; advance booking advisable

🐕   Admitted if kept under control

⎈   Tea kiosk next to Information
Centre, summer weekends

➜   Between Northchurch & Ringshall
just off B4506, 3m N of A41
[165: SP970131] *Bus:* Monument:
Red Rover 27 from BR Tring, alight
Aldbury, ½m; Beacon: 61
Aylesbury–Luton (passing close BR
Aylesbury & Luton) (tel. Aylesbury
(0296) 84919) *Station:* Monument:
Tring, 1¼m. Beacon: Cheddington
3½m

SHAW'S CORNER 🏠   ✉💾

Ayot St Lawrence, nr Welwyn AL6 9BX (tel. Stevenage (0438) 820307)

---

*The home of George Bernard Shaw from 1906 until his death in 1950; many literary and
personal relics in downstairs rooms, which remain as in his lifetime; kitchen and pantry
newly opened*

Note: Upstairs rooms (Shaw's bedroom & bathroom, & display room) open weekdays

◎   30 March to end Oct: Wed to Sat 2–6; Sun & BH Mon 12–6 Parties by written
appointment only, March to end Nov). Last admissions 5.30. On busy days
admission may be by timed ticket

£   £2.20. No reduction for parties which must book. Car park 50yds

♿   Garden and house, but some steps; please enquire about best times for visits;
unsuitable for severely disabled visitors

🐕   In car park only

➜   At SW end of village, 2m NE of Wheathampstead; approx. 2m from B653
[166: TL194167] *Bus:* Luton & District 304 St Albans–Hitchin (passing close
St Albans Abbey & close St Albans City), alight Gustardwood, 1¼m (tel. Hitchen
(0462) 38138) *Station:* Welwyn North 4m; Harpenden 5m

Humberside

Map of Humberside showing N. YORKS, S. YORKS, NOTTS, LINCS regions; towns Bridlington, Hornsea, Beverley, Hull, Withernsea, Goole, Scunthorpe, Grimsby; North Sea and River Humber; MAISTER HOUSE near Hull.

MAISTER HOUSE 🏛

160 High Street, Hull HU1 1NL (tel. Hull (0482) 24112)

Rebuilt in 1744, superb staircase hall designed in the Palladian manner; ironwork by Robert Bakewell; let as offices

Staircase and entrance hall only: all year: Mon to Fri 10–4; closed BH, Good Fri & 1 Jan

50p, incl. guidebook. Indoor photography by permission only. Unsuitable for parties. No parking at property. No WCs

Hull city centre. *Bus:* Local services to within 100yds (tel. Hull (0482) 222222); services from surrounding areas (tel. Hull (0482) 27146) *Station:* Hull ¾m

Isle of Wight

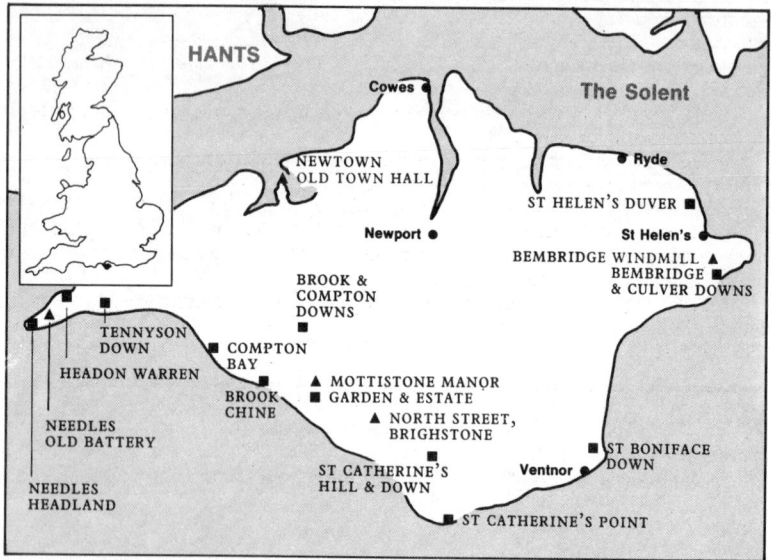

HANTS

Cowes

The Solent

NEWTOWN
OLD TOWN HALL

Ryde

ST HELEN'S DUVER ■

Newport ●

St Helen's ●

BEMBRIDGE WINDMILL ▲
BEMBRIDGE ■
& CULVER DOWNS

BROOK &
COMPTON
DOWNS

TENNYSON
DOWN

COMPTON
BAY

HEADON WARREN

▲ MOTTISTONE MANOR
■ GARDEN & ESTATE

BROOK
CHINE

▲ NORTH STREET,
BRIGHSTONE

NEEDLES
OLD BATTERY

■ ST BONIFACE
DOWN

ST CATHERINE'S
HILL & DOWN

Ventnor ●

NEEDLES
HEADLAND

■ ST CATHERINE'S POINT

COAST AND COUNTRY

The Trust owns more than 3,500 acres of the Island, much of it beautiful chalk downland and spectacular coastline, and nearly all of it freely accessible for visitors to enjoy.

The best-known landmark on West Wight is the Needles, the sharp points of rock stretching into the sea at the extreme west of the Island. Overlooking the famous rocks the Trust owns the **Needles Headland** [196: SZ300848], as well as the Needles Old Battery (see p. 132) and three coastguard cottages, let as holiday homes (see p. 19). The Needles can also be seen from **Headon Warren** [196: SZ310851], a gorse and heather-covered heath; and from here Trust land extends to the chalk cliffs of **Tennyson Down** [196: SZ330855], where the Poet Laureate walked every day when he lived at nearby Farringford.

Following south-east from West Wight the Trust also owns much land along the Back of the Wight. On the coast **Compton Bay** [196: SZ378840], one of the Island's most popular bathing beaches, is protected by the Trust (dogs not allowed on beach from Aug to mid Sept), as is **Brook Chine** [196: SZ385835]. Behind the sea, following the chalk 'hog's back', the Trust owns **Compton Down** and **Brook Down** [196: SZ376850/ SZ395891]. The Trust's **Mottistone Estate** [196: SZ405837] is further east and includes the Manor, the gardens (see p. 131), farmland, woodland, Mottistone Down and most of Mottistone village. The Trust's properties have recently been added to with the bequest of **North Street, Brighstone**, including the local post office and gift shop.

At the southernmost tip of the Island is **St Catherine's Point** [196: SZ495755], where there is another National Trust holiday cottage. Inland, **St Catherine's Hill** and **St Catherine's Down** [196: SZ494772/495785] give magnificent views over both the

130

eastern and western ends of the Island. Also in the south, the Trust protects much of the Ventnor Downs, including the highest point on the Island, **St Boniface Down** [196: SZ565782] which rises steeply to 764ft and is renowned for its holm oak forest.

On the east of the Island the Trust owns **Bembridge & Culver Downs** [196: SZ624869], which overlook to the north the village of Bembridge and its windmill (see p. 131). [&] Stretching almost across Bembridge harbour mouth is **St Helen's Duver** [196: SZ637891], a wide sand and shingle spit which used to be a golf course and now has a nature trail for disabled people. The Club House has been converted to a holiday cottage, also adapted for disabled visitors.

The Trust has acquired a spacious Edwardian holiday cottage next to the sea at Cowes on the north of the Island. On the north-west coast the ancient borough of **Newtown** [196: SZ424906] is now reduced to a small village, although the outlines of the 13th century town are still clearly visible. The Trust owns the Old Town Hall (see p. 132) and protects much of the old borough and the entire river estuary, which is now a nature reserve managed by the Isle of Wight County Council.

The Trust publishes a free visitors' guide to all the coast and countryside it protects on the Isle of Wight, Copies are available from 35a St James' Street, Newport, PO30 1LB (tel. 0983 526445).

BEMBRIDGE WINDMILL 🗙   🏠

Bookings and enquires to the Custodian, Mill Reach, Kings Road, Bembridge, Isle of Wight PO35 5NT (tel. Isle of Wight (0983) 873945 during opening hours)

Dating from around 1700, the only windmill to survive on the island; much of the wooden machinery can still be seen

🔲🔲   29 March to 3 Nov: daily except Sat (but open Easter Sat & daily in July & Aug) 10–5. Last admissions 4.45. Conducted school parties and special visits March to end Oct (but not July or Aug), by written appointment. Small shop

£   £1. No reduction for parties. All school parties are conducted by a NT guide; special charge applies. Parking 100yds. No WCs. Picnic field

→   ½m S of Bembridge on B3395 [196: SZ639874] *Bus:* Southern Vectis 8 BR Ryde Esplanade–Sandown (tel. IoW (0983) 62264) *Station:* Brading (U) 2m by footpath *Ferry:* Ryde (Wightlink Ltd) 6m; E. Cowes (Red Funnel), 13m

MOTTISTONE MANOR GARDEN 🏵

Bookings and enquiries to the Custodian, 3 Winkle Street, Calbourne, Newport, Isle of Wight PO30 4JF

Fine gardens laid out in the 1970s providing a setting for the medieval and Elizabethan manor house

🔲   **Garden:** 1 April to 25 Sept: Wed only & BH Mon 2–5.30. Last admissions 5. **House open:** 26 August only. Parties by written appointment

£   Garden £1.50, house £1 extra. No reduction for parties. Parking 50yds. No WCs

🐕   Dogs on leads   *continued*

131

→ At Mottistone, 2m W of Brighstone on B3399 [196: SZ406838] *Bus:* Southern Vectis 1B Newport–Freshwater (tel. IoW (0983) 523831). *Ferry:* Yarmouth (Wightlink Ltd) 6m; W. Cowes (Red Funnel) 12m

---

THE NEEDLES OLD BATTERY

Bookings and enquiries to the Custodian, 3 Winkle Street, Calbourne, Newport, Isle of Wight PO30 4JF (tel. Isle of Wight (0983) 754772 during opening hours)

A Victorian coastal fort built 1862, 250ft above sea level; 200ft tunnel to spectacular views of Needles Rocks and lighthouse; original gun barrel mounted on carriage in the parade ground; the laboratory, searchlight position and two position finder cells have been restored; exhibition on the history of the Headland; children's exhibition

29 March to 3 Nov: daily except Fri & Sat (but open daily Good Fri 29 March to 11 April and from 25 May to 3 Oct) 10.30–5. Last admissions 4.30. 10 Nov to 22 Dec: Sun 10.30–3.30. 27 Dec to 5 Jan: daily 10.30–3.30. Last admissions 3. Conducted school parties and special visits March to end Dec (but not July & Aug) by written appointment

Shop open as Battery

£1.60. No reduction for parties; all parties are conducted by a NT guide; a special charge applies. No vehicular access to Battery. Parking 1m away at Alum Bay, bus hourly to Battery, see below. Children and dogs must be kept under strict control because of the cliffs

Tea-room open as Battery (but only open daily during July & Aug) mid-morning to mid-afternoon

→ At Needles Headland, W of Freshwater Bay and Alum Bay (B3322) [196: SZ300848] *Bus:* Southern Vectis 42 Yarmouth–Needles, May to Oct only; otherwise any service to Alum Bay, thence ¼m. (tel. IoW (0983) 523831) *Ferry:* Yarmouth (Wightlink Ltd) 5m; W Cowes (Red Funnel), 16m

---

OLD TOWN HALL, NEWTOWN

Bookings and enquiries to the Custodian, Gays Folly, Amos Hill, Totland Bay, Isle of Wight PO39 0DP

The small , now tranquil, village of Newtown once sent two members to Parliament, and the Town Hall was the setting for these often turbulent elections

29 March to end Sept: Mon, Wed & Sun (but open Good Fri, Easter Sat and Tues & Thur in July & Aug) 2–5. Last admissions 4.45. Guided tours by written appointment

£1. No reduction for parties. No WCs

→ Between Newport and Yarmouth, 1m N of A3054 [196: SZ424905] *Bus:* Southern Vectis 7 Newport–Freshwater (passing Yarmouth Ferry Terminal), alight Barton's Corner, 1m (tel. IoW (0983) 523831) *Ferry:* Yarmouth (Wightlink Ltd) 5m; West Cowes (Red Funnel) 6m

Kent

ST JOHN'S
JERUSALEM
GARDEN ▲
Westerham
QUEBEC HOUSE
KNOLE
OLD SOAR MANOR
IGHTHAM
MOTE
EMMETTS GARDEN
CHARTWELL
SPRIVERS GARDEN
SCOTNEY CASTLE
GARDEN
E. SUSSEX

● Gravesend
OWLETTS
▲
TUDOR YEOMAN'S HOUSE

● Maidstone
▲ STONEACRE
WOOL HOUSE

▲ SISSINGHURST CASTLE
GARDEN
▲ SMALLHYTHE PLACE

Thames
Estuary

Canterbury ●

● Ashford

SOUTH FORELAND ▲
LIGHTHOUSE

BUILDINGS & GARDENS

COAST

The Trust owns 450 acres of land on either side of Dover; 67 acres of cliff and farmland with fine walks to the south west at **Great Farthingloe** [179: TR2902393], 52 acres of clifftop grassland behind the port of Dover and the remainder at St Margaret's Bay to the north-east, including **Bockhill Farm** which together with Kingsdown Leas incorporates about a mile of the famous white cliffs. [♿] Paths across Bockhill Farm are suitable for wheelchair users – (a strong pusher is needed) [179: TR372448].

[👤] Further north at **Sandwich Bay** [179: TR347620] and **Pegwell Bay** [179: TR343627] are 550 acres of coastal saltmarsh, sand dunes, mudflats and foreshore, managed for the Trust as a nature reserve by the Kent Trust for Nature Conservation and forming part of a Site of Special Scientific Interest (SSSI). Guided walks can be arranged from the Sandwich Bay Bird Observatory. Formed by the serpentine river Stour which

KITTIWAKE

133

finally reaches the sea at Pegwell Bay, the saltings, mudflats and freshwater marshes attract migrant waders as well as British sea and shore birds, including some rare species. One of the footpaths is suitable for wheelchairs and leads to an accessible birdhide. Access to this is from the Pegwell Bay side. Send an s.a.e. for a leaflet to the KTNC, The Annexe, 1A Bower Mount Road, Maidstone, Kent ME16 8AX (tel. Maidstone (0622) 753017).

COUNTRYSIDE

The Trust owns a row of 16th- and 17th-century houses in the lovely village of **Chiddingstone** near Edenbridge, including the Castle Inn, the post office and stores. There is public footpath access to the **Chiding Stone** standing on half an acre of land given to the Trust by Lord Astor of Hever.

East of Trottiscliffe (now popularly spelt Troseley) is **Coldrum Long Barrow** [188; TQ654607], a megalithic burial chamber surrounded by standing stones. The tomb was opened in 1910 and 22 skeletons were found, dating from 3,000 BC – the New Stone Age. Not far away south-west of Wrotham at **Oldbury Hill** [188: TQ582561] is the southern half of an Iron Age hill-fort, where flint implements have been found, thought to date back to Neanderthal times. At **Wrotham Water** [188: TQ629597] are 335 acres of farmland with footpath access including part of the North Downs Way.

At **Toys Hill,** south of Brasted [188: TQ465517] and on the neighbouring **Ide Hill** the Trust owns some 400 acres of heath and woodland including several viewpoints on Toys Hill where there is also a wheelchair route . The Trust's founder, Octavia Hill, knew this area well, and 100 acres of woodland given by the Sevenoaks District Council here bears her name. Part of the area is a Site of Special Scientific Interest. *Note:* These areas were badly devastated by the storm of October, 1987; and some woodlands no longer exist.

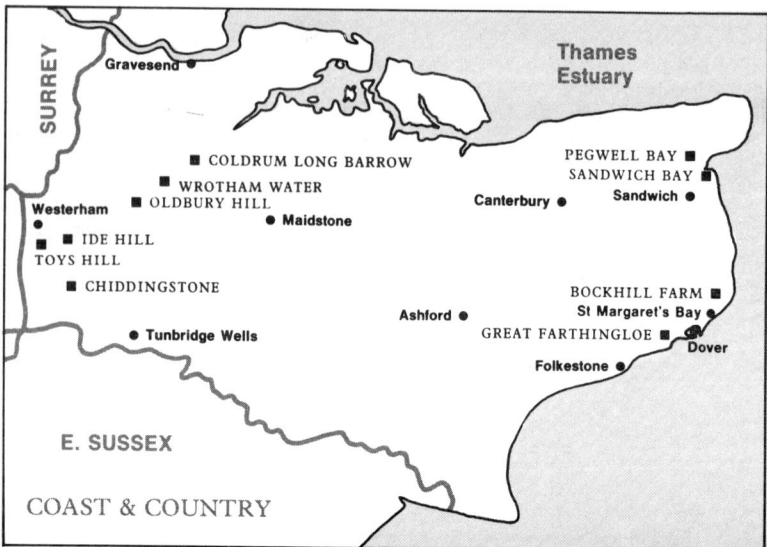

COAST & COUNTRY

CHARTWELL 🏠 ❀   ✕ ◩ ▦

Westerham TN16 1PS (tel. Edenbridge (0732) 866368)

Home of Sir Winston Churchill from 1924: the rooms, left as they were in his lifetime, evoke his career and interests, with pictures, maps, documents and personal mementoes; a museum of his many gifts and uniforms; terraced gardens and lake with the famous black swans; the garden studio contains many of Sir Winston's paintings

Note: Owing to the large numbers visiting Chartwell, entry to the house is by timed, numbered ticket; the waiting time may be spent in the garden, but visitors are warned that occasionally in summer the delay in gaining admission to the house is considerable

🄾   **House only:** 2–28 March & Nov: Sat, Sun & Wed only 11–4.30. **House, garden & studio:** 30 March to end Oct: Tues, Wed & Thur 12–5.30: Sat, Sun & BH Mon 11–5.30. Last admissions ½hr before closing. Closed Good Fri and Tues following BH. Group reduction for pre-booked parties on Tues am only (except after BH) until 12 noon (tel. Administrator)

🄲   Shop open same times as house

£   House only (March & Nov) £2.20. House and garden £3.70; children £1.90. Garden only £1.50; children 80p. Studio 50p, no reduction. Pre-booked parties (Tues am) £3. Parking 500yds, hilly; steps

♿   Tel. Administrator for special parking; ground floor accessible; small lift to first floor; garden difficult; ♿ WC in coach park

🐕   In grounds only, on leads

🍴♿   Coffee, lunches and teas; licensed self-service restaurant (no spirits). Open same days as house March & Nov: 10.30–4; April to end Oct: 10.30–5

     Events: 14–15 June, 'Dance the Night Away'; 26 July, Sheepdog trial; for details contact NT Regional Office (tel. Lamberhurst (0892) 890651). ♿

➡   2m S of Westerham, fork left off B2026 after 1½m [188: TQ455515] *Bus:* London & Country 320 BR Bromley N–Westerham (passing BR Bromley S) (tel: 081-668 7261); Kentish Bus 20/3 Sevenoaks–Westerham (passing BR Sevenoaks) (tel: Gravesend (0474) 321300). On both, alight Westerham, 2m. *Station:* Edenbridge (U) 4m; Edenbridge Town 4½m; Sevenoaks 6½m

EMMETTS GARDEN ❀

Ide Hill, Sevenoaks TN14 6AY (tel. Ide Hill (073 275) 367 or 429)

5-acre hillside garden; one of the highest gardens in Kent with splendid views over the Weald, noted for its fine collection of rare trees and shrubs; lovely spring and autumn colours; rose and rock gardens now open and further restoration work in progress

🄾   29 March to end Oct: Wed to Sun & BH Mon: 2–6. Last admissions 5

£   £2. Pre-booked parties £1.50, children 80p   *continued*

135

⬥🖼 Most of garden; golf buggy (seats 3) available from car park to ticket hut only; ♿ WC. Fountain & waterfall; scented azaleas in spring and roses in summer. Beware sheer drop at end of shrub garden

🐕 On leads only

☕♿ Tea-room, open 2–5 on same days as garden

Events: 17–18 Aug, Country Fair (tel. Lamberhurst (0892) 890651). ♿

➡ 1½m S of A25 on Sundridge to Ide Hill road, 1½m N of Ide Hill off B2042, leave M25 at exit 5, then 4m [188: TQ477524] *Bus:* Nu-Venture 404 from BR Sevenoaks, alight Ide Hill, 1½m (tel. Maidstone (0622) 882288) *Station:* Sevenoaks 4½m; Penshurst (U) 5½m

IGHTHAM MOTE 🏰✤✝   ✈✉

Ivy Hatch, Sevenoaks TN15 0NT (tel. Plaxtol (0732) 810378)

A beautiful medieval moated manor house with important later additions; features include the Great Hall; Old Chapel and crypt c.1340; Tudor chapel with painted ceiling c.1520; drawing room with Jacobean fireplace and frieze; 18th-century Palladian window; major new exhibition in Billiards Room

Notes: The house may be very busy on Sun between 2 & 4: visitors may be asked to wait. Large scale repairs in progress; an excellent opportunity to see conservation in action

◎ **👤** 29 March to end Oct: daily except Tues & Sat, weekdays 12–5.30; Sun & BH Mon 11–5.30. Last admissions 5. Pre-booked guided tours for groups of 20 or more (no reduction), on open weekdays am only; tel. Administrator

🛍 **❄** Shop as house. Also 6 Nov to 21 Dec: Wed to Sat 11–4

£ Weekdays £3. Sun & BH. £3.50, children £1.80. Pre-booked parties of 20 or more weekdays £2.50, children £1.30 (no reduction Sun & BH)

👶 Baby feeding/changing facilities available

♿ Garden, courtyard, Great Hall, tea-bar and part of shop only; special parking available; apply to ticket kiosk; ♿ WC

☕ Tea-bar open as house but closes 5

Events: 5 & 6 July, 'Midsummer Magic' concert; for details contact NT Regional Office (tel. Lamberhurst (0892) 890651). ♿

➔ 6m E of Sevenoaks, off A25, and 2½m S of Ightham, off A227 [188: TQ584535] *Bus:* Maidstone & District 222/3 BR Borough Green–BR Tunbridge Wells, alight Ivy Hatch, ¾m (tel. Medway (0634) 832666); Auto-Reps 306 Sevenoaks–BR Borough Green, alight Ightham Common, 1½m (tel. Gravesend (0474) 327207) *Station:* Borough Green & Wrotham 3½m; Hildenborough 4m

---

KNOLE 🏰 ♠ ❄   ✂ ✗

Sevenoaks TN15 0RP (tel. Sevenoaks (0732) 450608)

One of the largest English houses, dating from 1456; enlarged in 1603 by Thomas Sackville, 1st Earl of Dorset, to whom it was granted by Elizabeth I; state rooms with collection of portraits, including works by Reynolds and Gainsborough; silver; tapestries, hangings and important collection of 17th-century English furniture; deer park

◎ **👤** **House:** Good Fri 29 March to end Oct: Wed to Sat and BH Mon 11–5; Sun 2–5. Last admissions 4. Extra rooms shown on Fri (except Good Fri). Guided tours for pre-booked groups of 25 or more on Tues only throughout season (except Tues following BH Mon); no reduction. **Garden:** May to Sept: first Wed in each month only. **Park:** open daily to pedestrians by courtesy of Lord Sackville

🛍 **❄** Shop open as house. Also 6 Nov to 21 Dec: Wed to Sat 11–4

£ £3 (Fri £3.50, children £1.80). Pre-booked parties of 25 or more accepted on Wed, Thur & Sat £2. Garden only 50p. Parking (NT members free) £5.50 (Fri £6) includes one admission to house. Park free to pedestrians. Only vehicles carrying visitors to the house are allowed in the park

♿ **🦽** Great Hall, park and garden only. Herb and wilderness garden

☕ Tea-room opening in 1991

🐕 In park only, on lead

➔ At S end of Sevenoaks town; just E of A225 [188: TQ532543] *Bus:* From surrounding areas to bus station, ¼m (tel. Gravesend (0474) 312300) *Station:* Sevenoaks 1½m

OLD SOAR MANOR ▣   ✉

Plaxtol, Borough Green TN15 0QX

The solar block of a late 13th-century knight's dwelling

Old Soar is in the guardianship of English Heritage

⊙   29 March to end Sept: daily 9.30–6.30

£   Free. No WCs. Exhibition on Manor and surrounding areas

🐕   On leads only

➔   2m S of Borough Green (A25); approached via A227 and Plaxtol; narrow lane, unsuitable for coaches [188: TQ619541] *Bus:* Maidstone & District 222 BR Borough Green–BR Tunbridge Wells, alight E end of Plaxtol, thence ¾m by footpath (tel. Medway (0634) 832666) *Station:* Borough Green & Wrotham 2½m

OWLETTS ▣❀   ✉✉

Cobham, Gravesend DA12 3AP

A modest red brick Charles II house with contemporary staircase and plasterwork ceiling; small pleasure and kitchen gardens; property administered and largely maintained on the Trust's behalf by the tenant

⊙   April to end Sept: Wed & Thur only, 2–5. Last admissions 4.30

£   £1.20. No reduction for children or parties. Parties by arrangement; please write to tenant. No WCs

➔   1m S of A2 at W end of village, at junction of roads from Dartford and Sole Street [177: TQ665687] *Station:* Sole Street 1m

QUEBEC HOUSE ▣   ✉✉

Westerham TN16 1TD (tel. Westerham (0959) 62206)

General Wolfe spent his early years in this gabled, red brick 17th-century house; four rooms containing portraits, prints and memorabilia relating to Wolfe's family and career are on view; in the Tudor stable block is an exhibition about the Battle of Quebec and the parts played by Wolfe and his adversary, the Marquis de Montcalm

⊙   29 March to end Oct: daily except Thurs & Sat 2–6. Last admissions 5.30. Parties only by prior arrangement with Custodian

£   £1.70, children 90p. Pre-booked parties £1.20 (prices include exhibition). No picnicking. Car parking nearby

▣   In village, not NT

PLEASE REFER TO PAGES 5–9

→ At E end of village, on N side of A25, facing junction with B2026 Edenbridge road [187: TQ449541] *Bus:* All services quoted for Chartwell (page 135) passing close to the House *Station:* Sevenoaks 4m; Oxted 4m

ST JOHN'S JERUSALEM GARDEN ❖ 🏠   ✂

Sutton-at-Hone, Dartford DA4 9HQ

Large garden, moated by the River Darent; the house, formerly a Knight's Hospitallers' church, was later rebuilt as a private house; a small section was retained for family worship, but later was converted into a billiard room; only this section and the garden are open; administered and largely maintained for the Trust by the tenant

🅾 **Former chapel & garden only:** April to end Oct: Wed only, 2–6. Last admissions 5.30

💷 80p. No reduction for children or parties. Parties by arrangement; please write to tenant. No coaches

♿ Garden only accessible

→ 3m S of Dartford at Sutton-at-Hone, on E side of A225 [177: TQ558703] *Bus:* Kentish Bus 13–15 from Dartford (passing BR Dartford) (tel. Gravesend (0474) 312300) *Station:* Farningham Road ¼m

SCOTNEY CASTLE GARDEN ❖ 🏛   ✂

Lamberhurst, Tunbridge Wells TN3 8JN (tel. Lamberhurst (0892) 890651)

One of England's most romantic garden landscapes; surrounding the ruins of a 14th-century moated castle, old castle open during summer months

🅾 **Garden only:** 30 March to 10 Nov: Wed to Fri 11–6; Sat, Sun & BH Mon 2–6, or sunset if earlier. Last admissions ½hr before closing. **Old Castle:** May to 25 Aug: same times

🏠❖ Shop open as garden. Also 12 Nov to 20 Dec: Tues to Fri 11–4   *continued*

139

£ Wed to Fri £2. Sat, Sun & BH Mon £2.80. Pre-booked parties £1.60, children £1; (no party reduction on Sat, Sun or BH Mon). Hilly approach to garden. Picnicking in car park area

♿ ◉ Garden partly accessible to wheelchair users, but strong companion necessary; path very steep in places. Herb garden

Events: 28–31 Aug, Shakespeare play (for details contact NT Regional Office (tel. Lamberhurst (0892) 890651)

♨ In Goudhurst village (not NT)

➜ 1m S of Lamberhurst on A21 [188: TQ688353] *Bus:* Maidstone & District 256 Tunbridge Wells–Wadhurst (passing BR Tunbridge Wells), alight Lamberhurst Green, 1m (tel. Medway (0634) 832666) *Station:* Wadhurst 5½m

---

SISSINGHURST CASTLE GARDEN ❀ ⌂ ⌂ ✗ ✗ ⊞

Sissinghurst, nr Cranbrook TN17 2AB (tel. Cranbrook (0580) 712850)

The famous connoisseurs' garden created by the late Vita Sackville-West and her husband, Sir Harold Nicolson, between the surviving parts of an Elizabethan mansion; also the study where Vita Sackville-West worked, and the long library

Note: The garden may be very busy at around 3pm; visitors may be asked to wait. As paths are narrow and uneven visitors are asked to leave pushchairs at the entrance; baby back carriers are available. No tripods in garden

◯ Good Fri 29 March to 13 Oct: Tues to Fri 1–6.30; Sat, Sun & Good Fri 10–6.30. Closed all Mon, incl. BH. Last admissions 6

⌂ ❄ Shop same days as garden. Tues to Fri 12–6.30; Sat & Sun 10–6.30. Also open 23 Oct to 21 Dec: Wed to Sat 11–4

£ Tues to Sat £4; Sun £4.50, children £2.30. Coaches and parties by appointment only; reduction on weekdays. (No coaches Sat or Sun pm.) Tel. Administrator for details

♿ Admission restricted to two chairs at any one time because of narrow and uneven paths. Disabled visitors may be set down at garden entrance. Plan of recommended wheelchair route available. ♿ WC

♨ ❄ Coffee, lunches, teas in Granary Restaurant (no spirits) Tues to Fri 12–6, Sat & Sun 10–6. Also open 23 Oct to 21 Dec: Wed to Sat 11–4. Picnicking in the car park and in grass field in front of castle only

➜ 2m NE of Cranbrook, 1m E of Sissinghurst village (A262) [188: TQ8138] *Bus:* Maidstone & District 4/5 Maidstone–Hastings (passing BR Staplehurst), alight Sissinghurst, 1¼m (tel. Medway (0634) 832666) *Station:* Staplehurst 5½m

SMALLHYTHE PLACE 🏠 ❀   ⊠ ⊠ ⊠

Smallhythe, Tenterden TN30 7NG (tel. Tenterden (058 06) 2334)

The Ellen Terry memorial; early 16th-century half-timbered house; home of Ellen Terry from 1899 to 1928; many personal and theatrical mementoes

O   Good Fri 29 March to end Oct: daily except Thur & Fri (open Good Fri) 2–6, or dusk if earlier. Last admissions ½hr before closing

£   £1.80. Pre-booked parties Tues am only; no reduction; no parties at other times. Max. 25 people in the house at any one time, garden has shelter for a further 25. No picnicking. 🦮 Guide dogs admitted when house is not busy

➔   2m S of Tenterden, on E side of the Rye road (B2082) [189: TQ893300]
Bus: Fuggles 312 BR Rye–Tenterden (tel. Cranbrook (0580) 240522)
Station: Rye 8m; Appledore 8m; Headcorn 10m

SOUTH FORELAND LIGHTHOUSE 🏠

St Margaret's-at-Cliffe

A distinctive landmark on the White Cliffs of Dover with views to France; built in 1843 and used by Marconi for first radio communications as an aid to navigation in 1898; tower only open, the cottage is tenanted

Note: There are no parking facilities at the lighthouse which can be reached on foot from NT car park at Langdon Cliffs (2 miles) or from St Margaret's village

O   30 March to end Oct: Sat, Sun & BH Mon 2–5.30. Last admissions 5

£   £1. No reduction for parties, which must pre-book with the Regional Office (tel. Lamberhurst (0892) 890651)

➔   At St Margaret's at Cliffe [179: TR359433] *Bus:* East Kent 90/A Folkestone– Deal (passing BR Dover Priory & Walmer) (tel. Thanet (0843) 581333)
Station: Martin Mill 2½m

SPRIVERS GARDEN ❀   ⊠

Horsmonden TN12 8DR (tel. Brenchley (089272) 3553)

Flowering and foliage shrubs, herbaceous borders, old walls, spring and summer bedding; tenanted property; administered and largely maintained on the Trust's behalf by the tenant

O   Garden only May to 25 Sept: Wed only 2–5.30. Last admissions 5

£   £1.10. No reduction for children or parties. Parking limited; space for one coach only. No WCs

➔   2m N of Lamberhurst on B2162 [188: TQ6940] *Bus:* Maidstone & District 297 BR Tunbridge Wells–Tenterden (tel. Medway (0634) 832666)
Station: Paddock Wood 4m

KENT

STONEACRE 🏠❀🐴 ✈✉

Otham, Maidstone ME15 8RS (tel. Maidstone (0622) 862871)

A small half-timbered mainly late 15th-century manor house, with great hall and crownpost; garden; tenanted property; administered and largely maintained on the Trust's behalf by the tenant

🅾   April to end Oct: Wed & Sat 2–6. Last admissions 5

💷   £1.40. No reduction for parties

👁   Garden recommended to accompanied visually handicapped visitors

➡   At N end of Otham village, 3m SE of Maidstone, 1m S of A20 [188: TQ800535] *Bus:* Maidstone & District 12, 812 Maidstone–Tenterden (passing close BR Maidstone E & W), to within 1m (tel. Medway (0634) 832666) *Station:* Bearsted 2m

TUDOR YEOMAN'S HOUSE 🏠🐴 ✉

Sole Street, Cobham DA12 3AX

A yeoman's house of timber construction; tenanted property; administered and largely maintained on the Trust's behalf by the tenant

🅾   Main hall only, by written application to tenant

💷   50p. No reduction for children or parties. No WCs

➡   1m SW of Cobham, on W side of B2009, just N of Sole Street Station [177: TQ657677] *Station:* Sole Street, few yds

WOOL HOUSE 🏠🐴 ✉

Wells Street, Loose, Maidstone ME15 0EH

A 15th-century half-timbered house, thought to have been used for the cleaning of wool; tenanted property; administered and largely maintained on the Trust's behalf by the tenant

🅾   April to end Sept by written application to tenant

💷🐴   50p. No reduction for children or parties. No WCs

➡   3m SE of Maidstone, ¼m W of the Cranbrook Road (A229) [188: TQ755521] *Bus:* Maidstone & District 4/5 Maidstone–Hastings (passing close BR Maidstone E & W) (tel. Medway (0634) 832666) *Station:* Maidstone E 3m; Maidstone W 3m

Lancashire

BANK HOUSE FARM
JACK SCOUT AND
GEORGE'S LOT
■ EAVES & WATERSLACK WOODS
● Carnforth

N. YORKS

Irish
Sea

● Lancaster

● Blackpool

▲ GAWTHORPE HALL
● Burnley

● Preston

● Blackburn

River Ribble

W. YORKS

STUBBINS ESTATE ■
● Ramsbottom

Southport
●
▲ RUFFORD
  OLD HALL
● Ormskirk

GREATER MANCHESTER

MERSEYSIDE

COAST AND COUNTRY

The Trust owns nearly 200 acres of land at **Silverdale**, overlooking the saltmarshes of the
Kent estuary just over the Cumbrian border. Silverdale village was once on the River
Kent, but the river changed its course in the 1920s and now flows some 4 miles away.
Fifty-seven acres of **Bank House Farm** [97: SD460752] on the northern fringe of the
village are owned by the Trust with neat limestone walls enclosing a patchwork of small
fields and spinneys. The shoreline is marked with low limestone cliffs and the fields are
full of daffodils in the spring time. A coastal footpath crosses this property. **Jack Scout,** 16
acres of cliff and foreshore on the fringe of Morecambe Bay, was the first coastal property
north of the River Ribble to be owned by the Trust [97: SD459737]. It was acquired in
1983, and has much to interest historians, scientists, botanists, birdwatchers and
country-lovers. There are extensive views from the clifftops to the Lake District hills
across the Kent estuary.

143

More recently still the Trust acquired **George's Lot,** a 9-acre cliff field, to extend the length of foreshore open to the public [97: SD459750]. 🏛 All this coastal limestone pasture and scrub is crossed by public footpaths, and a little further inland 106 acres of **Eaves and Waterslack Woods** present a fine variety of trees and other flora, with many woodland birds and animals and a 2-mile nature walk [97: SD465758].

North of Bury, astride the B6214, is the **Stubbins Estate,** 436 acres of agricultural land with numerous public footpaths through fields and woodland full of interesting wildlife and flowers. The estate, given to the Trust in 1943, provides access from the industrial Rossendale Valley to Holcombe Moor, a bleak area of rough grassland and heath, notable especially for its numerous bird species [109: SD785177].

GAWTHORPE HALL 🏛 ❄   ✖ ✉ ✏ 📷

Padiham, nr Burnley, Lancashire BB12 8UA (tel. Padiham (0282) 78511)

House built in 1600–1605; one-time home of the Shuttleworth family; restored by Sir Charles Barry in the 1850s; Barry's designs recently re-created in the principal rooms; display of Rachel Kay-Shuttleworth textile collections; private study by arrangement; collection of portraits from the National Portrait Gallery; 17th-century estate building, recently restored, houses a broad programme of art, craft and management courses

Let to Lancashire County Council

[O] [❄]   **Hall:** Good Fri 29 March to 3 Nov: daily except Mon & Fri, but open Good Fri & BH Mon, 1–5. Last admissions 4.15. **Garden:** all year: daily 10–6

[🛍] [❄]   Craft gallery and shop. Open 29 March to 22 Dec: Tues to Fri 11–5, Sat & Sun 1–5

[£]   House and garden £2. Parties by prior arrangement. Free parking 150yds. We regret house is not suitable for baby backpacks or pushchairs

[♿]   Access across cobbled yard to shop and coach house gallery. Unisex [♿] WC in same area. Limited access to ground floor of hall, via ramps (prior warning of visit is essential). Some steps inside ground floor. Access to grounds and garden incl. rose garden and top terrace; some steps and gradients. Cars may bring passengers to front door of Hall, and to courtyard, for shop and tea-room

⬛✿ Tea-room open as shop. Please check in advance; seating limited. Run by Gawthorpe Enterprises Ltd

➡ On E outskirts of Padiham; ¼m drive to house on N of A671 [103: SD806340] *Bus:* Ribble 150 Preston–Burnley (passing BR Blackburn); also frequent services from Burnley. All pass close BR Burnley Barracks & Burnley Manchester Road. (tel. Preston (0772) 263333) *Station:* Rose Grove (U) 2m

RUFFORD OLD HALL ⌂✿ ✉📷

Rufford, nr Ormskirk L40 1SG (tel. Rufford (0704) 821254)

One of the finest 15th-century buildings in Lancashire, the late medieval half-timbered hall is remarkable for its ornate hammer-beam roof and screen; here, and in the Carolean Wing, altered in 1821, there are fine collections of 17th-century oak furniture, 16th-century arms, armour and tapestries

🅾 **House:** 30 March to 3 Nov: daily except Fri 1–5. Last admissions 4.30. **Garden:** same days 12–5.30; Sun 1–5.30

🏠✿ Shop open as garden. Also 5 Nov to 19 Dec: daily except Mon & Fri 12.30–5 (Sun 2–5)

£ Hall and garden £2.30, children £1.20. Garden only £1.20. Reduction for pre-booked parties, not Sun. We regret house is not suitable for baby backpacks and pushchairs

♿ Garden only. ✿ House & garden suitable if escorted

🐕 In grounds only, on leads

⬛✿ Light lunches and teas; available 12–5; Sun 2–5 (teas only). 5 Nov to 19 Dec, as shop, see above. Picnic site adjacent to car park

Events: Please send s.a.e. for details

➡ 7m N or Ormskirk, in village of Rufford on E side of A59 [108: SD463160] *Bus:* Ribble/N Western 101 Liverpool–Preston (tel. Preston (0772) 263333) *Station:* Rufford (U), not Sun, ½m; Burscough Bridge 2½m

145

Leicestershire

STAUNTON HAROLD CHURCH ✝ ♠   ✈ ✉

Staunton Harold, Ashby-de-la-Zouch (tel. Melbourne (0332) 863822)

One of the very few churches to be built during the Commonwealth, erected by Sir Robert Shirley, an ardent Royalist; interior retains original 17th-century cushions and hangings; wrought-iron screen by Robert Bakewell; fine panelling and painted ceilings; parkland setting, and adjacent Staunton Harold Hall, not NT

O	30 March to end Oct: Wed to Sun & BH Mon 11–1 & 2–5 or sunset if earlier
£	Free; collection box. No WCs
♿	Church and park largely suitable
⬛	Light refreshments available at Hall and in Stable Block (not NT)
➔	5m NE of Ashby-de-la-Zouch, W of B587 [128: SK379208] *Bus:* Kinch X8 Birmingham–Nottingham (tel. Sileby (0509) 816161); also Paul James 99 Nottingham–Coalville (tel. Leicester (0533) 313391). Both pass close BR Nottingham. On both alight Lount, 1m. Trent 68/9 BR Derby–Melbourne (passing close BR Derby) thence 3m (tel. Derby (0332) 292200)

146

Lincolnshire

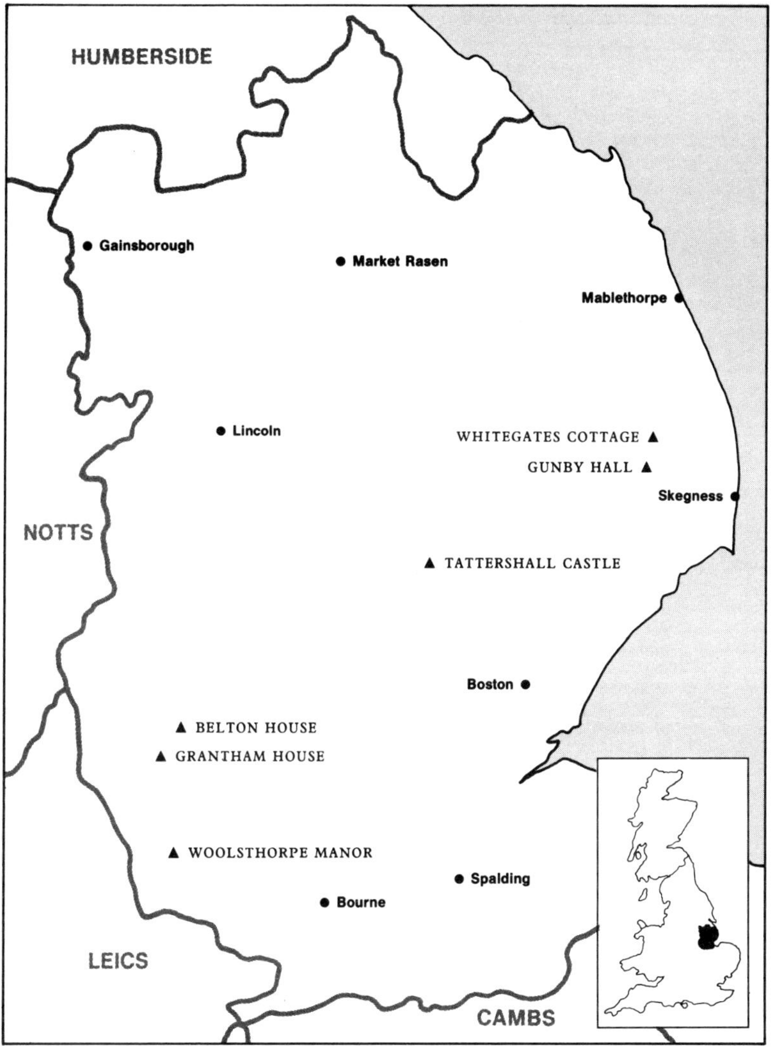

HUMBERSIDE

● Gainsborough

● Market Rasen

Mablethorpe ●

● Lincoln

WHITEGATES COTTAGE ▲

GUNBY HALL ▲

Skegness ●

NOTTS

▲ TATTERSHALL CASTLE

Boston ●

▲ BELTON HOUSE

▲ GRANTHAM HOUSE

▲ WOOLSTHORPE MANOR

● Spalding

● Bourne

LEICS

CAMBS

147

LINCOLNSHIRE

BELTON HOUSE 🏠❄️🏠♠✝ ⊠

Grantham NG32 2LS (tel. Grantham (0476) 66116)

The crowning achievement of Restoration country house architecture, built 1685–88 for Sir John Brownlow; alterations by James Wyatt in the 1770s, plasterwork ceilings by Edward Goudge, wood carvings of the Grinling Gibbons school; portraits, furniture, tapestries, oriental porcelain; family silver gilt and Speaker Cust's silver; exhibition focusing on the abdication of Edward VIII; formal gardens; orangery; landscaped park with Bellmount Tower; children's TV series 'Moondial' filmed here; fine church (not NT) with family monuments; lakeside walk

O **House:** 30 March to end Oct: Wed to Sun & BH Mon 1–5.30. **Garden & Park:** 11–5.30. Last admissions 5. Free access to Park on foot only from Lion Lodge gates all year (this does not give admittance to house, garden or Adventure Playground). Access to Bellmount Woods and Tower from separate car park. Park may be closed occasionally for special events

   Notes: Educational visits from school parties welcomed (Education Liaison Officer, schoolroom and teacher's pack available); also 'grounds only' arrangements available for school parties; contact Administrator for details

🗑️❄️ Shop same days as house 12–5.30. Also Nov to 22 Dec: Sat & Sun 12–4

£ House & garden £3.50. Parties £2.60 (incl. free admission for organiser)

🎢 Extensive Adventure Playground, incl. under-6 'corral'; miniature train rides in summer; ♿ access to refreshment kiosk, but rough paths to playground; difficult in wet weather

♿ House difficult; please arrange with Administrator to visit Wed to Fri when less busy. Park, garden, restaurant and shop accessible; car parking by prior arrangement; ♿ WC

🐕 In parkland only, on leads

🍴♿ Lunches & teas in licensed restaurant open as shop. Open for functions and booked parties throughout year

   Events: Belton Horse Trials (6–7 April); concerts in summer; occasional events in the Park; special exhibitions; details from Administrator; s.a.e. please

➡️ 3m NE of Grantham on the A607 Grantham-Lincoln road, easily reached, and signposted from the A1 [130: SK929395] *Bus:* Road Car 601 Grantham–Lincoln; 609 Grantham–Sleaford (both pass close BR Grantham) (tel. Lincoln (0522) 532424 *Station:* Grantham 3m

GRANTHAM HOUSE 🏠❄️♠ ⊠✖

Castlegate, Grantham NG31 6SS

The house dates from 1380, but has been extensively altered and added to throughout the centuries, resulting in a pleasant mixture of architectural styles; the walled gardens run down to the river; on opposite bank Sedgwick Meadows, also NT, form an open space in the centre of town

🅾 Ground floor only April to end Sept: Wed 2–5 by written appointment only
with the tenant, Major-General Sir Brian Wyldbore-Smith

💷 ♿ £1. Due to size of the rooms, numbers in parties should not exceed seven.
No WCs

➡ Immediately E of Grantham Church [130: SK916362] *Bus:* Road Car 601
Grantham–Lincoln, to within ¼m (tel. Lincoln (0522) 532424)
Station: Grantham 1m

GUNBY HALL 🏠🌸🎨   ✖

Gunby, nr Spilsby PE23 5SS

Red brick house with stone dressings, built in 1700 and extended in 1870s; early 18th-century wainscoting and fine oak staircase; English furniture; portraits by Reynolds; contemporary stable block; walled kitchen and flower garden; sweeping lawns and borders

🅾 **Ground floor of house & garden:** 30 March to end Sept: Wed 2–6. Last
admissions 5.30. Closed public holidays. Garden also open Thur 2–6. House &
garden also open Tues, Thur and Fri by written appointment only with
J. D. Wrisdale at above address

💷 House & garden £2. Garden only £1. No reduction for parties. Access roads
unsuitable for coaches which must park in layby at gates ½m from Hall

♿ 🏵 Garden only. Rose & herb garden

🐕 In garden only, on leads

Events: Occasional concerts

➡ 2½m NW of Burgh-le-Marsh, 7m W of Skegness on S side of A158 (access off
roundabout) [122: TF467668] *Bus:* Road Car 6 Skegness–Lincoln (passing
close BR Skegness) (tel. Lincoln (0522) 532424) *Station:* Skegness 7m

TATTERSHALL CASTLE 🏰🏠   ✖

Tattershall, Lincoln LN4 4LR (tel. Coningsby (0526) 42543)

Built c.1440 for Ralph Cromwell, Lord Treasurer of England, an important example of early brick building; tower containing state apartments rescued from dereliction and restored by Lord Curzon 1911–14; four great chambers with ancillary rooms, brick vaulting and late Gothic fireplaces, tapestries; new information displays in turret rooms

🅾🌸 29 March to end Oct: daily 10.30–6. Nov to end March 1992, incl. 1 Jan: daily
12–4.30. Last admissions ½hr before closing. Closed 25 & 26 Dec

🏪🌸 Shop open same times as Castle

💷 £1.80. Parties £1.40. Advance booking essential for coach parties

♿🏵 Ground floor of castle and grounds. ♿ WC with nappy-changing facility

🐕 In car park only on leads   *continued*

149

Notes: Castle is particularly suitable for school groups. Lincoln Cathedral and Boston 'Stump' visible from Castle on clear days. Picnicking welcome in grounds. Limited number of floodlit evening visits available for organised parties £2.50, children £1.20 (incl. NT members). Min charge £100

➡️ On S side of A153, 15m NE of Sleaford; 10m SW of Horncastle [122: TF209575] *Bus:* Brylaine Boston–Woodhall Spa (passing close BR Boston) (tel. East Kirkby (079 03) 212 *Station:* Ruskington (U) 10m

WHITEGATES COTTAGE 🏠

Mill Lane, Gunby Hall Estate, Bratoft, nr Spilsby

A small cottage built c.1770 to provide accommodation adjacent to land distant from the main body of the farm; constructed in the once common, now extremely rare, Lincolnshire vernacular tradition of mud and stud walling under a long-straw thatch roof; recently restored using traditional methods and materials

🅾️ April to end Sept: Wed 2–6 by written appointment only with the tenant, Mr Zaremba

💷 £1. Because of the small size of the rooms in the cottage, numbers in parties visiting the property should not exceed six at any one time. WCs at Gunby Hall

➡️ 2m W of Burgh le Marsh, 8m W of Skegness. Approached by Gunby Lane off A158 just W of the roundabout N of Gunby Hall. *Public transport:* as for Gunby Hall (see p. 149)

WOOLSTHORPE MANOR 🏛️   ✖️

Woolsthorpe, Colsterworth, nr Grantham (tel. Grantham (0476) 860338)

Small 17th-century farmhouse, birthplace and family home of Sir Isaac Newton; some of his major work was formulated here, during the Plague years (1665–66) 'in the prime of my age for invention'; early edition of his Principia Mathematica, *pub. 1687, on display*

🅾️ 30 March to end Oct: Sat to Wed incl. BH Mon 1–5.30. Last admissions 5

Notes: In the interests of preservation, numbers of visitors admitted to rooms at any one time may be limited; particularly at peak weekends and Bank Holidays

💷 ♿ £2. No reduction for parties which must book in advance with the Custodian. Parking for coaches limited to one at a time. Picnicking in car park only

♿ Limited access to ground floor only (assistance required)

🐕 In car park only, on leads

➡️ 7m S of Grantham, ½m NW of Colsterworth, 1m W of A1 (not to be confused with Woolsthorpe near Belvoir) [130: SK924244] *Bus:* Road Car 606–8 Grantham–South Witham (passing close BR Grantham) (tel. Lincoln (0522) 532424) *Station:* Grantham 7m

London

HERTS

ESSEX

● Harrow

Romford ●

▲ FENTON HOUSE

▲ SUTTON HOUSE   ▲ EASTBURY
                      HOUSE
BLEWCOAT SCHOOL   ▲ RAINHAM
       ▲ 'ROMAN'BATH   HALL

▲ OSTERLEY   ▲ GEORGE INN
  PARK   ● Greenwich
       ▲
   CARLYLE'S HOUSE

Hounslow ●

Kingston-upon-Thames
       ■ EAST SHEEN COMMON
       ▲ HAM HOUSE

   ●   Merton ●   Bromley ●   PETTS WOOD
MORDEN HALL PARK ■   ■
                   ■ WATERMEADS   ■ — CHISLEHURST
                                                COMMON
               Croydon ●   & HAWKWOOD
                   ■ SELSDON WOOD

                                        KENT

SURREY

COUNTRYSIDE

Kent Border: The Trust owns two small strips of **Chislehurst Common,** acquired as part of a scheme for preserving the Common. It also has 88 acres of wood and heathland at neighbouring **Petts Wood** [177: TQ450681] which was bought by public subscription in 1927 as a memorial to the founder of British Summer Time, William Willett. Adjoining this land, at **Hawkwood,** is a further 245 acres of farm and woodland.

Surrey Border: Adjoining Richmond Park, 53 acres of **East Sheen Common** [176: TQ197746] are managed for the Trust by the London Borough of Richmond-upon-Thames. There are nature reserves at **Selsdon Wood** south-east of Croydon [177: TQ357615], and at **Watermeads** on the River Wandle in Mitcham where a key may be obtained from the Warden for a small deposit and annual subscription. The Trust also owns **Morden Hall Park** [176: TQ259687] in the London Borough of Merton. This is a delightful oasis of 124 acres of parkland alongside the River Wandle and new visitor facilities are planned for 1991.

151

LONDON

BLEWCOAT SCHOOL 🏠🛍

23 Caxton Street, Westminster SW1H 0PY (tel. 071-222 2877)

Built in 1709 at the expense of William Green, a local brewer, to provide an education for poor children; in use as a school until 1926, the building was bought by the Trust in 1954 and restored in 1975; now NT London Information Centre and Shop

O ❄ 🛍 All year: Mon to Fri 10–5.30 (23 & 24 Dec closes 4.30); late night shopping Thur until 7; also Sat 7, 14, & 21 Dec 11–4.30. Closed BH Mon, 25–31 Dec, 1 Jan & Good Fri

£ 🐕 Free

→ Near the junction with Buckingham Gate *Bus:* Frequent local services (tel. 071-222 1234) *Station:* Victoria ¼m. *Underground:* St James's Park, few yds

CARLYLE'S HOUSE 🏠 ✖✖

24 Cheyne Row, Chelsea SW3 5HL (tel. 071–352 7087)

18th-century town house, home of Thomas and Jane Carlyle from 1834 until their deaths; contains furniture, books, personal relics and portraits

O 30 March to end Oct: Wed to Sun & BH Mon 11–5. Last admissions 4.30

£ £2.20. No reduction for students or parties, which should not number more than 20. All parties must book in advance with Custodian

Note: Certain rooms have no electric light. Visitors wishing to make close study of interior of the house should avoid dull days early and late in the season

→ Off Cheyne Walk, between Battersea and Albert Bridges on Chelsea Embankment, or off Oakley Street [176: TQ272777] *Bus:* Frequent local services (tel. 071-222 1234) *Station:* Victoria 1½m *Underground:* Sloane Sq 1m

PLEASE REFER TO PAGES 5–9

152

EASTBURY HOUSE

Barking, Essex IG11 9SN

An important example of a medium-sized Elizabethan manor house

Eastbury House is let to the London Borough of Barking and Dagenham

By written appointment only with the Controller of Development & Technical Services, Town Hall, Barking IG11 7LU

Free. No WCs. Very limited access to ground floor

In garden only

In Eastbury Square, ¼m S of Upney station [177: TQ457838]
Bus: Frequent local services (tel. 071-222 1234) *Station:* Barking, thence one stop on Underground District line to Upney ¼m

FENTON HOUSE

Windmill Hill, Hampstead NW3 6RT (tel. 071-435 3471)

Late 17th-century house; walled garden; outstanding collection of porcelain and early keyboard instruments

March: Sat & Sun only 2–6; 30 March to end Oct: Sat to Wed (incl. BH Mon) 11–6. Last admissions 5. Parties during March on weekdays by written appointment

£2.80. No reduction for parties which must book. No parking facilities

Ground floor only

Events: Concerts; s.a.e. for details please

continued

Note: For permission to use the early keyboard instruments, apply in writing to the Custodian

→ Visitors' entrance on W side of Hampstead Grove *Bus:* Frequent local services (tel. 071-222 1234) *Station:* Hampstead Heath 1m. *Underground:* Hampstead 300yds

GEORGE INN 🏠

77 High Street, Southwark SE1 (tel. 071-407 2056)

Only remaining galleried inn in London; famous as a coaching terminus in 18th and 19th centuries; mentioned by Dickens in Little Dorrit

O ❄ During licensing hours

▸ Bar food daily; à la carte restaurant Mon to Fri & Sat evening

→ On E side of Borough High Street, near London Bridge stn *Bus:* Frequent local services (tel. 071-222 1234) *Station & Underground:* London Bridge, few min. walk

HAM HOUSE 🏠❄ ✖✗

Ham, Richmond TW10 7RS (tel. 081-940 1950)

Outstanding Stuart house, built about 1610, redecorated and furnished in 1670s in the most up-to-date style of the time by the Duke and Duchess of Lauderdale; much of this furniture is still in its original rooms today; restored 17th-century garden

Notes: Prices and opening times are subject to alteration as it is the intention that the management of the house and garden will be transferred from the Victoria and Albert Museum to the National Trust. Necessary conservation work is likely to take place on the house during 1991/2 which accounts for the extra months of closure

O ❄ **House:** April to end Sept: daily except Mon 11–5.30. Closed Oct to end March 1992. **Garden:** all year: daily except Mon 11–5.30. **Shop:** as house 11–5

£ House £2; garden free. Pre-booked adult parties £1.20. Parking 400yds

♿ House & garden. Disabled visitors may park near entrance; ♿ WC in garden

▸ Teas and light lunches in garden restaurant (not NT) April to end Oct 11.30–5.30; please check in advance (tel. 081-940 1950). ♿ access difficult

➡️ On S bank of Thames, W of A307, at Petersham [176: TQ172732]
Bus: LT 65 Ealing Broadway–Kingston; 71 Richmond–Chessington Zoo (both passing BR Richmond & Kingston, 71 also passing BR Surbiton) (tel. 071-222 1234) *Station:* Richmond 1½m by footpath, 2m by road; Kingston 2m

OSTERLEY PARK 🏠🌳   ☒

Isleworth, Middlesex TW7 4RB (tel. 081-560 3918)

Elizabethan mansion transformed by Robert Adam 1760–80; with Adam decorations and furniture; 140 acres of parkland

Notes: Prices and opening times are subject to alteration as it is the intention that the management of the house will be transferred from the Victoria and Albert Museum to the National Trust. Necessary conservation work is likely to take place on the house during 1991/2 which accounts for the extra months of closure

🅾️❄️ **House:** 30 March to end Oct: Wed to Fri 1–5; Sat, Sun & BH Mon 11–5. March 1992: Sat & Sun 11–5. Last admissions 4.30
Park: all year 9–7.30 or sunset if earlier. Car park closed 25 & 26 Dec

💷🚶 £2.50. Parties must book; rates on application to Administrator. Park free. Car park, 250yds, £1. Guided tours may be arranged in advance with the Administrator

♿ House & park; special parking arrangements; ♿ WC

🐕 In park only, not allowed on specified areas of lawn to E & S of house (guide dogs excepted)

🍴♿ Teas & light lunches in stables, 1 March to end Oct: Tues to Sun & BH Mon 12–5

➡️ N of Osterley station (Piccadilly line); access from Syon Lane, N side of Great West Road (A4[T]), or from Thornbury Road (¼m E of station) [176: TQ146780] *Bus:* LT 91 Hounslow–Wandsworth ½m. (tel. 071-222 1234) *Station:* Syon Lane, 1¾m *Underground:* Osterley ¾m

RAINHAM HALL 🏠 ✈ ✉

The Broadway, Rainham, Essex RM13 9YN

Attractive red-brick house with stone dressing on symmetrical plan, built in 1729; contemporary wrought iron gates and panelling

O April to end Oct: Wed & BH Mon 2–6; also Sat by written application to tenant

£ £1.80. No reduction for parties. Parking limited to 5 cars. No WCs. ♿ Guide dogs by special arrangement with tenant

→ Just S of the church, 5m E of Barking [177: TQ521821] *Bus:* Frequent local services (tel. 071-222 1234) *Station:* Rainham, few yds

'ROMAN' BATH 🏠

5 Strand Lane WC2

The remains of a bath, restored in the 17th century, believed by some to be Roman

The 'Roman' Bath is administered and maintained by Westminster City Council

O Bath visible through window from pathway all year. Otherwise May to end Sept: every Wed 1–5 by appointment only (24 hours' notice) (tel: 071-798 2063) during office hours

£ 50p. Children under 16 and OAPs 25p. No WCs

→ Just W of Aldwych (Piccadilly Line) station, approach via Surrey Street [176: TQ309809] *Bus:* Frequent local services (tel. 071-222 1234) *Station:* Blackfriars or Charing Cross, both ½m *Underground:* Temple, not Sun, few yds; Embankment ½m

SUTTON HOUSE 🏠

2 & 4 Homerton High Street, Hackney E9 6JQ (tel. 081-986 2264)

An early 16th-century house of red brick built on the familiar H-plan with later additions and alterations; contains original panelling, fireplaces, wall paintings and other features

Note: Sutton House is undergoing substantial repairs and refurbishment; however, on viewing days at least part of the building will be accessible to visitors

O All year: 1st Sun in each month 2–5.30 for viewing prior to complete refurbishment. Special events will be advertised in the Thames & Chilterns NT Regional Newsletter

£ 50p. Parties must book in advance with the Project Manager (tel. 081-986 2264) and may also be admitted by prior arrangement at other times

→ At the corner of Isabella Road and Homerton High Street [176: TQ352851] *Bus:* Frequent local services (tel. 071-222 1234) *Station:* Homerton ¼m; Hackney Central ¼m; Hackney Downs ½m

Merseyside

COAST AND COUNTRY

Formby: see entry on p. 158.

On the north bank of the Mersey at **Speke Hall** (see p. 158), the Trust now owns the remainder of the historic landscape surrounding the Hall, consisting of the **Home Farm and Stocktons Wood** [108: SJ423826]. Research indicates that this wood has never been cultivated, which accounts for its rich variety of insects.

The Wirral Peninsula has a 12-mile long Country Park, several parts of which are owned by the Trust. **Caldy Hill** [108: SJ224855] gives views across the mouth of the River Dee where bird-watchers will find many varieties of duck and waders in large numbers. It has been estimated that over 20,000 oystercatchers roost here. At **Heswall** [108: SJ246825] are 40 acres of meadow and farmland on the Dee Estuary with fine views to Wales.

The acid heathland of **Thurstaston Common** [108: SJ244853] is rich in insect life.

FORMBY 🏛

Victoria Road, Formby (tel. Formby (07048) 78591)

The Trust owns about 500 acres of dune, foreshore and pinewood between the sea and the town of Formby, 2 miles inland; red squirrels can frequently be seen in the pine trees and the shoreline attracts waders such as oystercatchers and sanderlings

O **❋** All year

£ Entrance per car: 30 March to 3 Nov: £1.20; 4 Nov to end March 1992: weekdays 50p, Sat & Sun £1.20. Coaches £2.50 all year. No refreshments or WCs. Two picnic sites

♿ Wheelchair walkway across dunes; hard surface paths to red squirrel reserve and Cornerstone Walk

🐕 Dogs on leads through squirrel reserve

→ 15m N of Liverpool, 2m W of Formby, 2m off A565 [108: SD275080] *Bus:* Merseytravel Circular 4/A, 161/4 BR Formby–BR Freshfield, to within ½m (tel. 051-236 7676) *Station:* Freshfield 1m

SPEKE HALL 🏛❋🏺   ✖ ✖

The Walk, Liverpool L24 1XD (tel. 051-427 7231)

One of the most famous half-timbered houses in the country; the Great Hall evokes the communal living of Tudor times while the small rooms, some with Morris wallpapers, show the Victorian preference for privacy and comfort; fine plasterwork and priestholes; fully equipped Victorian Kitchen and Servants' Hall; restored garden with bluebell walks in woodland area, rhododendrons, rose garden and summer border

Speke Hall is administered and financed by the National Trust with the help of a grant from the National Museums & Galleries on Merseyside

O **❋** **X** **House:** 30 March to 1 Nov: daily except Mon (open BH Mon) 1–5.30. 2 Nov to 15 Dec: Sat & Sun 1–4.30. Guided tours, school visits and evening tours by prior arrangement with Administrator.
Garden: 30 March to 1 Nov: as house. Nov to March 1992: daily except Mon 12–4 (closed 24–26, 31 Dec & 1 Jan).

🛍 **❋** Shop open as house

£ £2.50. Family £6.25. Garden only 50p. Reduction for parties. Car park 200yds

♿ Ground floor (includes most principal rooms); special car parking by arrangement; ♿ WC

🍴♿ Light refreshments and teas; tea-room open from noon; lunches 12–2; parties should book. Picnics in orchard

→ On N bank of the Mersey, 8m SE of Liverpool, 1m S of A561, on W side of Liverpool Airport [108: SJ419825] *Bus:* Merseybus 80, 180 BR Liverpool Lime St–Liverpool Airport (passing BR Garston), 89 BR Garston–Liverpool Airport, thence ½m (tel. 051-236 7676) *Station:* Garston 2m; Hunt's Cross 2m

Norfolk

COAST

There are entries in the following pages for the major coastal estates belonging to the Trust: **Blakeney Point**, p. 160, and **Brancaster**, p. 161.

COUNTRYSIDE

The Trust owns more than 2000 acres at **Horsey:** including **Horsey Windpump** (see p. 163), marshland, marrams, farmland and **the Mere.** There is restricted access to the mere, part of the Norfolk Broads, with brackish water because of seepage from the nearby sea, although it is separated from it by sand dunes. Car park and WCs.

At **West Runton** between Sheringham and Cromer the Trust owns about 70 acres, known locally as the Roman Camp and including the highest point in the county [133: TG184414]. Adjoining **Beeston Regis Heath** is about 30 acres of heathland and woodland giving fine views of the coastline. There is access to the long distance coastal footpath. Car parking for both properties at West Runton ('Roman Camp'). (See also **Sheringham Park**, p. 164.)

PLEASE REFER TO PAGES 5–9

BLAKENEY POINT 🏛️👤🧍

Warden's address: 35 The Cornfield, Langham, Holt, Norfolk NR25 7DQ
(tel. April to Sept: Cley (0263) 740480; Oct to March: Binham (0328) 830401)

A 3½ mile long sand and shingle spit, summer home for over eleven species of seabird, including common and sandwich tern, oystercatcher and ringed plover; winter visitors include large flocks of brent geese; common seal colony

O ✲ All year

£ No landing fee. Access on foot from Cley Beach (3½m) or by ferry from Morston and Blakeney (tidal). Restricted access to certain areas of the Point during the main bird breeding season (May to July)

🧍 For pre-booked school parties and special interest groups (small charge)

🐕 Must be on leads

♿ A 400ft-long wheelchair walkway leads to the bird hide on the Point; local boatmen will help disabled visitors with wheelchairs; please give advance warning of a visit to Warden (address above)

☕ Light refreshments and exhibition in the Old Boathouse (April–Sept)

Note: Information centre at Morston Quay. Car park 50p (NT members free). Adjoining properties at Morston and Stiffkey comprise 1,000 acres of saltmarsh and intertidal mudflats. In July the marshes are coloured purple with sea lavender; breeding ground for waders in the summer and visited by large flocks of brent geese in the winter

→ Morston Quay, Blakeney [133: TG0046] and Cley are all off A149 Cromer to Hunstanton road *Station:* Sheringham 8m

BLICKLING HALL 🏛️✲🏠🌳🧍 ✉️🚫

Blickling, Norwich NR11 6NF (tel. Aylsham (0263) 733084)

17th-century red brick house with fine furniture, pictures, tapestries; great gallery has Jacobean plaster ceiling; notable garden with early 19th-century orangery; parkland with good walks, and lake

O **House:** 30 March to 27 Oct: Tues, Wed, Fri, Sat, Sun & BH Mon 1–5.
Garden: same days as house (daily in July & Aug) 12–5. **Park:** daily all year

🏠 ✲ Shop open same days as garden. Also Nov to 22 Dec: Thur to Sun 11–4; 4 Jan to end March 1992: Sat & Sun 11–4. Plant Sales centre in Old Orchard open daily throughout year 10–5 (closed 25 & 26 Dec, 1 Jan & Good Fri)

£ House & garden £4.50. Garden only £2. Parties £3.50, please book with s.a.e. to Administrator. Private guided tours available outside normal opening hours, details from Administrator. Coarse fishing in lake; permits available from Warden at 1 Park Gates (tel. Aylsham (0263) 734181). Cycle hire in Old Orchard on house open days. Free access to South Front, shop and restaurant on open days

⚠ 👶 Children's guide. Baby slings available

♿ Parking immediately E of Hall; entrance gate from car park to grounds is ramped. House: ramped entrance, then ground floor on one level. A lift enables disabled visitors to see the upper floor. ♿ WCs

🐕 In park and picnic area only, on leads

🍽 ♿ 🌸 Lunches & teas in restaurant all season on open days 11–5 (Nov to 23 Dec & 4 Jan to end March 1992: 11–3.30); table licence (parties by arrangement). ♿ Tea-room has a ramp. Picnic area in old walled garden

Notes: Suite of Conference Rooms for hire: contact Conference Rooms Manager for details. B & B accommodation at the Buckinghamshire Arms, Blickling (tel. Aylsham (0263) 732133)

➜ On N side of B1354, 1½m NW of Aylsham on A140, 15m N of Norwich, 10m S of Cromer [133: TG178286] *Bus:* Eastern Counties 751/8/9 Norwich–Sheringham (passing close BR Norwich), alight Aylsham, 1½m (tel. Norwich (0603) 613613) *Station:* North Walsham (U) 8m

BRANCASTER ⛺ 🦀 🏛 🐕 🚶

Warden's address: Dial House, Brancaster Staithe, Kings Lynn PE31 8BW (tel. Brancaster (0485) 210719)

2,000 acres of beach with 4½ miles of tidal foreshore, sand dunes, and saltmarsh, including the site of the Roman Fort of Branodunum.

🅾 🌸 All year. Information Centre and cycle hire at Brancaster Staithe Harbour, April to end June: Sat & Sun 10–6; July & Aug: daily 10–6. Golf club car park at Brancaster Beach, parking charge (incl. NT members)   *continued*

🚹 Information Centre only

🐕 Under control at all times and not on Scolt Head Island from mid April to mid Aug

Notes: A boat can be hired at Brancaster Staithe (weather permitting) to take visitors to the National Nature Reserve on Scolt Head Island. It is managed for the Trust by the Nature Conservancy Council (NCC Warden: tel. Brancaster (0485) 210330). The Island is an important breeding site for four species of tern, oystercatcher and ringed plover. Nature Trail. It is inadvisable to walk at low tide over the saltmarshes and sand flats. Dial House Basecamp available for hire, sleeps 20, contact NT Warden for further details

🍴 Near the Harbour (not NT)

➔ Brancaster Staithe is halfway between Wells and Hunstanton on A149 coast road [132: TF800450] *Bus* Goldline Hunstanton–Wells-next-the-Sea, with connections from King's Lynn (passing close BR King's Lynn) (tel. Norwich (0603) 613613)

FELBRIGG HALL 🏠✝️✳️🌳🖼️👤🏛️ ✉️

Norwich NR11 8PR (tel. West Runton (026 375) 444)

One of the finest 17th-century houses in Norfolk, with its original 18th-century furniture and pictures and an outstanding library; walled garden, including a restored dovecote, has a traditional layout of herbaceous plants and fruit trees; walks in fine, mature woodland and around lake

🅾️✳️ **House:** 30 March to 27 Oct: Mon, Wed Thur, Sat & Sun 1.30–5.30.
Garden: same days 11–5.30. Woodland walks all year (except Christmas Day): daily, dawn to dusk

🏠✳️ Shop same days as house 12–5.30. Also 28 Oct to 22 Dec: Mon, Wed, Thur, Sat & Sun 11–4

💷 House & garden £4. Garden only £1.50. Parties £3, Mon, Wed & Thur only, please book with s.a.e. to Administrator

📖👶 Children's guidebook. Baby slings available. Parent & baby room

♿🔘 Parking in front of house for disabled drivers only. Disabled visitors may be set down at house. Access to ground floor only, shop and restaurant. ♿ WC. Woodland & lakeside walks

🐕 In park only, on leads

🍴✳️ Park Restaurant 30 March to 27 Oct: daily 11–5.15; also 28 Oct to 22 Dec: as shop, but 11–3.30; (waitress service lunches 12–2, booking advisable, tel. West Runton (026 375) 8237). 4 Jan to end March: Sat & Sun 11–3.30

Events: For details of musical and other events send s.a.e. to Administrator

➔ Nr Felbrigg village, 2m SW of Cromer; entrance off B1436, signposted from A148 and A140 [133: TG193394] *Station:* Cromer (U) or Roughton Road (U), both 2¼m

PLEASE REFER TO PAGES 5–9

4 SOUTH QUAY, GREAT YARMOUTH 🏠   ✉

Great Yarmouth NR30 2SH (tel. Great Yarmouth (0493) 855746)

16th-century building with panelled rooms and 19th-century frontage; leased to Norfolk Museums Service as museum of domestic life

O ❋ All year: Mon to Fri (& Sun June to end Sept) 10–1 & 2–5.30

£ ♿ Adults 50p summer, 25p winter; children 20p; students 40p summer, 20p winter

➜ [134: TG523073] *Bus:* Local services (tel. Great Yarmouth (0493) 844928); also from surrounding areas (tel. Great Yarmouth (0493) 842341) *Station:* Yarmouth ½m

HORSEY WINDPUMP ✖

Horsey, Great Yarmouth NR29 4EF

A drainage windmill that was working until 1943 when lightning severely damaged it; acquired by the Trust in 1948 and restored

O 30 March to 30 Aug: daily 11–5 (July & Aug 11–6)

£ £1. No reduction for parties. Car park £1. Unsuitable for disabled or visually handicapped visitors; difficult staircase. ♿ WC

🐕 On leads only

➜ 2½m NE of Potter Heigham, 11m N of Yarmouth near B1159 [134: TG457223] *Bus:* Eastern Counties 626 Great Yarmouth–Martham (passing close BR Yarmouth), alight W Somerton School, 1¼m (tel. Great Yarmouth (0493) 842341) *Station:* Acle (U) 10m

OXBURGH HALL 🏠✝❋👤   ✖✉✎

Oxborough, nr King's Lynn PE33 9PS (tel. Gooderstone (036 621) 258)

Moated house built in 1482 by the Bedingfeld family, who still live here; the rooms show the development from medieval austerity to Victorian comfort; magnificent Tudor gatehouse; embroidery worked during her captivity by Mary Queen of Scots; garden with lawns, fine trees and colourful borders; French parterre; delightful woodland walk

O **House:** 30 March to end Sept: daily except Thur & Fri 1.30–5.30; BH Mon 11–5.30; Oct: Sat & Sun 1.30–5.30. **Garden:** 30 March to end Oct: daily except Thur & Fri 12–5.30

🏠❋ As house 1.30–5; also 2 Nov to 22 Dec: Sat & Sun 11–4

£ £3.30. Pre-arranged parties £2.50, please book with s.a.e. to Administrator

👶🅰 Baby slings available. Children's guidebook   *continued*

163

Access to house 200yds; shallow ramp to 4 ground floor rooms; WC in west wing of house. Easy access to tea-room and shop. 2 shallow steps to Chapel, 100yds from Hall

Light lunches and teas in Old Kitchen 12–5 on open days (2 Nov to 22 Dec: Sat & Sun 12–3.30). Table licence

At Oxborough, 7m SW of Swaffham on S side of Stoke Ferry road [143: TF742012] *Station:* Downham Market 10m

ST GEORGE'S GUILDHALL

27 King Street, King's Lynn PE30 1HA (tel. King's Lynn (0553) 774725)

Largest surviving English medieval guildhall; adjoining medieval warehouse and Tudor house

All year (when not in use as a theatre): Mon to Fri (closed Good Fri), 10–5; Sat 10–12.30. Closed 25 & 26 Dec & 1 Jan

Free

Events: King's Lynn Festival and annual programme of events from the General Manager at above address (tel. King's Lynn (0553) 773578)

On W side of King Street close to the Tuesday Market Place [132: TF616202] *Bus:* From surrounding areas (tel. King's Lynn (0553) 772343) *Station:* King's Lynn ½m

SHERINGHAM PARK

Gardener's Cottage, Sheringham Park, Upper Sheringham NR26 8TB (Warden: tel. Sheringham (0263) 823778)

770 acres including the outstanding 90-acre landscaped park by Humphry Repton, with fine, mature, mixed woodland. Spectacular views of coast and countryside from viewing towers. Large area of species rhododendrons and azaleas, flowering late May–June

All year round, dawn to dusk. Numerous waymarked walks through woodland, parkland and to the coast; leaflet on sale in car park

Sheringham Hall is privately occupied. Limited access is available to selected rooms only, April to Sept by written appointment with the leaseholder

£2 per car, incl. all passengers. Coaches £5; please book in advance with Warden

Raised walkway from car park to park viewpoints. WC

On leads in park

Refreshments and shop at nearby Felbrigg Hall during open hours (see p. 162)

2m SW of Sheringham, access for cars off A148 Cromer–Holt road; 5m W of Cromer; 6m E of Holt [133: TG135420] *Station:* Sheringham (U) 2m

Northamptonshire

CANONS ASHBY HOUSE 🏠 ❄ ♠ ✝   ✂

Canons Ashby, Daventry NN11 6SD (tel. Blakesley (0327) 860044)

Home of the Dryden family since the 16th century; a manor house, c.1550, added to in the 1590s, and altered in the 1630s and c.1710; largely unaltered since; Elizabethan wall paintings and outstanding Jacobean plasterwork; English furniture; formal garden with terraces, walls and gate-piers of 1710; medieval priory church; 70-acre Park

⬛ **House:** 30 March to end Oct: Wed to Sun & BH Mon (closed Good Fri) 1–5.30 or dusk if earlier. Last admissions 5. **Park:** open as house, access through garden   *continued*

☐ Shop open as house

£ £2.50; children £1.20. Parties £2. Donation box for church. Parking 200yds; coaches and parties should pre-book in writing with the Administrator

♿ 👁 Access to garden and ground floor via 3 steps. House difficult but please telephone Administrator for special arrangements. ♿ WC. Taped guide for visually handicapped and guidebook for deaf visitors

🐕 On leads, in Home Paddock only

Events: Concerts in church; occasional garden fêtes; details from Administrator; please send s.a.e.

☕ ♿ Afternoon tea in Brewhouse 1–5; same days as house. Party bookings for light lunches by prior arrangement

➡ On B4525 Northampton-Banbury road [52: SP577506] *Station:* Banbury 10m

LYVEDEN NEW BIELD 🏠 ✚

nr Oundle, Peterborough (tel. Benefield (083 25) 358)

Shell of an uncompleted 'lodge' or garden house, begun c.1595 by Sir Thomas Tresham: design based on a cross; the exterior incorporates friezes inscribed with religious quotations and signs of the Passion; Sir Thomas died before building was completed; his son, Francis Tresham, was then imprisoned in connection with the Gunpowder Plot; viewing platform at south window

⭕ ❄ All year: daily. Parties by arrangement with the Custodian, Lyveden New Bield Cottage, Oundle, Peterborough PE8 5AT

£ 80p. Limited roadside parking; access on foot ½m along farm track; no parking for coaches which may drop and return to pick up passengers. No WCs

On leads only

→ 4m SW of Oundle via A427, 3m E of Brigstock, just off Harley Way [141: SP983853] *Bus:* United Counties X65 Northampton–Peterborough (passing close BR Peterborough); alight Lower Benefield, 2m by bridlepath; United Counties 8 Kettering–Corby, alight Brigstock, 2½m. Both pass close BR Kettering (tel. Kettering (0536) 512411) *Station:* Kettering 10m

PRIEST'S HOUSE 🏠 ✕ ✕

Easton-on-the-Hill, nr Stamford, Lincolnshire

Pre-Reformation priest's lodge; specialist architectural interest; small museum of village bygones upstairs

By appointment only with Mr R. Chapman, Glebe Cottage, 45 West Street, Easton-on-the-Hill, Stamford PE9 3LS (tel. Stamford (0780) 62506)

£ Free. Unsuitable for coaches

Ground floor room only

→ Approx. 2m SW of Stamford off A43 [141: TF011045] *Bus:* Midland Fox 180, Blands 7/10 from Stamford (passing close BR Stamford), alight Easton, ½m (tel. Stamford (0780) 65555 or Leicester (0533) 511411) *Station:* Stamford 2m

PLEASE REFER TO PAGES 5–9

Northumberland

SCOTLAND

LINDISFARNE CASTLE

ST CUTHBERT'S CAVE ■

■ FARNE ISLANDS

■ ST AIDAN'S DUNES

Seahouses ●

■ BEADNELL LIME
KILNS & DUNES

ROS CASTLE
■

LOW NEWTON-BY-THE-SEA ■
AND NEWTON POOL   ■ ▲ DUNSTANBURGH
                              CASTLE

EMBLETON LINKS

North
Sea

LADY'S WELL ■

CRAGSIDE HOUSE &
▲ COUNTRY PARK ● Alnmouth

DRURIDGE BAY ■

WALLINGTON ▲   Morpeth ●

HADRIAN'S WALL ▲
& HOUSESTEADS FORT

▲ GEORGE STEPHENSON'S
   BIRTHPLACE

■   ▲   TYNE & WEAR
ALLEN BANKS   ● Hexham ▲

CUMBRIA   CHERRYBURN

DURHAM

COAST

Here is one of the most beautiful stretches of English coastline, with its castles – some ruined, some in splendid repair – its miles of sandy beaches, links, and sand dunes, and its nature reserves and rocky offshore islands.

⚑ If you are visting Northumbria or Scotland by car, the A189 from the A1 north of Newcastle will take you within easy reach of **Druridge Bay** [81: NZ2896]; here the Trust owns a mile of coastline with 99 acres of golden sand dunes and grassland, and further north there are dunes at **Alnmouth**. The A189 road rejoins the A1 at Alnwick, but B roads lead to the starkly dramatic ruin of **Dunstanburgh Castle** (see p. 171). From here the Trust owns a 4-mile stretch of coastline, including **Embleton Links** [75: NU243235] and **Low Newton-by-the-Sea** [75: NU241246]. Almost the whole of the square at Low Newton is owned by the Trust as well as **Newton Pool** [75: NU243240], a freshwater lake behind the dunes. This nature reserve is home to breeding birds such as blackheaded gull, teal, mute swan, dabchick, sedge warbler and reed bunting and in winter goldeneye and

168

pochard. ⑤ Two hides are provided for birdwatchers, one adapted for disabled visitors with a wheelchair pathway. There are parking bays for disabled visitors at Low Newton. From Craster to Low Newton there is a beautiful 2½-mile walk along the rocky coastline and the dunes. Information boards have been placed at the access points to help introduce this coastline to visitors.

The road leads on to **Beadnell Harbour** where the Trust owns the 18th-century sandstone **Lime Kilns** and just to the north, a ½ mile of sand dunes [75: NU237286]. From Beadnell the B1340 hugs the coast for about 6 miles to Bamburgh, passing **St Aidan's Dunes** [75: NU211327] with spectacular views of the **Farne Islands** (see p. 172) on clear days. On the way, at Seahouses, is a Trust Information Centre and Shop – and access to the Farnes. The Trust's coastal holdings in Northumberland culminate at **Lindisfarne Castle** on Holy Island (see p. 174) from where there are views not only seawards, but inland to the Cheviot Hills.

EIDER DUCK

COUNTRYSIDE

⚐ The Allen and Tyne rivers meet 3 miles west of Haydon Bridge off the A69 near Hexham, and nearby the Trust owns **Allen Banks** [86/87: NY799630] – nearly 200 acres of hill and river with woodland and riverside walks along the steep banks of the Allen, and a picnic site in the car park. From the top of the eastern bank is a view northwards across the Tyne valley to **Hadrian's Wall**. Roe deer and red squirrels can be found here and a small tarn is home to various species of wildfowl. Four miles north on the B6318 is access to the Trust's **Hadrian's Wall Estate** (see p. 173). More than 2,000 acres of farmland, 4½ miles of the course of the Roman wall, including stretches of the stone wall and ditch, **Housesteads Fort**, several milecastles and, at Shield on the Wall, one of the best preserved sections of the Vallum, form one of the Trust's most fascinating and breathtaking antiquities. ⑤ WC at **Housesteads** car park.

Seven miles west of Rothbury at Holystone on the edge of the Cheviots is **Lady's Well** which has probable associations with St Ninian [81: NT953029]. Views of the Cheviots, Lindisfarne, Chillingham Park (not NT) and Bamburgh Castle (not NT) can be seen from the hilltop of **Ros Castle** [75: NU081253] near Wooler between the A1 and the A697. North-east of Wooler near Holburn Grange is a natural stone cave in the Kyloe Hills – **St Cuthbert's Cave**, where the saint's body is said to have rested on its journey from Lindisfarne to Durham [75: NU059352].

⚐ At **Wallington** (see p. 175), the Trust owns 13,000 acres of beautiful countryside. The land is farmed, but with the agreement of the farmers, circular walks are open during the summer months for visitors to the Estate. Walks leaflets are available at Wallington and they introduce the walker to the geology, history, flora and fauna of the area. ⚐ The 900-acre **Cragside House and Country Park** (see p. 170) is a must for walkers: 40 miles of footpaths and carriage drives are available. The Power Circuit, a 1½-mile circular walk, highlights the industrial archaeology of Cragside. It includes the restored hydraulic and hydro-electric machinery at the Ram and Power Houses and the Iron Bridge, one of the first steel bridges in the world. Walks leaflets are available at the Visitor Centre. During June, the Country Park comes alive with a superb display of rhododendrons and azaleas and in the autumn the colours are quite breathtaking. The latest attraction is the Armstrong Energy Centre, an exhibition of energy technology over the past 100 years, and into the future.

CHERRYBURN

Mickley Square, Stocksfield NE43 7DB (tel. Stocksfield (0661) 843276)

Birthplace of Northumbria's greatest artist, wood engraver and naturalist, Thomas Bewick in 1753; family cottage restored; small museum on Bewick's life and works; demonstrations of hand printing from wood blocks in Printing House; farmyard with animals

29 March to end Oct: daily except Mon but open BH Mon 1–5.30. Last admission 5. Small shop selling Thomas Bewick mementoes and prints

£1.80. No reduction for parties

Wheelchair access. WC

11m W of Newcastle and 11m E of Hexham on A695. 200yds signed from Mickley Square [88: NZ075627] *Bus:* Northumbria 602 Newcastle-upon-Tyne–Hexham (passes BR Newcastle) (tel: 091-232 4211) *Station:* Prudhoe 1½m, Stocksfield 1½m

TAWNY OWL *(Thomas Bewick)*

CRAGSIDE HOUSE AND COUNTRY PARK

Rothbury, Morpeth NE65 7PX (tel. Rothbury (0669) 20333)

A Victorian mansion, mainly designed by R. Norman Shaw, in a 900-acre park created by the 1st Lord Armstrong; 30 rooms open; the first house in the world lit by hydro-electricity; the system was developed by Armstrong with man-made lakes and underground piping; he also planted millions of trees and shrubs and built 40 miles of drives and footpaths; 'The Power Circuit', a 1½-mile circular walk, includes the restored Ram and Power Houses with their hydraulic and hydro-electric machinery, and in the Visitor Centre, the Armstrong Energy Centre

House: 29 March to end Oct: daily except Mon but open BH Mon, 1–5.30. Last admissions 5. **Country Park:** 29 Mar to end Oct: daily 10.30–7. Nov to March 1992: Sat & Sun 10.30–4

Visitor Centre (including Shop, Vickers Room Restaurant, Information Centre & Armstrong Energy Centre): 29 March to end Oct: daily 10.30–5.30; Nov & Dec: Tues, Sat & Sun 10.30–4; Feb to end March 1992: Sat & Sun 12–4. Tel. Rothbury (0669) 20448

House, Country Park & Visitor Centre £3.50; pre-booked parties £3. Country Park & Visitor Centre only £2; pre-booked parties £1.50. Car park 100yds from house (7 car parks in Country Park). Coach park 350yds (advance booking essential)

Notes: Trout fishing from boats on Tumbleton Lake; bird hides at Blackburn Lake; for fishing bookings tel. Rothbury (0669) 21051 (answerphone)

No backpacks in house; front sling baby carriers available; please enquire about other facilities for mothers and babies. Playground at Dunkirk car park; Education Room/School party base at Visitor Centre

House (lift to first floor) & Visitor Centre; special car park & ♿ WC at Visitor Centre, House and Crozier Drive car park; wheelchair path, adapted picnic tables & special parking at Nelly's Moss Upper Lake; adapted fishing pier at Tumbleton Lake; for details tel. Rothbury (0669) 20266 (Country Park office)

In Country Park only

Morning coffee, lunches and teas in Vickers Rooms Restaurant in Visitor Centre. Tel. Rothbury (0669) 20134. Picnicking in all car parks and around Nelly's Moss Lakes

Events & Guided Walks: For list send s.a.e. to Administrator

13m SW of Alnwick (B6341) and 15m NW of Morpeth-Wooler road turn left onto B6341 at Moorhouse Crossroads, entrance at Debdon Gate, 1m N of Rothbury, public transport passengers enter by Reivers Well Gate from Morpeth Road (B6344) [81: NU073022] *Bus:* Northumbria 514/6 Morpeth–Thropton (passing BR Morpeth) with connections from Newcastle (passing Tyne & Wear Metro Haymarket), alight Reivers Well Gate, ¾m (tel. 091-232 4211)

DUNSTANBURGH CASTLE

Craster, Alnwick (tel. Embleton (066 576) 231)

The castle was built in 1316 by Thomas Earl of Lancaster and enlarged later by John of Gaunt; the dramatic ruin encloses 11 acres of dolerite promontory with sea cliffs to the north

Dunstanburgh is in the guardianship of English Heritage

Good Fri 29 March to end Sept: daily 10–6. Oct to end March 1992: Tues to Sun 10–4. Closed 24–26 Dec and 1 Jan. Shop in Craster (Council car park) April: Sat, Sun & Easter week 11–4; May to end Sept: daily 10.30–5.30; Oct: Sat & Sun 11–4.30   *continued*

£   Admission prices subject to review. 85p; OAPs, students and UB40 holders 65p; children 40p. NT information caravan in Council car park at Craster, 1m. Embleton car park, 1½m (no coaches at Embleton). ⓑ Castle unsuitable; ⓑ WC at Craster car park; parking 30p; free to NT members; coaches £1 (NB 1990 prices)

🐕   On leads only

🍴   In Craster (not NT)

→   9m NE of Alnwick, approached from Craster on S and Embleton on N (pedestrians only) [75: NU258220] *Bus:* Northumbria 501 Alnwick–Berwick-upon-Tweed (passing close BR Berwick-upon-Tweed) with connections from Newcastle (passing Tyne & Wear Metro Haymarket), alight Craster, 1½m (tel. 091-232 4211) *Station:* Chathill (U), not Sun, 5m from Embleton, 7m from Castle; Alnmouth, 7m from Craster, 8¼m from Castle

FARNE ISLANDS 🏛️🐦✝️🚶   ❌

The islands provide a summer home for over 17 different species of seabirds, including puffin, kittiwake, eider duck, guillemot, fulmar, tern; the islands also provide a base for a large colony of grey seals. St Cuthbert died on Inner Farne in 687; chapel built to his memory in 14th century and restored 1845

Notes: Public car park in Seahouses opposite harbour. NT Information Centre & Shop at 16 Main Street, Seahouses (tel. Seahouses (0665) 721099). WC on Inner Farne. Visitors to the islands are particularly asked to keep to the rules which have been made to preserve these islands as a bird sanctuary

O Inner Farne and Staple Islands only are open to visitors. 29 March to 30 April & Aug to end Sept daily 10–6. During breeding season (1 May to 31 July) access is restricted: Staple 10.30–1.30, Inner Farne 1.30–5. Visitors are advised to wear hats!

£ May to end July £2.80; school parties £1.30. At other times £2; school parties £1. Admission fees do not include boatmen's charges. Tickets may be bought from Warden on landing and boat tickets from boatmen in Seahouses Harbour. No landing in bad weather. Enquiries about landing answered by Warden/ Naturalist, The Sheiling, 8 St Aidan's, Seahouses, Northumberland NE68 7SR. Nature walks on Inner Farne & Staple Island. Islands are difficult for disabled or visually handicapped visitors and unsuitable for wheelchairs. 🅮 WC on Inner Farne

🍴 In Seahouses (not on islands), not NT

➔ 2–5m off the Northumberland coast, opposite Bamburgh: trips every day from Seahouses Harbour, weather permitting [75: NU2337] *Bus:* As for Dunstanburgh Castle (page 171) but alight Seahouses *Station:* Chathill, (U), not Sun, 4m (Postbus connects Seahouses with trains)

HADRIAN'S WALL & HOUSESTEADS FORT 🏛🖼

Bardon Mill, Hexham NE47 6NN (EH Custodian, tel. Bardon Mill (049 84) 363)

The Trust owns 4½ miles of the Wall including the stretch from Steel Rigg to Housesteads and Housesteads itself, the best preserved of the Roman Wall forts; Roman Wall display in Housesteads Information Centre

Housesteads Fort is in the guardianship of English Heritage

Note: Opening arrangements and admission charges subject to alteration

O ❋ **Hadrian's Wall:** at all times. **Housesteads Museum & Fort:** Good Fri 29 March to end Sept: daily 10–6. Oct to end March 1992: daily 10–4. Closed 24–26 Dec & 1 Jan

🏠 ❋ Shop & Information Centre at Housesteads car park: March: Sat & Sun 11–5; April & Oct: daily 11–5, May to end Sept: daily 10–6, Nov: Sat & Sun 11–dusk. Tel. Bardon Mill (049 84) 525

£ Hadrian's Wall & Information Centre free. Housesteads Museum & Fort £1.40; OAPs, students and UB40 Holders £1.05; children (under 16) 70p. Car & coach parks at Housesteads, ½m; 30p, and at the western end at Steel Rigg, managed by the National Park Authority. No access for vehicles to Housesteads Fort

🅮 Information Centre only, parking available near Housesteads Fort; ask Information Centre Manager for details. 🅮 WC at Information Centre. Housesteads Fort not suitable for wheelchairs

🐕 On leads only

🍴 ❋ Hot and cold drinks and ice cream at Information Centre. Picnicking at Information Centre

Events: For details of guided walks send s.a.e. to Information Centre   *continued*

NORTHUMBERLAND

➡️ 6m NE of Haltwhistle, 4m N of Bardon Mill railway station; ½m N of B6318; best access from car parks at Housesteads and Steel Rigg [86/87: NY790688] *Bus:* Rochester & Marshall 890 Hadrian's Wall summer service BR Hexham– BR Haltwhistle (tel. Hexham (0434) 600263) *Station:* Bardon Mill (U) 4m

LINDISFARNE CASTLE 🏰❀🎫🛗 ✉️📷

Holy Island, Berwick-upon-Tweed TD15 2SH
(tel. Berwick-upon-Tweed (0289) 89244)

Built in 1550 to protect Holy Island Harbour from attack; restored and converted into a private house by Sir Edwin Lutyens in 1903. Small walled garden designed by Gertrude Jekyll; 19th-century lime kilns

🅾️🔑 Good Fri 29 March to end Sept: daily except Fri (but open Good Fri) 1–5.30 (at selected times guided tours only). Oct: Wed, Sat & Sun 1–5.30. Last admissions 5. Admission to garden only when gardener is in attendance

🛍️ NT shop in Main Street, Holy Island Village. Tel. Berwick-upon-Tweed (0289) 89253

£ £2.80. Parties of 15 or more by prior arrangement only with Administrator; no reduction. No WCs. Public car park, ½m, 70p, incl. NT members

✝ No backpacks in Castle (including framed baby carriers); front sling baby carriers available

🐾 On leads as far as Lower Battery only

☕ In Holy Island Village (not NT)

Notes: It is impossible to cross the island between the 2 hours before high tide and the 3½ hours following. Tide tables are printed in local newspapers, and displayed at the causeway

→ On Holy Island, 6m E of A1 across causeway [75: NU136417]
Bus: Northumbria 477 from Berwick-upon-Tweed (passing close BR Berwick-upon-Tweed). Times vary with tides; check in advance: (tel. Berwick-upon-Tweed (0289) 307283) *Station:* Berwick-upon-Tweed 10m from causeway

---

STEPHENSON'S BIRTHPLACE 🏠🏢   ✉

Wylam NE41 8BP (tel. Wylam (0661) 853457)

A small stone tenement built c.1760 to accommodate four pitmen's families; furnishings reflecting the age of George Stephenson's birth here in 1781

O Good Fri 29 March to end Oct: Thur, Sat & Sun, BH Mon & Good Fri 1–5.30. Last admissions 5. Other times by appointment with the custodian

£ 60p. Access by foot and bicycle through Country Park. No parties. No WCs. Parking by War Memorial in Wylam village, ½m

→ 8m W of Newcastle, 1½m S of A69 at Wylam. Access on foot and bicycle through Country Park, ½m E of Wylam [88: NZ126650] *Bus:* OK Motor Services 684 Newcastle–Ovington, alight Wylam, 1m (tel. 091-261 0707) *Station:* Wylam (U) ½m

---

WALLINGTON 🏠❄🖐🚶   ✉🏢

Cambo, Morpeth NE61 4AR (tel. Scot's Gap (067 074) 283)

Built on the site of a medieval castle in 1688 and altered in the 1740s; exceptional plasterwork and porcelain; 19th-century Central Hall with paintings by William Bell Scott; collection of dolls' houses; museum; terraced walled garden and conservatory; coaches in West Coach House; Estate Room with exhibition; 100 acres of woodlands and lakes

Note: Visitors to the house will be asked to leave bulky objects in the entrance hall and remove sharp-heeled shoes

O ❄ **House:** 29 March to end Oct: daily except Tues 1–5.30. Last admissions 5.
Walled Garden: 29 March to end Sept: daily 10.30–7; Oct to March 1992 daily 10.30–4. **Grounds:** all year during daylight hours   *continued*

🛍️ ❄️ Shop & Information Centre open 29 March to end Oct: daily 10.30–5.30; Nov & Dec: Wed to Sun 12.30–4.30; Feb & March 1992: Sat & Sun 12.30–4.30. Tel Scot's Gap 067 074) 249

£ House, walled garden & grounds £3. Parties £2.60. Walled garden & grounds £1.50; parties £1. Parties must book in advance

🚼 ⚠️ No backpacks in house; front sling baby carriers available; please enquire about other facilities for mothers and babies. Dolls' houses and toy soldier collections

♿ ◉ Ground floor of house only; apply to parking attendant for special reserved bays; most of grounds, conservatory and Walled Garden terrace accessible, but no wheelchair access to Walled Garden; electric 3-wheeler for hire (contact Administrator for details); steep slope and steps. ♿ WC. Scented roses in garden

🐕 In walled garden on leads, and in grounds only

🍴 ❄️ Coffee, lunches & teas in Clock Tower Restaurant same times as shop, see above. Tel. Scot's Gap (067 074) 274. ♿ in Harness Room. Picnics in car park and West Woods

Events: Send s.a.e. to Administrator for details of walks and events ♿

Note: New circular walks open on the Wallington Estate; leaflets available at the shop

➡️ 12m W of Morpeth (B6343), 6m NW of Belsay (A696), take B6342 to Cambo [81: NZ030843] *Bus:* Northumbria/Vasey 419 from Morpeth (Wed, Fri, Sat only) (passing close BR Morpeth); otherwise Snaith 808 from Newcastle (passing close BR Newcastle), alight Shielhill Cross Roads, 1¼m; National Express 370 or Scottish Citylink 170 from Newcastle (passing close BR Newcastle), alight Capheaton Road End 2m (tel. Northumberland CC Morpeth (0670) 514343)

Nottinghamshire

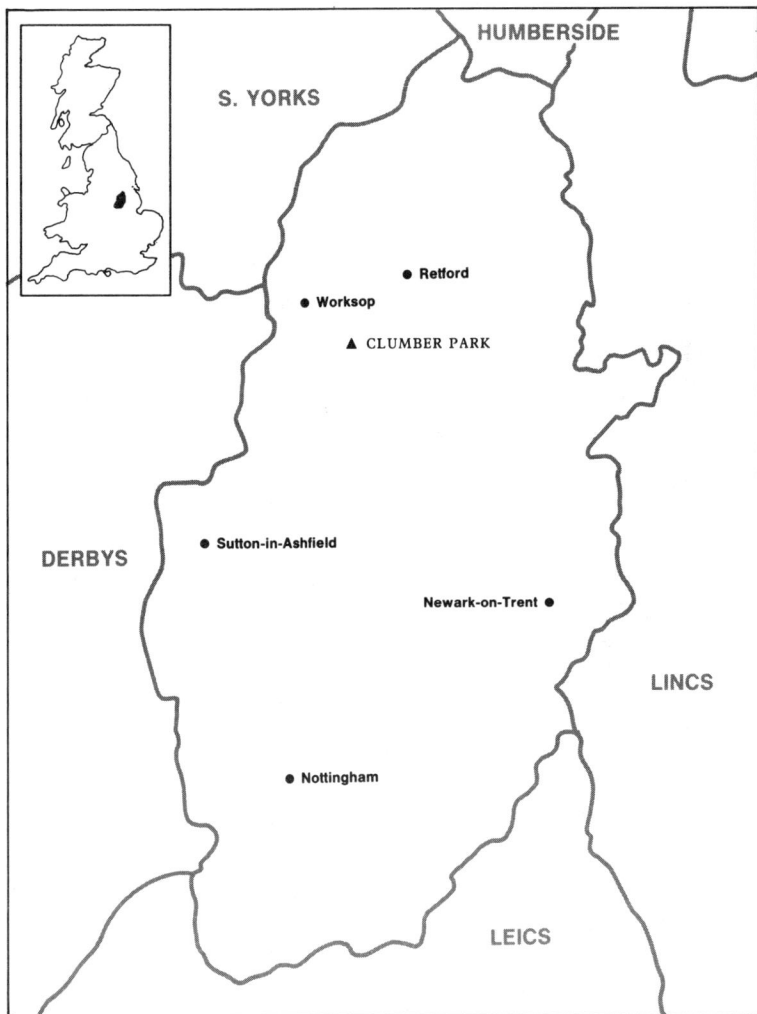

HUMBERSIDE

S. YORKS

● Retford

● Worksop

▲ CLUMBER PARK

DERBYS

● Sutton-in-Ashfield

Newark-on-Trent ●

LINCS

● Nottingham

LEICS

CLUMBER PARK ⊕ ✚ 🏠 🚶 ✿   ⊠

The Estate Office, Clumber Park, Worksop S80 3AZ (tel. Worksop (0909) 476592)

3,800 acres of parkland with double lime avenue; fine Gothic Revival Chapel built 1886–89

NOTTINGHAMSHIRE

for 7th Duke of Newcastle; house demolished 1938; superb 80-acre lake with foot ferry; stable block with restaurant, shop and information point; Classical bridge, temples, lawned Lincoln Terrace and pleasure grounds; Walled Kitchen Garden & Tools Exhibition; Clumber Conservation Centre

Park: open all year during daylight hours. **Chapel:** all year: daily (except 25 Dec) to end Sept 10–5; Oct to Easter 10–4 (donation box). **Walled Kitchen Garden & Tools Exhibition:** April to end Sept: Sat, Sun & BH Mon and some weekdays during summer school holidays 10–5. Last admissions 4.30; telephone Visitor Liaison Officer to check details

Clock Tower Shop open all year daily: Jan to 30 March 10.30–5; 31 March to 26 Oct 10.30–6; 27 Oct to 22 Dec 10.30–5; Jan to end March 1992 10.30–5

Pedestrians free; cars, motorbikes & caravanettes £2; cars with caravans, mini coaches £3; coaches midweek £5, weekends and BH £10. Exemption for NT members only. Parking 100yds from visitor facilities. Bicycle hire (identification essential) including cycles with child carriers £2 for 2hrs; (mid-week party bookings for min. 20 cycles) book through Visitor Liaison Officer. Orienteering by arrangement. Horse riding by permit. Fishing bank: 16 June to 14 March; 7am to dusk; day ticket £2; season ticket £30. Day tickets available on the bank from fishing bailiff. Walled Kitchen Garden & Tools Exhibition 50p

13 miles of tarmac roads; most areas accessible; Walled Kitchen Garden & Tools Exhibition fully accessible. Restaurant & shop accessible. Wheelchairs (incl. child size) available to borrow (identification required) from NT shop. WCs

Self-service cafeteria: daily Jan to 30 March: 10.30–5; 31 March to 26 Oct: 10.30–6; 27 Oct to 22 Dec: 10.30–5; Jan to end March 1992 10.30–5. Restaurant open as above; closed Christmas week. Open for functions and booked parties throughout the year. Bookings and enquiries: tel. Worksop (0909) 484122

Events: 18 & 19 May, Clumber Park Horse Trials; 23 June, NT Clumber sponsored Walk and Country Pursuits Show; concerts; details from Visitor Liaison Officer; please send s.a.e. accessible over grassland

Notes: All enquiries to Visitor Liaison Officer. Guided walks may be booked for parties throughout the summer. Information point open April to Oct afternoons (tel. (0909) 484977). 150-berth caravan site run by Caravan Club; open to non-members. NT & Caravan Club members have priority (tel. Worksop (0909) 484758). Camp site run by Camping & Caravanning Club of Great Britain: tents only, showers, hot water: April to end Sept (tel. Worksop (0909) 482303). Clumber Conservation Centre for school and other groups (book with Head Warden): open weekends April to end Oct and other times by arrangement

4½m SE of Worksop, 6½m SW of Retford, 1m from A1/A57, 11m from M1 Jn 30. [120: SK645774 or 120: SK626746] *Bus:* E Midland 33 Worksop–Nottingham (passing close BR Worksop), alight Carburton, 1¾m (tel. Chesterfield (0246) 211007); Sherwood Forester service in summer months (tel. Nottingham (0602) 824268) *Station:* Worksop 4½m; Retford 6½m

Oxfordshire

COUNTRYSIDE

The **Buscot and Coleshill** estates extend to about 7,500 acres of farmland and woodland [163: SU2694]. This beautiful, rural area includes **Badbury Hill,** at which there is a car park. An Iron Age hill-fort gives fine views over the upper Thames Valley and south to the Berkshire Downs on which is **White Horse Hill.** Buscot is an attractive stone village close to the Thames, with a popular picnic area at Buscot Weir. You may park in the village a short walk away. There is also a picnic site and small car park by the Thames to the west of Buscot on the road to Lechlade. Coleshill village is a typical estate village of Cotswold stone-and-tile houses and cottages. The dry stone walls and box hedges are an attractive feature of the village.

A mile south-east of Watlington, on an escarpment of the Chilterns, **Watlington Hill** [175: SU702935] rises to 700ft and gives splendid views over much of Oxfordshire. The scenery alone is rewarding, and for the naturalist the area offers much fascination. This chalk and flint hill is overlaid with clay and flints, so the vegetation includes both clay

179

and chalk loving plants. There is a fine yew forest, and whitebeam, dogwood, hawthorn and the wayfaring tree grow in profusion. The hill is skirted by the Upper Icknield Way. It is an ideal spot for picnics or simply enjoying the view.

An interesting feature to look out for on the side of the hill is the White Mark, a triangle cut out of the chalk and kept free of vegetation. Just south of the hill lie **Watlington Woods**, which are especially attractive at bluebell time. There is a small car park for both the hill and woods off the Watlington to Northend road.

Aston Wood [165: SU740973], to the west of Stokenchurch, is a pleasant pocket of Chiltern woodland. An area rich in wildlife, it adjoins the Nature Conservancy Council's National Nature Reserve at Aston Rowant. There is parking in a layby beside the A40.

There are some excellent archaeological monuments in the open countryside south of Uffington, south-west Oxfordshire. The famous landmark of **White Horse Hill** has a 360ft long figure of a horse cut in the chalk. At the foot of the hill is a sheltered grassy area known as 'The Manger', where traditionally the horse comes to feed! The origin of the White Horse is unknown, but it is probably early Iron Age and is certainly one of the oldest such figures in Britain. Above it is an ancient barrow. The hill is crowned by the Iron Age hill-fort of **Uffington Castle**, which dates from the 1st century BC and is surrounded by a strong defensive bank and ditch. The smaller, flat-topped **Dragon Hill** is nearby. It is traditionally the site where St George slew the dragon, and legend has it that the distinctive bare patch is where the dragon's blood was spilled on the earth.

All three monuments [174: SU301869] belong to the Trust but are in the care of English Heritage. This fascinating area may be approached on foot from the Ridgeway path or by car from the B4507. There is a large car park 500 yards away from the monuments.

South of White Horse Hill, there is much pleasant countryside to be explored at **Ashdown Woods** [174: SU283824], adjoining the 17th-century **Ashdown House** (see page 180), and **Weathercock Hill** on the opposite side of the B4000. There is a car park 250 yards from the house. Please note that the estate and car park are closed to the public for estate management purposes on Fridays throughout the year.

ASHDOWN HOUSE 🏠 ❇ 🐾 𝕏   ✖ 🐾

Lambourn, Newbury, Berkshire RG16 7RE

17th-century house built by 1st Lord Craven and by him 'consecrated' to Elizabeth, Queen of Bohemia; great staircase rising from hall to attic; portraits of the Winter Queen's family; access to roof; fine views, box parterre and lawns; avenues and woodland walks

🅾 ❇	**Hall, stairway, roof and grounds only:** April to end Oct: Wed & Sat 2–6. Closed Easter & BH Mon. Guided tours only; at 2.15, 3.15, 4.15 & 5.15 from front door. Last admissions to house 5.15. **Woodlands:** all year: Sat to Thur dawn to dusk
💷 ♿	Grounds, hall, stairway & roof £1.80. No reduction for parties, which should book **in writing.** Woodland free. Car park 250yds. No WCs or refreshments available. No picnicking.
♿	Grounds only; house not accessible to wheelchair users
🐎	Woodland only (not in house or grounds)

PLEASE REFER TO PAGES 5–9

➡️ 2½m S of Ashbury, 3½m N of Lambourn, on W side of B4000 [174: SU282820]
Bus: Thamesdown 47 Swindon–Lambourn, not Sat (passing close BR
Swindon) with connections for Newbury on Bee Line 108, (tel. Swindon
(0793) 523700). On Sat, Bee Line 108 Swindon–Newbury (tel. Newbury
(0635) 40743)

BUSCOT OLD PARSONAGE 🏠✳️ ✖️✖️

Buscot, Faringdon SN7 8DQ

Early 18th-century house of Cotswold stone on bank of Thames; small garden

🅾️ April to end Oct: Wed only 2–6 by appointment in writing with tenant

💷 £1. Not suitable for parties. No WCs

➡️ 2m from Lechlade, 4m from Faringdon on A417 [163: SU231973]
Bus: Swanbrook 64 Swindon–Carterton, or Thamesdown 77 Swindon–
Cirencester (both passing close BR Swindon), alight Lechlade, 1½m (tel.
Wiltshire C C Trowbridge (0225) 753641)

BUSCOT PARK 🏠✳️🌷 ✖️✖️✖️

Faringdon SN7 8BU (tel. Faringdon (0367) 240786, not weekends)

*18th-century house with Faringdon Collection of fine paintings and furniture; park setting
with Harold Peto water garden and recently replanted walled garden*

Buscot Park is administered for the National Trust by Lord Faringdon

🅾️ Good Fri 29 March, 30 & 31 March, then 3 Apr to end Sept: Wed, Thur, Fri
2–6. Also open every 2nd & 4th weekend 2–6 (i.e. 13 & 14, 27 & 28 April;
11 & 12, 25 & 26 May; 8 & 9, 22 & 23 June; 13 & 14, 27 & 28 July; 10 & 11,
24 & 25 Aug; 14 & 15, 28 & 29 Sept). Last admissions 5.30

💷 House & grounds £3.20. Grounds only £2.20. No reduction for parties which
must book in writing to the Housekeeper. Unsuitable for wheelchair users due
to gravel paths throughout grounds and steep flight of steps to house

🍴 Afternoon teas in tea-room. Teas and lunches for parties by prior arrangement
only, with housekeeper (tel. Faringdon (0367) 242094). Also plant sales next
to car park; both open when house & grounds are open

➡️ Between Lechlade and Faringdon, on A417 [163: SU239973]
Bus: As Buscot Old Parsonage, above, but 2¾m walk from Lechlade

GREAT COXWELL BARN 🏠

Great Coxwell, Faringdon

*13th-century monastic barn, stone-built with stone-tiled roof which has interesting timber
construction*   *continued*

181

OXFORDSHIRE

O ❋	All year: daily at reasonable hours
£ ♿	50p. No WCs
🐕	On leads only
➜	2m SW of Faringdon between A420 and B4019 [163: SU269940] *Bus:* Swindon & District 66 Swindon–Oxford (passing close BR Swindon & passing BR Oxford), alight Great Coxwell turn, ¼m (tel. Swindon (0793) 522243) *Station:* Swindon 10m

GREYS COURT 🏠❋🏠 ✉🏛

Rotherfield Greys, Henley-on-Thames RG9 4PG
(tel. Rotherfield Greys (049 17) 529)

Jacobean house with Georgian additions set amid the remains of the courtyard walls and towers of a 14th-century fortified house; Tudor donkey wheel well-house; garden contains Archbishop's Maze

O	30 March to end Sept: **house:** Mon, Wed & Fri: 2–6; **garden:** daily except Thurs & Sun 2–6. Last admissions 5.30
£	House & garden £3.20. Garden only £2.20. No reduction for parties, which must book. Parking 220yds
🐕	In car park only
☕	Teas in Cromwellian stables, 1 April (BH Mon) then April & May: Wed & Sat 2.30–5.15; June to end Sept: Mon, Wed, Fri & Sat 2.30–5.15
➜	3m W of Henley-on-Thames, east of B481 [175: SU725834] *Bus:* Bee Line 136/7 from Reading (passing close BR Reading), alight Peppard Common, 2m (tel. Reading (0734) 581358) *Station:* Henley-on-Thames 3m

PRIORY COTTAGES 🏠 ✉

1 Mill Street, Steventon, Abingdon OX13 6SP

Former monastic buildings, converted into two houses; South Cottage contains the Great Hall of the original priory

O	The Great Hall in South Cottage only, April to end Sept: Wed 2–6; by written appointment with tenant
£	£1. No reduction for parties. No WCs
	Note: very small house, unsuitable for coach parties
➜	4m S of Abingdon, ¼m W of A34 on corner of The Causeway and Mill Street, entrance in Mill Street [164: SU466914] *Bus:* Oxford Minibus 32/A Oxford–Steventon (passing close BR Oxford) (tel. Oxford (0865) 727000) *Station:* Didcot Parkway 5m

Shropshire

COUNTRYSIDE

Perhaps one of the most famous landmarks in this border county is the **Long Mynd** [137: SO430940] a heather-covered upland, of which the Trust owns some 5,500 acres. A good starting point is the **Carding Mill Valley** (see p. 185) from which paths lead to the high moorland and its prehistoric remains which include burial mounds, hill-forts and the ancient Port Way track which traverses the hill. Vehicle access is by a steep road which is liable to congestion in summer. On fine days there are views from the summit to Snowdonia, the **Brecon Beacons** (see p. 271), the **Clent Hills** (see p. 121) and the Cotswolds. ♿ Wheelchair users may reach some viewpoints on the Long Mynd, and visit the shop and restaurant at Carding Mill Valley.

The patchwork of heather provides a home for the red grouse (the Long Mynd is the most southerly grouse moor in the country) and for a variety of other upland birds, including raven, buzzard and dipper, which are joined by wheatear and ring ouzel in the summer months.

Since 1981 the Trust has acquired about 370 acres of **Wenlock Edge** including **Easthope Wood** [138: SO570965], **Harley Bank** [127: SO605002] and **Blakeway Coppice** [138: SO595988]. This wooded limestone escarpment runs from Craven Arms to Ironbridge and is internationally famous for its geology, in particular its coral reef exposures. A rich limestone flora includes the wild service tree and nine species of orchid. Public and permitted paths traverse the Edge; the road along the escarpment gives extensive views and passes close by the Elizabethan **Wilderhope Manor** (see p. 187).

ATTINGHAM PARK 🏛️🔆🚻   ✕ ✕

Shrewsbury SY4 4TP (tel. Upton Magna (074 377) 203)

An elegant neo-Classical house with magnificent state rooms, Italian furniture, Regency silver and impressive picture collection; good walks all year through landscaped deer park

🅾️❄️ **House:** 30 March to end Sept: Sat to Wed 1.30–5; BH Mon 11–5. Oct: Sat & Sun 1.30–5. Last admissions to house 4.30. **Deer park & grounds:** open daily except Christmas Day

🛍️ Shop open as house

💷 House & Park £2.70. Family £6.75; Park & grounds only 80p. Parties by arrangement. Evening opening for pre-booked parties £80 min. charge for party of 20, or £4 per person incl. guided tour. Parking 120yds

🏫🚼 Education room available for pre-booked parties (max. 30 children); contact Administrator for details. Mother & baby room

♿👁️ Prior notice of visit appreciated; disabled visitors may be driven to entrance; ♿ WC at brewhouse. 👁️ Braille guide. Tea-room access difficult

🐕 Dogs in grounds only, on leads (no dogs in deer park)

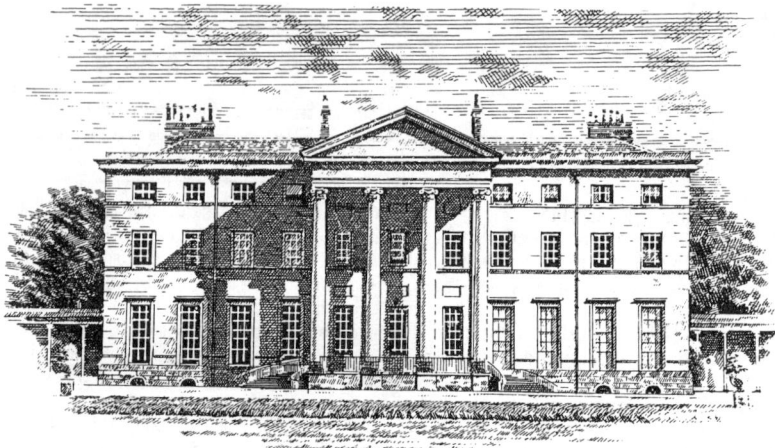

◼ Home-made refreshments in tea-room same days as house 12.30–5. BH Mon 11–5. Licensed. Lunches & suppers at other times for pre-booked parties. Separate tea-room available. Picnic sites along Mile Walk

Events: Details from Administrator; send s.a.e.

➡ 4m SE of Shrewsbury, on N side of the Telford road (A5) [126: SJ550099] *Bus:* Williamsons X96 Shrewsbury–Telford (passing close BR Shrewsbury & Wellington Telford West (tel. 0345 056 785) *Station:* Shrewsbury 5m

BENTHALL HALL 🏠🕸✚ ✄✉

Broseley TF12 5RX (tel. Telford (0952) 882159)

16th-century stone house with mullioned windows and moulded brick chimneys; intricately carved oak staircase, decorated plaster ceilings and oak panelling; plantsman's garden; Restoration church

◯ 31 March to end Sept: Wed, Sun & BH Mon 1.30–5.30. Last admissions 5. House and/or garden for parties at other times by arrangement

£ £2.00. No reduction for parties. Garden £1. Joint ticket with Moseley Old Hall (see p. 199) £3.75. Parking 150yds. Coaches by appointment

♿ Ground floor and parts of garden

Events: Church services most Suns 3.15. Visitors welcome

➡ 1m NW of Broseley (B4375), 4m NE of Much Wenlock, 6m S of Wellington [127: SJ658025] *Bus:* Tellus/Crystal Motors 9 from Wellington (passing close BR Wellington Telford West), alight Broseley, 1m (tel. 0345 056 785) *Station:* Telford Central 7½m

CARDING MILL VALLEY & LONG MYND 🏞

Chalet Pavilion, Carding Mill Valley, Church Stretton SY6 6JG (tel. Church Stretton (0694) 722631)

5,500 acres of moorland, part of the Long Mynd, extending for 4 miles, and including the Carding Mill Valley where the Trust has a café, shop & Information Centre in the Chalet Pavilion. The land rises to 1,700ft, providing magnificent views of the Shropshire and Cheshire plains and the Black Mountains

◯🕸 Moorland: all year. **Chalet Pavilion (café, shop & information centre):**
🏠◼ 30 March to end June, & Sept: Tues to Sat 2–5; Sun & BH Mon 10.30–5.30; July to end Aug: Mon to Sat 2–5.30; Sun & BH Mon 10.30–5.30. Oct: Sat & Sun 2–5. Booked parties at other times by arrangement

£ Entrance charge per car, £1. Coaches free

♿ Café, shop & information centre. Parking immediately outside building

🐕 Must be kept under control on moorland; not admitted to the Chalet Pavilion

◼♿ Light lunches & teas at the Chalet Pavilion   *continued*

185

→ 15m S of Shrewsbury, W of Church Stretton valley and A49; approached from Church Stretton and, on W side, from Ratlinghope or Asterton [137: SO443945] *Bus:* Midland Red West 435 Shrewsbury–Ludlow, alight Church Stretton, ½m (tel. 0345 212 555) *Station:* Church Stretton (U) 1m

DUDMASTON 🏠🏵🖼 ✉🖼

Quatt, nr Bridgnorth WV15 6QN (tel. Quatt (0746) 780866)

Late 17th-century house with fine furniture; Dutch flower paintings, modern pictures, watercolours and botanical art, modern sculpture, family and natural history; lakeside garden and walk through the Dingle

◉ 31 March to end Sept: Wed & Sun only 2.30–6. Last admissions 5.30. Special opening for pre-booked parties only, Thur pm

🛍 Shop open as house

£ House & garden £2.50. Family £6.25. Garden only £1.50. Parking 100yds

♿ Ramp to entrance; access to main and inner halls, Library, Oak Room, No 1 & Darby galleries and Old Kitchen. Special access arrangements; apply to Administrator; ♿ WC by car park

🐕 In garden and Dingle only, on leads

☕♿ Home-made teas 2.30–5.30

→ 4m SE of Bridgnorth on A442 [138: SO746887] *Bus:* Midland Red West 297 Kidderminster–Bridgnorth (passing close BR Kidderminster) (tel. 0345 212 555) *Station:* Bridgnorth (Severn Valley Rly) 4m; Kidderminster 10m

MORVILLE HALL 🏠♿ ⊠

nr Bridgnorth WV16 5BN

Elizabethan house of mellow stone, converted in 18th century, in fine setting; attractive garden under restoration

O ❄ By written appointment only with the tenant, Mrs J. K. Norbury

♿ Ground floor and most of garden

→ [138: SO668940] *Bus:* Midland Red West 436/7 Shrewsbury, Bridgnorth (passing close BR Shrewsbury & Severn Valley Rly Bridgnorth) (tel. 0345 212 555) *Station:* Bridgnorth (Severn Valley Rly) 3½m

WILDERHOPE MANOR 🏠♿🚶 ⊠

Easthope, Much Wenlock TF13 6EG (tel. Longville (069 43) 363)

Stands on southern slope of Wenlock Edge in remote country with views down to Corvedale; the limestone house dates from 1586, and is unaltered but unfurnished; let to the Youth Hostels Association; circular walk through farmland and woods

O ❄ April to end Sept: Wed & Sat 2–4.30. Oct to end March 1992: Sat only 2–4.30

£ £1. No reduction for parties. ♿ Access to house difficult

🍴 Longville Arms, Longville (not NT); home-cooked food

🐕 Dogs on leads in area around Manor

→ 7m SW of Much Wenlock, 7m E of Church Stretton, ½m S of B4371 [138: SO545929] *Station:* Church Stretton (U) 8m

Somerset

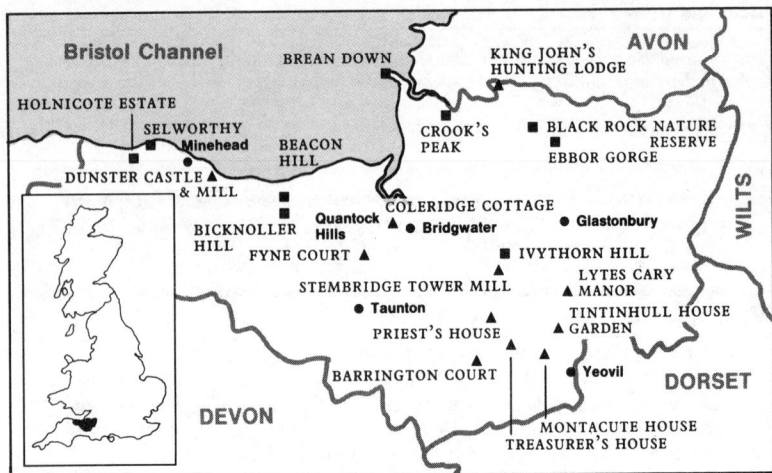

Map of Somerset showing: Bristol Channel, AVON, BREAN DOWN, KING JOHN'S HUNTING LODGE, HOLNICOTE ESTATE, SELWORTHY, Minehead, BEACON HILL, CROOK'S PEAK, BLACK ROCK NATURE RESERVE, EBBOR GORGE, DUNSTER CASTLE & MILL, COLERIDGE COTTAGE, BICKNOLLER HILL, Quantock Hills, Bridgwater, Glastonbury, FYNE COURT, IVYTHORN HILL, WILTS, STEMBRIDGE TOWER MILL, LYTES CARY MANOR, Taunton, TINTINHULL HOUSE GARDEN, PRIEST'S HOUSE, BARRINGTON COURT, Yeovil, DORSET, DEVON, MONTACUTE HOUSE, TREASURER'S HOUSE

COAST AND COUNTRY

[🛈] Just over the Somerset/Avon border, south-west of Weston-super-Mare, **Brean Down** forms the southern arm of Weston Bay, jutting out into the Bristol Channel [182: ST2959]. A steep path with steps cut into the hillside leads to the top of this limestone headland, once the site of a Roman temple. The ruins of a large 19th-century fort remain at the seaward end, built when it was feared that the French might sail up the Bristol Channel to attack the mainland. There is a bird sanctuary here, and good sea fishing from the rocks.

Further to the south-west on the southern edge of Bridgwater Bay the beautiful range of the Quantock Hills meets the sea at Quantoxhead. The Trust owns more than 1,100 acres of these hills; probably the more important parts are **Beacon and Bicknoller Hills,** east of Williton – some 630 acres of moorland with the Iron Age fort of **Trendle Ring** which is an Ancient Monument. From these hills are magnificent views over the Bristol Channel, the Vale of Taunton Deane and Exmoor [181: ST125410/124397]. [🛈] At **Fyne Court** (see p. 191) there are three walks over the eastern Quantocks, taking in heathland, forest and farmland.

Inland to the east of the Quantocks the long low ridge of the Polden Hills overlooks Sedgemoor and Athelney – the large wetland area of Somerset once drained and used for agricultural purposes by the monks of Glastonbury Abbey. One of the several small properties owned by the Trust in this area is **Ivythorn Hill,** 88 acres of high land and woodland on the A39 which runs the length of the Poldens [182: ST474348].

[🛈] On Exmoor on the Somerset/Devon border the Trust owns the 12,400-acre **Holnicote Estate** [181: SS8844], including the high tors of Dunkery and Selworthy Beacons with breathtaking views in all directions, 15 farms and part or all of many small villages and hamlets, one of which is the beautiful model village of **Selworthy** with its cream cob walls, thatched roofs and lovely cottage gardens. There is a shop and information centre at Selworthy open 30 March to 27 Oct: Mon to Sat 10–5, Sun 2–5. Tel. 0643 862745. The estate covers 4½ miles of coastline between Porlock Bay and Minehead. The South-West Peninsula Coastal Path which begins at Minehead curves inland to avoid the possibility of landslips in the Foreland sandstone which predominates either end of the property at Greenaleigh Point and Hurlstone Point. The Trust has, however made a new but tougher footpath on the lower slopes which is recommended to more experienced walkers. There is a circular nature walk which begins and finishes at the car park at Webber's Post.

On the limestone Mendip Hills above Wells a smaller but no less interesting valley vies with the famous Cheddar Gorge (caves not NT). ⓘ & **Ebbor Gorge** offers two nature walks, one takes ½ hour and is recommended to wheelchair users; the other takes 1½hrs and climbs to 800ft giving superb views. In this woodland badgers are plentiful and birds of prey such as buzzard and sparrowhawk may be seen. The caves are home to greater and lesser horseshoe bats [182: ST525485]. ⓘ The Trust also owns the **Black Rock Nature Reserve** at Cheddar and the northern slopes of Cheddar Gorge; a circular walk from the B3135 road at Black Rock Gate traverses plantations, natural woodland, limestone scree and rough downland [182: ST468543].

BARRINGTON COURT 🏠🏠

nr Ilminster TA19 0NQ (tel. South Petherton (0460) 40601/52242)

Tudor manor house restored in 1920s by Colonel Lyle. Now sub-let to Stuart Interiors, the furniture reproducers

As this Handbook went to press major changes were taking place at Barrington Court due to the sale of the remaining years of the lease by the tenant. This means that previous access to the adjacent, privately created garden, which had been agreed informally between the Trust and its then tenant cannot be offered in 1991

🅾 **Court House only:** April to Sept: Wed only 2–5

£ £1

➡ In Barrington village, 5m NE of Ilminster, off A303, 6m S of Curry Rivel on A378 between Taunton and Langport [193: ST397182] *Bus:* Southern National 32/3 Ilminster–South Petherton with connections from Taunton (passing close BR Taunton) (tel. Somerset CC: 0345 078 718) *Station:* Crewkerne 7m

COLERIDGE COTTAGE 🏠 ✈️ ✂️

35 Lime Street, Nether Stowey, Bridgwater TA5 1NQ
(tel. Nether Stowey (0278) 732662)

Coleridge's home for three years; where he wrote The Ancient Mariner *and part of*
Christabel

[O] [✳] 26 March to 29 Sept: Tues to Thur, & Sun 2–5 (parlour and reading room only
shown). In winter by written application to the Custodian. Parties please book

[£] £1.20. No reduction for parties

[🍴] In village (not NT)

[→] At W end of Nether Stowey, on S side of A39, 8m W of Bridgwater [181:
ST191399] *Bus:* Southern National 15 Bridgwater–Nether Stowey (passing
close BR Bridgwater) (tel. Taunton (0823) 272033) *Station:* Bridgwater 8m

DUNSTER CASTLE 🏰 ✳ ♠ ✂️

Dunster, nr Minehead TA24 6SL (tel. Dunster (0643) 821314)

*Fortified home of the Luttrell family for 600 years; castle dating from the 13th century,
remodelled by Anthony Salvin in the 19th century; fine 17th-century staircase and plaster
ceilings; terraced garden of rare shrubs; 28-acre park*

[O] **Garden:** 1 March to 3 Nov: daily 11–5 or dusk if earlier. **Castle:** 25 March to
30 Sept: Sat to Wed 11–5. Oct: Sat to Wed 12–4. Open BH Mon

[🏠] [✳] Open daily 1–30 March: 11–4.30; 31 March to 27 Oct: 11–5. 2 Nov to
15 Dec: Sat & Sun only 11–4. Tel. Dunster (0643) 821626

💷   Castle & garden £4; children (under 16) £2. Parties £3.50 by written arrangement with the Administrator. Garden & grounds only £1.90; children (under 16) 80p. 10-min. steep climb to Castle from car park

♿   Castle situated on a steep hill and access is difficult, but not impossible with a willing helper. Areas of the house can be visited and assistance given if needed. Special parking by arrangement. ♿ WC

🐕   In car park and park area only

🍽   In Dunster village (not NT). Picnics in car park and park only

➜   In Dunster, 3m SE of Minehead on A396, just off A39 [181: ST995435]
Bus: Southern National 28 Taunton–Minehead (passing BR Taunton); 38/9 from Minehead. On all, alight Dunster Steep, ½m (tel. Taunton (0823) 272033)
Station: Dunster (W Somerset Steam Rly) 1m

DUNSTER WORKING WATERMILL 🖼   ✖

Mill Lane, Dunster, nr Minehead TA24 6SW (tel. Dunster (0643) 821759)

On the site of a mill mentioned in the Domesday Survey of 1086; the present mill dates from the 18th century and was restored to working order in 1979

🅾   Good Fri 29 March to end June: daily except Sat (open Easter Sat) 11–5. July & Aug: daily 11–5. Sept & Oct: daily except Sat 11–5

💷   £1.30. Family tickets available: party rates by prior arrangement. The mill is run and maintained by private funding; NT members must pay normal admission charge. Parking, ¼m

🍽   Tea-room and tea-garden (not NT)

➜   On River Avill, beneath Castle Tor; approach via Mill Lane or Castle Gardens on foot; from car park in Dunster village or in old park [181: ST995435]
Bus & Station: As Dunster Castle, above

FYNE COURT 🖼🏠🌳👤   ✖

Broomfield, Bridgwater TA5 2EQ (tel. Kingston St Mary (0823) 451587)

Headquarters of the Somerset Trust for Nature Conservation and visitor centre for the Quantocks; the former pleasure grounds of the now demolished home of the pioneer electrician, Andrew Crosse

🅾 ❄   All year: daily 9–6 or sunset if earlier

💷   Free. Car park charge. Coach parking by prior arrangement only. Shop (not NT) open Easter to Christmas daily 2–5

♿   Trail for disabled visitors. ♿ WC

🍽♿   Teas on Sun and Bank Holidays during summer (not NT). Picnic sites

➜   6m N of Taunton at Broomfield; 9m SW of Bridgwater [182: ST222321]
Station: Taunton 6m

KING JOHN'S HUNTING LODGE 🏠

The Square, Axbridge BS26 2AP (tel. Axbridge (0934) 732012)

Early Tudor merchant's house extensively restored in 1971; museum of local history and archaeology, run by volunteers for Sedgemoor District Council

O   Easter to end Sept: daily 2–5

£   Free; guided tours by written arrangement. Council car park, 2 min. walk

●   In Axbridge (not NT)

→   In the Square, on corner of High Street [182: ST431545] *Bus:* Badgerline 126/7 , 826 Weston-super-Mare–Wells (passing close BR Weston-super-Mare) (tel. Weston-super-Mare (0934) 621201) *Station:* Worle 8m

LYTES CARY MANOR 🏠➕✿

Charlton Mackrell, Somerton TA11 7HU

Manor house with 14th-century chapel; 15th-century hall and 16th-century great chamber; home of Henry Lyte, translator of Niewe Herball *(1578); hedged gardens*

O   30 March to 30 Oct: Mon, Wed & Sat 2–6 or dusk if earlier; last admissions 5.30

£   £2.50, children £1.30. No reduction for parties. No WCs. Plants for sale

     Note: Large coaches cannot pass the gate piers so must stop in road, ¼m walk

♿   Garden only. ● Scented plants in herbaceous borders

→   1m N of Ilchester bypass A303; signposted from roundabout at junction of A303, A37 & A372 [183: ST529269] *Bus:* Badgerline Bristol–Yeovil (passing BR Bristol Temple Meads); Southern National 54 Yeovil–Taunton (passing close BR Taunton). Both pass within ¾m BR Yeovil Pen Mill. On both, alight Kingsdon, 1m (tel. Somerset CC: 0345 078 718) *Station:* Yeovil Pen Mill 8½m; Castle Cary 9m; Yeovil Junction 10m

MONTACUTE HOUSE 🏠❀♣ ✉

Montacute TA15 6XP (tel. Martock (0935) 823289)

Late 16th-century house; H-shaped ground plan and many Renaissance features, including contemporary plasterwork, chimneypieces and heraldic glass; fine 17th- and 18th-century furniture; exhibition of samplers dating from 17th century; Elizabethan and Jacobean portraits from the National Portrait Gallery displayed in the Long Gallery and adjoining rooms; formal garden; landscaped park

O ❀ **House:** 30 March to 3 Nov: daily except Tues 12–5.30. Last admission 5. Other times by arrangement with Administrator. **Garden and park:** 30 March to end March 1992: daily except Tues 11.30–5.30 or dusk if earlier

▢ ❀ Open daily except Tues. Closed Good Fri. 4–28 March & 4 Nov to 22 Dec 11.30–4.30; 30 March to 3 Nov 11.30–5.30. Tel. Martock (0935) 824575. Plant centre (not NT) selling interesting and unusual locally grown plants: April to end Sept: daily except Tues 2–6

£ House, garden & park £4. Garden & park only £2 (30 March to 3 Nov), £1 (4 Nov to end March 1992). Parties £3.50, children £1.70. Party organisers please book visits, lunches and teas by writing to Administrator (s.a.e. please)

♿ Garden, restaurant & shop only; ♿ WC. ♦ Braille guide

🐕 In park only, on leads

▣ ♿ Licensed restaurant; light lunches and teas open as shop (last orders 5).
❀ Tel. Martock (0935) 826294

➔ In Montacute village, 4m W of Yeovil, on S side of A3088, 3m E of A303 near Ilchester [183 & 193: ST499172] *Bus:* Safeway/Stennings Yeovil–South Petherton (passing within ¼m BR Yeovil Pen Mill) (tel. Somerset CC: 0345 078 718) *Station:* Yeovil Pen Mill 5½m; Yeovil Junction 7m; Crewkerne 7m

PRIEST'S HOUSE ⬚ ✕✕

Muchelney, Langport TA10 9DQ (tel. Langport (0458) 250672)

Late medieval hall house with large Gothic windows; originally residence of priests serving the parish church across the road; tenant's own collection of furniture and paintings

O   Normally by appointment, but please note that major conservation work is planned for part of 1991 during which the house will be closed. All enquiries to the National Trust Wessex Regional Office (see p. 22)

→   1m S of Langport [193: ST429250] *Bus:* Southern National 54 Yeovil–Taunton (passing close BR Taunton & within ¼m Yeovil Pen Mill), alight Huish Episcopi, ¼m (tel. Taunton (0823) 272033)

STEMBRIDGE TOWER MILL ⬚ ⬚

High Ham TA10 9DJ (tel. Langport (0458) 250818)

The last thatched windmill in England, dating from 1822 and in use until 1910

O   31 March to 29 Sept: Sun, Mon & Wed 2–5; special arrangements may be made for coach and school parties

£   £1.40. Parties by prior appointment with the tenant; no reduction. Parking for coaches ¼m. No WCs

→   2m N of Langport, ½m E of High Ham [182: ST432305]; take road opposite cemetery in High Ham, Mill is ¼m along on right
Station: Bridgwater 10m

TINTINHULL HOUSE GARDEN ⬚ ⬚

Tintinhull, nr Yeovil BA22 9PZ

Twentieth-century formal garden surrounding a 17th-century house; the layout, divided into areas by walls and hedges, has border colour and plant themes; shrub roses and clematis; kitchen garden

[O]	30 March to end Sept: Wed, Thur, Sat & BH Mon 2–6
[£]	£2.50. No reduction for parties or children. Coach parties by arrangement with tenant
[&] [◉]	Special parking by arrangement. Roses, honeysuckles and other scented plants
[♥]	In courtyard, not NT
[→]	5m NW of Yeovil, ½m S of A303, on E outskirts of Tintinhull [183: ST503198] *Bus:* Southern National 52 from Yeovil (passing within ¼m BR Yeovil Pen Mill) (tel. Yeovil (0935) 76233) *Station:* Yeovil Pen Mill 5½m; Yeovil Junction 7m

TREASURER'S HOUSE [🏠]

Martock TA12 6JL

Small house dating from 13th and 14th centuries with medieval hall and kitchen

[O] [✳]	By written appointment with tenant (s.a.e. please)
[£]	Medieval hall and kitchen only £1.20. No reduction for children or parties. No WCs
[♥]	In Martock (not NT)
[→]	Opposite church in middle of village; 1m NW of A303 between Ilminster and Ilchester [193: ST462191] *Bus:* Southern National 52 from Yeovil (passing within ¼m BR Yeovil Pen Mill) (tel. Yeovil (0935) 76233) *Station:* Crewkerne 7½m; Yeovil Pen Mill 8m

195

Staffordshire

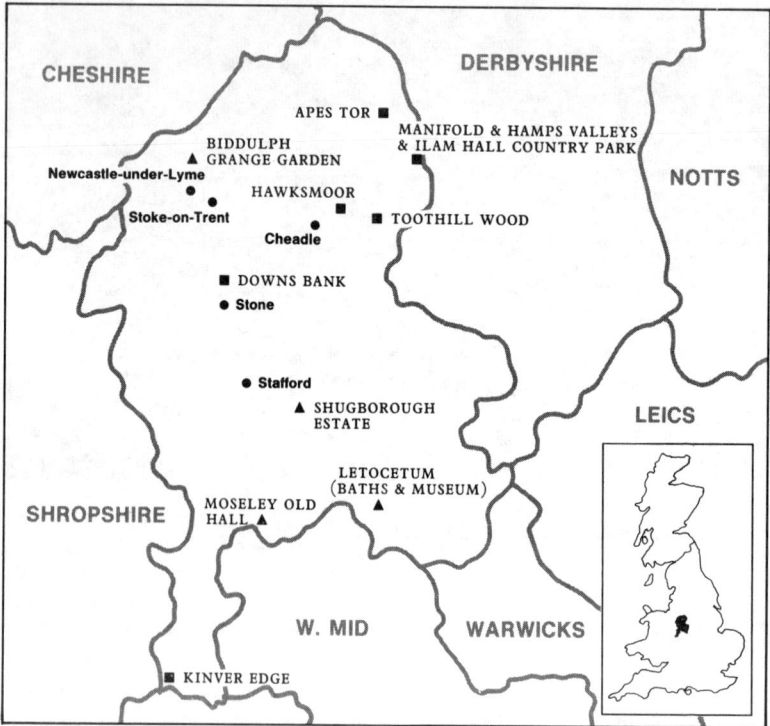

CHESHIRE

DERBYSHIRE

APES TOR ■

MANIFOLD & HAMPS VALLEYS
& ILAM HALL COUNTRY PARK

BIDDULPH
▲ GRANGE GARDEN

Newcastle-under-Lyme
●

NOTTS

HAWKSMOOR

Stoke-on-Trent
●

■ TOOTHILL WOOD

Cheadle ●

■ DOWNS BANK

● Stone

● Stafford

▲ SHUGBOROUGH
ESTATE

LEICS

LETOCETUM
(BATHS & MUSEUM)

MOSELEY OLD
HALL ▲

▲

SHROPSHIRE

W. MID

WARWICKS

■ KINVER EDGE

COUNTRYSIDE

On the Staffordshire/Derbyshire Peak District borders is **Apes Tor,** a rock face in the gorge of the River Manifold below Hulme End [119: SK100586]. It is of particular geological interest since it shows clearly the folding and faulting processes that have formed this part of the southern Peak District landscape.

The Trust owns over 1,000 acres of farmland and rock hills on the Staffordshire side of the **Manifold** and **Hamps Valleys** and **Dovedale** (see also p. 82). The Manifold and Hamps are beautiful, but lesser known perhaps than their sister river, the Dove. In dry summers they vanish underground down 'swallet' holes in the limestone, leaving a dry water-course for some miles until they reappear at Ilam. These river valleys support a wide range of limestone loving plants, and dippers and kingfisher haunt their waters. At Wetton Mill (NT) on the Manifold is a car park and refreshments (not NT). A well-surfaced, disused railway with adjacent car parks, gives good access to the Manifold and Hamps Valleys. The Dove joins the Manifold near **Ilam Hall** (see p. 198).

⌘ A fourth river, the Churnet, flows through **Hawksmoor** [128: SK035445], an area of some 300 acres of woodlands and farmland. There are several walks through Hawksmoor, including a nature trail.

Further south near Alton Towers (not NT), a recent gift to the Trust was 10 acres of **Toothill Wood** [128: SK066425]. The property includes part of the Staffordshire Way long-distance footpath, and the viewpoint of Toothill Rock.

To the south-west and not far from the industrial landscape of Stoke-on-Trent is **Downs Banks** [127: SJ902370] just north of Stone – undulating moorland with a stream, given to the Trust as a war memorial in 1946.

At the extreme south-west of the county, **Kinver Edge** [138: SO835830] gives views across the Severn Valley to the Shropshire Hills. The Trust owns 285 acres of this wood- and heath-covered sandstone ridge. A particularly interesting feature is the cave dwellings at Holy Austin Rock, which were, unbelievably, inhabited until the 1950s. In the 19th century some of these primitive homes were given a veneer of modernity in the shape of brick fronts and tiled gables, but these have gone, leaving only empty holes. There is wheelchair access to a limited part of the property, near the Warden's house.

BIDDULPH GRANGE GARDEN

Biddulph Grange, Biddulph, Stoke-on-Trent ST8 7SD
(tel. Stoke-on-Trent (0782) 517999

An exciting and rare survival of a high Victorian garden, acquired by the Trust in 1988 and focus of an extensive restoration project. Conceived by James Bateman, the 15 acres are divided into a number of smaller gardens designed to house specimens from his extensive and wide-ranging plant collection. An Egyptian Court, Chinese Pagoda, Joss House, Bridge and Pinetum together with many other settings all combine to make the garden a miniature tour of the world

1 May to 3 Nov: Wed to Fri 12–6, Sat, Sun & BH Mon 11–6. Last admissions 5.30 or dusk if earlier. Pre-booked guided tours at 10 on Wed, Thur & Fri. Also open 9 Nov to 18 Dec: Sat & Sun 12–4

Shop open as garden

£3. Family ticket £7.50. Pre-booked guided tours £5 (NT members incl.). Free car park 50yds

Access for disabled visitors difficult. Please contact Head Gardener for details. WC

Tea-room serving coffee, home-made teas and light refreshments open as garden

5m SE Congleton, 7m N of Stoke-on-Trent. Access from A527 (Tunstall Road). Entrance on Grange Road [118:SJ895591]. *Bus:* C-Line 87/8 from Congleton (passing BR Congleton) (tel. Chester (0244) 602666) *Station:* Congleton 2½m

PLEASE REFER TO PAGES 5–9

ILAM HALL COUNTRY PARK 🟢🧑‍🦯🚻✝

Ilam, Ashbourne, Derbyshire DE6 2AZ (tel. Thorpe Cloud (033 529) 245)

84 acres of attractive park and woodland on both banks of the river Manifold, in the South Peak Estate, with magnificent views towards Thorpe Cloud and the entrance to Dovedale

O ❄ **Grounds and Park:** all year, daily. Hall is let to YHA and is not open.

□ ❄ Shop and Information Centre with an exhibition on Ilam and the South Peak Estate. Jan to 30 March: Sat & Sun 10–4; 31 March to 26 Oct; daily 10–6; 27 Oct to 22 Dec: Sat & Sun 10–4; Jan to end March 1992: Sat & Sun 10–4

£ Free. Car park 60p (NT members free); minibuses & coaches £1.20; no coaches Sun or BH Mon

🐕 On leads only

♿ Access to Information Centre

🍽 ❄ Manifold Restaurant open as shop for hot and cold lunches, refreshments and teas. Booked parties by arrangement

Notes: Guided walks around the estate may be booked by groups; contact Head Warden (tel. Thorpe Cloud (033 529) 503). Day visit room for booked school, youth and adult groups; service provided jointly by NT and Peak National Park offers illustrated talks, guided walks, farm visits and fieldwork. Further details from the National Park Study Centre, Losehill Hall, Castleton, Derbyshire S30 2WB (tel. Hope Valley (0433) 20373). 55 berth caravan site run by Caravan Club: open to non-members of Caravan Club: Easter to mid Oct (tel. Thorpe Cloud (033 529) 310). Backpackers – lightweight camp site; no facilities. Groups book with Head Warden; see above

➔ 4½m NW of Ashbourne [119: SK132507] *Bus:* Warrington 443 from Ashbourne, Thur, Sat only, with connections from Derby, also various services from BR Buxton and Derby, summer Suns only; otherwise Shearings 201 Derby–Manchester (passing close BR Derby & Macclesfield), alight Ilam Cross Roads, 2m (tel. Derby (0332) 292200 for all services)

LETOCETUM (BATHS & MUSEUM) 🏛

Watling Street, Wall, nr Lichfield (tel. Shenstone (0543) 480768)

Excavated bath-house of a Roman posting station on Watling Street; the most complete example of its kind in Britain; interesting museum

Letocetum is in the guardianship of English Heritage

O ❄ Good Fri 29 March to end Sept: daily 10–6. Oct to end March 1992: daily except Mon: 10–4. Shop

£ Museum & site 95p. OAPs and UB40 holders 75p. Parties of 11 or more 15% discount. Schools free bookings (tel. Wolverhampton (0902) 765105)

Note: Informal talk given in museum for small parties only, on prior request

♿ Museum only. Site on uneven ground

🐕 On leads only

➔ 2m SW of Lichfield, on N side of A5 [139: SK099066] *Station:* Shenstone 1½m

---

MOSELEY OLD HALL 🏠 ❄ ✻   ✉ ✉ ✉

Moseley Old Hall Lane, Fordhouses, Wolverhampton WV10 7HY
(tel. Wolverhampton (0902) 782808)

Elizabethan house with later alterations. Charles II hid here after the battle of Worcester; the bed in which he slept is on view, also the hiding place he used; small garden reconstructed in 17th-century style with formal box parterre; 17th-century plants only grown; Sandford Heritage Education Award winner

🔅 16 March to end Oct: Wed, Sat, Sun & BH Mon; also Tues in July & Aug 2–5.30. Pre-booked parties at other times incl. evening tours

🛒 Shop open as house. Also 10 Nov to 15 Dec: Sun only 2–4.30

£ £2.50. Family £6.25. All parties by previous arrangement; joint ticket with Benthall Hall (see p. 185) £3.75

🎓 Educational facilities

♿ Ground floor (3 rooms) and garden only; ♿ WC in garden

🍽 Licensed restaurant in 18th-century barn. Teas, as house; and 10 Nov to 15 Dec: Sun only 2–4.30. Lunches, suppers and candlelit suppers at other times for pre-booked parties. ♿ Two tables on ground floor

➔ 4m N of Wolverhampton; S of M54 between A449 and A460; traffic from N on M6 leave motorway at Shareshill, then A460; 2½m S of Shareshill island; traffic from S on M6 & M54 take Jn. 1 to Wolverhampton; coaches **must** approach via A460 to avoid low bridge [127: SJ932044] *Bus:* Chaserider 870–2 Wolverhampton–Cannock (passing close BR Wolverhampton), alight Bognop Road, ¾m; W Midlands Travel 532/3 from Wolverhampton, thence ¾m (all pass close BR Wolverhampton) (tel. 021–200 2601) *Station:* Wolverhampton 4m

SHUGBOROUGH ESTATE 🏛 ❄ 🏠 🌳 📷 ⚔   ⨯

Milford, nr Stafford ST17 0XB (tel. Little Haywood (0889) 881388)

The Shugborough Estate is being restored as a 19th-century working estate. Shugborough Hall is the 18th-century home of the Earls of Lichfield; enlarged c.1750, altered by Samuel Wyatt 1790–1806; collections of French and English china, silver, paintings and furniture; rococo plasterwork by Vassalli; in the stable block is the Staffordshire County Museum with recreations of 19th-century life including original kitchens, laundry and working brew-house; in the parkland is a Georgian farmstead built in 1805 for Thomas, Viscount Anson as home farm for the estate, now working farm museum with rare breeds and demonstrations of traditional farming methods; extensive parkland with neo-Classical monuments; Victorian terraces and rose gardens; garden and woodland walks

Shugborough is financed and administered by Staffordshire County Council. NT members are entitled to free entry to Mansion House only and must pay vehicle entry charge and any special event charge which may be in operation. Admission charges and opening arrangements may vary when special events are held. Telephone property for details of 1991 events programme

🅾 ❄ House, museum, farm and gardens: Good Fri 29 March to 27 Oct: daily 11–5. Open from 10.30 on weekdays for booked parties. 28 Oct to 27 March 1992: booked parties only (museum, farm, gardens and conservation tours of house: tel. property for details)

£ Parkland £1 per vehicle (NT members incl.) giving access to parkland, gardens, picnic area and walks and trails. Free car park at farm for farm visitors. House, museum & farm £6 (otherwise £2.50 per site); children, OAPs, registered unemployed and parties £3 (otherwise £1.50 per site); family ticket (2 adults and 2 children) £12. Guided walks and trails for booked parties throughout the year £1 per head. Evening visits for booked parties (min. 30) £3 per site plus cost of supper. Guided tours available for school parties at £1 per head per site (all 3 sites for £2.50); working demonstrations available from Oct to Easter £2 per head per demonstration; schools must book in advance

🏠 ❄ NT shop at house and farm. Tel. Little Haywood (0889) 881388

🅰 'Noah's Park' at farm gives children chance to see and touch domestic and rare breeds of animal and poultry. Games gallery in corn mill. Farm quiz book. Children's play area. Activity Days in August

♿ Museum and farm accessible (reduced admission charge); access can be arranged to ground floor of house if prior notice is given. ♿ WC

🐕 Dogs on lead in parkland only. Guide dogs admitted to house and museum

🍽 ♿ ❄ Lunches, high teas and snacks in tea-room near museum; dinners available to pre-booked parties (min. 20). Tea-room at farm for light refreshments open as house. Picnic sites by main and farm car parks

➜ 6m E of Stafford on A513; entrance at Milford [127: SJ992225]
Bus: Chaserider 822–5 Stafford–Lichfield (passing close BR Stafford & Lichfield) (tel. Stafford (0785) 58388)

Suffolk

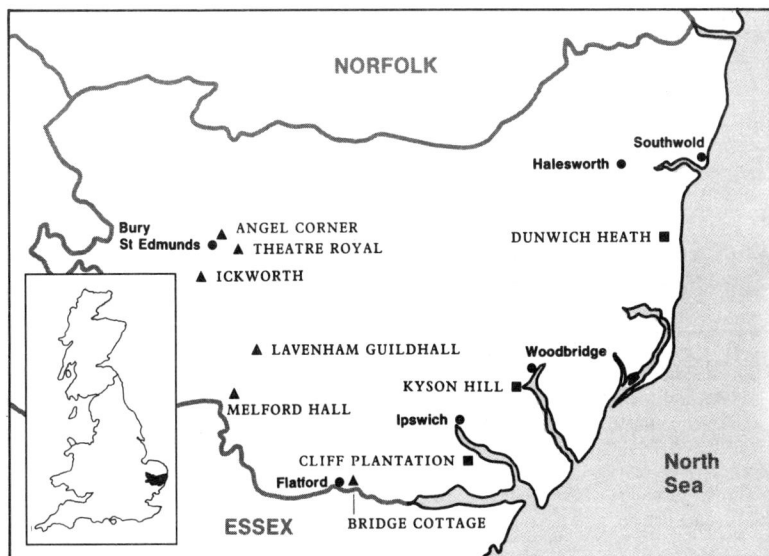

COAST AND COUNTRYSIDE

Dunwich Heath is described fully in the entry on p. 202. At **Kyson Hill** just south of Woodbridge, there are lovely views of the winding River Deben from 4 acres of parkland, with fine walks [169: TM269477].

Further south near Chelmondiston Village on the Orwell is the **Cliff Plantation** east of **Pin Mill**, a well-known beauty spot for visitors from Ipswich. This natural woodland is accessible on foot in any weather, and there are fine views of the river and an extremely varied collection of fishing boats, Thames barges and pleasure craft of all types are drawn up on the shore [169: TM214380].

LINNET

ANGEL CORNER 🏠 ✉

8 Angel Hill, Bury St Edmunds
(tel. Bury St Edmunds (0284) 757072) (weekdays); 763436 (weekends))

A Queen Anne house containing the Gershom-Parkington collection of clocks and watches

O ❄	All year: daily 10–5, (Sun 2–5). Closed Good Fri, 24, 25 & 26 Dec	
£	Free; donations welcome. Parties requiring a lecture should book with the Curator. No WCs	
☕	Tea and coffee	
➜	[155: TL855643] *Bus:* From surrounding areas (tel. Bury St Edmunds (0284) 766171) *Station:* Bury St Edmunds ½m	

BRIDGE COTTAGE 🏠 ☕

Flatford, East Bergholt, Colchester, Essex CO7 6OL
(tel. Colchester (0206) 298260/298865)

Just upstream from Flatford Mill, the restored thatched cottage houses a display about John Constable, several of whose paintings depict this property; tea garden; shop; boats for hire; Information Centre

O	30 March to end May & Oct: Wed to Sun & BH Mon 11–5.30. June to end Sept: daily 11–5.30	
🛍 ❄	Shop open as cottage. Also 31 Oct to 22 Dec: Thur to Sun 11–3.30	
£	Parking 200yds; private car park, charge (NT members included). Free admission to Bridge Cottage	
🐕	On leads only	
♿	Special car parking; please ask for temporary permit. Access to tea garden and shop	
☕ ❄	Teas & light lunches as cottage; also 31 Oct to 22 Dec: Sat & Sun only 11–3.30	
➜	On N bank of Stour, 1m S of East Bergholt (B1070). [168: TM077332] *Bus:* Eastern Counties, 92–6 Ipswich–Colchester (passing BR Ipswich and close BR St Botolphs), alight E Bergholt, ¾m (tel. Ipswich (0473) 253734) *Station:* Manningtree 1¾m by footpath, 3½m by road	

DUNWICH HEATH ☕ 🏞 🐕 👤

Dunwich, Saxmundham IP17 3DJ (tel. Westleton (072 873) 505)

215 acres of sandy cliffs and a fine example of Sandlings heathland with a mile of beach; nature walk and access to public hides at the adjacent RSPB Minsmere reserve

O ❄	All year: dawn to dusk; introductory talks available for group visits	

202

⬜🏵 Shop, April, May, June, Sept & Oct: Wed to Sun 11–5; July & Aug: daily 11–5. Nov to 22 Dec: Thur to Sun 11–4. Jan to end March: Sat & Sun only, 11–4

💷 Parking fees: cars £1; coaches £5; season tickets £5

♿ Car park viewing point and some footpaths accessible. Please contact the Warden for further information. Adapted ♿ WC at coastguard cottages; stairlift to viewing room. Batricar available. Holiday flat for disabled guests at the coastguard cottages

🍴♿ Tea-room in coastguard cottages, open as shop (Nov to end March: 11–3.30)
🏵

🐕 Must be on leads

Notes: Information Room in coastguard cottages; day and season tickets for coarse fishing; sea angling; 3 holiday flats for rent

➡ 1m S of Dunwich, signposted off Dunwich to Westleton road [156: TM475683] *Station:* Darsham 6m

---

ICKWORTH 🏛🏵🍴👤🏛   ✕🚫

Ickworth, The Rotunda, Horringer, Bury St Edmunds IP29 5QE
(tel. Bury St Edmunds (0284) 735270)

Begun about 1794, completed 1830, the house is an eccentric elliptical rotunda connected by two curved corridors to flanking wings; sumptuous state rooms with 18th-century and late Regency furniture; magnificent silver; picture collection; formal garden; several miles of waymarked woodland and park walks; old walled garden and summer-house; deer enclosure

⭕ **House:** 30 March to end April: Sat, Sun & BH Mon 1.30–5.30. May to end
🏵 Sept: Tues, Wed, Fri, Sat, Sun & BH Mon 1.30–5.30. Oct: Sat & Sun 1.30–
5.30. **Park:** all year: daily 7–7   *continued*

🏠❄ Shop same days as house 12–5.15. Also 1 Nov to 22 Dec: Fri to Sun 12–3.30

💷 House, garden & park £3.50, children £1.50. Parties £3 (no party rate Sun & BH Mon). Access to park & garden £1 (access to shop & restaurant with park ticket). 35 min. tape guide to house available

🅰️🚼 Children's playground next to car park. Childrens guide. Baby slings available

♿👁 Disabled visitors may be taken up to the house. Access to house via 2 steps; then all ground floor rooms are level. Much of garden accessible, but gravel drive and paths. ♿ WC. Shop & restaurant in basement; regret not accessible to wheelchair users. 👁 Braille guide

🐕 In park only, on leads

🍽 Lunches & teas; table licence, open as shop

➡ In Horringer, 3m SW of Bury St Edmunds on W side of A143 [155: TL8161] *Bus:* Eastern Counties 141–4 Bury St Edmunds–Haverhill (passing close BR Bury St Edmunds) (tel. Bury St Edmunds (0284) 766171) *Station:* Bury St Edmunds 3m

LAVENHAM GUILDHALL 🏠❄ ✖ ✖

Market Place, Lavenham CO10 9QZ (tel. Lavenham (0787) 247646)

Early 16th-century timber-framed Tudor building; overlooks and dominates the market place; originally hall of the Guild of Corpus Christi; display of local history, farming and industry including a unique exhibition of 700 years of the medieval woollen cloth trade; garden

🅾 30 March to 3 Nov: daily 11–5. Parts of the building may be in use for community purposes but it is otherwise open to the public

🏠❄ Shop open as Guildhall. Also 7 Nov to 22 Dec: Thur to Sun 11–4

💷 £1.80, children 60p. Parties £1.50: please book with s.a.e. to Custodian-in-Charge. School parties 50p by prior arrangement. ♿ Shop & tea-room only

🅰️ Children's guide

🍽♿ Tea-room for coffee, light lunches & teas (closed some Mon & Tues for community purposes). Also 9 Nov to 1 Dec: Sat & Sun 11–4

➡ A1141 and B1071 [155: TL917494] *Bus:* Chambers 1/2/8 Bury St Edmunds–Colchester (passing close BR Bury St Edmunds & Sudbury) (tel. Bures (0787) 227233) *Station:* Sudbury (U) 7m

MELFORD HALL 🏠 ❋ 🗙 🖾

Long Melford, Sudbury CO10 9AH (tel. Sudbury (0787) 880286)

A turreted brick Tudor mansion, little changed since 1578 with the original panelled banqueting hall, an 18th-century drawing room, a Regency library and a Victorian bedroom, showing fine furniture and Chinese porcelain; garden; special Beatrix Potter display

◉ 30 March to end April: Sat, Sun & BH Mon 2–5.30. May to end Sept: Wed, Thur, Sat, Sun & BH Mon 2–5.30. Oct: Sat & Sun 2–5.30

£ Principal rooms & garden £2.40. Pre-arranged parties £2 Wed & Thur only, please book with s.a.e. to Administrator

🄰 Children's guide.

♿ Disabled visitors may be driven to the Hall. Ground floor rooms easily accessible; stairlift available to first floor; some steps in garden. ♿ WC (by main entrance)

☕ In Long Melford

➜ In Long Melford on E side of A134, 14m S of Bury St Edmunds, 3m N of Sudbury [155: TL867462] *Bus:* Theobolds/Chambers various services (but frequent) from Sudbury (passing BR Sudbury) (tel. Suffolk CC Ipswich (0473) 265676 *Station:* Sudbury (U) 4m

THEATRE ROYAL 🏠 🖾

Westgate Street, Bury St Edmunds IP33 1QR
(tel. Bury St Edmunds (0284) 755127)

Built in 1819 by William Wilkins, a rare example of a late Georgian playhouse with fine pit, boxes and gallery; working theatre, still used

◉ ❋ All year: daily except Sun, 10–6. Closed Good Fri & BH Mon. No access to auditorium if theatrical activity is in progress. The theatre may be closed altogether during parts of Aug when no performances are being staged. To avoid disappointment visitors should enquire by letter or telephone

£ Free. Tour for parties by prior arrangement with the Administrator, £20. Limited parking in Westgate Street. No parking in front of the theatre

☕ Meals; licensed bar in theatre for evening performances

Events: For 1991 events programme please send s.a.e. to Administrator. Box Office Bury St Edmunds (0284) 769505

➜ In Westgate Street on S side of A134 from Sudbury (one-way system) [155: TL855637] *Bus:* From surrounding areas (tel. Bury St Edmunds (0284) 766171) *Station:* Bury St Edmunds ¾m

PLEASE REFER TO PAGES 5–9

Surrey

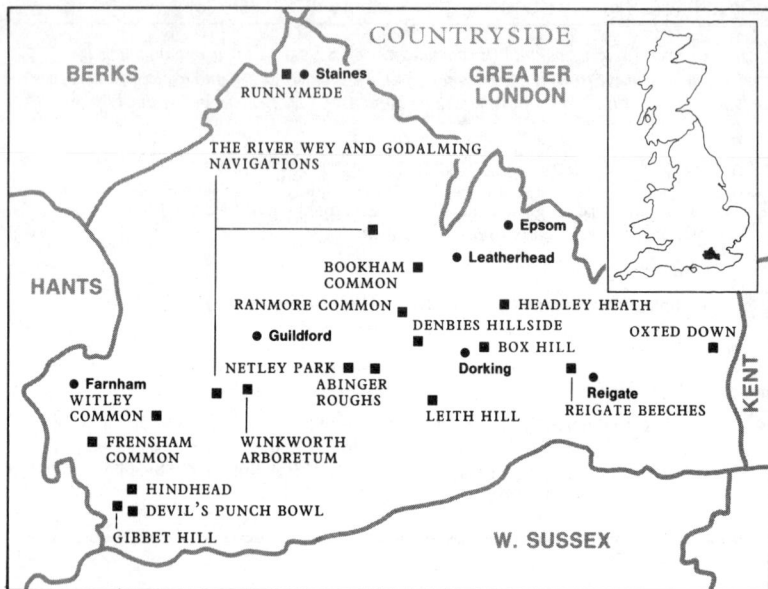

COUNTRYSIDE

BERKS

GREATER LONDON

■ ● Staines
RUNNYMEDE

THE RIVER WEY AND GODALMING
NAVIGATIONS

● Epsom

● Leatherhead

BOOKHAM ■
COMMON

RANMORE COMMON ■

HANTS

HEADLEY HEATH

DENBIES HILLSIDE

● Guildford

OXTED DOWN ■

NETLEY PARK ■ ■

■ BOX HILL

Dorking ●

● Farnham
WITLEY
COMMON ■

ABINGER
ROUGHS

Reigate

KENT

REIGATE BEECHES

■ LEITH HILL

■ FRENSHAM
COMMON

WINKWORTH
ARBORETUM

■ HINDHEAD
■ ■ DEVIL'S PUNCH BOWL
GIBBET HILL

W. SUSSEX

COUNTRYSIDE

The Trust owns a great deal of common land in Surrey and some famous viewpoints such as **Box Hill** (see p. 208) and **Leith Hill, Coldharbour Common, Duke's Warren and the Rhododendron Wood** (see p. 210). There are many lesser known properties, which are just as beautiful. ⟨i⟩ **Bookham and Banks Commons** west of Leatherhead [187: TQ1256] are of particular interest for their rich bird life. The manor of Bocheham is known to have been owned by Chertsey Abbey as early as 666 AD, and in the Domesday Survey the commons are listed as providing pannage – the right to graze pigs on acorns – for the Abbey. Access is by footpaths and bridle ways and there are parking facilities. Not far away **Ranmore Common** [187: TQ1451] and **Denbies Hillside** [187: TQ145503] bound the southern edges of the Polesden Lacey estate (see p. 211) and offer good walks on the south slopes of the North Downs.

North of Abinger Hammer, and 4 miles west of Dorking there is a car park from which you can explore on foot the wooded ridge of **Abinger Roughs** and **Netley Park** [187: TQ111480]. Sadly, many of these areas were damaged in the great storms of October 1987 and January 1990.

Nearer London, between **Reigate** and Banstead Heath [187: TQ250520] are 360 acres of open down, copse and beechwood on the North Downs with views towards the South Downs. This includes **Colley Hill, Reigate Fort, Reigate Beeches**, a short strip of the **Pilgrim's Way, Margery Wood, Juniper Hill**, and wood and parkland at **Gatton**.

Four miles south of Epsom, near Box Hill, some 530 acres of **Headley Heath,** including

MALLARD AND MOORHEN

the Lordship of Headley Manor [197: TQ2053] were originally grazed by sheep and other stock; continuing management by the Trust enables the various habitats to be maintained for the benefit of a great variety of plants, trees, birds and insects.

Much further south at **Hindhead** are more than 1,400 acres of heathland and woodland [186: SU8936]. [⚐] There are nature walks through the **Devil's Punch Bowl** and **Gibbet Hill**; from the latter are panoramic views to the Chilterns and over the Weald to the South Downs.

Astride the A287 Hindhead to Farnham road is **Frensham Common** [169: SU8540], now part of a country park managed by Waverley Borough Council in which the Trust owns about 1,000 acres, including Frensham Great and Little Ponds. There is a wide variety of wildlife, including wildfowl.

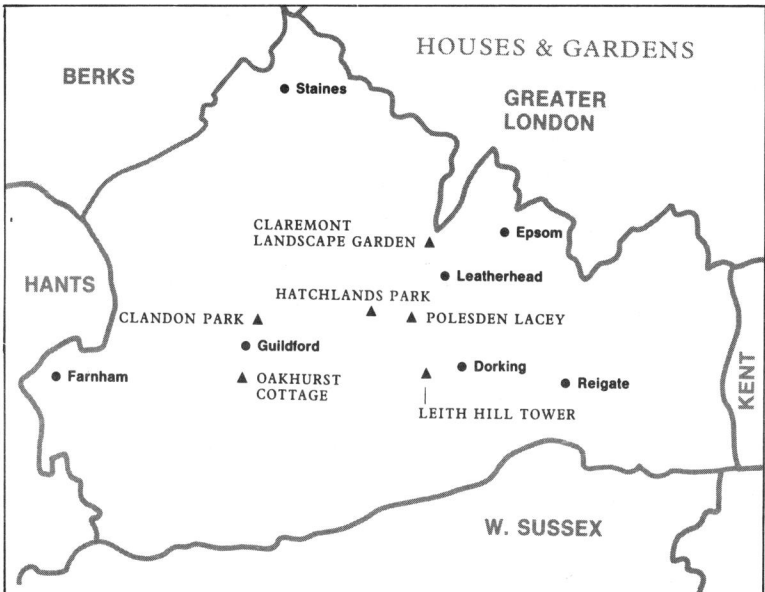

BOX HILL ⚒️🚶🏠

(General enquries: tel. Dorking (0306) 885502)

On the edge of the North Downs, rising 400ft from the River Mole; more than 800 acres of woods and chalk downland with magnificent views to the South Downs; a designated Country Park with nature walks; summit buildings include an exhibition room and 1890s' fort currently being restored

O ❄️ All year

🏠 ❄️ Shop & Information Room: Good Fri 29 March to end Oct: Wed to Sun & BH Mon 11–5.30; Nov to mid Dec: Wed to Sun 12–4

£ Countryside free. Coaches must not use the zig-zag road from Burford Bridge on W side of the hill as a weight restriction applies, but must approach from E side of the hill B2032 or B2033; car/coach parks at top of hill; pay & display £1 (free to NT members displaying membership cards)

♿ Summit area including shop & restaurant. Special parking by restaurant. Wheelchair path to viewpoint. ♿ WCs near NT shop

🐕 Must be kept under control, sheep grazing

🍴 ❄️ Morning coffee, lunches and teas. Licensed restaurant open all year, daily (except Mon & Tues, but open BH Mon): April to end Sept: 11–5.30; Oct to end March: 11–4. Closed 25 & 26 Dec. Booking advisable for lunches at weekends (tel. Dorking (0306) 888793). Servery (take-away) April to end Sept: daily 10.30–5.30 (open BH Mon). Oct to end March: daily 10.30–4. Closed 25 & 26 Dec.

Events: 30 June, Country Day (car park £1 incl. NT members)

→ 1m N of Dorking, 2½m S of Leatherhead on A24 [187: TQ171519] *Bus:* Epsom Buses 516 BR Leatherhead–Box Hill; 551 Dorking–Box Hill (passing BR Betchworth) (tel. Epsom (037 27) 28201) *Station:* Boxhill, Dorking & Westhumble ½m

CLANDON PARK 🏠❄️🏠   ☒

West Clandon, Guildford GU4 7RQ (tel. Guildford (0483) 222482)

Built in early 1730s for the 2nd Lord Onslow by the Venetian architect, Giacomo Leoni; two-storeyed Marble Hall; Onslow family pictures and furniture and Gubbay collection of porcelain, furniture and needlework; old kitchens; Queen's Royal Surrey Regimental Museum; garden with parterre, grotto and Maori House

O Good Fri 29 March to end Oct: daily except Thur & Fri (but open Good Fri) 1.30–5.30; BH Mon and preceding Sun 11–5.30. Last admissions 5

🏠 ❄️ Shop open as house. Also open for Christmas shopping and some weekends in March. Tel Guildford (0483) 211412

£ 🏃 House, garden & museum £3. Parties, Mon to Wed only, £2.50; parties and guided tours by prior arrangement with Administrator. Parking 300yds

[icon] Nappy-changing table available

[icon] Parking near front of house for disabled **drivers** only; disabled visitors may be set down at house; [icon] WC on lower ground floor; ramp to garden

[icon] On leads in picnic area and car park only

[icon][icon] Licensed restaurant in house on days house is open. Lunches 12.30–2; teas
[icon] 3.15–5.30 available for visitors to house only. Also open some weekends in March and pre-Christmas. Prior booking for lunch advisable (tel. Guildford (0483) 222502). Picnic area

Notes: The house is available for non-residential private and commercial functions, and a series of concerts is held in the Marble Hall; the Administrator welcomes enquiries. The park is not owned by the National Trust and is not open to the public. Garden Centre (not NT); tel. Guildford (0483) 222925 for opening times

[icon] At West Clandon on A247, 3m E of Guildford; if using A3 follow signposts to Ripley to join A247 via B2215 [186: TQ042512] *Bus:* Blue Saloon 532 BR Bookham–Guildford (passing BR Clandon) (tel. Guildford (0483) 64226); London & Country 408 W Croydon–Guildford (passing close BR Guildford), alight W Clandon Cross Roads, ¼m (tel. 081-668 7261) *Station:* Clandon 1m

CLAREMONT LANDSCAPE GARDEN [icon]   [icon]
Portsmouth Road, Esher, KT10 9JG

One of the earliest surviving English landscape gardens, restored by NT; begun by Sir John Vanbrugh and Charles Bridgeman before 1720, extended and naturalised by William Kent; Capability Brown also made improvements; lake, island with pavilion; grotto; turf amphitheatre, viewpoints and avenues; house not NT

[icon][icon] All year: daily. March: 9–5. April to end Oct: 9–7. (10–14 July garden closes 4). Nov to end March 1992: 9–5 or sunset if earlier. Last admissions ½hr before closing. Closed 25 Dec & 1 Jan

[icon][icon] Shop: March: Sat & Sun 11–4.30; April to end Oct: daily (except Mon) 11–5.30; Nov to 15 Dec; daily except Mon 11–4.30; 11 Jan to end March 1992: Sat & Sun 11–4.30

[icon][icon] Sun & BH Mon £2, Mon to Sat £1.20; no reduction for parties. Guided tours (min. 15 persons) £1 extra per person by prior booking: tel. Esher (0372) 469421. All coach parties must book; **no coaches on Sun**. Parking at entrance
continued

209

⛼ Level pathway around lake; and level grassland. ⛼ WC in car park

✖ Dogs not admitted April to end Oct

☕⛼ Tea-room serving morning coffee, hot and cold lunches and home-made teas.
❄ Open as shop. Last orders ½ hr before closing.

Events: 10–14 July, Fête Champêtre; postal applications only (s.a.e. please)
from 15 April to: Claremont Box Office, Polesden Lacey, Dorking, Surrey
RH5 6BD (tel. enquiries from 28 May: Bookham (0372) 457223). ⛼ Special
car parking for disabled drivers only. Please note garden closes 4pm on 10–14
July

➔ On S edge of Esher, on E side of A307 (no access from Esher bypass) [187:
TQ128634] *Bus:* Green Line 715 Oxford Circus–Guildford (passing close BR
Esher) (tel. 081-668 7261) *Station:* Esher 2m; Hersham 2m; Hinchley Wood
2½m

HATCHLANDS PARK 🏛❄   ✖ ✖ ✖

East Clandon, Guildford GU4 7RT (tel. Guildford (0483) 222787)

*A handsome brick house built in 1750s by Stiff Leadbetter for Admiral Boscawen, hero of the
Battle of Louisberg; splendid interiors by Robert Adam; in 1988 the Cobbe collection of fine
keyboard instruments, paintings and furniture was installed and the house was extensively
redecorated; the garden, by Repton and Gertrude Jekyll, is being restored*

🅞 31 March to 20 Oct: Tues, Wed, Thur, Sun & BH Mon (and Sat in Aug) 2–5.30

🗋 ❄ Shop open as house. Also for Christmas shopping

£ £2.80. Parties £2.30, Tues, Wed & Thur only. Parking 150yds

🧍 Facilities in ladies' cloakroom for nursing mothers; nappy-changing table

⛼ Ground floor, terrace and part of garden. Special car parking for disabled
drivers only, by prior arrangement with Administrator; disabled visitors may
be set down at house

☕ Light lunches 12.30–2 and home-made teas 2.30–5 same days as house.
⛼ Alternative easier access for wheelchair users

Events: Recitals are held in the house; please apply to Administrator for details

➔ E of East Clandon, N of A246 Guildford-Leatherhead road [187: TQ063518]
Bus: As Clandon Park, p. 208, but all services pass house
Station: Clandon 2½m, Horsley 3m

LEITH HILL TOWER 🏛🥾

(Tel. at Tower during opening hours: Dorking (0306) 712434)

*An 18th-century tower on the highest point in south-east England; the top of the tower is
1,029ft above sea level and provides magnificent views to the North and South Downs. The
beautiful Rhododendron Wood is ¾m to the south-west, best April/May*

[O] [✴] Good Fri 29 March to end Sept: Wed 2–5; Sat, Sun & BH 11–5. Last admissions 4.30. Also open fine weekends Oct to end March. Due to repair work on the outside of the Tower, access may be limited during certain periods

[£] [𝒻] Tower: 50p. No reduction for parties. Rhododendron Wood: donations welcome. Parking in designated areas along road at foot of the hill, ½ mile walk from Tower, some steep gradients. No direct vehicular access to summit. No coaches. Information room in tower

[♿] Limited access to Rhododendron Wood

[🐕] In woodland and countryside only, not in Tower

[☕] Light refreshments open same times as Tower

[→] On summit of Leith Hill, 1m SW of Coldharbour A29/B2126 [187: TQ139432]. Rhododendron Wood: [187: TQ131427] *Bus:* Tillingbourne 22 Guildford–Dorking (passing close BR Guildford and passing BR Chilworth and Dorking), alight Holmbury St Mary, 2½m (tel. Cranleigh (0483) 276880) *Station:* Holmwood (U), not Sun, 2½m; Dorking 5½m

OAKHURST COTTAGE [🏠]   [✖]

Hambledon, nr Godalming (tel. Wormley (0428) 684733)

A very small timber-framed cottage, restored and furnished as a cottager's dwelling

[O] 30 March to end Oct: Wed, Thur, Sat, Sun & BH Mon 2–5. Small groups by special appointment only with Mrs E. Hardy (tel. no. above)

[£] £1.70. No reduction for parties. Max. 6 visitors per party. Property too small for coach parties. Parking 200yds. No WCs

POLESDEN LACEY [🏠][✴][♠]   [✖]

nr Dorking RH5 6BD (tel. Bookham (0372) 458203 or 452048)

Originally an 1820s' Regency villa, remodelled after 1906 by the Hon. Mrs Ronald Greville, well-known Edwardian hostess; fine paintings, furniture, porcelain and silver; photographs from Mrs Greville's albums. Extensive grounds, walled rose garden, lawns; views; King George VI and Queen Elizabeth (now the Queen Mother) spent part of their honeymoon here

[O][✴] **House:** March & Nov: Sat & Sun only 1.30–4.30; 29 March to end Oct: Wed to Sun (incl. Good Fri) 1.30–5.30; also open BH Mon & preceding Sun 11–5.30. **Grounds:** daily all year: 11–sunset. Last admissions to house ½hr before closing

[🛍][✴] Shop open same days as house from 11. Also open for Christmas shopping. Tel. Bookham (0372) 57230

[£] Garden only 29 March to end Oct £2; Nov to 24 March 1992 £1.20; house Sun & BH Mon £3 extra; other open days £2 extra. Parties £3.50 (house & garden) weekdays only by prior arrangement with Administrator. No prams or pushchairs in house. Parking 150yds

[👶] Nappy-changing table in ladies' WC. High chair available in restaurant

continued

211

All showrooms and parts of garden; some fairly firm gravel paths . Disabled drivers may park near shop, restaurant and house with permission of Administrator; [&] WC near restaurant. Rose & lavender gardens

No dogs in formal gardens or on lawns. Allowed in rest of grounds on leads. Good walks on estate

Coffee, lunches and home-made teas in licensed restaurant in courtyard. Jan to March (light refreshments): Sat & Sun only 1.30–4.30. 29 March to end Oct: Wed to Sun & BH Mon 11–5.30 (closed 2–2.30). Also open as shop Nov & Dec. Last orders ½hr before closing. Evening functions by special arrangement (tel. Bookham (0372) 456190). Snack bar serving light refreshments at peak times. Picnic site by main car park

Events: 19 June to 7 July, open-air theatre: postal applications only (s.a.e. please) from 15 April to PLOAT Box Office, Polesden Lacey, Dorking, Surrey RH5 6BD (tel. enquiries from 28 May: Bookham (0372) 457223) [&]. 7 July Polesden Fair; extra entrance charge, incl NT members

Notes: Estate includes a YHA hostel and a Camping Club members' site. Coaches approaching from Dorking should not turn off through Westhumble, but take A246 at Givons Grove roundabout before Leatherhead

5m NW of Dorking, 2m S of Great Bookham, off A246 Leatherhead-Guildford road [187: TQ136522] *Bus:* London & Country 408 Guildford–West Croydon, (passing close BR Guildford & Leatherhead), alight Great Bookham, 2m (tel. 081-668 7261) *Station:* Boxhill & Westhumble 2½m via scenic path through NT park; Bookham 2½m

---

THE RIVER WEY & GODALMING NAVIGATIONS

Navigation Manager, Dapdune Lea, Wharf Road, Guildford GU1 4RR
(tel. Guildford (0483) 61389)

One of the earliest historic waterways, built in 1670; a tranquil river retaining its old locks and weirs; supports many species of water birds and a varied flora and fauna; extending from the River Thames at Weybridge to Godalming Wharf, a distance of 19½ miles, and presently the most southerly point of the inland waterway system

|O| |❄| Towing path for walkers, free visitors' moorings, and the 19½-mile waterway throughout the year (except Christmas Day) during daylight hours, subject to stoppages for major maintenance purposes

|£| Towing path: walkers and moorings for visiting boats, no charge. Navigation licences (including all lock tolls) are payable on all powered and non-powered craft issued for the year or for 7- or 21-day visits, with 10% reduction for 7 or 21 days only, for visiting NT members on production of current membership card. Check on insurance and outboard engine size before visiting property

|🐕| Must be kept under control

|→| Access from A3 & M25. Visiting craft can enter from the Thames at Shepperton or slipways at Guildford or Pyrford *Station:* Addlestone, Byfleet & New Haw; Guildford, Farncombe & Godalming all lie close to the navigation

RUNNYMEDE 🖼

(tel. Egham (0784) 432891)

188 acres of historic meadows where King John sealed the Magna Carta in 1215; 110 acres of wooded slopes of Cooper's Hill overlook the meadows, giving fine views of the surrounding countryside; memorials dedicated to the Magna Carta, John F. Kennedy and the Air Forces

|O| |❄| All year. Riverside car park open April to end Sept weather permitting. Tea-room car park open all year

|🛍| |🏪| Magna Carta tea-room and shop open April to end Sept: daily 10.30–5.30 (or later at peak times)

|£| Car park 80p; coaches £3. Fishing: day permits only. April to end Sept available from main entrance car park. Oct to 15 March by post (with s.a.e.) to NT Warden, Langham Farm House, Langham Place, Egham, Surrey

|♿| Access to tea-room and meads by prior arrangement. Good vehicle access to riverbank

|→| On the Thames, ½m W of Runnymede Bridge, on S side of A308 (M25, Junction 13). *Bus:* From surrounding areas (tel. 081-668 7261). *Station:* Egham, ½m

WINKWORTH ARBORETUM 🌸🖼

General enquiries to NT Regional Office, Polesden Lacey, Dorking, Surrey RH5 6BD (tel. Bookham (0372) 453401)

Hillside woodland with two lakes, many rare trees and shrubs; peak displays: spring for bluebells and azaleas, autumn for colour; fine views

|O| |❄| All year: daily during daylight hours

|🛍| Shop open 29 March to 16 Nov: daily except Mon 2–6 or dusk if earlier

|£| |🐕| £1.50 donation. No reduction for parties. Coach parties must book with Concessionaire (see 🏪 for address) to ensure parking space. Car parking charge may be introduced in 1991 *continued*

213

♿ Limited access; viewpoint and lake from lower entrance are accessible

🍴 Tea-room for light refreshments near upper car park; opening times as for shop but also open daily in May & Oct 11–6 for light lunches and teas. Booking with Concessionaire, Winkworth Arboretum, nr Godalming, Surrey (tel. Hascombe (048 632) 265 when tea-room open)

→ Near Hascombe, 2m SE of Godalming on E side of B2130 [169, 170 or 186: SU990412] *Bus:* Tillingbourne 43/4/6 Godalming–Guildford (passing close BR Godalming) (tel. Cranleigh (0483) 276880) *Station:* Godalming 2m

WITLEY COMMON INFORMATION CENTRE ♿ 🚻 👤

Keeper's Cottage, Haslemere Road, Witley, Godalming GU8 5QA
(tel. Wormley (0428) 683207)

A purpose-built Nature Information Centre set in pinewoods on edge of common; audio visual programme and exhibition explaining history, natural history and management of Witley Common; nature trails, interesting and varied flora and fauna

🅾 **Information Centre:** 30 March to end Oct: daily except Mon & Fri but open BH Mon 11–1 & 2–5. Nov: Wed, Thur, Sat & Sun 1–4.30. **Common:** open at all times

🛍 ❄ Shop open as Centre. Also for Christmas shopping

£ 🎫 Free to Centre. Guided parties £1.50 (min. charge £10); children 80p (min. charge £10); party charge also gives access to audio-visual programme and guided tour of a nature trail. Parking 100yds from Centre. All groups must pre-book with Centre Manager

🔺 Arrangements for schools and parties, please book with s.a.e. to Manager

♿ Ground floor of Centre and one nature trail

🐕 Must be kept on leads on trails; no dogs in Centre

🍴 Refreshments open same times as Centre 30 March to end Oct

Events: ♿ Series of guided walks throughout the season, some of which are suitable for disabled visitors (details from Centre Manager; s.a.e. please)

→ 7m SW of Guildford between London-Portsmouth A3 and A286 roads, 1m SW of Milford [186: SU9341] *Bus:* Alder Valley 267, 272/4, 292 Guildford–Hindhead (passing close BR Godalming) (tel. Guildford (0483) 575226) *Station:* Milford 2m

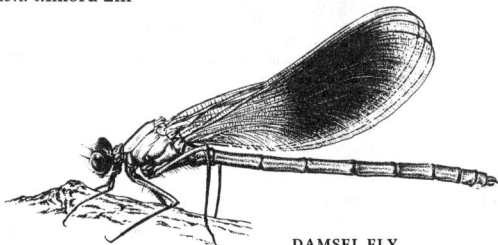

DAMSEL FLY

Sussex (East)

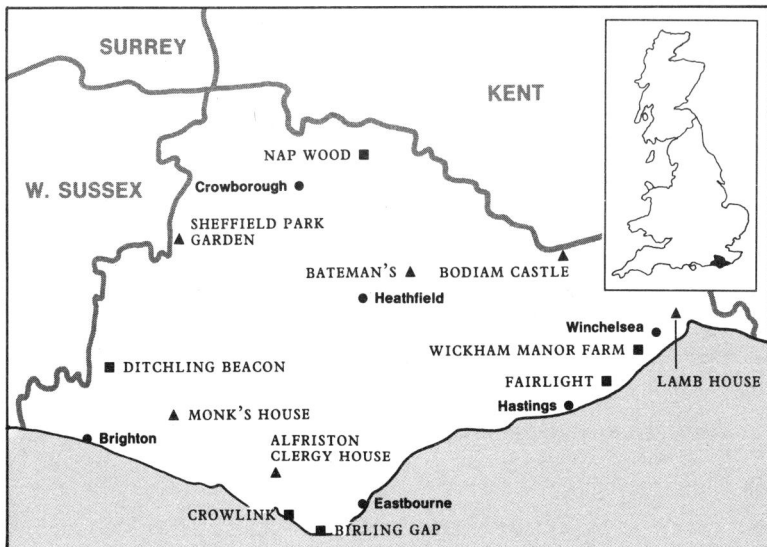

COAST

The South Downs dip down into the sea at Beachy Head just to the west of Eastbourne and the adjoining Seven Sisters, forming one of the best known and loved lengths of coast in England; just as famous as the White Cliffs of Dover. At **Crowlink** and **Birling Gap** the Trust owns some 770 acres of chalk downland and cliffs; here, and on the neighbouring downland are some of the most delightful walks and unspoilt views. 🚶 The downs at Crowlink have gradual slopes and short turf over which wheelchairs may be pushed; there are no designated wheelchair routes and visitors may wander where they wish. The beach at Birling Gap remains relatively uncrowded. The coastal strip is a Site of Special Scientific Interest [199: TV5497]. Car parking at both Crowlink and Birling Gap. To the east of Hastings, public footpaths give access to more Trust-owned cliffland at **Fairlight** near Hastings [199: TQ884127].

COUNTRYSIDE

North of Brighton are the remains of **Ditchling Beacon** hill-fort [198: TQ332131], which lie across the South Downs Way; from the NT car park there is a splendid view across the Weald. On a clear day the North Downs can be seen, and nearer at hand Ashdown Forest and Crowborough Beacon.

215

At Winchelsea, once on the coast, and now slightly inland, is **Wickham Manor Farm** which includes a large portion of the relics of the original town.

[⚡] Near Tunbridge Wells, the Sussex Wildlife Trust leases 107 acres of woodland from the Trust. **Nap Wood** [188: TQ585330] on the A267 is mostly oak woodland maintained as a nature reserve. Footpath and limited parking.

ALFRISTON CLERGY HOUSE 🏠✿   ✖✉

The Tye, Alfriston, Polegate BN26 5TL (tel. Alfriston (0323) 870001)

The first building acquired by the Trust, a 14th-century Wealden hall house, half-timbered and thatched; medieval Hall, exhibition room and two other rooms shown; exhibition on display all season; cottage garden

O	29 March to end Oct: daily 11–6 or sunset if earlier. Last admissions ½hr before closing
🛍✿	Shop open as house. Also 6 Nov to 22 Dec: Wed to Sun 11–4
£	March, April, May, Sept & Oct: £1; pre-booked parties 70p; children 40p. June to end Aug £1.50; children 80p; pre-booked parties £1.10; children 60p. WCs and parking in car park at other end of village (not NT). 🦽 House unsuitable for wheelchair users
☕	In village (not NT)
➜	4m NE of Seaford, just E of B2108, in Alfriston village, adjoining The Tye and St Andrews Church [189: TQ521029] *Bus:* Southdown 726 Eastbourne–Brighton (passing close BR Polegate & Seaford) (tel. Eastbourne (0323) 27354) *Station:* Berwick 2½m

BATEMAN'S 🏠🏠✿✖   ✖✉✎

Burwash, Etchingham TN19 7DS (tel. Burwash (0435) 882302)

Rudyard Kipling's home, 1902–36; built by a local ironmaster in 1634; Kipling's rooms and study as they were during his lifetime; garden; watermill grinds corn for flour; alongside is one of the oldest working water-driven turbines in the world, installed by Kipling; his 1928 Rolls Royce is on show in its original garage

☐ **House, mill and garden:** Good Fri 29 March to end Oct: daily except Thur & Fri but open Good Fri 11–5.30. Last admissions 4.30. The mill grinds corn every Sat at 2 in the open season.

☐ ✳ Shop as house. Also 6 Nov to 21 Dec: Wed to Sat 11–4

£ Weekdays £3, parties £2.40. Weekends, BH Mon & Good Fri: £3.50, children £1.80; parties £2.80. Parties only by arrangement with Administrator

♣ Nappy-changing facilities

♿ The mill is not suitable for wheelchair users, but ground floor of house and garden are accessible; there are routes which avoid the steps. ♿ WC in car park

☐♿ Morning coffee, light lunches and teas in tea-room. Picnicking in Quarry Garden and copse adjacent to car park

Events: Bailey's Summerstage concert 3 Aug

→ ½m S of Burwash (A265); approached by road leading S from W end of village or N from Woods Corner (B2096) [199: TQ671238] *Bus:* Autopoint 318 Hurst Green–Heathfield (passing BR Etchingham) (tel. Herstmonceux (0323) 832430) *Station:* Etchingham 3m

BODIAM CASTLE ▮▮

Bodiam, nr Robertsbridge TN32 5UA (tel. Staplecross (0580) 830436)

Built in 1385 against a French invasion which never came, Bodiam was 'slighted' in the 17th century and has been uninhabited ever since. Nevertheless it remains remarkably intact; the best example of its type in the country; floors have been replaced in some of the towers so that visitors can view the interior; audio-visual presentation

☐ ✳ 29 March to end Oct: daily 10–6 or sunset if earlier. Nov to end March 1992: Mon to Sat 10–sunset. Closed 25–27 Dec. Last admissions ½hr before closing

☐ ✳ Shop open 29 March to 22 Dec: daily 10–½hr before Castle closes. 28 Dec to end March 1992: Mon to Sat 10–½hr before Castle closes

£ £1.70; children 90p. Parties £1.20. Car park ¼m 50p (NT members free). Audio-visual presentation on life in a medieval castle   *continued*

SUSSEX

♿ The car park, shop and restaurant/tea-room are on level ground; ♿ WC in car park. The castle (but not its towers) is accessible to wheelchair users, but it is ¼ mile from the car park over uneven ground; for alternative access details please telephone Administrator before visiting

🍽♿ Lunches, teas and snacks in car park restaurant/tea-room 29 March to 22 Dec: daily 10.30–½hr before Castle closes. Picnicking in castle grounds

🐕 Dogs on leads in grounds only

➡ 3m S of Hawkhurst, 1m E of A229 [199: TQ782256] *Bus:* Hastings Buses 326, 349/50 Hastings–Tunbridge Wells (passing BR Hastings & Tunbridge Wells) (tel. Hastings (0424) 433711) *Station:* Robertsbridge 5m

LAMB HOUSE 🏠✿

West Street, Rye TN31 7ES

The home of the writer Henry James from 1898 to 1916 where he wrote the best novels of his later period; the walled garden, staircase, hall and three rooms on the ground floor containing some of James's personal possessions are on view; tenanted property, administered and largely maintained on the Trust's behalf by tenant

🅾 April to end Oct: Wed & Sat only 2–6. Last admissions 5.30

£ £1.40. No reduction for parties or children. No WCs or car park

➡ In West Street, facing W end of church [198: TQ920202] *Bus:* From surrounding areas to Rye (tel. Hastings (0424) 433711) *Station:* Rye ¼m

MONK'S HOUSE 🏠✿

Rodmell, Lewes BN7 3HF

A small village house and garden; home of Leonard and Virginia Woolf from 1919 until his death in 1969; house and garden administered and largely maintained by tenant on Trust's behalf

🅾 30 March, April & Oct: Wed & Sat 2–5. May to end Sept: Wed & Sat 2–6. Last admissions ½hr before closing

£ £1.70. No reduction for children or parties; max. 15 people in house at a time. Parties only by prior arrangement with the tenant. Car park 50 yds; village street too narrow for coaches; drivers please set passengers down at main road junction, and park elsewhere

→ 4m SE of Lewes, off former A275 (now unclassified) in Rodmell village, near church (no access from A26) [198: TQ421064] *Bus:* Southdown 123 Lewes–Newhaven (passing BR Lewes) (tel. Lewes (0273) 474441 *Station:* Southease (U) 1¼m

SHEFFIELD PARK GARDEN ✿♿ 💢
Uckfield TN22 3QX (tel. Danehill (0825) 790655)

100-acre landscape garden with five lakes laid out in 18th century by Capability Brown; mature trees, rare shrubs and water lilies; beautiful at all times of year

○ 30 March to 10 Nov: Tues to Sat 11–6 or sunset if earlier, Sun & BH Mon 2–6, or sunset if earlier, closed Good Fri & Tues following BH Mon. Open from 1 to sunset on Sun in Oct & Nov. Last admissions 1hr before closing

☐✿ Shop as garden. Also 13 Nov to 21 Dec: Wed to Sat 11–4

£ March, April & June to end Sept £3.10, children £1.60; parties £2; May, Oct & Nov £3.60, parties £2.50; children £1.30. No reduction for parties on Sat, Sun & BH Mon

♿ Most parts of garden accessible. ♿ WC. Car parking near entrance; follow access sign at entrance

→ Midway between East Grinstead and Lewes, 5m NW of Uckfield, on E side of A275, ½m from Sheffield Park station (Bluebell line) [198: TQ415240] *Bus:* Southdown 769 from BR Haywards Heath (peak days); RDH 121 from Lewes (Sat only); otherwise, Southdown 781 Eastbourne–Haywards Heath (passing BR Haywards Heath and Uckfield), alight Chailey Crossroads, 1¾m (tel. Lewes (0273) 474441) *Station:* Sheffield Park (Bluebell Rly) ¾m; Haywards Heath 7m; Buxted 7m

Sussex (West)

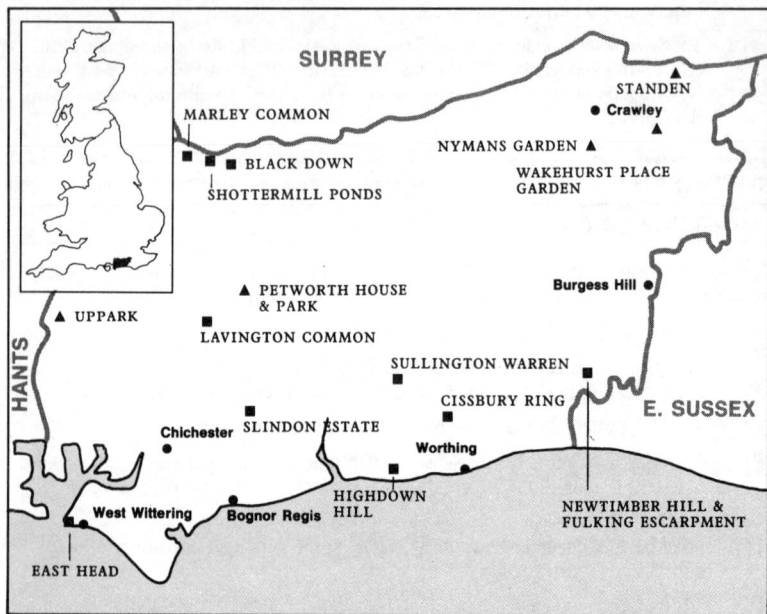

SURREY

STANDEN
● Crawley

MARLEY COMMON

NYMANS GARDEN ▲

■ ■ ■ BLACK DOWN
SHOTTERMILL PONDS

WAKEHURST PLACE
GARDEN

▲ PETWORTH HOUSE
& PARK

Burgess Hill ●

▲ UPPARK

■
LAVINGTON COMMON

SULLINGTON WARREN
■

HANTS

CISSBURY RING

E. SUSSEX

Chichester ■ SLINDON ESTATE

Worthing

HIGHDOWN
HILL

NEWTIMBER HILL &
FULKING ESCARPMENT

West Wittering Bognor Regis

EAST HEAD

COAST

[人] At West Wittering is the 110-acre sand and shingle spit of **East Head** east of the entrance to Chichester Harbour [181: SU766990]. Vulnerable to the constant battering it receives from the sea and, indeed, from the feet of visitors, East Head is important because it demonstrates how the sea has shaped this part of the coastline, and because it supports a variety of wildlife. The Trust has fenced off part of the spit, while marram grass has been introduced to 'bind' the dunes, but there is a nature walk, and naturalists come to see the waders, the plant and marine life, and the insect population.

COUNTRYSIDE

On the Surrey/Sussex borders a large acreage of sandstone moorland at **Black Down and Marley Common** gives fine views south to the South Downs and the English Channel. [人] The heights of Black Down are covered with gorse and heather, Scots pine and silver birch, and the down supports both heath and woodland birds: linnet and yellowhammer in the upland gorse, and woodpecker, warbler and tree pipit on the lower wooded slopes. At the foot of Marley Lane are two hammer ponds: **Shottermill Ponds** [186: SU883324]. **Lavington Common** [197: SU950190], and **Sullington Warren** [198: TQ096144] are heather-clad heathland properties, well supplied with footpaths and car parking areas. A famous landmark, **Cissbury Ring** [198: TQ140082] near Findon, gives views to Beachy Head and the Isle of Wight. There was a flint mining industry on the Ring in Neolithic times and its remains can still be seen at the western end of the hill. One of the largest Iron Age hill-forts in the country is on the summit. **Newtimber Hill** [198: TQ2712] and the adjacent **Fulking Escarpment** are two downland properties providing spectacular views over the weald and to the sea. Rich in downland flora and fauna, these properties lavishly reward those who leave the beaten track to seek them out. **Harting Down**, near Petersfield [197: SU798184] is a newly acquired 520-acre stretch of chalk downland. Magnificent views, good walks, traversed by South Downs Way, rich in downland flora and fauna.

Another archaeologically important site is **Highdown Hill** near Ferring [197/198: TQ092043]. This has a late Bronze Age settlement, and an Early Iron Age hill-fort with a pagan Saxon cemetery within its ramparts. Excavations were carried out in the summer of 1988.

The **Slindon Estate** north of Bognor Regis [197: SU9608] includes much of Slindon village with its 17th-century brick and flint cottages. Within the once famous Beech Wood which was devastated by the great storm of October 1987, can be found a shingle beach, 130ft above sea level, which proves that the sea once reached here – it is now 5 miles away! Other archaeological sites on the estate include the Neolithic causewayed enclosure of Barkhale and the largest surviving section – 3½ miles – of Stane Street, which took the Roman legions to Chichester, past Bignor Hill. The park and Bignor Hill are open daily and access to the remainder of the 3,500-acre estate is by public footpaths and bridleways.

NYMANS GARDEN 🏵 🏠 🧍

Handcross, nr Haywards Heath RH17 6EB
(tel. Handcross (0444) 400321 or 400002)

One of the great gardens of the Sussex Weald; rare and beautiful plants, shrubs and trees from all over the world; azaleas, rhododendrons, eucryphias, hydrangeas, magnolias, camellias and roses; walled garden, hidden sunk garden, pinetum, laurel walk; romantic ruins

🅞	Good Fri 29 March to end Oct: daily except Mon & Fri (but open BH Mon & Good Fri) 11–7 or sunset if earlier. Last admissions 1hr before closing
🗋	Shop & exhibition 12–6 on same days as garden
£	£2.80. Parties £2.30. Car park at entrance; space limited so coaches must book. Leaflets on sale for spring, summer & autumn walks
♿ 🐕	Garden accessible; special wheelchair route indicated. ♿ WC. Old roses and other scented flowers and plants
🐕	In car park only *continued*

📋♿ Sandwiches, cakes & teas in tea-house near car park

➡️ On B2114 at Handcross, 4½m S of Crawley, just off London–Brighton M23/
A23 [187: TQ265294] *Bus:* Brighton & Hove/Greenline 773 Brighton–BR
Gatwick (passing BR Crawley), alight Handcross ¼m–¾m according to direction
(tel. Brighton (0273) 206666) *Station:* Balcombe 4½m; Crawley 5½m

PETWORTH HOUSE 🏠🌳 ✖✖

Petworth GU28 0AE (tel. Petworth (0798) 42207)

*Magnificent late 17th-century house in beautiful deer park (see following entry); important
collection of pictures (many by Turner and Van Dyck), sculpture and furniture; carving by
Grinling Gibbons; archive room; many of the fine specimen trees in the pleasure grounds were
lost in the storm of October 1987 but restoration is now in progress*

Note: Visitors are asked to note that the North Gallery is being restored during 1991
and that other rooms are in the course of rearrangement

⭕ **House:** Good Fri 29 March to end Oct: daily except Mon & Fri (but open Good
Fri & BH Mon, closed Tues following) 1–5.30; **gardens and car park:** 12.30–
5.30. Last admissions to house 5. Extra rooms shown Tues, Wed & Thur

🗂️❄️ Shop open same days as house 12.30–5.30. Also open for Christmas shopping

💷 £3.30. Parties, Tues, Wed, Thur & Sat £2.50, by prior written arrangement with Administrator. Guided tours mornings only by arrangement with the Administrator (additional charge). No prams in house; pushchairs admitted. Coach parties alight at Church Lodge entrance, coaches then park in NT car park. NB car park is 750yds from house. Courtesy carriage available to ferry disabled and infirm visitors to house

👶 Baby feeding/changing facilities; high chair

♿ Disabled visitors may be set down at the Church Lodge entrance. Disabled drivers should make arrangements with the Administrator. See 💷 for note on courtesy carriage. All ground floor public rooms accessible; ♿ WC in Servants' Block

🍽️♿ Light lunches in licensed restaurant 12.30–2.30; teas 3–5.30 same days as house. Also open as shop in Nov & Dec

➡️ In centre of Petworth (A272/A283) [197: SU976218]; car park well signposted *Station:* Pulborough 5¼m

---

PETWORTH PARK 🌳

As Petworth House, above

Beautiful 700-acre deer park, with lake, landscaped by Capability Brown and immortalised in Turner's paintings

⭕❄️ All year: daily 8 to sunset. Closed 28–30 June

💷 Free. Car park for park only on A283, 1½m N of Petworth. No vehicles in park. Height restriction of 6ft 9in in car park

♿ Car park and part of park accessible with care; some uneven paths

🐕 Must be kept under control

➡️ Pedestrian access from Petworth town and on A272 & A283
Station: Pulborough 5¼m

STANDEN 🏠✿📧   ✕

East Grinstead RH19 4NE (tel. East Grinstead (0342) 323029)

A family house of the 1890s, designed by Philip Webb, friend of William Morris; the remarkably complete interior has been carefully restored; Morris textiles and wallpapers; good furniture, pottery and pictures of the period; original electric light fittings; billiard room; conservatory; beautiful hillside garden with fine views across the Medway valley

O — 29 March to end Oct: Wed to Sun & BH Mon (closed Tues following), **house:** 1.30–5.30; **garden:** 12–5.30. Last admissions 5

🗓✿ — Shop open as house. Also for Christmas shopping

£ — House & garden £3.20. Garden only £1.60. Parties £2 weekdays only; other times by prior booking with Administrator. Parking 180yds

👶 — 2 baby carriers available; suitable for children aged up to 16 months; pushchairs not allowed in house

♿ — Several rooms and part of garden; some steps in house; disabled drivers may park on forecourt of house but deep gravel; steps and gravel paths in garden

🐕 — In car park and woodland walks only

🍽♿ — Light lunches & afternoon teas. Open as garden. Also open as shop in Nov & Dec. Light lunches available for coach parties by prior arrangement with Administrator. No picnics in garden

➡ — 2m S of East Grinstead, signposted from B2110 (Turners Hill road) [187: TQ389356] *Bus:* London & Country SW 474 E Grinstead–Crawley (passing close BR E Grinstead & passing BR Three Bridges), alight Saint Hill, ½m (tel. 081-668 7261) *Station:* E Grinstead 2m

UPPARK ✿📧

South Harting, Petersfield, Hampshire GU31 5QR (tel. Harting (0730) 825317)

This late 17th-century house was partially destroyed by fire on 30 August 1989. The attic and first floor were completely gutted but the structure of the state rooms and basement survives largely intact. Many of the 18th-century contents were saved and are now in safe storage. Restoration work will be in progress throughout 1991. The garden was landscaped by Repton, and there are magnificent views southwards

O 🗓 — 31 March to end Sept: Sun only 1.30–5.30. Last admissions 5. Small shop and temporary exhibition

£ — 50p. No refreshments

Note: Arrangements are temporary and liable to change. It is essential to telephone the property to check details

➡ — 5m SE of Petersfield on B2146, 1½m S of South Harting [197: SU775177] *Bus:* Hants & Sussex 61 BR Petersfield–Midhurst (with connections from BR Chichester), alight S Harting, 1½m uphill walk (tel. Chichester (0243) 372045) *Station:* Petersfield 5½m

WAKEHURST PLACE GARDEN ❀   ✖

Ardingly, Haywards Heath RH17 6TN (tel. Ardingly (0444) 892701)

A superb collection of exotic trees, shrubs and other plants; many displayed in a geographic manner; extensive water gardens; Winter Garden; Rock Walk and many other features including the Loder Valley Nature Reserve

Notes: Wakehurst Place is leased to the Ministry of Agriculture and is administered and maintained by the Royal Botanic Gardens, Kew. Prices and opening times may be subject to alteration

[O] [❀]   All year: daily (except 25 Dec & 1 Jan). Nov to end Jan: 10–4; Feb & Oct 10–5; March: 10–6; April to end Sept: 10–7. Last admissions ½hr before closing. Bookshop (not NT) open all year

[£]   £2, children (16 and under) £1. Parties £1.50; parties of children 60p (prices subject to review). Parking 400yds from Mansion. Exhibition in Mansion

[♿]   Most of upper garden accessible, but much uneven ground elsewhere. [♿] WC

[🍴]   Easter to mid Oct: self-service tea-room (not NT); other times light refreshments from bookshop. Pre-booked seasonal lunches during Christmas season

[→]   1½m NW of Ardingly, on B2028 [187: TQ339314] *Bus:* London & Country 472 Haywards Heath–Crawley (passing BR Haywards Heath & Crawley) (tel. 081-668 7261) *Station:* Balcombe 5m; E Grinstead 6½m; Horsted Keynes (Bluebell Rly) 3¾m

Tyne & Wear

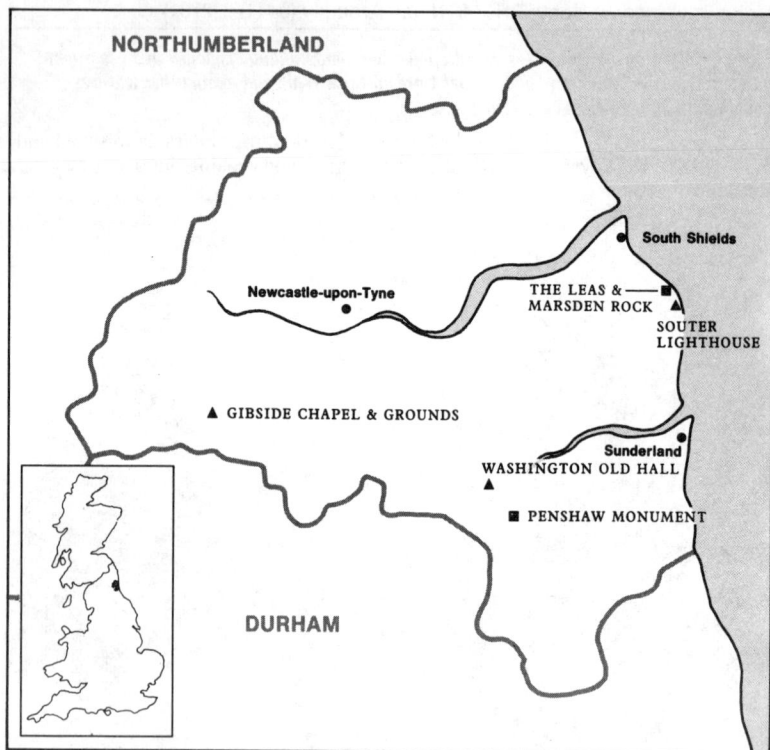

NORTHUMBERLAND

South Shields

Newcastle-upon-Tyne

THE LEAS &
MARSDEN ROCK

SOUTER
LIGHTHOUSE

▲ GIBSIDE CHAPEL & GROUNDS

Sunderland
WASHINGTON OLD HALL

■ PENSHAW MONUMENT

DURHAM

COAST AND COUNTRYSIDE

At South Shields, the Trust owns 2½ miles of spectacular coastline, from Trow Point to Lizard Point [88: NZ400650]. The property consists of **The Leas**, a large open area of grassland, bordered on the east by limestone cliffs, and **Marsden Rock**, with its famous bird colony of kittiwakes, cormorants and fulmars. Guided walks with the Warden take place on a regular basis during the season. At he southern end of this area is the recently acquired **Souter Lighthouse** (see p. 227) with its complex of buildings [88:NZ641408].

Inland from The Leas can be found the well-known landmark of **Penshaw Monument** [88: NZ334544]. A Doric temple, built in 1844 to commemorate the first Earl of Durham, it can be seen from miles around. It is situated near the village of Penshaw and is just off the A183 Sunderland road; car parking in disused road at foot of monument.

PLEASE REFER TO PAGES 5–9

226

GIBSIDE CHAPEL & GROUNDS ✚ ♠ ⛱ ♦ ☒

nr Rowlands Gill, Burnopfield, Newcastle-upon-Tyne NE16 6BG
(tel. Consett (0207) 542255)

The finest example of Palladian Church architecture in the North East; built as a mausoleum for the Bowes family between 1760 and 1812; restored 1965; Chapel lies at end of the Great Walk leading to the coloumn of British Liberty; splendid 2½-mile walk with views of the ruined Hall, River Derwent and landscaped park

Note: There is no access to the Banqueting House or to Gibside Hall which is a dangerous ruin

O Good Fri 29 March to end Oct: daily except Mon but open BH Mon 11–5. Last admissions 4.30

£ £1.50. Parties £1.20 by appointment with Custodian. WCs

♿ Please contact Custodian for special arrangements

🐕 In the grounds, on leads

🛍 🏠 Shop, tea-room and picnic area in car park

Events: Service in Chapel 1st Sunday each month at 3. National Trust annual service, 2 June, 3. Programme of concerts and guided walks; apply to Custodian for further details, s.a.e. please

➔ 6m SW of Gateshead, 20m W of Durham; entrance on B6314 between Burnopfield and Rowlands Gill [88: NZ172583] *Bus:* Go-Ahead Northern 607/8/11 Newcastle–Rowland's Gill; 745 Newcastle–Consett (all passing close BR Newcastle). On all alight Rowlands Gill, ½m (tel. 091-232 5325) *Station:* Blaydon (U) 5m

SOUTER LIGHTHOUSE 🏠 🖼 ♿ ⚐ ✖ 🏢

Coast Road, Whitburn, Sunderland (tel. 091-529 3161)

Shore-based lighthouse and associated buildings built in 1871; first lighthouse to be powered by alternating electric current; acquired by Trust in 1990 so in first stages of development; access to Engine Room; Light Tower; information display and Fog Signal Station

O 29 March to end Oct: daily except Mon but open BH Mon 11–5. Last admission 4.30. Guided tours only to top of Light Tower (approx every ½ hr)

£ £1.20. Pre-booked parties £1. Car and coach park 100yds

🏠 🛍 Shop and refreshments same times as lighthouse. Picnicking in grounds

Events: For list of events and guided walks please send s.a.e. to Custodian

♿ Wheelchair access. ♿ WC. All areas except Light Tower accessible

➔ 2½m S of South Shields on A183, 5m N of Sunderland on A183 [88:NZ641408] *Bus:* from surrounding areas (tel. 091-232 5325) *Station:* East Boldon (U) 3m

WASHINGTON OLD HALL 🏛️ ❁   ✉

The Avenue, Washington Village NE38 7LE (tel. 091-416 6879)

From 1183–1288 the home of George Washington's direct ancestors, remaining in the family until 1613; due for demolition in 1936, it was rescued, restored and given to the Trust

Washington Old Hall is administered by the National Trust and leased to Sunderland Borough Council which maintains the property

🅾️	Good Fri 29 March to end Oct: daily except Fri, (but open Good Fri) 11–5. Last admissions 4.30
🛍️	Small shop in entrance hall, open as house
💷	£1.50. Parties £1 on application to Custodian. Coaches must park on the Avenue
🐕	In grounds only, on leads
♿	Ground floor only
☕	Teas can be arranged; telephone Custodian for details

Events: 4 July; American Independence Day Celebrations; ♿

➡️	5m W of Sunderland, 2m E of A1, S of Tyne tunnel, follow signs, Washington New Town, District 4, then Washington village; situated on E side of Avenue [88: NZ312566] *Bus:* Go-Ahead Northern X85/9, 194, 293–4, 297 from Tyne & Wear Metro Heworth; also other services from surrounding areas (tel. 091-232 5325) *Station:* Heworth (Tyne & Wear Metro) 4m; E Boldon (U) 6m; Newcastle 7m

Warwickshire

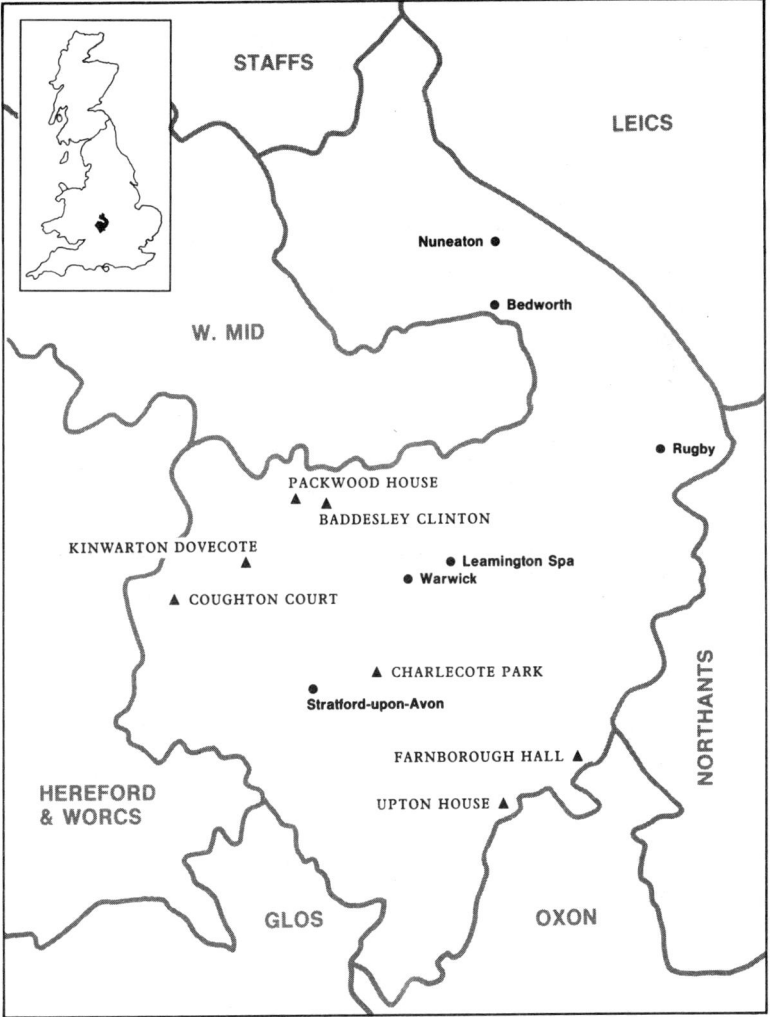

STAFFS

LEICS

Nuneaton ●

● Bedworth

W. MID

● Rugby

PACKWOOD HOUSE
▲ ▲
BADDESLEY CLINTON

KINWARTON DOVECOTE
▲
● Leamington Spa
● Warwick

▲ COUGHTON COURT

▲ CHARLECOTE PARK
●
Stratford-upon-Avon

FARNBOROUGH HALL ▲

UPTON HOUSE ▲

NORTHANTS

HEREFORD
& WORCS

GLOS

OXON

PLEASE REFER TO PAGES 5–9

BADDESLEY CLINTON 🏛 ✤ ♣ ✝   ✗ ✉

Knowle, Solihull B93 0DQ (tel. Lapworth (0564) 783294)

A romantically sited medieval moated manor house; dating from 14th century; little changed since 1634; family portraits; chapel; garden; ponds and lake walk

[O] 6 March to end Sept: Wed to Sun & BH Mon (closed Good Fri) 2–6 (grounds open from 12.30). Oct: Wed to Sun 12.30–4.30. Last admissions to house ½hr before closing

[□][✤] Shop open as grounds. Also 1 Nov to 15 Dec: Wed to Sun 12.30–4.30

[£] £3.10. Family ticket £8.50. Grounds only £1.80. Parties of 15 or more and coaches (weekdays only) by prior written arrangement. Free parking. No perambulators or push-chairs in house. Timed tickets issued to control numbers in house

[♿] Access to ground floor and most of garden. [♿] WC near shop

[♨][✤] Lunches (licensed), refreshments & teas; same days as house 12.30–5.30. Also Nov & Dec as shop. No picnicking in garden

[→] ¼m W of A4141 Warwick/Birmingham road, at Chadwick End, 7½m NW of Warwick, 15m SE of central Birmingham [139: SP200715] *Station:* Lapworth (U), not Sun, 2m; Dorridge, not Sun except May to Sept, 4m; Birmingham International (BR & Airport) 9m

CHARLECOTE PARK 🏛 ✤ ♣ ⚓ 🔍   ✗ ✉

Wellesbourne, Warwick CV35 9ER (tel. Stratford-upon-Avon (0789) 470277)

Home of Lucy family since 1247; present house built in 1550s and later visited by Queen Elizabeth I; park landscaped by 'Capability' Brown, supports herd of red and fallow deer, reputedly poached by Shakespeare, and a flock of Jacob sheep, first introduced in 1756; principal rooms altered 1830s in Elizabethan Revival style

[O] 30 March to end Oct: daily except Mon & Thur (open BH Mon) 11–6 (house closed 1–2). Last admissions to house 5. Evening guided tours for pre-booked parties 2nd Wed in each month 7.30–9.30; full price (incl. NT members)

[□][✤] Shop open as house. Also 2 Nov to 15 Dec: Sat & Sun 12–4

[£] £3.20. Family ticket £8.80. Parties of 15 or more (60 max.) and school parties, by prior arrangement with Administrator. Car and coach park 300yds. Video film of life at Charlecote Park in the Victorian period

[♿][♠] Access to all open rooms, except the Gatehouse Museum. [♿] WC behind Orangery. Arrangements can be made at the kiosk to drop off disabled visitors or park near house. The video can be viewed in the gatehouse. [♠] Braille guide

[♨][♿] Morning coffee, light lunches, afternoon teas in the Orangery Restaurant open as shop. Picnicking in deer park only

Events: 30 May: special open day. 21–26 June, Midsummer Music Festival; details from Administrator

→ 1m W of Wellesbourne, 5m E of Stratford-upon-Avon, 6m S of Warwick on N side of B4086 [151: SP263564] *Bus:* Midland Red 18 Leamington Spa–Stratford-upon-Avon (tel. Rugby (0788) 535555) *Station:* Stratford-upon-Avon, not Sun, except May–Sept, 5½m; Warwick, not Sun except May–Sept, 6m; Leamington Spa 8m

COUGHTON COURT 🏠🌳   ✂🖼

nr Alcester B49 5JA (tel. Alcester (0789) 762435)

Impressive central gatehouse dating from 1509; during the Civil War this formerly moated and mainly Elizabethan house was attacked by both Parliamentary and Royalist forces; it suffered damaged again in James II's reign; contents of the nine-roomed South Wing include some notable furniture, porcelain, portraits and relics of Throckmorton family who have lived here since 1409; tranquil lake and riverside walk *continued*

[O] 30 March to 4 April: daily 1.30–5.30. April: Sat & Sun 1.30–5.30. May to end Sept: daily except Mon & Fri (open BH Mon but closed 9–19 Aug) 1.30–5.30. Oct: Sat, Sun & 22–24 (half-term) 1.30–5. Last admissions to house ½hr before closing

[shop] Shop open as house

[£] £2.40. Family ticket £6.60. Parties of 15 or more (except BH) by prior arrangement. Evening guided tours for pre-booked parties Tues to Thur. Full price, incl. NT members, for evening visits. School parties Tues to Thur mornings by prior arrangement

[access] One room on ground floor, and shop. WC with handrail, otherwise unadapted

[dogs] Dogs on leads in grounds only

Events: Concerts; details from Administrator

[→] 2m N of Alcester on E side of A435 [150: SP080604] *Bus:* Midland Red West X6, 146, 166 Birmingham–Evesham (passing BR Redditch & close BR Evesham) (tel. 0345 212 555) *Station:* Redditch 6m

FARNBOROUGH HALL [icons]

Banbury, Oxfordshire OX17 1DU

A classical mid 18th-century stone house, home of the Holbech family for 300 years; notable plasterwork; the entrance hall, staircase and 2 principal rooms are shown; the grounds contain charming 18th-century temples, a ¾-mile terrace walk and an obelisk

The tenants, Mr & Mrs Holbech, are responsible for the opening arrangements

[O] **House, grounds & terrace walk:** April to end Sept: Wed & Sat 2–6, also 5 & 6 May 2–6. **Terrace walk only:** Thur & Fri 2–6. Last admissions 5.30

[£] House, grounds & terrace walk £2.20. Garden & terrace walk £1.30. Terrace walk only (Thur & Fri) 80p. Parties by written arrangement only, no reduction. Coach and car park. Strong shoes advisable for terrace

[access] House and garden accessible (terrace walk is very steep)

[dogs] Welcome on leads in grounds only

[→] 6m N of Banbury, ½m W of A423 [151: SP430490] *Bus:* Midland Red 509/10 from Banbury (passing close BR Banbury) (tel. Rugby (0788) 535555) *Station:* Banbury 6m

KINWARTON DOVECOTE [icon]

A circular 14th-century dovecote; fine ogee doorway; retains its potence; a rare feature

[O] 30 March to end Oct: daily 9–6 or sunset if earlier. Other times by prior appointment only with Severn Regional Office (address on p. 22). Key obtainable from Glebe Farm next door

[£] 50p

→ 1½m NE of Alcester, just S of B4089 [150: SP106585] *Bus:* As Coughton Court, page 232, but alight Alcester, 1½m *Station:* Wilmcote (U), not Sun except May to Sept, 5m; Wootton Wawen (U), not Sun, 5m

PACKWOOD HOUSE 🏠 🚹 ❀   ✕ ✉

Lapworth, Solihull B94 6AT (tel. Lapworth (0564) 782024)

Mainly built about 1560, the timber-framed Tudor house contains a wealth of interesting tapestry and furniture; gardens include a Carolean formal garden and a notable yew garden

🅾 30 March to end Sept: Wed to Sun & BH Mon 2–6. Oct: Wed to Sun 12.30–4. Last admissions to house ½hr before closing

🏠 Shop open as house

💷 £2.50. Family ticket £6.90. Garden only £1.70. Parties of 15 or more by written arrangement. Morning and evening guided tours for pre-booked parties by arrangement. Free car and coach park

♿ Access to part of garden and ground floor

☕ Picnic site. Refreshments available at Baddesley Clinton (see p. 230) from 12.30.

→ 2m E of Hockley Heath (on A3400), 11m SE of central Birmingham [139: SP174722] *Bus:* Midland Red X20/X50 Birmingham–Stratford-upon-Avon, alight Hockley Heath, 1¾m (tel. Rugby (0788) 535555) *Station:* Lapworth (U), not Sun, 1½m; Dorridge, not Sun except May–Sept, 2m; Birmingham International 8m

PLEASE REFER TO PAGES 5–9

UPTON HOUSE 🏠 ❀   ✕ ✕ ✕

Banbury, Oxfordshire OX15 6HT (tel. Edge Hill (0295 87) 266)

*The house, built of a mellow local stone, dates from 1695, but the outstanding collections in
the house are the chief attraction: assembled this century by the 2nd Lord Bearsted, they
include paintings by English and Continental Old Masters, Brussels tapestries, Sèvres
porcelain, Chelsea figures and 18th-century furniture; fine garden including terraces,
herbaceous borders, fruit, vegetable and water gardens, lakes*

🅾	30 March to end April & Oct: Sat, Sun & BH Mon 2–6. May to end Sept: Sat to Wed, incl. BH Mon 2–6. Last admissions to house 5.30
🗋 ❀	Shop open as house. Also 2 Nov to 15 Dec: Sat & Sun 2–4
£	£3.10. Family ticket £8.50. Garden only £1.80. Parties of 15 or more & evening guided tours by written arrangement (no reduction). Free parking
🚼	Mothers' room
♿	Ground floor rooms and part of garden. ♿ WC. Special parking near house for disabled drivers. Motorised buggy with driver available for access to/from lower garden, manned by volunteers from Banbury NT Centre
☕ ♿ ❆	Tea-room in house. Also open as shop in Nov & Dec
→	On A422, 7m NW of Banbury, 12m SE of Stratford-upon-Avon [151: SP371461] *Station:* Banbury 7m

West Midlands

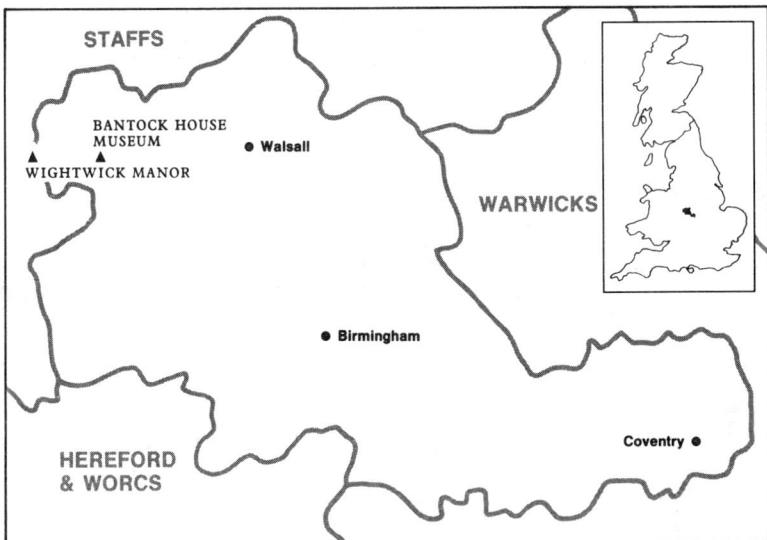

THE BALSTON COLLECTION, BANTOCK HOUSE MUSEUM ⬛

Bantock Park, Bradmore Road, Wolverhampton WV3 9LQ
(tel. Wolverhampton (0902) 312132)

Thomas Balston's collection of Victorian Staffordshire portrait figures, which he presented to the Trust in 1960, is on permanent view at Bantock House Museum (not NT); also on view are the town's important collections of 18th-century English enamels; Georgian and Victorian japanned tin and papier mâché; good collections of Worcester porcelain, dolls and toys, and some local history

All year: Mon & Thur 10–7; Tues, Wed, Fri & Sat 10–5; Sun 2–5. Closed Good Fri, Easter Sun, 1 Jan and 25 & 26 Dec; other days at Christmas, Bank & public holidays subject to arrangement. Tours by arrangement

£ Free. Parking outside museum for cars; 300yds for coaches, access via Finchfield Road

Children's holiday activities are arranged during each long holiday. Please enquire in advance

Ground floor only, includes the Balston Collection; cars may draw up to the front door, access via Bradmore Road

SW of Wolverhampton town centre on B4161; access via Bradmore Road
Bus: W Midlands Travel 513/4, 542/3 from BR Wolverhampton (tel. 021-200 2601) *Station:* Wolverhampton 2m

WIGHTWICK MANOR 🏠 ✿ ✉ ⌀

Wightwick Bank, Wolverhampton WV6 8EE (tel. Wolverhampton (0902) 761108)

Begun in 1887, the house is a notable example of the influence of William Morris, with many original Morris wallpapers and fabrics; Kempe glass, de Morgan ware and other pre-Raphaelite works of art; Victorian/Edwardian gardens with yew hedges and topiary, terraces and two pools

House: March to 31 Dec: Thur & Sat 2.30–5.30. Also open BH Sun & Mon 2.30–5.30. (ground floor only, no guided tours). **Garden:** same days as house 2–6. Closed 25 & 26 Dec. Also open for pre-booked parties Wed & Thur. Admission to house by timed ticket. Owing to the fragile nature of contents and the requirements of conservation, some rooms cannot always be shown; tours will therefore vary during the year

£3. Students £1.65. Garden only £1. No reduction for adult parties, which must book. Parking: limited space; only room for one coach. Pottery and bookshop (not NT). Coffee and soft drinks available

5 rooms & garden (but site slopes)

In garden only, on leads

3m W of Wolverhampton, up Wightwick Bank (A454), beside the Mermaid Inn [139: SO869985] *Bus:* W Midlands Travel 542/3 from Wolverhampton to within 600 yds; Tellus Midland Red West 890 Wolverhampton–Bridgnorth (all pass close BR Wolverhampton) (tel. 021-200 2601) *Station:* Wolverhampton 3m

Wiltshire

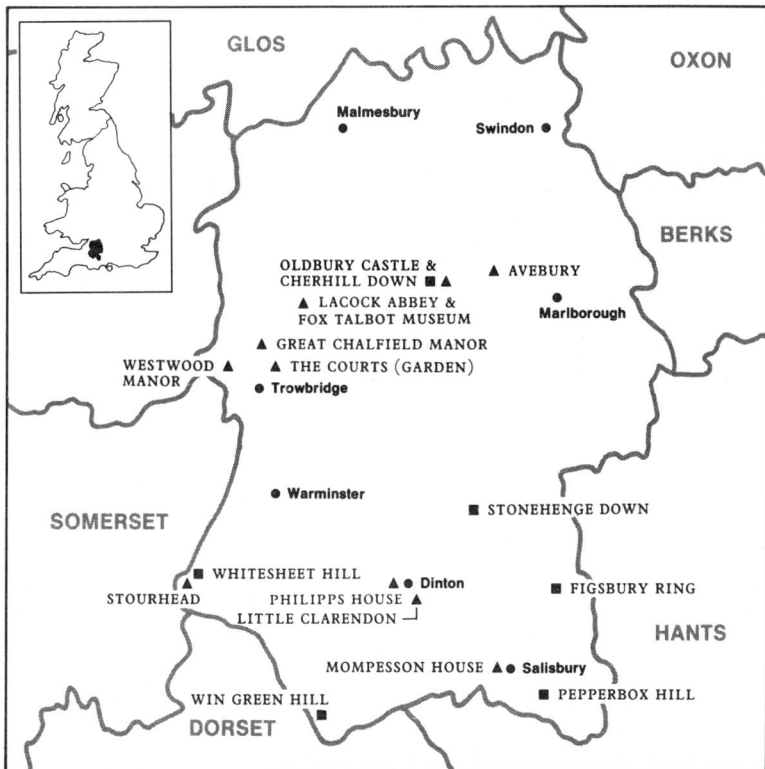

GLOS

OXON

Malmesbury
●

Swindon ●

BERKS

OLDBURY CASTLE &
CHERHILL DOWN ■ ▲   ▲ AVEBURY

▲ LACOCK ABBEY &
FOX TALBOT MUSEUM   Marlborough
                            ●

▲ GREAT CHALFIELD MANOR

WESTWOOD ▲   ▲ THE COURTS (GARDEN)
MANOR

● Trowbridge

● Warminster

■ STONEHENGE DOWN

SOMERSET

▲■ WHITESHEET HILL   ▲ ● Dinton
STOURHEAD   PHILIPPS HOUSE ▲   ■ FIGSBURY RING
           LITTLE CLARENDON ┘

HANTS

MOMPESSON HOUSE ▲● Salisbury

WIN GREEN HILL   ■ PEPPERBOX HILL
                ■
DORSET

COUNTRYSIDE

As well as the important ancient monument of **Avebury** (see p. 238) the Trust owns other notable antiquities in Wiltshire. **Figsbury Ring**, north-east of Salisbury and giving fine views over this city, is an Iron Age hill-fort [184: SU188338]. The Trust's land at Stonehenge is described in the entry on p. 242.

West of Avebury, between Calne and Bockhampton, are **Cherhill Down** and **Oldbury Castle** [173: SU046694]. The Trust owns the earthwork of Oldbury Castle with about 190 acres of the unimproved downland and the Iron Age hill-fort on the down. From the ridge are fine views over the Marlborough Downs to the east, south to Devizes and west to Chippenham. The Trust also owns **Whitesheet Hill** with its Iron Age hill-fort on the Stourhead Estate.

In the extreme south of Wiltshire the highest point in Cranborne Chase is **Win Green Hill**, 911ft [184: ST925206], crowned with a clump of beech trees shielding a bowl

237

barrow; from the summit are views south-east to the Isle of Wight and north-west to the Quantocks.

From **Pepperbox Hill** on the Southampton road (A36) [184: SU215248] there are spectacular views over Salisbury. The octagonal tower, which gives its name to these 72 acres is a 17th-century folly.

AVEBURY 🏛

nr Marlborough SN8 1RF

One of the most important Megalithic monuments in Europe, 28½-acre site with stone circles enclosed by a ditch and external bank; approached by an avenue of stones; Alexander Keiller Museum (EH); Wiltshire Life Society's display of Wiltshire rural life in the Great Barn; the NT also owns 912 acres, which provide the setting for the stone circle

The Museum, Stone Circle and Avenue, and Windmill Hill (tel. Avebury (067 23) 250) are under the guardianship of English Heritage; the Great Barn and adjoining refreshment room are administered by the Wiltshire Life Society (tel. Avebury (067 23) 555)

O ❄	Stone Circle: daily
🗂	Open daily 25–30 March: 11–4, 31 March to 26 Oct: 11–6. 27 Oct to 15 Dec: Sat & Sun only 11.30–4.30. Tel. Avebury (067 23) 384
£	For museum admission charges tel. Avebury (067 23) 250. Admission also charged for Great Barn (NT member incl.)
♿	Museum, Barn and parts of Circle (access for disabled drivers to barn area)
🐕	In Stone Circle only
◨	Lunches & teas at licensed Stones Restaurant and Red Lion Inn (not NT)
→	6m W of Marlborough, 1m N of the Bath road (A4) on A4361 and B4003 [173: SU102699] *Bus:* Thamesdown 49 Swindon–Devizes/Marlborough (passing close BR Swindon) (tel. Swindon (0793) 523700); Wilts & Dorset 5 Salisbury–Swindon (tel. Salisbury (0722) 336855) *Station:* Pewsey, no practical Sun service, 10m

---

THE COURTS (GARDEN) 🎛   ✖

Holt, nr Trowbridge BA14 6RR (tel. Trowbridge (0225) 782340)

18th-century house (not open to the public); with an ornamental façade, flanked by a 7-acre garden of mystery

O	**Garden only:** 29 March to end Oct: daily except Sat 2–5. Out of season by appointment
£ ♿ 🗂	£1.50, children 50p. Parties by arrangement in advance with the Head Gardener. No WCs. NT shop in Melksham, 4m (tel. Melksham (0225) 706454)

➡️ 3m SW of Melksham, 3m N of Trowbridge, 2½m E of Bradford on Avon, on S side of B3107 [173: ST861618] *Bus:* Badgerline 237 Chippenham–Trowbridge (passing close BR Chippenham & Trowbridge) (tel. Bath (0225) 464446) *Station:* Bradford-on-Avon 2½m; Trowbridge 3m

GREAT CHALFIELD MANOR 🏠❄️✝️🗡️ ❌❌❌

nr Melksham SN12 8NJ

Dating from 1480, the manor house is set across a moat between parish church and stables. Restored early this century by Major R. Fuller, whose family still lives here

🅾️ April to end Oct: Tues to Thur by guided tours only, starting 12.15, 2.15, 3, 3.45 & 4.30. Closed on public holidays

Note: Members of historical and other societies wishing to visit the Manor in organised parties can usually be shown the church, house and garden on other weekdays, by written appointment with Mrs Robert Floyd

💷 £2.80. No reduction for children or parties. No WCs

➡️ 3m SW of Melksham via Broughton Gifford Common (sign for Atworth – drive on left) [166: ST860630] *Bus:* Badgerline 237 Chippenham–Trowbridge (passing close BR Chippenham & Trowbridge), alight Holt, 1m by footpath or Broughton Gifford 1½m (tel. Bath (0225) 464446) *Station:* Bradford-on-Avon 3m

LACOCK ABBEY 🏠✝️♣️ ❌❌

nr Chippenham SN15 2LG (tel. Lacock (024 973) 227)*

Abbey founded in 1232 and converted into a country house after 1539; medieval cloisters, sacristy and chapter house; 16th-century stable court, tower and chimneys; Gothick hall built in 1754; home of the Talbot family who gave the Abbey and village to the Trust

🅾️❄️ **House:** 30 March to 3 Nov: daily except Tues 1–5.30. **Cloisters & grounds:** 30 March to 3 Nov: daily 12–5.30. Last admissions 5 *continued*

[🏠] [❄] In village. 1–30 March: Tues to Sat 11.30–4. 31 March to 26 Oct daily 10.30–5.30. 27 Oct to 22 Dec daily 11.30–4. 2 Jan to 28 March 1992: Tues to Sat 11.30–4. Tel. Lacock (024 973) 302*

[£] House, cloisters & grounds £3.50, children £1.70, parties £3. Cloisters & grounds £1.40

[♿] Grounds and cloisters; house is less easy; special car parking arrangements; wheelchairs available at Museum; [♿] WC at house. Pre-booked guided parties for visually handicapped visitors; taped guides

[🍴] In village (not NT)

[→] 3m S of Chippenham, just E of A350 [173: ST919684] *Bus:* Badgerline 234/7 264/5 Chippenham–Trowbridge–Bath (passing close BR Chippenham & Trowbridge and passing BR Bath Spa) (tel. Bath (0225) 464446) *Station:* Chippenham 3½m

From April 1991 tel. nos. will be Abbey: Chippenham (0249) 730227; Shop: Chippenham (0249) 730302

LACOCK: FOX TALBOT MUSEUM [🏛] [✶]

Lacock, nr Chippenham SN15 2LG (tel. Lacock (0249) 73459)*

A museum of photography commemorating the achievements of William Henry Fox Talbot (1800–77)

[🔵] March to 3 Nov: daily except Good Fri 11–5.30. Last admissions 5

[🏠] Shop selling photographic books, films, postcards. Open as museum

[£] £2. Parties £1.70

[♿] Ground floor only accessible; apply to curator for further facilities, and see Lacock Abbey, above; [♿] WC at Abbey & in Red Lion car park

[🍴] In village (not NT)

[→] At entrance gates to Lacock Abbey (see p. 239) *Bus & Station:* as for Lacock Abbey

From April 1991 tel. no. will be Chippenham (0249) 730459

LITTLE CLARENDON [🏛] [✶] [✉]

Dinton, Salisbury SP3 5OZ

Tudor house

[🔵] [❄] By prior written appointment with tenant

[£] £1.20. No reduction for children or parties. House not suitable for pushchairs or prams. No coaches

[→] ¼m E of Dinton Church [184: SU015316] *Bus & Station:* As for Philipps House, below

MOMPESSON HOUSE 🏠✿

The Close, Salisbury SP1 2EL (tel. Salisbury (0722) 335659)

One of the finest 18th-century houses in the Cathedral Close; notable plasterwork; elegant oak staircase; fine period furniture; important Turnbull collection of 18th-century English drinking glasses; china collection: attractive walled garden

🅾   25 March to 3 Nov: daily, except Thur & Fri 12–5.30. Last admissions 5

💷   £2.30, children £1.20. Parties £2. Visitor sitting room. Parking in Cathedral
🛍   Close (a charge is made by the Dean & Chapter). Coach parking in Central Car
Park. Shop at 41 High Street (tel. Salisbury (0722) 331884)

♿   Ground floor & garden only

🍴   Teas in Garden Room when house open

➡   On N side of Choristers' Green in the Cathedral Close, near High Street Gate
[184: SU142295] *Bus:* From surrounding areas (tel. Salisbury (0722)
336855) *Station:* Salisbury ½m

PHILIPPS HOUSE 🏠♣

Dinton, Salisbury SP3 5HJ (tel. Teffont (072 276) 208)

Neo-Grecian house by Jeffry Wyattville, completed in 1816; let to, and administered and maintained by, the Young Women's Christian Association and used as art centre

🅾✿   By prior written arrangement only with the Warden

💷   £1.20. No reduction for children or parties

♿   Grounds and ground floor

🍴   Penruddocke Arms and Swordsman Inn, Dinton (not NT)

➡   9m W of Salisbury, on N side of B3089 [184: SU009319] *Bus:* Wilts & Dorset
25–7 from Salisbury (passing BR Salisbury & Tisbury) (tel. Salisbury (0722)
336855) *Station:* Tisbury 5m

WILTSHIRE

STONEHENGE DOWN 🏛🏊🚶

Amesbury, nr Salisbury SP4 7DE (tel. Bristol (0272) 734472)

The Trust owns 1,500 acres of surrounding downland including some fine Bronze Age barrows; there are recommended walks and an archaeological leaflet available at Stonehenge shop, not NT

The henge monument is owned and administered by English Heritage

🅾 £ Monument opening details are obtainable from the address and tel. no. above.
❄   NT members free. NT downland open at most times, subject to the farming calendar

➔   Monument 2m W of Amesbury, at Jn of A303 & A344/A360 [184: SU1242]
    Bus: Wilts & Dorset 3 BR Salisbury–Stonehenge (tel. Salisbury (0722) 336855) *Station:* Salisbury 9½m

STOURHEAD ❄🏠🌳   ✗🕹

Stourton, Warminster BA12 6QH (tel. Bourton (0747) 840348)

Landscape garden laid out 1741–80, with lakes and temples, rare trees and plants; house begun 1721 by Colen Campbell contains furniture by the younger Chippendale, and fine paintings; King Alfred's Tower, a red-brick folly built in 1772 by Flitcroft at the edge of the estate is 160ft high giving fine views over neighbouring counties of Somerset, Dorset and Wiltshire

🅾 ❄ **Garden:** all year: daily 8–7 or sunset if earlier (except 24–27 July when garden will close at 5). **House:** 25 March to 3 Nov: Sat to Wed 12–5.30 or dusk if earlier. Last admissions 5. Other times by written appointment with Administrator. **King Alfred's Tower:** 5 March to 3 Nov: daily except Fri & Mon (open BH Mon) 2–5.30 or dusk if earlier. Tower is 2m by road from Stourhead House; parking 100yds; level walk to Tower. Dogs may be tied up outside, but are not allowed up Tower. Tel. Maiden Bradley (09853) 785

242

▢✳ Open daily 1–30 March & 27 Oct to 22 Dec 11–4, 31 March to 26 Oct 11–6, Jan to end March 1992 11–4. Tel. Bourton (0747) 840591

£ House £3.50, children £1.70. Parties £3 by written appointment only. Garden March to 30 Oct £3.50, children £1.70, parties £3; Nov to end Feb £2.30, children £1.20; no reduction for parties. Parking ¼m from house, garden & facilities. King Alfred's Tower £1.20, children (5–15) 60p

♿ Garden accessible, but 13 steps up to house then ground floor rooms on one level; special parking arrangements at house and garden; 1½m-long path round lake is recommended to wheelchair users who are advised to avoid congested times at weekends and in May & June; ♿ WC in Spread Eagle courtyard. Scented azaleas in early summer

🐕 No dogs in garden except Nov to end Feb; in woods throughout year

🍴♿ Spread Eagle Inn (NT) at garden entrance (tel. Bourton (0747) 840587) open all year. Lunches, bar snacks, dinner; 4 bedrooms with bathrooms en suite (winter breaks). Village hall restaurant (self-service): coffee, light lunches, teas. Open 3–24 March: Sun only 11–4; 25–30 March: daily 11–4; 31 March to 26 Oct: daily 10.30–5.30 (tel. Bourton (0747) 840161). Picnicking in car park & garden

Events: Fête Champêtre 24–27 July. Tickets (tel. Bourton (0747) 840142). Only ticket holders to the fête will be admitted to the garden after 5

➡ At Stourton, off B3092, 3m NW of Mere (A303) [183: ST7834]
Bus: Leathers 20 BR Gillingham–Stourton (Wed & Sat only); Southern National 59 from BR Gillingham, alight Zeals, 1¼m (tel. Wiltshire CC: Trowbridge (0225) 753641) *Station:* Gillingham 6½m; Bruton (U) 7m

WESTWOOD MANOR 🏠✳   ✖✖✖

Bradford on Avon BA15 2AF (tel. Bradford on Avon (02216) 3374)

15th-century stone manor house, altered late 16th century, with late Gothic and Jacobean windows and Jacobean plasterwork; modern topiary garden

Westwood Manor is administered for the National Trust by a tenant

◯ 31 March to end Sept: Sun, Tues & Wed 2–5. House unsuitable for children under 10. Other times parties of up to 20 by written application with s.a.e. to tenant

£ £2.50. No reduction for parties or children. No WCs

➡ 1½m SW of Bradford on Avon, in Westwood village, beside the church; village signposted off Bradford on Avon to Rode road (B3109) [173: ST812590]
Bus: From surrounding areas to Bradford on Avon, thence 1½m (tel. Bath (0225) 464446) *Station:* Avoncliff (U), 1m; Bradford on Avon 1½m

PLEASE REFER TO PAGES 5–9

Yorkshire (North)

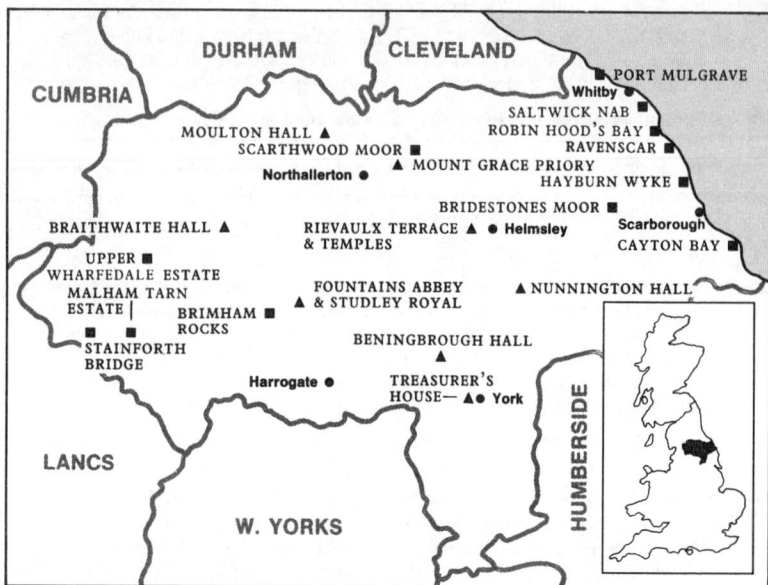

DURHAM   CLEVELAND
PORT MULGRAVE
CUMBRIA   Whitby ●
SALTWICK NAB ■
MOULTON HALL ▲   ROBIN HOOD'S BAY ■
SCARTHWOOD MOOR ■   RAVENSCAR ■
Northallerton ●   ▲ MOUNT GRACE PRIORY
HAYBURN WYKE ■
BRIDESTONES MOOR ■
BRAITHWAITE HALL ▲   RIEVAULX TERRACE ▲ ● Helmsley   Scarborough
& TEMPLES   CAYTON BAY ■
UPPER ■
WHARFEDALE ESTATE
MALHAM TARN   FOUNTAINS ABBEY   ▲ NUNNINGTON HALL
ESTATE | ▲ & STUDLEY ROYAL
BRIMHAM ■
■ ROCKS
STAINFORTH   BENINGBROUGH HALL
BRIDGE   ▲
Harrogate ●   TREASURER'S
HOUSE— ▲● York
LANCS
W. YORKS
HUMBERSIDE

COAST

The Trust's many holdings on the North Yorkshire coast are crossed by the Cleveland Way long distance footpath. An alternative route for the Cleveland Way has now been completed via NT property at **Cayton Bay**, south of Scarborough [101: TA063850]. This provides an ideal opportunity to see the variety of habitats contained within its 90 acres. Extensive woodland and grassland management schemes are being undertaken to improve their nature conservation interest. [101: TA063850]. Six miles north of Scarborough, at **Hayburn Wyke**, 65 acres of high cliffs overlook the Trust-owned bay and rocky beach. A stream provides a small waterfall to this attractive beach. 🖫 **Robin Hood's Bay** is perhaps the best known feature of the North Yorkshire coast. Here the Trust's ownership is greatest with the whole of the headland north of the village of Robin Hood's Bay, **Boggle Hole** and most of the southern end and headland of the Bay including the clifftop south of **Ravenscar** above the magnificent and dramatic Beast Cliff. Steps have been built and experiments are being conducted to encourage vegetation to regrow on bare areas. The remains of the Peak Alum Works just north of Ravenscar are being investigated by an archaeologist and team of assistants. A spur from the Cleveland Way gives access to two information panels which explain the alum industry and the Trust's consolidation work on site [94: NZ973024]. A trail begins at the Trust's Coastal Centre at Ravenscar. Guided walks. Leaflet available. The Coastal Centre and shop are open 10.30–5.30: 29 March to 7 April daily; April, May & Sept weekends, BH Mon (& Tues following); 25 May to 31 Aug daily; Oct weekends if weather fine. Refreshments available in village. [94: NZ980025].

Port Mulgrave, 5 miles north of Whitby: 38 acres of cliff and undercliff surrounding the harbour and the northern headland of the bay [94: NZ796175]. Saltwick Nab, just south of Whitby is home to a wide variety of wild flowers and insects. The Nab, an inhospitable stack of alum shale, is only accessible after a difficult scramble at low tide, when the remains of an old jetty are visible. Accessible from the Cleveland Way. [94: NZ914112]. Newbiggin Cliffs, 25 acres on the Cleveland Way, 2 miles north-east of Filey [93: TA827105]; guillemot and razorbill nest here.

COUNTRYSIDE

The 4,000-acre Malham Tarn Estate between Ribblesdale and Wharfedale [98: SD8966] includes several farms and Ewe Moor, a dry valley of fissured limestone above Malham Cove. The Tarn and its wetlands are internationally important as a nature reserve, and Tarn House is let by the Trust to the Field Studies Council. The nature reserve is jointly managed by the National Trust and the Field Studies Council. The area has a rich flora and has characteristic upland breeding birds such as wheatear, curlew, lapwing and redshank. Great crested grebes, coots and tufted ducks breed on the Tarn and can be seen from a bird hide situated at the north-west corner of the Tarn. The Pennine Way runs through the middle of the estate, skirting the eastern and northern shores of the Tarn. Access to the Tarn on foot only. The old drovers' road, Mastiles Lane, approaches the Tarn from Kilnsey, 5 miles away across the moors, and the great caravanserai of the drovers was at Great Close. Towards Malham village, the Trust owns the popular waterfall of Janet's Foss, part of the Malham Tarn Estate. 🚹 Access for disabled people from the Polegate to the south-east of the Tarn, along the estate road for about 1½ miles, passing the Tarn shore.

To the north east of the Malham Tarn Estate is the recently acquired Upper Wharfedale Estate, amounting to some 5,200 acres with grazing rights over approximately a further 2,000 acres. This estate comprises the finest features of Dales landscape, including meadowland in the valley of the River Wharfe, limestone pasture and acid moorland stretching above the steep hillsides to over 2,000ft. The estate is criss-crossed with stone walls dividing eight farms, and also includes 400 acres of magnificent woodlands, waterfalls and a former deer park.

At Stainforth, the Trust owns a 17th-century single span packhorse bridge across the River Ribble; once part of the route from Ripon to Lancaster [98: SD818672].

Near the Cleveland Hills to the north, Scarthwood Moor gives fine views of the Pennines [94 & 100: SE465995] from its moorland heights. It provides a popular picnic site beside the stream at its valley floor.

🚹 Bridestones Moor [94: SE8791] lies within the North York Moors National Park on the edge of Dalby Forest, 12 miles south of Whitby, 7 miles north-east of Pickering and a mile east of the A169. Part of the property is a Nature Reserve which can be reached by taking the Forestry Commission's Dalby Forest Drive, for which a small charge is made. A car park [94: SE879904] is situated 3 miles north-east of Low Dalby with WCs. The reserve contains a variety of plants and animals typical of the North York Moors, in addition to the Bridestones, which are impressive and oddly shaped sandstone outcrops. The Trust is currently carrying out important conservation work on this area of considerable natural history interest. Nature walk leaflet available.

Crosscliff and Blakey Topping. Crosscliff is an area of heather moorland ½ mile north of Bridestones Moor, situated approximately 1½ miles east of Pickering–Whitby road, A169, 11 miles south of Whitby. At the northern end of the property lies Blakey Topping, a curiously shaped conical hill, rising to a height of 875ft above sea level. There are impressive all-round views from this point. The nearest car parking is either at the

245

National Park car park at the Hole of Horcum on the A169 [101: SE852938] or the Forestry Commission's Crosscliff viewpoint car park, just off the Dalby Forest Drive [101: SE896915].

[†] **Brimham Rocks**, [99: SE2165] 8 miles south-west of Ripon, off B6265, 10 miles north-west of Harrogate off B6165, strange and fantastic rock formations, set in open moorland overlooking Nidderdale. Shop, refreshment kiosk and Information Centre are open 11–5: 29 March to 7 April daily; 8 April to 24 May weekends & BH Mon; 25 May to 31 Oct daily. Admission: cars £1; minibuses £1.50; coaches £4. [&] WC; special car parking by arrangement with Warden. Dogs must be on leads in April, May & June, and thereafter under strict control; grazing animals. Tel. Harrogate (0423) 780688.

BENINGBROUGH HALL 🏛 ✿ 📷 ☂   ✖ ✂ 🗑

Shipton-by-Beningbrough, York YO6 1DD (tel. York (0904) 470666)

John Bourchier built this imposing Georgian hall in 1716; set in 365 acres, it has exquisite carving; plasterwork; over 100 pictures on loan from the National Portrait Gallery; cantilevered staircase; furniture and porcelain; servants exhibition; well-equipped Victorian laundry; 7-acre garden; Pike Ponds walk; potting shed

🅾	Good Fri 29 March to end Oct: daily except Mon & Fri (but open BH Mon and Good Fri) 12–6 or dusk if earlier. Also open Fri in July and Aug. Last admissions 5.30
🏠 ✿	Open as house. Also Nov to 22 Dec: Sat & Sun 12–5
£	House, garden & exhibitions £3.40; family £8.50; parties £2.80. Garden & exhibitions only £2.20; family £5.50. School groups and parties by prior arrangement. For conservation reasons pushchairs are not allowed in the house
♿ 🚼	Baby-changing facilities. High chairs in restaurant. Wilderness play area
♿	Ground floor only, by ramp; level garden paths (embedded gravel); special parking spaces. [&] WC in stable block
🍴 ♿	Hot & cold lunches, teas, in restaurant open as shop 12–5.30. Special functions by arrangement. Picnic area in walled garden

Events: Contact Administrator for full range of events. Guided garden walks most weekends

➡️ 8m NW of York, 2m W of Shipton, 2m SE of Linton-on-Ouse (A19) [105: SE516586] *Bus:* Yorkshire Pullman from York (passing close BR York), to within 1m (tel. York (0904) 622304) *Station:* York 8m

BRAITHWAITE HALL 🏠✲　　　　　　　　　❌🍴

East Witton, Leyburn DL8 4SY (tel. Wensleydale (0969) 40287)

17th-century hall, now a working farmhouse; 748 acres of moor and farmland

🅾️ By arrangement with tenant, Mrs David Duffus

💷 50p, incl. leaflet. No access for coaches. No WCs

➡️ 1½m SW of Middleham, 2m W of East Witton (A6108) [99: SE117857] *Bus:* Dalesbus 803 from Leeds, summer only (passing close BR Harrogate), alight East Witton, 2m (tel. Harrogate (0423) 566061)

FOUNTAINS ABBEY & STUDLEY ROYAL ✝✲♣　　❌

Fountains, Ripon HG4 3DZ (tel. Ripon (0765) 86333)

Fountains Abbey on the banks of the River Skell, founded by Cistercian monks in 1132 and the largest monastic ruin in Britain; the Abbey ruins provide the dramatic focal point of the 18th-century landscape garden at Studley Royal; water garden, temples, follies, vistas, deer park; small museum; St Mary's church, built by William Burges 1871-8

🅾️✲ **Abbey & Garden:** daily except 24 & 25 Dec and Fri in Nov, Dec & Jan. Jan to March and Nov & Dec: 10-5 or dusk if earlier. April to June & Sept: 10-7. July & Aug: 10-8. Oct: 10-6 or dusk if earlier. **Deer Park:** all year during daylight hours. **Fountains Hall:** daily, April to end Sept: 11-6; Oct to end March 1992: 11-4. **St Mary's Church:** 29 March to end Sept 1-5.

🎟 Guided tours available April to end Oct daily at 2.30

📷✲ Studley Royal shop: daily 10-6. Abbey shop: Easter to end Oct daily 10-6; Nov & Dec weekends 10-6

⚐£⚐ Hall, deer park and church free. Abbey and garden only: 1–28 March & Nov to
end Dec: £2.40, children £1. Family £5.80. Groups (over 15) £2, children 80p.
Group (over 40) £1.80, children 70p. 29 March to end Oct: £2.70, children
£1.20. Family £6.60. Groups (over 15) £2.30, children 90p. Group (over 40)
£2, children 80p. Car parking free at Abbey; £1 at Studley Royal, refundable
on purchase of admission ticket; coaches free; motorcycles 30p

♿ Abbey precincts and Studley Royal garden; powered 'runarounds' available at
both entrances by prior booking only; ♿ WC in Studley car park and next to
tea-room at lakeside and in Abbey car park

🐾 On leads only

🍴♿ Easter to Oct. Light lunches, sandwiches etc, teas, coffee, cold drinks. Lakeside
tea-room at Studley Royal: daily 10–5.30. Abbey tea-room, Easter to end Oct:
10.30–5.30. Picnic areas available

Events: Second weekend in July: Music by Moonlight. For full programme of
events contact Events office (tel. Ripon (0765) 86333)

➡ 4m W of Ripon off B6265 to Pateley Bridge [99: SE271683] *Bus:* United 145
from Ripon (with connections from BR Harrogate) Thur & Sat only (tel.
Darlington (0325) 468771); Dalesbus 806 from Leeds, summer only (passing
close BR Harrogate) (tel. Harrogate (0423) 566061)

MOULTON HALL 🏛🛈   ✄✄✄

Moulton, Richmond (tel. Barton (032 577) 227)

Rebuilt about 1650, with fine carved wood staircase

🅾✿ By arrangement with tenant, the Hon J. D. Eccles

£ 50p. Unsuitable for coaches. No WCs

♿ Please enquire about access when arranging a visit

➡ 5m E of Richmond; turn off A1 ½m S of Scotch Corner [99: NZ235035]
Bus: United 25 Darlington–Richmond (passing close BR Darlington), alight
Moulton village, ½m (tel. Darlington (0325) 468771) *Station:* Darlington 9½m

MOUNT GRACE PRIORY ✝   ✄

Osmotherley, Northallerton DL6 3JG (tel. Osmotherley (060 983) 494)

*The greater part of the remains of a 14th-century priory; the most important Carthusian ruin
in England; reconstructed and furnished cell on show; exhibition on the Carthusians and
NT/EH information room*

Mount Grace Priory is in the guardianship of English Heritage

🅾✿ Good Fri 29 March to end Sept: daily 10–6. Oct to end March 1992: daily
except Mon 10–1 and 2–4. Last admissions ¾ hr before closing

£1.40; OAPs, students and UB40 holders £1.05; children (under 16) 70p. Parties of 11 or more 15% discount. School visits Mon to Fri, free, but must be booked with EH (tel. York (0904) 622902). Bulky bags and pushchairs may be left in reception

6m NE of Northallerton, ½m E of A19 and ½m S of its junction with A172 [99: SE449985] *Bus:* United/Tees & District 90/A Northallerton–Middlesbrough (passing close BR Northallerton), alight Priory Road End, ½m (tel. Middlesbrough (0642) 210131) *Station:* Northallerton 6m

NUNNINGTON HALL

Nunnington, York YO6 5UY (tel. Nunnington (043 95) 283)

Manor house on the banks of the River Rye, partly 16th-century, but mainly late 17th-century; the principal reception rooms include a magnificent panelled hall with a fine carved chimneypiece; panelled bedrooms, fine tapestries; china; Carlisle Collection of Miniature Rooms fully furnished in different periods; garden

30 March to 4 April and weekends in April: 2–6. May, June, Sept & Oct: Tues to Thur, Sat & Sun 2–6. July & Aug: Tues to Thur 2–6; Sat & Sun 12–6. Open BH Mon 2–6. Last admission 5. School parties Tues & Wed 10–12 by appointment

Open as house

House & garden £2.50; children £1.20. Garden only £1. Parties £2. For conservation reasons pushchairs and prams are not allowed in the house. Car parking 50yds; unsuitable for trailer caravans

Collection of miniature rooms *continued*

⬥ House: ground floor and tea-room only; ramp to main garden; loose gravel paths; for special parking apply at Reception; ⬥ WC

⬥ In car park only

⬥ ⬥ Tea-room open as shop. Lunches, Sat & Sun in July & Aug. Indoor tea-room and tea-garden

Events: Contact Administrator for details (also for educational activities)

➔ In Ryedale, 4½m SE of Helmsley (A170) Helmsley-Pickering road; 1½m N of B1257 Malton-Helmsley road [92: SE670795] *Bus:* Scarborough & District 128 Scarborough–Helmsley (passing close BR Scarborough & Seamer), alight Wombleton, 3m (tel. Scarborough (0723) 375463)

RIEVAULX TERRACE & TEMPLES ⬥⬥⬥

Rievaulx, Helmsley YO6 5LJ (tel. Bilsdale (043 96) 340)

Half-mile long grass-covered terrace and adjoining woodlands with vistas over Rievaulx Abbey (English Heritage) and Rye valley to Ryedale and the Hambleton Hills; two mid 18th-century temples; the Ionic Temple has elaborate ceiling paintings and fine 18th-century furniture; permanent exhibition in the basement on English landscape design in the 18th century

Note: No access to Abbey from Terrace. No access to property Nov to end March

⬥ 29 March to end Oct: daily 10.30–6 or dusk if earlier. Last admissions 5.30. Ionic Temple closed 1–2

⬥ Shop and Information Centre open same times

⬥ £1.70, children 80p. Parties £1.50; children 70p. Parking at reception, but coach park 200yds; unsuitable for trailer caravans

⬥ Terrace recommended; access to temples not possible because of steps. Unadapted WCs. Powered 'runaround' available

⬥ On leads only

⬥ Teas at Nunnington Hall, 7m (see entry, above)

➔ 2½m NW of Helmsley on B1257 [100: SE579848] *Bus:* United 294 from Middlesbrough (passing close BR Middlesbrough), Fri only (tel. Middlesbrough (0642) 210131); otherwise Scarborough & District 128 Scarborough–Helmsley, thence 2½m (tel. Scarborough (0723) 375463)

TREASURER'S HOUSE ⬥⬥   ⬥⬥⬥

Chapter House Street, York YO1 2JD (tel. York (0904) 624247)

Elegant 17th/18th-century town house on the site of the former residence of the Treasurers of York Minster; a fine collection of furniture; small formal garden; exhibition and video film show development of the house from Roman times and some of its associated personalities

⬥ 29 March to end Oct: daily 10.30–5. Last admissions 4.30

⬜ Open as house. Tel. York (0904) 646757. Also NT shop at 32 Goodramgate open all year Mon to Sat 9–5.30

£ 𝕂 £2.30, children £1. Parties £2, children 80p. No reduction on Sun or BH Mon. Guided tours by arrangement. Evening opening for pre-booked parties £3.50 (min. charge £80) incl. guided tour; contact Administrator. No parking facilities

👶 Facilities for babies & nursing mothers on request; high chair. For conservation reasons pushchairs are not allowed in the house

♿ Ground floor only; steps at back door to part of basement and tea-room; strong helper needed. Cars may set down disabled passengers at door. Braille guide

🍴 ♿ Licensed tea-room open as house (tel. York (0904) 646757); coffee, lunches & teas. Open for pre-booked parties during and outside normal opening hours and for private functions. ♿ see above

Events: Coffee by Candlelight evenings and outdoor events; apply to Administrator for details. ♿ outdoor events only

➡ In Minster Yard, on N side of Minster [105: SE604523] *Bus:* From surrounding areas (tel. York (0904) 624161) *Station:* York ½m

Yorkshire (South) see Derbyshire & Peak District p. 81

251

Yorkshire (West)

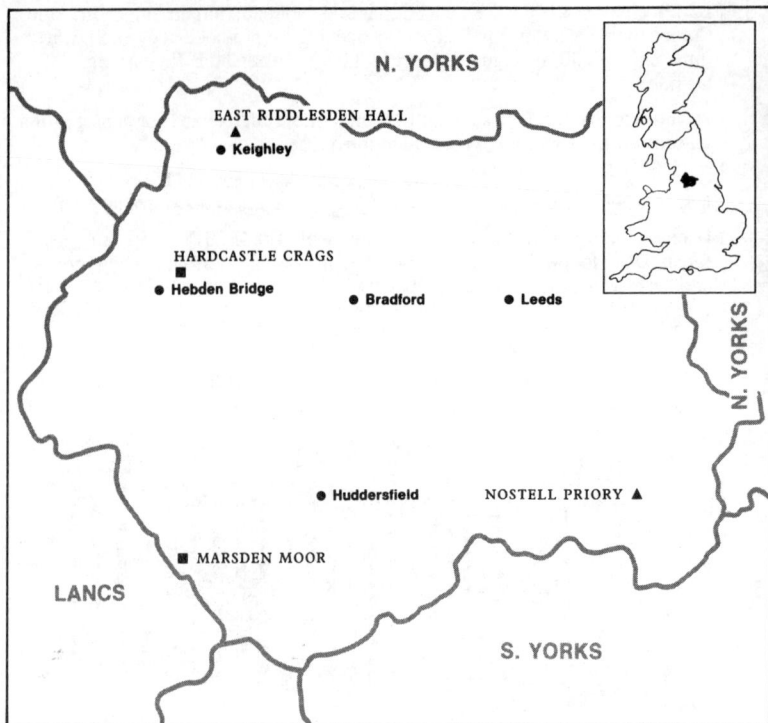

COUNTRYSIDE

[🚶] **Hardcastle Crags**, $1\frac{1}{2}$ miles north-west of Hebden Bridge, comprises two steep wooded valleys, each with a stream running through it. The woodland is predominantly broadleaved, with areas of conifers. Rock outcrops (the Crags) and millponds are attractive features. Riverside walks beside Hebden Water take you through the deciduous woodland and past a disused 19th-century cotton mill. [♿] The main path is accessible to wheelchair users, but most of the property is not negotiable. There is a fine variety of wild flowers. The woodlands are inhabited by wood ants and red squirrels. The Slurring Rock at the highest point of one of the woodland walks, is so called because children once slid or 'slurred' down its slopes in wooden clogs, often carved from locally grown alder or 'clog wood'. Three self-guided walks enable the more adventurous walker to explore the woodlands in depth. A leaflet covers all three walks and the area in general. Always open. Guided walks available, please contact the Warden (tel. Halifax (0422) 844518). Parking at entrance; coaches by arrangement only; information caravan (seasonal). Picnic sites. Public WCs available outside entrance to property. [103: SD988291].

Open moorland at **Marsden Moor** almost surrounding the town of Marsden, stretches from Buckstones Moor on the A640 to Wessenden Moor, north of the A635 [109: SE0210/0611]. This is wild, open moorland country, yet it has a surprising diversity of interest; valleys, reservoirs, peaks and crags and a wealth of archaeological remains dating from pre-Roman settlements to the great engineering structures of the railway and canal developments. Guided walks are organised throughout the year. Details from the Warden at Unit 24, Colne Valley Workshops, Linthwaite, Huddersfield HD7 5QG (please send s.a.e.).

EAST RIDDLESDEN HALL 🏛️❀🏛️ ✉️🎨

Bradford Road, Keighley BD20 5EL (tel. Keighley (0535) 607075)

A traditional 17th-century West Yorkshire manor house with panelled rooms, fine plasterwork and mullioned windows, providing an ideal setting for pewter, domestic utensils and Yorkshire oak furniture; formal walled garden, now restored to original design; monastic fishpond and grounds running down to River Aire; Great Barn, 120ft long, with collection of traditional agricultural machinery

🅾️ 29 March to 3 April and weekends in April: 12–5.30. May to Oct: Sat to Wed 12–5.30. Last admissions 5

📷❀ Shop and information area in Bothy open as house. Also Nov to 22 Dec: Sat & Sun 12–4

💷 £2. Parties £1.70; children 80p. Parking 100yds; coaches must book as space limited. School groups and parties on weekdays by arrangement. No large bags allowed in the house; pushchairs, rucksacks etc must be left at Reception. Evening openings for pre-booked parties: contact Administrator

👶🔺 Facilities for babies & nursing mothers; high chairs in tea-room. Children's guide

♿ Ground floor and garden; some uneven surfaces; loose gravel paths. For special parking facilities apply at Reception. Shop accessible via some steps. Tea-room on first floor of Bothy, but teas may be brought down to disabled visitors. Unadapted WC with access via some steps. 🔊 Braille guide   *continued*

253

⊞ In grounds only, on leads

⊞ ✻ Tea-room open as property, also open Nov to 22 Dec, Sat & Sun 12–4. Open for pre-booked parties during and outside normal opening hours, and for private functions. ⊞ see above. Picnic area in field

Events: Details from Administrator (also information on educational activities and Living History Days). 'Riddlesden Revels' on first Sun in each month

➔ 1m NE of Keighley on S side of the Bradford road close to Leeds & Liverpool Canal [104: SE079421] *Bus:* Frequent services from BR Bradford Interchange, Bingley & Keighley (tel. Leeds (0532) 457676) *Station:* Keighley 1m

NOSTELL PRIORY ⊞ ✻   ✗ ⊠ ⊠

Doncaster Road, Nostell, nr Wakefield WF4 1QE (tel. Wakefield (0924) 863892)

A fine Palladian house, built for the Winn family in 1733; an additional wing and many of the state rooms were designed by Adam; the Priory houses one of England's finest collections of Chippendale furniture, which was specially made for the house; large grounds

🅞 30 March to end April, May, June, Sept & Oct: Sat 12–5; Sun 11–5. July & Aug: daily except Fri 12–5, Sun 11–5. Also open on following public holidays: Easter Mon & Tues; May Day Mon; Spring BH Mon & Tues; Aug BH Mon (Mon 11–5, Tues 12–5). Gift shop (not NT)

£ 🏃 House & grounds £3. Grounds only £2. Parties £2.50, children £1.30. Pre-booked parties welcome outside published opening times (no reduction and charge made for NT members). Min. charge of £75 is made if party numbers less than 30. Guided tours only on weekdays (last tour 4); free-flow visiting at weekends. Parking 350yds. NT members will be expected to pay additional charge for events. For conservation reasons pushchairs must be left in reception

♿ Disabled visitors may usually be driven to front door. Lift to first floor; grounds accessible; ♿ WC. ⊞ Braille guide

⊞ In grounds only

⊞ ♿ Light lunches and teas in Stable Block (not NT). Meals available to parties, by arrangement (tel. Wakefield (0924) 862205). Picnic site

➔ On the A638 out of Wakefield towards Doncaster [111: SE407172] *Bus:* W Riding 485/Yorkshire Rider 498 Wakefield–Doncaster; W Riding 122/3 from Wakefield; 183 Castleford–S Elmsall; Yorkshire Traction 245 from Pontefract (tel. Leeds (0532) 457676) *Station:* Fitzwilliam 1½m

Wales: Clwyd

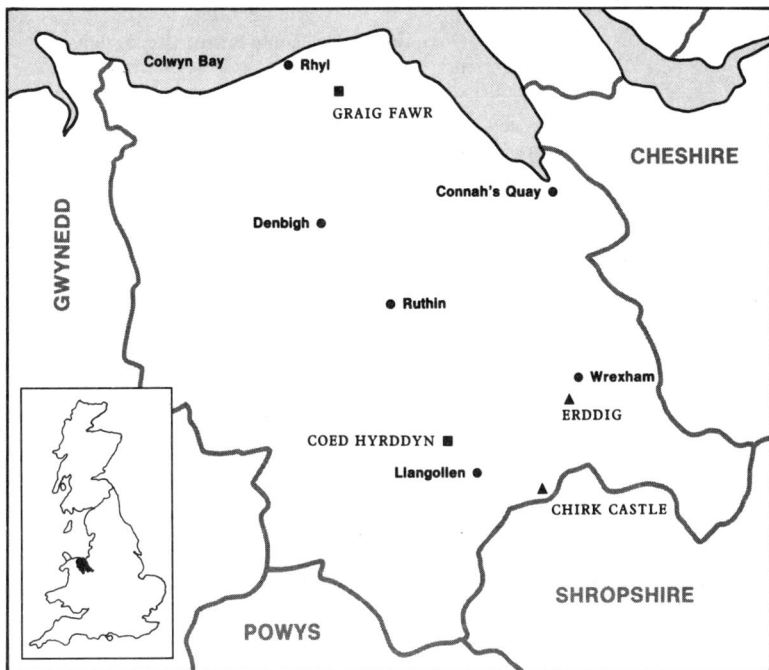

COUNTRYSIDE

[†] **Graig Fawr**, a large limestone hill, south of Prestatyn [116: SJ060805] is a Site of Special Scientific Interest with many marine fossils and a treasure trove of lime-loving plants, such as harebells, small scabious, bird's-foot trefoil and hoary rock-rose. The common blue butterfly delights the visitors to this popular viewpoint. Leaflet from North Wales Regional Office (address on p. 22); s.a.e. please.

Above the road from Llangollen to the Horseshoe Pass is **Coed Hyrddyn** (or Velvet Hill) [117 & 125: SJ200440], giving fine views.

CHIRK CASTLE 🏰 ❄ ♠   ⚔ ✗ ▨

Chirk, Clwyd LL14 5AF (tel. Chirk (0691) 777701)

Marcher fortress, completed in 1310, commanding fine views over the surrounding countryside; elegant state rooms with elaborate plasterwork, superb Adam-style furniture, tapestries and portraits; formal gardens with clipped yews and a variety of flowering shrubs; entrance gates by the Davies brothers, 1721; 18th-century parkland   continued

🅾 28 March to 29 Sept: daily except Mon & Sat but open BH Mon; 5 Oct to 3 Nov: Sat & Sun only. **Castle:** 12–5; **grounds:** 12–6. Last admissions: 4.30

🛍 Shop open as Castle

💷 £3. Pre-booked parties of 20 or more £2.40. Family ticket (max. 2 adults, 2 children) £7.50. Connoisseurs' Tours, Tues mornings by prior arrangement only for parties of min. 20. Car park 200yds

♿ ⬛ Parts of castle & garden only (very limited access). Special parking arrangements. ⬛ Braille guide

🚼 Baby facilities. Baby carriers for loan. Highchair in tea-room

☕ Licensed tea-room: light lunches and teas. Picnicking in car park

➡ ½m W of Chirk village off A5; additional 1½m of private driveway to Castle [117: SJ269381] *Bus:* Crosville Wales 2 Wrexham–Shrewsbury, alight Chirk village, 1½m (tel. Wrexham (0978) 261361) *Station:* Chirk (U) 1½m

ERDDIG 🏠 ❀ ♠ 🏠   ✕ 🏛

nr Wrexham, Clwyd LL13 0YT (tel. Wrexham (0978) 355314)

Late 17th-century house with 18th-century additions, retaining most of its original furniture; the range of outbuildings includes kitchen, laundry, bakehouse, stables, sawmill, smithy and joiners' shop; large walled garden restored to its 18th-century formal design; 10 min. video programme

🅾 Good Fri 29 March to 13 Oct: daily, except Thur & Fri (open Good Fri) 11–6 (house 12–5). Last admissions 4. School and youth groups Mon to Wed mornings only by prior arrangement

🛍 Joiners shop manufacturing quality garden furniture for sale; open same times as property; catalogue available

£ Family rooms (incl. Belowstairs, outbuildings & garden) £4. Parties £3.20. Belowstairs (incl. outbuildings & garden) £2.50. Parties £2. Family ticket (max. 2 adults, 2 children) £6.25. Parking 200yds

& Ground floor, garden (ramps) and out-buildings only; not an easy property for wheelchairs, please discuss visits in advance with Administrator. 🔲 WC in main yard, wheelchair provided. ◀ Braille guide.

🔲 👶 Babyfeeding and changing facilities. Highchair in tea-room. Baby carriers on loan. Children's guide

🐕 In grounds only on lead

▣ Licensed tea-room: light teas and lunches. Picnicking in car park area

Events: Contact Administrator. Meet the Gardener Tours available by prior arrangement

Notes: Most rooms have no electric light; visitors wishing to make a close study of pictures and textiles should avoid dull days early and late in the season. Due to the extreme fragility of their contents, the Tapestry and Chinese Rooms are open on Wed and Sat only

➔ 2m S of Wrexham, signposted A525 Whitchurch road, or A483/A5152 Ruabon road [117: SJ326482] *Station:* Wrexham Central (U) 1½m; Wrexham General 2m via Erddig Road & footpath

---

ERDDIG VISITOR CENTRE 🏠 🔲 🌳 ♿ 👤   ✈

nr Wrexham (tel. Wrexham (0978) 264470)

Houses an exhibition depicting the changes on the Erddig Estate; 17th-century demountable barn in and around which is a collection of local farm machinery, mainly from second half of the 19th century; parkland; Open Days with farming demonstrations during season; conservation project in park won Prince of Wales Award in 1988

O April to 13 Oct: Sat & Sun only 10–5 (but open Good Fri & BH Mons). School and youth groups Wed & Thur only by prior arrangement. Last admissions 4.30

£ Free

& ◀ Access to Centre, barn, conservation area in park and nature trails. 🔲 WC next to ticket office. ◀ Nature trails

➔ *Station:* Wrexham Central (U) 1m; Wrexham General 1½m

257

Dyfed

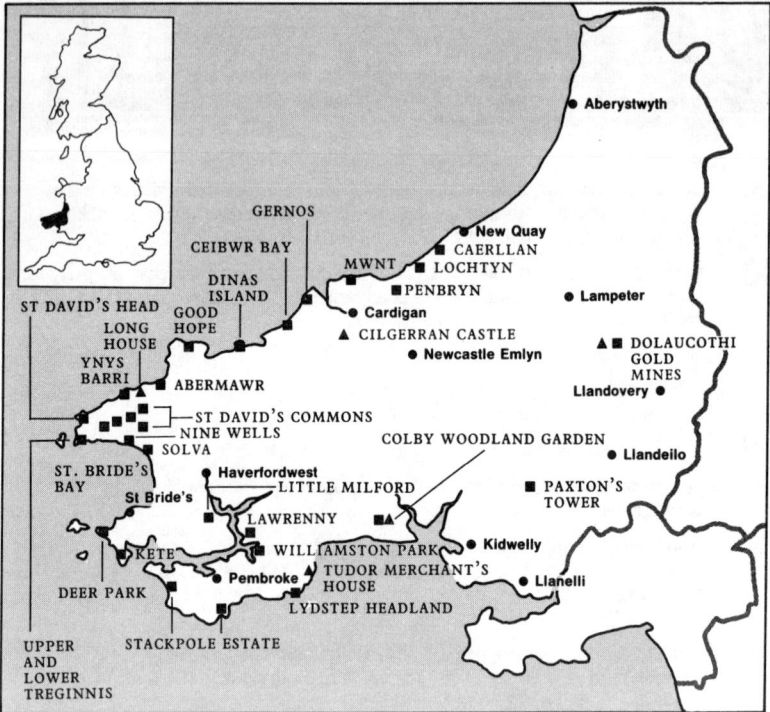

ABERYSTWYTH map with labels: GERNOS, CEIBWR BAY, MWNT, New Quay, CAERLLAN, LOCHTYN, DINAS ISLAND, PENBRYN, Lampeter, ST DAVID'S HEAD, GOOD HOPE, LONG HOUSE, Cardigan, CILGERRAN CASTLE, DOLAUCOTHI GOLD MINES, YNYS BARRI, Newcastle Emlyn, ABERMAWR, Llandovery, ST DAVID'S COMMONS, NINE WELLS, SOLVA, COLBY WOODLAND GARDEN, Llandeilo, ST. BRIDE'S BAY, Haverfordwest, LITTLE MILFORD, PAXTON'S TOWER, St Bride's, LAWRENNY, KETE, WILLIAMSTON PARK, Kidwelly, DEER PARK, Pembroke, TUDOR MERCHANT'S HOUSE, Llanelli, LYDSTEP HEADLAND, UPPER AND LOWER TREGINNIS, STACKPOLE ESTATE

COAST

The 168-mile long Pembrokeshire Coast Path begins at Amroth on Carmarthen Bay and ends at St Dogmaels, a village on the outskirts of Cardigan. It traverses Trust property for much of its length, beginning with the 980-acre **Colby Estate** at Amroth, giving views of Somerset, Caldy and Gower. 1½ miles east of Manorbier is **Lydstep Headland** [158: SS090976] accessible by footpath from Lydstep village. NT shop in Pembroke.

The 2,000-acre **Stackpole Estate,** 4 miles south of Pembroke [158: SR977693] includes freshwater lakes at Bosherston, thick with waterlilies in summer; woods, 8 miles of cliffs, two beaches, farmland and sand dunes. From the tiny and beautiful Stackpole Quay where the Trust has several holiday cottages, you can walk over the headland to Barafundle Bay where there is a wide sweep of pale golden sand and good bathing. ♿ An adventure area near the Quay has been developed for able-bodied and disabled people. There are car parks at Stackpole Quay and Broadhaven – the second of the bathing beaches. About a mile from Broadhaven is St Govan's Chapel (not NT), a tiny 13th-century building clinging to a crevice half way down three steep cliffs and reached by a long flight of extremely uneven stone steps. The Ministry of Defence controls access and closes the road at certain times when the nearby firing ranges are in use. At Freshwater West, the Trust owns a farm and a large part of **Kilpaison Burrows**, one of the finest sand dune systems in Pembrokeshire

On the northern side of Milford Haven at **Kete**, west of Dale, the Trust owns 168 acres, giving views of Skomer and Skokholm Islands [157: SM800045]. From here is a good walk to the cliffs of St Anne's Head.

The Trust owns about 15½ miles of the coastline at **St Bride's Bay**, including the **Deer Park** at Marloes which is separated from the adjacent headland by a high stone wall built at the beginning of the 19th century, although deer were never introduced. It provides a suitable feeding habitat for certain coastal sea bird species, such as chough. There are marvellous views of Skomer and Skokholm to the south [157: SM78091]. Car park, information panel and WCs.

[ẋ] Nearby at **Marloes Sands** [157: SM7707] a 2½-mile walk can be followed along the Pembrokeshire coastal path. It takes in the sandstone cliffs, an Iron Age fort and Marloes Mere; raven, chough and grey seal may be seen; the mere is an exciting place to watch birds. Leaflet from DWT, 7 Market Street, Haverfordwest, Dyfed SA61 1NF (45p by post). The area is also mentioned in National Park publications.

[ẋ] In the **St David's** area [145: SM740278] the National Trust owns land extending from west of Newgale Beach to St David's Head [145: SM721278], incorporating 1,309 acres of unspoilt coastline with four farms, and 2,150 acres of commons, all within the Pembrokeshire Coast National Park. The landscape is one of rocky outcrops, coastal plateau and spectacular coastline, important for geology and natural history. The views are extensive and beautiful along the coast to Marloes, west to Ramsey Island and north towards Strumble Head. NT shop at **Solva** (seasonal); visitor centre with shop at St David's.

Further acquisitions have added to the Trust's ownership on the North Pembrokeshire coastline. 200 acres of coastal farmland at **Ynys Barri**, Llanrhian [151(157): SM805328] includes 2 miles of coastland between Porthgain Harbour and Abereiddy. Near Abercastle, **Long House Farm** [157: SM853337] comprises 151 acres of farmland with 2½ miles of scenic rugged coastline. Two small islands are included with the land: Ynys-y-Castell and Ynys Deullyn. There is an Iron Age promontory fort on the property. **Dinas Island Farm** [157: SM0140] lies 5 miles east of Fishguard and 18 miles west of Cardigan; 414 acres of farmland with 2½ miles of coastline lying within the Pembroke-shire Coast National Park. Just to the east of Strumble Head, 3 miles north-west of Fishguard, on the Pembrokeshire coast is 97 acres of rugged coastal outcrop and largely unimproved pasture, known as **Good Hope** [157: SM912407]. 6½ acres are owned at **Ceibwr Bay**, Moylegrove [139(168): 109485]. **Abermawr**, [157: SN891347] is 10 miles from St Davids and a little to the south of Strumble Head; 268 acres comprising a shingle beach backed by a freshwater marsh lying in a wooded valley and forming about half a mile of coast. At **Gernos**, St Dogmaels, Cardigan [145: SM1340], the National Trust protects 2 more miles of the North Pembrokeshire coast; 106 acres to the west of Cemmaes Head, near St Dogmaels, including the promontory of Pen-yr-Afr.

Between Cardigan and Newquay the Trust owns **Mwnt** [145: SN1952], a family beach with parking, lavatories and a refreshment kiosk; **Penbryn** [145: SN295519], just north-east of Tresaith with extensive beaches, car parking, lavatories and café/refreshment facilities (no dogs at Mwnt and Penbryn beaches between 1 May and 30 Sept); **Caerllan** at Cwmtudu [145: SN355577], with 1½ miles of cliff walks to Newquay; and **Lochtyn** [145: SN315545], a rocky headland near the village of Llangranog; from the highest point, **Pen-y-Badell**, splendid views can be seen across Cardigan Bay to the Llyn Peninsula and Snowdonia. **Penparc Farm** consists of 120 acres south-west of Cwmtudu including one mile of coastline and ¼ mile of valley bluff.

Recent acquisitions on the Pembrokeshire coast include 4 farms, comprising over 800 acres of farmland, and further areas of coastal land, totalling some 10 miles of coastline.

COUNTRYSIDE

Two rivers, the Western and Eastern Cleddau, begin in the Preselli Hills and meet south-east of Haverfordwest, to form a fascinating 10-mile long estuary, finally reaching the sea beyond Milford Haven. The Trust owns two areas of woodland here; one at **Little Milford** on the Western Cleddau, south of Haverfordwest [158: SM967118] with public foot-paths; the other a 71-acre hanging wood at **Lawrenny** on the east side of Castle Reach.

Two other rivers which enter this estuary are the Creswell and the Carew. **Williamston Park,** a promontory between these rivers south-east of Lawrenny, is one of the two deer parks of Carew Castle – now a dramatic ruin (not NT). The Park is a Nature Reserve, managed by the Dyfed Wildlife Trust; access is by footpath only [158: SN030057].

The Trust owns 15 acres at **Paxton's Tower,** 7 miles east of Carmarthen [159: SN541191]. This folly was once known as Nelson's Tower, and was built in the early 19th century on a hill giving fine views over the countryside.

CILGERRAN CASTLE 🏛

nr Cardigan

13th-century ruin, an inspiration to many artists, including Turner

Cilgerran Castle is in the guardianship of Cadw (Welsh Historic Monuments)

O £ Please telephone Cadw (Cardiff (0222) 465511) for opening times and admission prices

→ On rock above left bank of the Teifi, 3m SE of Cardigan, 1½m E of A478 [145: SN195431] *Bus:* Davies Bros 460/2 BR Carmarthen–Cardigan, alight Llechryd. 1¾m by footpath (tel. Dyfed CC Carmarthen (0267) 233333)

COLBY WOODLAND GARDEN 🌸🌿🏵🏛　　　　　　🐕

Colby Bothy, Amroth, Narberth SA67 8PP
(Enquiries: tel. (Saundersfoot (0834) 811725; also Llandeilo (0558) 822800)

Woodland garden; the early 19th-century house is not open; (Mr & Mrs A. Scourfield Lewis kindly allow access to the walled garden during normal visiting hours); walks through secluded valleys along open and wooded pathways, one of which links the property with the nearby coastal resort of Amroth

O 30 March to 2 Nov: daily 10–5. Also open in winter during daylight hours

🛍 Shop open 30 March to 2 Nov: daily 10–5

£ £1.25, children 60p. Parties (min. 15) £1. No coaches, due to narrow approaches

♿ Parts of garden accessible; disabled visitors may park closer to the garden on request

🍵 Light refreshments open as shop

→ Adjoining Amroth beside Carmarthen Bay [158: SN155080] *Station:* Kilgetty (U) 2½m

DOLAUCOTHI GOLD MINES 🔣🔣🔣🔣

Pumsaint, Llanwrda SA19 8RR (tel. Pumsaint (055 85) 359)

Gold mines on the Dolaucothi Estate set amid wooded hillsides overlooking the beautiful Cothi valley, first exploited by the Romans, last worked in 1938; the Visitor Centre and Miners' Way explain the ancient and modern mine workings; underground tours in mid summer, miners' helmets and lamps give an authentic feeling to this exciting visit; displays of 1930s mining machinery in the mine yard

🅾   30 March to 2 Nov: daily incl. public holidays 10–6. Underground guided tours 25 May to 22 Sept: daily, every half hour. Last admissions 5

🔣🔣 New shop and restaurant open as property

    Note: Tour lasts about 1hr, involving rugged climbing; helmets with lights provided; stout footwear recommended. The underground tour is unsuitable for disabled or infirm visitors; the Trust regrets children under 5 are not admitted. Limited places are available on underground tours; tours are very busy during late July and Aug; please come early to avoid disappointment

💷   Visitors Centre, Miners' Way and Machinery: £2, children £1.20, NT members free. Group rates on application. Underground Tour (includes surface) £3.50, children £2. NT members half price. Parking 100yds

🐕   On leads, but not underground

➡   Between Lampeter and Llanwrda on A482 [146: SN6640]
    Station: Llanwrda (U), not Sun, except May to Sept, 8m

TUDOR MERCHANT'S HOUSE 🔣   🔣🔣

Quay Hill, Tenby SA70 7BX (tel. Tenby (0834) 2279)

A late 15th-century town house, characteristic of the building tradition of south-west Wales; the ground floor chimney at the rear of the house is a fine vernacular example; the original scarffed roof trusses survive; the furnishings of the house are of different periods; remains of early frescoes on three interior walls

🅾   31 March to 2 Nov: Mon–Fri 11–6; Sun 2–6. Closed Sat. Last admissions 15 min. before closing

💷   £1.25, children 60p. Group rate (min. 10 persons) £1. No WCs. Car parking in town. 🔣: Not recommended; difficult steps and stairs

➡   [158: SN135004] *Bus:* From surrounding areas (tel. Dyfed CC Carmarthen (0267) 233333). *Station:* Tenby 700yds

PLEASE REFER TO PAGES 5–9

Gwent

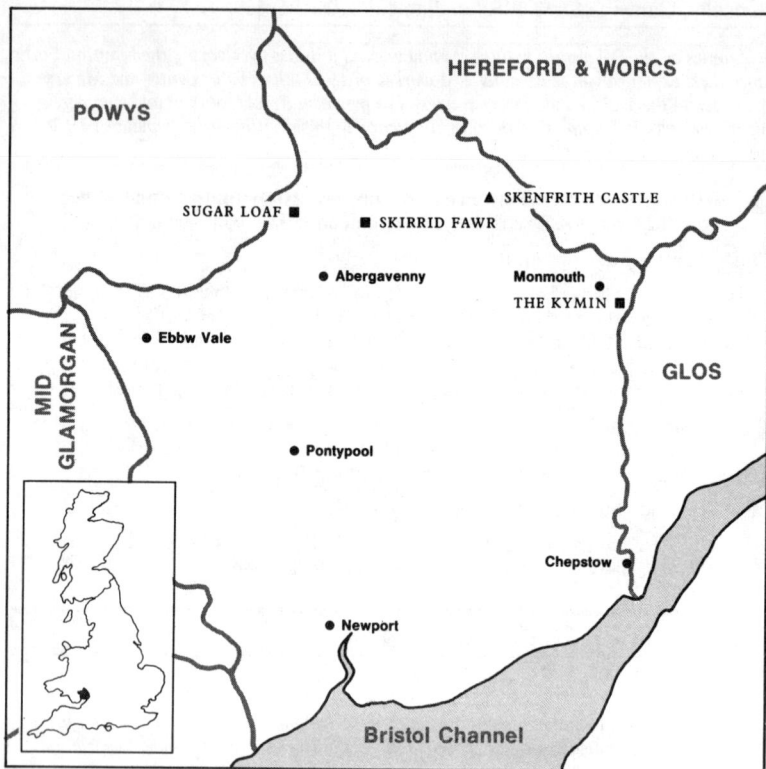

POWYS

HEREFORD & WORCS

SUGAR LOAF ■

■ SKIRRID FAWR

▲ SKENFRITH CASTLE

● Abergavenny

Monmouth

THE KYMIN ■

● Ebbw Vale

MID GLAMORGAN

GLOS

● Pontypool

Chepstow ●

● Newport

Bristol Channel

COUNTRYSIDE

A mile east of the border town of Monmouth is **The Kymin,** an 800ft high hill giving views over the valleys of the Wye and the Monnow. The 'first gentlemen in Monmouth' built a tower they called The Round House as a dining club on the summit, and also a bowling green and a Naval Temple which was visited by Nelson and Emma Hamilton in 1795 [162: SO02718]. Access from A4136.

The **Sugar Loaf** just west of Abergavenny [161: SO2718] is 2,000ft high and cone-shaped. There is access to the summit and footpaths across common land, open mountainside woodland and valleys. Another nearby viewpoint is **Skirrid Fawr** [161: SO330180], 1,600ft, giving views of the Sugar Loaf, the Usk valley and the Black Mountains.

PLEASE REFER TO PAGES 5–9

ROUND HOUSE ON THE KYMIN

SKENFRITH CASTLE 🏰

Skenfrith, nr Abergavenny

Norman castle built to command one of the main routes between England and Wales; a keep stands on the remains of the motte; 13th-century curtain wall with towers

Skenfrith Castle is in the guardianship of Cadw (Welsh Historic Monuments)

🅾 ✳ All year: at any reasonable time

💷 ♿ Free

➡ 6m NW of Monmouth, 12m NE of Abergavenny, on N side of the Ross road (B4521) [161: SO456203]

PLEASE REFER TO PAGES 5–9

Gwynedd

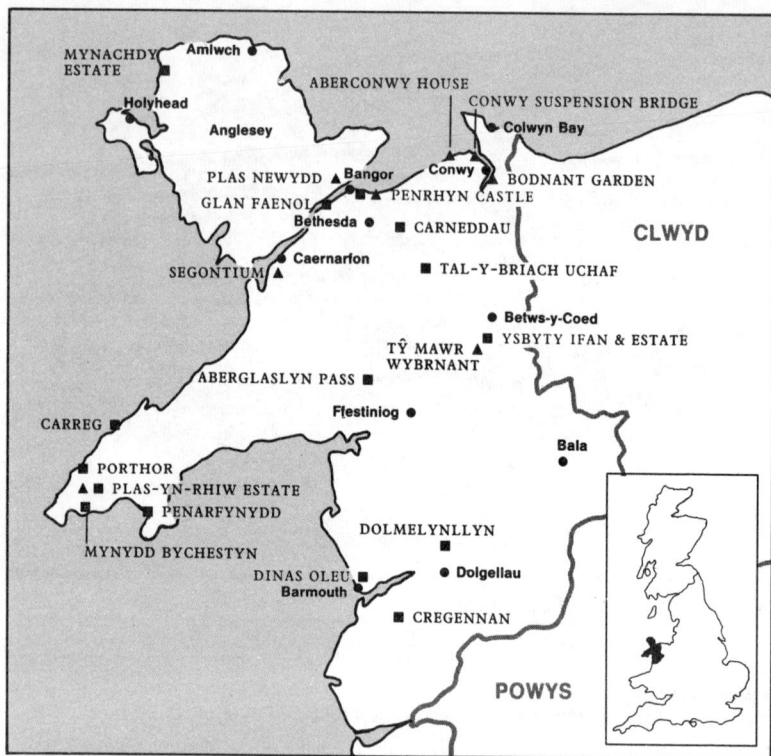

On the map:
- MYNACHDY ESTATE
- Amlwch
- ABERCONWY HOUSE
- Holyhead
- CONWY SUSPENSION BRIDGE
- Anglesey
- Colwyn Bay
- PLAS NEWYDD
- Conwy
- Bangor
- BODNANT GARDEN
- GLAN FAENOL
- PENRHYN CASTLE
- Bethesda
- CARNEDDAU
- CLWYD
- Caernarfon
- SEGONTIUM
- TAL-Y-BRIACH UCHAF
- Betws-y-Coed
- TŶ MAWR WYBRNANT
- YSBYTY IFAN & ESTATE
- ABERGLASLYN PASS
- CARREG
- Ffestiniog
- Bala
- PORTHOR
- PLAS-YN-RHIW ESTATE
- PENARFYNYDD
- DOLMELYNLLYN
- MYNYDD BYCHESTYN
- DINAS OLEU
- Dolgellau
- Barmouth
- CREGENNAN
- POWYS

COAST

It is fascinating to think that with all its vast holdings the Trust can never forget a small 4½-acre field above Barmouth, overlooking the wide sweep of Cardigan Bay with views of the Llŷn Peninsula: **Dinas Oleu**. This was the first property ever to be owned by the National Trust, given in 1895 [124: SH615158]. Since then the Trust has added many miles to its coastal properties in Gwynedd, including the beautiful **Mynachdy Estate** on the north-western coast of the island of Anglesey (*Note:* there is a covenanted area which is not Trust-owned; access to this area is totally banned between 15 Sept and 1 Feb). The Trust now owns 7½ miles of Anglesey's coastline including the section at **Plas Newydd**, the home of the Marquess of Anglesey (see p. 268). Recently acquired to protect the view across the Menai Strait from Plas Newydd, is **Glan Faenol** – more than 300 acres of farm and woodland stretching from Faenol Wood to Y Felinheli [114: SH530695].

Probably the most spectacular coastal scenery in North Wales can be seen from the gentle green slopes of the beautiful Llŷn Peninsula. The Trust's benefactresses on the Llŷn

– the Miss Keatings, were three sisters who gave **Plas-yn-Rhiw** (see p. 269), their lovely manor house and garden above Porth Neigwl. From 1950–66 they were tireless in their quest to rescue threatened land in the vicinity and present it to the Trust. The result is that the original estate of 416 acres has been reclaimed; 410 acres of which is coastal land. The Trust has kept up the Miss Keatings' good work by adding to the money they gave, a proportion of its Enterprise Neptune funds to acquiring more of the Llŷn coast – at **Penarfynydd, Mynydd Bychestyn, Porth Gwylan** and **Carreg**. The most recent acquisition of the Llŷn peninsula is **Porthor**, [123: SH166298] a delightful sandy cove protected by rocky promontories and backed by sand dunes. The beach is also known as 'Whistling Sands' owing to the whistling noise produced when the dry sand is walked on.

COUNTRYSIDE

The Trust owns well over 50,000 acres in this large county, dominated inland by the vast Snowdonia National Park. Many of its holdings are within this park, from **Aberglaslyn Pass** 🅐 in the south by the village of Beddgelert with the famous view north from the stone bridge, Pont Aberglaslyn [115: SH595463] to **Penrhyn Castle** at the extreme north of the area (see p. 267). By far the largest single estate owned by the Trust anywhere in England, Wales or Northern Ireland is the massive **Ysbyty Estate;** 42,000 acres transferred to the Trust through the National Land Fund in 1951. As well as Penrhyn Castle this vast holding includes **Carneddau**, south-east of Bangor on the A5 [115: SH6760] – 16,000 acres of high valley farms and some of the most exciting scenery in Snowdonia. The Trust owns ten of the main mountain peaks, including Tryfan where the first successful Everest climbers trained. South of Betws-y-Coed is **Ysbyty Ifan** [115/116: SH8448], 26,000 acres of hills, moor and valleys; a little to the north-west of this, in gentler country is **Tŷ Mawr** in the little valley of Wybrnant. 🅐 The Wybrnant Trail here is a short waymarked walk, a leaflet (s.a.e. please) is available from Tŷ Mawr (see p. 270). 🅐 Parts of Trail accessible from car park.

Several sheepwalks and mountain farms are owned in Snowdonia, notably **Tal-y-Braich Uchaf** – 1,057 acres of sheepwalk in the Ogwen valley [115: SH700602); and **Tŷ Gwyn** and **Ty'n y Maes Farms** in the Nant Ffrancon valley near Bethesda [115: SH642627].

🅐 The **Cwm Idwal** nature reserve, near Ogwen, is a mountain route around Llyn Idwal; the cwm or corrie has been famous since the 17th century for its rich variety of plants. The reserve is in the care of the Nature Conservancy Council, Penrhos Road, Bangor; send 10p and s.a.e. for leaflet.

At **Cregennan** [124: SH6614] are two lakes, hill farms and mountain land giving fine views to Cadair Idris where two sheepwalks are owned on the north face – **Tan-y-Gadair** and **Llyn-y-Gadair** [124: SH7013/7115] – both with spectacular views.

North-west of Dolgellau the **Dolmelynllyn** estate of 1,250 acres includes one of Wales's most spectacular waterfalls, Rhaeadr Ddu on the Gamlan, reached by footpath from the village of Ganllwyd; also two sheepwalks on **Y Llethr** [124: SH7222].

Details of guided walks programme from the Trust's North Wales office, (address on p. 22).

PLEASE REFER TO PAGES 5–9

ABERCONWY HOUSE 🏠 ✈ ⌧

Castle Street, Conwy, Gwynedd LL32 8AY (tel. Aberconwy (0492) 592246)

Medieval house, dating from the 14th century; now houses the Conwy Exhibition, depicting the life of the borough from Roman times to the present day; audio-visual presentation

🅾 28 March to 3 Nov: daily except Tues 11–5.30. Last admissions 5

📷 Shop open same days as house 9.30–5.30

💷 ♿ £1. Pre-booked parties of 20 or more 80p. Family (2 adults, 2 children) £2.50. No WCs

➡ At junction of Castle Street and High Street [115: SH781777] *Bus:* From surrounding areas (tel. Aberconwy (0492) 592111) *Station:* Conwy 300yds

BODNANT GARDEN 🍀 🏠 ✈

Tal-y-Cafn, Colwyn Bay, Clwyd LL28 5RE (tel. Týn-y-Groes (0492) 650460)

Among the finest gardens in the country, with magnificent collections of rhododendrons, camellias, magnolias, shrubs and trees; situated above the river Conwy, it extends for 80 acres and gives spectacular views of the Snowdonia range

🅾 16 March to end Oct: daily 10–5. Last admissions 4.30

💷 £2.50. Pre-booked parties of 20 or more £2.20. Car park 50yds from garden nursery

♿ 👁 The garden is steep in places, has many steps, and is not easy for wheelchairs. Scented roses and other plants. Braille guide

☕ Refreshment pavilion serving light lunches and teas open April to end Sept daily 11–5. Picnicking in car park area

→ 8m S of Llandudno and Colwyn Bay on A470, entrance ½m along the Eglwysbach R٫ad [115 & 116: SH801723] *Bus:* Bws Gwynedd 25 Llandudno–Eglwysbach (passing BR Llandudno Junction) (tel. Aberconwy (0492) 592111) *Station:* Tal-y-Cafn, not Sun, except July to Sept, 1½m

CONWY SUSPENSION BRIDGE [T]

Conwy, Gwynedd

Designed and built by Thomas Telford, the famous engineer; this elegant suspension bridge was completed in 1826, replacing the ferry, previously the only means of crossing the river

Note: Continued restoration work may involve the closure of the bridge during the 1991 season

[O] [❄] **Bridge:** night and day to pedestrians and cyclists only

[£] [&] Free: collecting box on the bridge for contributions. No WCs. Parking 50yds (50p to non-NT members)

→ 100yds from Conwy town centre, adjacent to Conwy Castle [115: SH785775] *Bus:* From surrounding areas (tel. Aberconwy (0492) 592111) *Station:* Conwy ¼m; Llandudno Junction ½m

PENRHYN CASTLE [M][T][❄]   [X][Ø]

Bangor, Gwynedd LL57 4HN (tel. Bangor (0248) 353084)

A huge neo-Norman castle (c.1820–1845) placed dramatically between Snowdonia and the Menai Strait; contains interesting 'Norman' furniture, panelling and plasterwork designed by the architect Thomas Hopper; fine pictures; industrial railway and doll museums; woodland; Victorian walled garden

[O] 28 March to 3 Nov: daily except Tues. **Castle:** 12–5 (July & Aug 11–5). **Grounds:** 11–6. Last admissions 4.30 (last audio-tour 4)   *continued*

🛍 Shop open as Castle

💷 £3.50. Booked parties of 20 or more £2.80. Family ticket £8.75 (max. 2 adults, 2 children). Audio tour for adults and children in Welsh and English; included in admission price (50p for NT members). Accompanied tours of roof of keep by prior arrangement. School and youth groups by arrangement. Parking 200yds

🚂 🧒 Industrial railway and doll museum. Adventure playground. Young Adventurers' audio-tour. Hands on educational facilities. Baby facilities. Baby carriers on loan

♿ 👁 All ground floor rooms; access ramps and handrail. Shop in basement; not accessible. Castle is least congested on Sat. Park paths are firm. Special parking by arrangement. Golf buggy, seating 3, for garden and park. ♿ WC. Braille guide

🐕 In grounds only on lead

☕ Light lunches and teas. Picnicking in grounds

➡ 1m E of Bangor, at Llandegai on A5122 [115: SH603720] *Bus:* Bws Gwynedd 5 Caernarfon–Llandudno (tel. Caernarfon (0286) 672556); 6/7 Bangor–Bethesda (tel. Bethesda (0248) 600207); 66 Bangor–Gerlan (tel. Bangor (0248) 600787). All pass close BR Bangor and end of drive to Castle *Station:* Bangor 3m

---

PLAS NEWYDD 🏠 ❋ ♣ 🏛   ⚔ ✉ 🎨

Llanfairpwll, Anglesey, Gwynedd LL61 6EQ (tel. Llanfairpwll (0248) 714795)

18th-century house by James Wyatt in unspoilt surroundings on the Menai Strait; magnificent views of Snowdonia; Rex Whistler's largest wall painting; military museum with relics of the 1st Marquess of Anglesey and the Battle of Waterloo; fine spring garden; beautiful lawn and parkland

⬛ 28 March to 29 Sept: daily except Sat 12–5 (garden 11–5 in July & Aug). 4 Oct to 3 Nov: Fri & Sun only 2–5. Last admissions 4.30

🗄 Shop open as garden

£ £3. Family ticket (max. 2 adults, 2 children) £7.50. Pre-booked parties of 20 or more £2.40. Parking ¼m

🅰 👶 Children's adventure playground. Youth groups by arrangement. Baby facilities. Baby carriers available on loan

♿ 👓 Ground floor accessible; ramps. Special parking, enquire at reception desk. Easy access to tea-room and shop. ♿ WC. Formal rose garden. Braille guide

🍴 Licensed tea-room: light lunches & teas; open as house (July & Aug opens 11)

➡ 1m SW of Llanfairpwll and A5 on A4080 to Brynsiencyn; turn off A5 at W end of Britannia Bridge [114 & 115: SH521696] *Bus:* Bws Gwynedd 42 Bangor–Llangefni (passing BR Bangor & Llanfairpwll) (tel. Holyhead (0407) 2002) *Station:* Llanfairpwll (U), no practical Sun service, except May to Sept, 1¼m

PLAS-YN-RHIW 🏠 ✽ 🏯 ✖ ✉

Rhiw, Pwllheli, Gwynedd LL53 8AB (tel. Rhiw (075 888) 219)

House with garden and woodlands on west shore of Porth Neigwl (Hell's Mouth Bay) on the Llŷn peninsula; small manor house, part medieval, with Tudor and Georgian additions; ornamental gardens with flowering trees and shrubs, divided by box hedges and grass paths; rising behind to the snowdrop wood

⬛ 28 March to 29 Sept: daily except Sat 12–5. 6 Oct to 3 Nov: Sun only 12–4. Last admissions ½hr before closing

Note: In the interests of preservation, numbers of visitors admitted to the house at any one time may be limited, particularly in July and August and BH Mon

🗄 Shop open as house

£ £1.50. Family ticket (max 2 adults, 2 children) £3.75. Pre-booked parties evenings only (incl. full guided tour) £2. Parking 80yds. No coaches

♿ Ground floor rooms only; most of garden very difficult for wheelchairs. ♿ WC

➡ 12m from Pwllheli on S coast road to Aberdaron (drive gate at the bottom of Rhiw Hill [123: SH237282] *Bus:* Bws Gwynedd 17 Pwllheli–Aberdaron (passing BR Pwllheli), alight Botwnnog, 3¾m (tel. Pwllheli (0758) 612458) *Station:* Pwllheli 10m

PLEASE REFER TO PAGES 5–9

SEGONTIUM 🏛 ⚔

Caernarfon, Gwynedd (tel. Caernarfon (0286) 5625)

Remains of Roman fort and museum containing relics found on site

Segontium is in the guardianship of Cadw (Welsh Historic Monuments)

O ❄ All year. March, April & Oct: Mon to Sat 9.30–5.30, Sun 2–5. May to end
Sept: Mon to Sat 9.30–6, Sun 2–6. Nov to end Feb: Mon to Sat 9.30–4, Sun
2–4. Closed 24–26 Dec, New Year's Day, Good Fri & May Day

£ ♿ Free. Parking on main road nearby

➜ On Llanbeblig road, A4085, on SE outskirts of Caernarfon, [115: SH485624]
Bus: From surrounding areas to Caernarfon, Bws Gwynedd 11 passes Museum,
on others alight Castle, ½m (tel. Caernarfon (0286) 672556) *Station:* Bangor
9m

TŶ MAWR WYBRNANT 🏠 🚹 ♨ ⚔

Penmachno, Betws-y-Coed, Gwynedd LL25 0HJ (tel. Penmachno (069 03) 213)

*The cottage is the birthplace of Bishop William Morgan (c.1545–1604), the first translator
of the Bible into Welsh; his translation is considered a masterpiece and became the foundation
of modern Welsh literature; the Wybrnant Nature Trail covers approximately 1 mile from
the house and back (see p. 265)*

O 28 March to 29 Sept: Wed, Thur, Fri & Sun 12–5. 4 Oct to 3 Nov: Fri & Sun
12–4. Last admissions ½hr before closing. May to end Aug: Fri evenings
6.30–8 by arrangement only

£ No access for coaches. £1. Parties (pre-booked of 20 or more) 80p. Family
(max 2 adults, 2 children) £2.50

🐕 In countryside only

➜ At the head of the little Wybrnant valley. 3½m SW of Betws-y-Coed; 2m W of
Penmachno [115: SH770524] *Station:* Dolwyddelau 3m (by footpath)

Powys

COUNTRYSIDE

The most famous mountains in Powys, the **Brecon Beacons** [160: SO010200] dominate the southern part of the county. The Trust was given over 8,000 acres of the main part of the range including the 2,900ft Penyfan, the highest peak in the Beacons by, aptly, Sir Brian Mountain, Chairman of the Eagle Star Insurance Company.

Henrhyd Falls, among the finest in the country, are in a beautiful spot near the edge of the South Wales coalfield, formed by the River Llech tumbling for 90ft through a deep wooded ravine. 🚹 Car park and circular walk. **Graigllech Woods,** are also Trust-owned [160: SN850119].

The Trust has more recently acquired 16,500 acres of **Abergwesyn Common** [127, 128 & 141: SN8359/9861]. This is a 12-mile stretch of high, beautiful, but wild and remote common land between Rhayader and the Irfon Gorge near Llanwrtyd Wells, accessible by public footpaths; but only recommended to the hardy hill walker! Dogs must be kept on a lead at all times.

POWIS CASTLE ▣✿♣ ✈✕✉▦

Welshpool, Powys SY21 8RF (tel. Welshpool (0938) 554336)

Medieval castle containing the finest country collection in Wales; built c.1200 by Welsh princes; the gardens are of the highest horticultural and historical importance; Clive Museum

O 28 March to end June & Sept to 3 Nov: daily except Mon & Tues. July & Aug: daily except Mon, but open BH Mon. **Castle:** 12–5. **Museum & garden:** 11–6. Last admissions ½hr before closing

£ 𝌘 Museum & garden £3. Family (max. 2 adults & 2 children) £7.50. Parties £2.40. Castle £2 extra. Tours, incl. dinner any evening by prior arrangement. Meet the Gardener tours available by prior arrangement

♿ 👁 Castle not possible for wheelchair users; access to tea-room, shop and parts of garden only. ♿ WC. Scented flowers, Braille guide

☕♿ Licensed tea-room: light lunches and teas

⬆ Baby feeding and changing facilities. Baby carriers available on loan. High chair

➜ 1m S of Welshpool, on A483; pedestrian access from High Street (A490); cars turn right 1m along main road to Newtown (A483); enter by first drive gate on right [126: SJ216064] *Bus:* Crosville Wales D71 Oswestry–Welshpool; D75 Shrewsbury–Welshpool, alight High Street, 1m (tel. Oswestry (0691) 652402) *Station:* Welshpool 1¼m via footpath in town

West Glamorgan

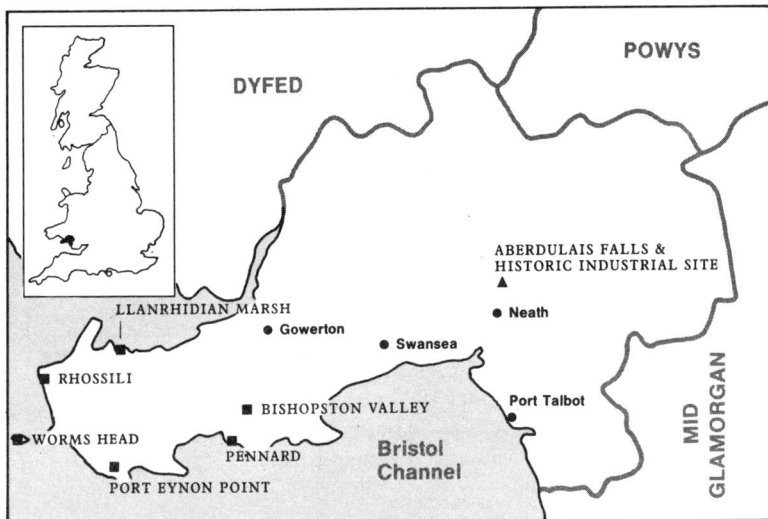

POWYS

DYFED

ABERDULAIS FALLS &
HISTORIC INDUSTRIAL SITE
▲

LLANRHIDIAN MARSH

● Gowerton

● Neath

● Swansea

RHOSSILI

Port Talbot

■ BISHOPSTON VALLEY

●WORMS HEAD

PENNARD

Bristol
Channel

MID GLAMORGAN

PORT EYNON POINT

COAST

The lovely and varied scenery of the Gower peninsula, the first area to be designated an Area of Outstanding Natural Beauty, lies just west of the coastal city of Swansea. It is renowned for its wildlife, sandy beaches and magnificent coast – yet much of it is remote, wild and unpopulated save for vast colonies of seabirds and waders. The Trust owns about 5,000 acres in Gower, ranging from saltmarsh at **Llanrhidian** on the north coast [159: SS490932] to the limestone cliffs between **Port Eynon** [159: SS468845] and **Rhossili**, see Visitor Centre entry, p. 274 🏃, with prehistoric caves and a medieval dovecote known as the Culver Hole; the lovely wooded valley at Bishopston; and the elongated rocky headland of **Worms Head** [159: SS383878] at the extreme westernmost point of the peninsula which is a National Nature Reserve and is leased to the Nature Conservancy Council.

DUNLIN

273

ABERDULAIS FALLS & HISTORIC INDUSTRIAL SITE ■■

Aberdulais, nr Neath SA10 8EU (tel. Neath (0639) 636674)

One of the most famous waterfalls in South Wales; long a favourite place for artists, writers and travellers; an important archaeological site with a unique blend of natural and human history; the waters of the falls powered a succession of industries for more than 400 years

Note: This property is undergoing a long-term programme of conservation and development. Visitors are asked to take particular care; children should be accompanied by an adult, or will be admitted at the discretion of the Project Manager

O ■ 30 March to 2 Nov: Mon to Fri 10–5; Sat, Sun & BH 11–6. 3 Nov to 24 Dec: daily 11–4. Last admissions ½hr before closing

■ ■ Shop open as property

£ ✗ £1.25. children 60p. Parties (min. 10 people) £1 by prior arrangement with the Warden; groups and school parties very welcome. Car park 200yds, at Aberdulais Tourist Information Centre, 2 min. walk. Guided tours during summer months. NT Information Centre in old stable area

♿ Southern and central part of site accessible, also Information Centre. ♿ WC at Tourist Information Centre. Car park 200yds; limited car parking on site

🐕 Must be kept on leads

■ Light refreshments are served by volunteers during public holidays and summer weekends. Teas, lunches & snacks at nearby Dulais Rock Hotel (not NT); also Aberdulais Basin Café March to end Sept 9–6. Picnic area on site, and elsewhere in the locality

➔ On A465, 3m NE of Neath [170: SS772995] *Bus:* S Wales 158 Swansea–Banwen (passing close BR Neath); 161, N10 from Neath. All pass close BR Neath (tel. Swansea (0792) 475511) *Station:* Neath 3m

---

RHOSSILI VISITOR CENTRE ■■■

Rhossili, Gower (tel. Gower (0792) 390707)

Situated adjacent to extensive NT ownership of the Raised Terrace, the Down, the beach, coastal cliffs and the Worms Head

O ■
■ 2–24 March: Sat & Sun 11–4; 28 March to 27 Oct: daily 10.30–5.30; 28 Oct to 10 Nov: daily 11–4; 16 Nov to 22 Dec: Sat & Sun 11–4

£ Free. Car park and WCs (not NT)

♿ Visitor Centre ground floor accessible. No separate parking facilities

■ Available nearby

➔ SW tip of Gower Peninsula approached from Swansea via A4118 and then B4247 *Bus:* South Wales 18/B/C from Swansea (passing close BR Swansea) (tel. Swansea (0792) 475511)

Northern Ireland

DOWNHILL CASTLE, MUSSENDEN TEMPLE,
BISHOP'S GATE & BLACK GLEN
NORTH ANTRIM CLIFF PATH
WHITEPARK BAY
GIANT'S CAUSEWAY
PORTSTEWART
STRAND
HEZLETT HOUSE ▲ Coleraine
LARRYBANE
FAIR HEAD
MURLOUGH BAY
Ballycastle
CUSHENDUN
CARRICK-A-REDE
● Londonderry
Ballymena
●
LIGHTHOUSE
ISLAND
▲ GRAY'S PRINTING PRESS
SPRINGHILL ▲
TEMPLETOWN
MAUSOLEUM
ORLOCK POINT
WELLBROOK
BEETLING MILL ▲
Lower Lough
Erne
Lough
Neagh
CROWN ▲
LIQUOR
SALOON Belfast
Bangor
THE ARGORY ▲
ARDRESS HOUSE
STRANGFORD LOUGH
WILDLIFE SCHEME
ROWALLANE ▲
GARDEN
KEARNEY
CASTLE
COOLE ▲
Ballynahinch
●
CASTLE WARD
FLORENCE COURT ▲
Armagh
CROM ESTATE ■
MURLOUGH NATURE RESERVE
Newry
●
Newcastle
MOURNE COASTAL
PATH
BLOCKHOUSE
AND GREEN ISLANDS
EIRE
MOUNT STEWART HOUSE,
GARDEN & TEMPLE OF THE WINDS

COAST

Most of the Trust's coastal holdings in Ulster are in Co. Down and Co. Antrim. The southernmost property in Co. Down is at the mouth of Carlingford Lough – **Blockhouse and Green Islands** [J254097]. These tiny islands total only 2 acres, but are important nesting sites for common, Arctic and roseate terns, and are leased to the Royal Society for the Protection of Birds. To the north of Carlingford Lough are the Mourne Mountains, and here the Trust owns two sections of the **Mourne Coastal Path** [J389269]. One runs south from Bloody Bridge at the foot of the highest mountain in the range, Slieve Donard, along the coast and past the site of St Mary's Ballaghanary, an early Celtic church; the other leads up the valley of the Bloody River, giving access to the mountains. 🚻 WC at car park, but the path is not recommended for wheelchairs.

On this same stretch of coast lies **Dundrum**, with the Widow's Row cottages and footpath along the old railway; also **Murlough National Nature Reserve**, near Newcastle, Ireland's first such reserve 🚶. The oldest dunes here are at least 5,000 years old and the

275

soil ranges from lime-rich to acid, supporting a wide variety of plants including pyramidal orchid, bell heather, primrose and dune burnet rose. Many birds nest in the spring sea buckthorn – reed bunting, stonechat, whitethroat; and in winter its orange berries attract thrushes and finches. Visitor facilities open June to mid Sept: daily 10–5, weather permitting. [access] There is a special slatted walkway across the dunes, suitable for wheelchair users, and the Warden organises guided walks for blind visitors (tel. Dundrum (039 675) 311 or 467 for details). Holiday cottages now available on shores of Dundrum Inner Bay. Dogs on leads only.

Strangford Lough the Trust's **Wildlife Scheme** here embraces the entire foreshore of Lough Strangford [J60615] and several islands, totalling about 5,400 acres. Vast flocks of wildfowl gather here, as well as nesting birds, seals and other marine animals. The wild flowers merit special attention. Bird hides and refuges are provided for study purposes. [access] Birdwatching facilities at Island Reagh, Castle Espie, at Mount Stewart Gas House and Anne's Point, Mount Stewart (tel. Saintfield (0238) 510721 or Strangford (039 686) 411). The Quoile Estuary and two riverside areas forming part of the Freshwater Quoile Pondage also comes under the Wildlife Scheme.

On the extreme easterly point of the Co. Down coastline is the former fishing village of **Kearney** [J650517] where the Trust owns 13 houses. **Ballymacormick Point** [J525837], is 1–3 miles north-east of Bangor on the south side of the entrance to Belfast Lough; there are 44 acres of rocky shore, and coastal heath of biological interest. **Orlock Point** [J559837] has wildfowl, wading birds and gulls. **Lighthouse Island** [J596858] is a 43-acre island with a bird observatory. Visits by arrangement with Mr Neville McKee, 67 Temple Rise, Templepatrick, Co. Down (tel. Templepatrick (084 94) 33068).

The North Antrim coastline is no less attractive, and is more dramatic than County Down. The Trust has a continuous series of coastal properties, beginning in the west with **Downhill** [C758363], (see p. 280).

Portstewart Strand consists of 2 miles of duneland west of Portstewart [C720360]. Parking £2. Visitor facilities June to end Aug: daily 10–6, weather permitting. [access] Beach accessible by car, but hard sand at low tide only. Dogs on leads only during summer months. **The Bar Mouth**, 5 miles north-west of Coleraine at the mouth of the River Bann [C792355] is a wildlife sanctuary with observation hide.

Between **Giant's Causeway** (see p. 281) and the ruins of **Dunseverick Castle** [C987445] the Trust now owns 104 acres of the **North Antrim Cliff Path**. East of Dunseverick is the beautiful curve of **Whitepark Bay**, 180 acres of white sand and white chalk cliff [D023440] with an information panel. Beyond this bay is the tiny stack of basalt connected in summer by a swinging rope bridge to the mainland; **Carrick-a-Rede**, the 'rock on the road'. This is the road the salmon take on their way to rivers in the north and there is a salmon fishery on the island [D062450]. Access to Carrick-a-Rede via cliff path from **Larrybane** where there is a car park, £1. Information Centre open April to June: weekends 11–6; July & Aug: daily 11–6, weather permitting. [access] WC. Adjoining are 58 acres of coastline with a disused basalt quarry and limeworkings [D051449].

The headland of **Fair Head** rises 636ft above the sea, giving views over **Murlough Bay**. Dogs on leads only. [access] Viewpoint car parks accessible. This is one of the most beautiful sections of the North Antrim coast [D185430/199418]. The Trust manages or owns 764 acres here, including wilderness and woodlands of outstanding interest for the geologist and botanist. Turning south again, the lovely village of **Cushendun** at the foot of Glendun [D248327] contains cottages designed and built by the architect of Portmeirion in North Wales, the late Clough Williams-Ellis. The harbour is also owned by the Trust. [info] Information Centre, tea-room and shop open Easter (29 March–7 April): daily 12–6; April, May, June & Sept: Sat, Sun & BH only 12–6; July & Aug: Mon to Sat 12–6, Sun 12–7. Light snacks at tea-room in basement of No. 1 Main Street; [access] ramp access at side and also to shop; [access] WC; car park nearby.

ARDRESS HOUSE 🏠📷🧍 ✉

64 Ardress Road, Portadown, Co. Armagh BT62 1SQ
(tel. Annaghmore (0762) 851236)

17th-century farmhouse, main front and garden façades added in 18th century by owner-architect George Ensor; fine neo-Classical plasterwork in drawing room; good furniture and pictures; display of farm implements and livestock in farmyard; garden; woodland walks

🔘 **House & farmyard:** Easter (29 March to 7 April): daily 2–6. April, May, June & Sept: Sat, Sun & BH 2–6. July to end Aug: daily except Tues 2–6

💷 🧍 House and farmyard £1.50; farmyard only £1. Parties £2 outside normal opening hours. Guided tours in Spanish and French by arrangement

🛝 Play area with tree swings

♿ Ground floor, picnic area and part of farmyard; ♿ WC in car park

🐕 In garden on leads

☕ Picnics welcome. Picnic area opens 12

➡ 7m from Portadown on Moy road (B28), 5m from Moy, 3m from Loughgall intersection 13 on M1, 9m from Armagh [H914559] *Bus:* Ulsterbus 67 Portadown–Kesquin Bridge (passing close NIR Portadown Stn) to within ¼m (tel. Craigavon (0762) 342511) *Station:* Portadown 7m

THE ARGORY 🏠🏠❀🧍♿🧍 ✉

(Co. Armagh) Moy, Dungannon, Co. Tyrone BT71 6NA (tel. Moy (086 87) 84753)

Set in over 300 acres of woodland overlooking the Blackwater river, the house dates from 1820 and was substantially changed in the 19th century; fascinating furniture and contents including an 1824 Bishop's barrel organ; imposing stable yard with a coach house and carriages, harness room, laundry and acetylene gas plant; sundial garden; extensive walks
continued

☉ Easter (29 March to 7 April): daily 2–6. April, May, June & Sept: Sat, Sun & BH 2–6. July to end Aug: daily except Thur 2–6. Open from 1–6 on all BH. Last tour 5.15

🛍 Shop open as house

💷 £1.50. Parties outside normal opening hours £2. Car park 50p. Parking 100yds. Coaches must book with Administrator

⚠ Adventure playground

♿ Ground floor of house, all driveways, walks & reception area; special car parking near east door of house (ramp); ♿ WC by reception area

🐕 In grounds & garden only, on leads

🍴♿ Light refreshments in tea-room, open as house. Picnics welcome

➔ 4m from Moy, 3m from M1, exit 14, NB: coaches must use exit 13; weight restrictions at Bonds Bridge [H872580] *Bus:* Ulsterbus 67, Portadown–Dungannon (passing close NIR Portadown Stn), alight Charlemont, 2½m (tel. Craigavon (0762) 342511)

CASTLE COOLE 🏠🌳👤 ✉

Enniskillen, Co. Fermanagh (tel. Enniskillen (0365) 322690)

Very fine neo-Classical late 18th-century house with wings connected by colonnades; original decoration and furniture; audio-visual display at reception

☉ Easter (29 March to 7 April): daily 2–6. April, May & Sept: Sat, Sun & BH only, 2–6. June to end Aug: daily except Thur 2–6. Last tour begins 5.15. Grounds open to pedestrians during daylight hours

💷 £2. Parties outside normal opening hours £2.65

🐕 In grounds on leads only

♿ Ground floor of house; disabled visitors may be set down at house. ♿ WC in reception building

🍴 Picnics welcome

➔ 1½m SE of Enniskillen on main Belfast-Enniskillen road (A4) [H260430] *Bus:* Ulsterbus 95, Enniskillen–Clones (tel. Enniskillen (0365) 322633)

CASTLE WARD 🏠🏡✿🌳🛏🚂👤 ✉

Strangford, Downpatrick, Co. Down BT30 7LS (tel. Strangford (039 686) 204)

700-acre country estate with woodlands, lake and seashore; unique 18th-century mansion with opposing façades in different styles; west front Classical, east front Gothick; Victorian laundry; formal and landscape gardens with specimen shrubs and trees; fortified towers; corn and sawmills; wildfowl collection; information centre, shop; theatre in stable yard; caravan park; holiday cottages; basecamp for young people; audio-visual shows

[O] **House:** Easter (29 March to 7 April): daily 1–6. April, Sept & Oct: Sat & Sun 1–6. May to end Aug: daily except Thur 1–6. Last tour 5.10. **Estate & grounds:** open all year dawn to dusk (charge for car park only). **Strangford Lough Barn:** open as house except May & June when open Sat, Sun & BH only 2–6

[🛍] Shop open same days as house: weekdays 1–5; Sat & Sun 1–6; BH 12–6

[£] £2. Parties outside normal opening hours £2.50. Three car parks; parking £2.50 (£1 when house and other facilities are closed). Coaches; booked parties to house, free; others £10. Horses (using bridlepath) £5 per single horsebox

[♿] Changing facilities in [♿] WC

[🎠] Adventure playground. Victorian Pastimes Centre; toys & dressing-up

[♿] Formal garden, house, restaurant, interpretation centre; disabled visitors may be set down at house; car park for disabled drivers behind stables; [♿] WC in stable yard

[🐕] In grounds on leads

[🍴][♿] Light refreshments, lunches and teas, open as shop. Party organisers should book visits and arrange teas in advance with Receptionist. Picnics welcome

[→] 7m NE of Downpatrick, 1½m W of Strangford village on A25, on S shore of Strangford Lough, entrance by Ballyculter Lodge [J752494] *Bus:* Ulsterbus 16 Downpatrick–Strangford, with connections from Belfast (passing close NIR Belfast Central Stn); alight Ballyculter Crossroads, 1m (tel. Downpatrick (0396) 612384)

CROM ESTATE [🍴][🌳][🏠]

Newtownbutler, Co. Fermanagh (tel. Newtownbutler (036 573) 8174)

1,350 acres of woodland, parkland and wetland on shores of Upper Lough Erne; one of Northern Ireland's most important nature conservation areas; buildings include Crom Old Castle and Crichton Tower

[O] 29 March to end Sept: daily 2–6

[£][🚶] Parking £1. Guided walks by arrangement

[🐕] Dogs on lead only

[🍴] Picnics welcome

[♿] [♿] WC. Property partially accessible

[→] · 3m W of Newtownbutler, on Newtownbutler–Crom road [J363245] *Bus:* Ulsterbus 95 Enniskillen–Clones (with connections from Belfast) alight Newtownbutler (tel. Enniskillen (0365) 322633)

PLEASE REFER TO PAGES 5–9

CROWN LIQUOR SALOON 🏠

Gt Victoria Street, Belfast (tel. Belfast (0232) 325368)

A magnificent High Victorian public house with rich ornamentation and fine woodwork, glass and tiles; built at the end of the 19th century; managed by Bass Ireland

O **🚻** Daily, during licensed hours 11.30am to 11pm; Sun 12.30pm to 2.30pm &
❋   7pm to 10pm

🍽 Full bar facilities, snack lunches

→ [J738332] *Bus:* From surrounding areas (tel. Belfast (0232) 246485 (Citybus)
   or 333000/320574 (Ulsterbus)) *Station:* Belfast Central ¼m

DOWNHILL CASTLE, MUSSENDEN TEMPLE, BISHOP'S GATE & BLACK GLEN 🏰🏠❋🚻🚶🚗

Bishop's Gate, 42 Mussenden Road, Castlerock, Co. Londonderry

Landscaped estate, laid out in the late 18th century by the energetic Earl Bishop, Frederick Hervey, Earl of Bristol and Bishop of Derry; includes Mussenden Temple perched on the cliff, ruins of his palatial house, family memorials, gardens, fish pond, woodland and cliff walks; panoramic views of Ireland's north coast

O **❋** **Temple:** Easter (29 March to 7 April): daily 12–6. April, May, June & Sept: Sat,
   Sun & BH 12–6. July & Aug: daily 12–6. **Grounds** open all year: dawn to dusk.
   Open for groups at other times by arrangement (tel. Coleraine (0265) 848728)

£ Free. Limited access for coaches. No WCs

Paths through garden; cars may be taken to Bishop's Gate

On leads

Picnics welcome

→ 1m W of Castlerock and 5M W of Coleraine on the Coleraine-Downhill coast road (A2) [J757357] *Bus:* Ulsterbus 134 Coleraine–Limavady (tel. Coleraine (0265) 43334) *Station:* Castlerock ½m

FLORENCE COURT

nr Enniskillen, Co. Fermanagh (tel. Florencecourt (036 582) 249/788)

One of the most important houses in Ulster, built in mid 18th century by John Cole, father of 1st Earl of Enniskillen; fine rococo plasterwork; pleasure grounds with ice house and water-powered sawmill; walled garden; fine views over surrounding mountains

○ Easter (29 March to 7 April): daily 1–6. April, May & Sept: Sat, Sun & BH only 1–6. June to end Aug: daily except Tues 1–6. Last admissions 5.15. Grounds open all year 10–1hr before dusk. Closed Christmas Day

Shop as house but June to Aug open from 12

£ £2. Parties outside normal opening hours £2.50. Parking 50yds. Information room

Garden & ground floor only; WC

In grounds and garden on leads

Teas & lunches downstairs in North Pavilion; open as shop. Picnics welcome

→ 8m SW of Enniskillen via A4 and A32 Swanlinbar Road [H175344] *Bus:* Ulsterbus 192 Enniskillen–Swanlinbar, to within 1m (tel. Enniskillen (0365) 322633)

GIANT'S CAUSEWAY

Bushmills, Co. Antrim BT57 8SU (tel. Bushmills (026 57) 31582)

Coast and cliff paths, unusual basalt and volcanic rock formations and a wealth of local and natural history; wreck site of Armada treasure ship Girona *(1588) at Port-na-Spaniagh; Visitors' Centre, with interpretative displays, audio-visual theatre and tourist information owned by Moyle District Council*

○ Giant's Causeway: all year. **Visitor Centre:** 15 March to end May: daily 11–5. June: daily 11–5.30. July & Aug: daily 10–7 (closing times may vary according to demand on Sun). Sept & Oct: Mon to Fri 11–5, Sat & Sun 10.30–5.30

Open as Visitor Centre

£ Free. Parking £1.50, incl. NT members (the car park is owned by Moyle District Council) *continued*

🖐   Parking access close to buildings; mini-bus with hoist for transport to Giant's Causeway during season; ramps to tea-room & Visitor Centre; 🖐 WC

🐕   On leads only, outdoors

💷🖐   Coffee, lunch, tea, snacks in tea-room at Visitor Centre (closes 6.15 in July & Aug)

➡️   On B146 Causeway–Dunseverick road [C945438] *Bus:* Ulsterbus 138 from Coleraine (passing NIR Coleraine Stn & connecting with trains from Belfast Central Stn); 172 Ballycastle–Portrush (tel. Coleraine (0265) 43334) *Station:* Portrush 8m

GRAY'S PRINTING PRESS 🏛️🔠   ✖️

49 Main Street, Strabane, Co. Tyrone BT82 8AU (tel. Strabane (0504) 884094)

18th-century printing press shop and stationers; it may have been here that John Dunlap, the printer of the American Declaration of Independence and James Wilson, grandfather of President Woodrow Wilson, learned their trade; collection of 19th-century hand printing machines; NT Information Centre in stationer's shop

🅾️   **Press:** April to end Sept: daily except Thur, Sun & BH 2–5.30. At other times by prior arrangement

🏪❄️   Shop (not NT) open all year same days as Press 9–1 & 2–5.30

💷🚶   £1. Public car park 100yds. 🖐 Shop only. Guided tours by arrangement

💷   In town, not NT

➡️   [H345977] *Bus:* Ulsterbus Express 273 Belfast–Londonderry (passing close NIR Londonderry Stn), alight Strabane town centre; few min. walk (tel. Strabane (0504) 382393)

HEZLETT HOUSE 🏛️   ✖️

Sea Road, Liffock, Castlerock, Co. Londonderry BT51 4RE (tel. Castlerock (0265) 848567)

17th-century thatched house; cruck-truss roof construction of particular interest

🅾️🚶   Easter (29 March to 7 April): daily 2–6. April, May, June & Sept: Sat, Sun & BH only 2–6. July & Aug: daily, except Tues 2–6. Guided tours by arrangement. Parties must book in advance (max. number in house 15 at any one time)

💷   £1. Parties outside normal opening hours £1.40. Cycles can be parked at side of house. No WCs

🖐   Ground floor only

🐕   In garden on leads

➡️   5½m W of Coleraine on Coleraine-Downhill coast road A2 [C772349] *Bus:* Ulsterbus 134 Coleraine–Limavady, alight Liffock crossroads, few min. walk (tel. Coleraine (0265) 43334) *Station:* Castlerock ¾m

MOUNT STEWART HOUSE, GARDEN & TEMPLE OF THE WINDS 🏠 ❋ 🏠 𝕴 ☒

Newtownards, Co. Down BT22 2AD (tel. Greyabbey (024 774) 387)

Fascinating 18th-century house with 19th-century additions, where Lord Castlereagh grew up; gardens largely created by Edith, 7th Marchioness of Londonderry, with an unrivalled collection of plants, colourful parterres and magnificent vistas; the Temple of the Winds, James 'Athenian' Stuart's banqueting hall of 1785, overlooks Strangford Lough

🔘	**House:** Easter (29 March to 7 April): daily 1–6. April, May, Sept & Oct: Sat, Sun & BH only 1–6. June to end Aug: daily except Tues 1–6. Last tour 5.15. **Garden:** Easter (29 March to 7 April): daily 12–6. April to end Aug: daily except Tues 12–6; Sept & Oct: Sat & Sun only 12–6. **Temple:** Same days as house but open 3–6 (last tour 5.30). Seasonal guided walks
📷	Open 12–6 same days as house (except June: weekends only). BH open 1–6
£	House, garden and Temple £3; booked parties £2.50. Parties outside normal opening hours £4. Garden (incl. Temple when open) £2.50. Parties outside normal opening hours £3.50. Parking 300yds
🚼	Changing facilities
♿	Ground floor of house and half garden; Disabled people may be set down at house; 🚻 WCs
🍴♿	Light refreshments and teas same times as shop
➡	15m E of Belfast A20 Newtownards-Portaferry road, 5m SE of Newtownards [J553695] *Bus:* Ulsterbus 9, 10, Belfast–Portaferry (passing close Belfast Central Stn) to within ¼m (tel. Newtownards (0247) 812391/2) *Station:* Bangor 10m

ROWALLANE GARDEN ❋

Saintfield, Ballynahinch, Co. Down BT24 7LH (tel. Saintfield (0238) 510131)

Fifty-two acres of natural garden; daffodils and rhododendrons in spring; summer flowering trees and shrubs and herbaceous plants, fuchsias and shrub roses in the Wall Garden; the rock garden with primula, meconopsis, heathers and dwarf shrubs is interesting throughout the year; several areas of natural wild flowers to attract butterflies

🔘❋	1–28 March: daily except Sat & Sun 9–5. 29 March to end Oct: daily (weekdays 10.30–6; weekends 2–6). Nov to end March 1992: daily except Sat & Sun 9–5. Closed 25, 26 Dec & 1 Jan
📷	Easter (29 March to 7 April): daily 2–6. April & Sept: Sat & Sun only 2–6. May to end Aug: daily 2–6
£ 𝕴	Easter to end Oct £2. Parties £1.50. Nov to end March £1. Parties 50p; outside normal opening hours £2.50. Parking on N side of garden. Guided walks at certain dates; telephone for details
♿	Garden accessible except for Spring and Rock gardens *continued*

🐕 On leads

🍵 Light refreshments in stable yard, open as shop, above

➔ 11m SE of Belfast, 1m S of Saintfield, W of the Downpatrick road (A7) [J412581] *Bus:* Ulsterbus 15, Belfast–Downpatrick (passing close NIR Belfast Central Stn) (tel. Downpatrick (0396) 612384)

SPRINGHILL 🏠 🏚 ❀ 🍴 🚹 ✉

20 Springhill Road, Moneymore, Magherafelt, Co. Londonderry BT45 7NQ
(tel. Moneymore (064 87) 48210)

17th-century 'Planter' house with 18th- and 19th-century additions; home of ten generations of a family which arrived from Ayrshire in the 17th century; house contains family furniture, refurbished nursery, paintings, ornaments and curios; 18th-century hand-blocked wallpaper; extensive outbuildings house a costume collection; walled gardens and woodland walks

🅾 Easter (29 March to 7 April): daily 2–6. April, May, June & Sept: Sat, Sun & BH 2–6. July & Aug: daily except Thur 2–6

🛍 Shop open as house

💷 £1.50. Parties outside normal opening hours £2. Parking 40yds

⊞ Changing facilities

⚠ Toy collection; children's costumes and activities

♿ ◉ All ground floor rooms; special car parking at rear of house and adjacent to costume museum; light refreshments; access to small sales point by arrangement with guiding staff; picnic area accessible; ♿ WC. Herb garden

🐕 In grounds on leads

▣ Light refreshments in Servants' Hall, open as house. Picnic areas in garden and woodland

➡ 1m from Moneymore on Moneymore-Coagh road (B18) [H866828]
Bus: Ulsterbus 110/20 Belfast–Cookstown (passing close NIR Antrim Stn), alight Moneymore Village, ¼m (tel. Magherafelt (0648) 32218)

TEMPLETOWN MAUSOLEUM 🐘

Templepatrick, Ballyclare, Co. Antrim

Built 1783 by Robert Adam in memory of the Hon. Arthur Upton

🅾 ❋ All year during daylight hours

£ 🐕 Free. No WCs

➡ In Castle Upton graveyard at Templepatrick on Belfast–Antrim road (A6) [J228859] *Bus:* Ulsterbus 120 Belfast–Ballymena (passing close NIR Belfast Central & Antrim Stns); alight Templepatrick village, few min. walk (tel. Belfast (0232) 333000 or 320574)

WELLBROOK BEETLING MILL 🐘 🐘 🐘 🐘

20 Wellbrook Road, Corkhill, Cookstown, Co. Tyrone BT80 9RY (tel. Tulnacross (064 87) 51735)

A hammer mill powered by water for beetling – the final process in linen manufacture; original machinery in working order; situated in attractive glen; wooded walks along the Ballinderry river and by the mill race

🅾 Easter (29 March to 7 April): daily 2–6. April, May, June & Sept: Sat, Sun & BH only 2–6. July & Aug: daily, except Tues 2–6

🗄 Shop open as Mill

£ £1. Parties outside normal opening hours £1.50; parties must book in advance. Parking. For information contact the Custodian (see tel. above)

◉ 'Touch and Sound' tour can be provided for visually handicapped visitors

🐕 In grounds only, on leads

➡ 4m W of Cookstown, ½m off Cookstown-Omagh road (A505), from Cookstown turn right at Kildress Parish Church [H750792] *Bus:* Ulsterbus 90 from Cookstown, with connections from Belfast (passing close NIR Antrim Stn) (tel. Magherafelt (0648) 32218)

Index

(Properties only mentioned in the general Coast and Countryside sections are not included)